LATINX TV IN THE TWENTY-FIRST CENTURY

Edited by Frederick Luis Aldama

THE UNIVERSITY OF
ARIZONA PRESS

TUCSON

The University of Arizona Press
www.uapress.arizona.edu

We respectfully acknowledge the University of Arizona is on the land and territories of Indigenous peoples. Today, Arizona is home to twenty-two federally recognized tribes, with Tucson being home to the O'odham and the Yaqui. Committed to diversity and inclusion, the University strives to build sustainable relationships with sovereign Native Nations and Indigenous communities through education offerings, partnerships, and community service.

ISBN-13: 978-0-8165-4501-8 (paperback)

Cover design by Leigh McDonald
Typeset by Sara Thaxton in 10.5/13.5 Warnock Pro with Futura Std

Library of Congress Cataloging-in-Publication Data
Names: Aldama, Frederick Luis, 1969– editor.
Title: Latinx TV in the twenty-first century / edited by Frederick Luis Aldama.
Other titles: Latinx pop culture.
Description: Tucson : University of Arizona Press, 2022. | Series: Latinx pop culture | Includes bibliographical references and index.
Identifiers: LCCN 2021038705 | ISBN 9780816545018 (paperback)
Subjects: LCSH: Hispanic Americans on television—History—21st century. | Television programs—History and criticism. | Hispanic Americans in television broadcasting—History—21st century.
Classification: LCC PN1992.8.H54 L38 2022 | DDC 791.45/652968073—dc23/eng/20211203
LC record available at https://lccn.loc.gov/2021038705

Printed in the United States of America
♾ This paper meets the requirements of ANSI/NISO Z39.48-1992 (Permanence of Paper).

LATINX TV IN THE
TWENTY-FIRST CENTURY

Latinx Pop Culture

SERIES EDITORS

Frederick Luis Aldama and Arturo J. Aldama

For Corina Villena-Aldama — and all our new-gen Latinx storytellers

CONTENTS

PART VI. #STREAMINGBROWN

CURATION; OR, IT'S ALL IN THE MIX

Forewords to the Televisual Delights of *Latinx TV in the Twenty-First Century*

i. Mama's Venom

"I was raised by a television," I used to say, and my mother, then very much alive, would retort with venom: "Thanks a lot!" Now that she's gone, I say it all the more as I attempt to translate into prose the nefarious, hedonistic twin pleasures and damaging pain of *televisual* entertainment.

Televisual? Because we are so beyond the rabbit-eared days of vacuum-tubed televisions.

Televisual over *television*, as TVs, smart or dumb, are almost an afterthought as streamed entertainments of all sorts and all species make their way from our smartphones to our synapses, tickling here, scarring there, and filling the time between cradle and grave with photon-borne distractions, communiques, hookup notifications, and god knows what else.

Which makes it such a delight to stumble upon Frederick Luis Aldama and crew's *Latinx TV in the Twenty-First Century*, which you now hold in your hand (in an indie bookstore? god love you! go buy it already) or spy on the screen. Aldama has *curated* a white hot mess (actually, better said, a #browntv hot mess) of madly diverting essays—and has done so in a way that captures the contemporary *now* of Latinas and Latinos and Latinxs in the televisual universe.

The key word there is "curate." I will save you a trip to the *Oxford English Dictionary* and tell you that the word's parentage is complex, filled with bastards and more: one part *cure*, as in the medical sense of being healed or cared for; one part *curé*, the paid deputy priest of a parish. Hence, the verb *curate*, as in to curate a museum; and the noun *curate*, a spiritual guide and ecclesiastic.

Now, I am not saying my good friend Fede Aldama is a priest (his old friends know him all too well), but he is one hell of a curator—and in both senses of the term, as this collection both *cures* the aching scars that make up the history of Latinx representation in the United States and beyond, and *curates* them like the best museum tour you've ever experienced: think the Tate Modern, but with a Mexy twist. More Joseph Cornell than Jackson Pollack, Aldama's assemblages of cutting-edge new scholars with masterblaster American Studies full profes like Fojas, Zamora, and Larry La Fountain-Stokes redefine the genre of the critical essay anthology, yielding a book that is as entertaining as it is informing, as pathway redefining as it is pathway establishing.

That's a tough trick.

And what will you glean? Laura Fernández's musings on the Latinx gaze (take that, Laura Mulvey!); Melissa Castillo Planas's thoughtful probings of *Cristela* and Tejana Cristela Alonzo; Yadira Gamez's unearthing of feminist codes in *George Lopez*; Katlin Marisol Sweeney's moving look at carceralized femmes in *Orange Is the New Black*; Muñoz, Reynoso-Franco, Perez-Palencia y Tovar's screening of Latinx mental health issues on the screen; Danielle Alexis Orozco's ode to the social justice work of decolonial women-of-color feminists, pleasure activists, and disability justice advocates; Cristina Rivera's outing of the ubiquitous forged Latinx facsimile *Dora the Explorer*; Mathew Sandoval's dissection of Disney's deathless/disembodied Día de Muertos confab *Elena of Avalor*; Mauricio Espinoza's exposé on Latinx cops; Carlos Gabriel Kelly González's great findings with regard to space bandidos in *The Mandalorian*; Camilla Fojas on Latinx undocumedia; Stacey Alex on undocumented Latinxs in *Party of Five*; Irma J. Zamora Fuerte's moving discoveries on the exclusion of immigrant narratives; Ryan Rashotte pondering tattoos, screened violence as narcotic, and more in Netflix's *Narcos*; J. V. Miranda on FX's *The Bridge*; Peyton Del Toro on lesbian Latina figuration; Héctor J. Pérez on *Vida*; Lawrence La Fountain-Stokes reading the stars alongside and for Walter Mercado, envisioning a "cuir, Caribglobal, transloca future"; David Schmidt's survey of the diverse world of streaming series from Latin America; Nicole Pizarro's contemplative inscriptions on *Siempre bruja*; and, last but not least, Peter Murrieta's tasty *charla* on Latinx TVLandia.

"Holy cultural studies, Batman," you might be saying to yourself, and you'd be right, as Aldama's nuanced curation of essays yields an experience that leaves readers on top of their game when it comes to Latinxs on TV, past, present, and future.

And now, as I was sad to be left out of this party (I always think of a good anthology as a party boat of sorts—think *The Love Boat* but with a Latinx cast!), I will leave you with a defining moment in the history of the televisual, at least for this Mexican American writer from Laredo, Texas. With a warning: it is utterly twentieth century, *not* twenty-first century, which is fitting, as I am a creature more of the last century than the present one. And so I end this introduction with my own turning point in the televisual history of Latinxs on the boob tube—and, owing to my generation, it is, of course, connected to MTV.

ii. Selena Quintanilla and Chrissie Hynde; or, How "Back on the Chain Gang" Becomes "Amor Prohibido" via Xicanosmosis

The silvery electronic synthesizers that open Selena's "Amor Prohibido" (1994) usher listeners into a lush (sweet, but not treacly) aural landscape every bit as unpredictable and split (between En-  glish and Spanish) as the South Texas coastal shores that gave birth to this singing goddess of conjunto and, after Cesar Chavez (or, maybe ahead of him), the most famous Mexican American the United States has ever known.

"Amor Prohibido" (Forbidden Love) segues into "No me queda mas" (I have nothing left, or nothing is left to me), a dreamy/sad meditation on loving and losing. The rest of the album is the stuff of memory, released just a few months before her callous assassination by Yolanda Saldívar, Selena's fan club president and agent for Selena's fashion line in Mexico.

The piece de résistance of the album, for me, however, is her cover/revision/rendition of the Pretenders' "Back on the Chain Gang," here subjected to Tex-Mex metamorphosis by Selena and her band as "Fotos y Recuerdos." The edge of Chrissie Hynde's cut is softened somewhat by the potentially cheesy synthesizer beat applied by Selena and band, but what emerges is actually a kind of conversation between white American rock and South Texas Tejano music, between the edgy precursor to alt rock and South Texas Chicano rhythms. You had no choice but to dance to the evocative catchy cadences of this next-world beat, this mestizo magic.

Selena's title transformation also foregrounds what the Pretenders version perhaps kept more obscure, the song being a paean to nostalgia and memory (facilitated by a photograph, that most weirdly fetishistic and ubiquitous of objects—Susan Sontag knew her shit).

When Selena's version was released, I had recently moved to the West Coast from the chilly, barren enigma (to me) of eastern Connecticut. I remember hearing Selena's "Fotos y Recuerdos" on the radio, as I bopped between Chula Vista and San Diego, San Ysidro, and L.A. in my 1980s-era VW Rabbit diesel. Here was a song that embodied what I came to call Xicanosmosis (Chicana/o + osmosis), where the jangling guitars and dangerous New Wave crooning of Hynde and her band was force-fused with a decidedly "Mexican" consciousness—"Mexican" *not* Mexican, as it came from WITHIN the United States, from a South Texas borderlands with a mind (and wit, and language) of its own.

Selena's untimely death led to her short-term apotheosis to the top of the music charts, but it also erased the possibility that her South Texas-born/borne sound would dominate the ear-space (and the Zeitgeist) of the United States. When J.Lo was chosen to play her in the requisite biopic (as if there was no difference between a Tejana and a New York Boriqua—you can imagine them in central casting: "well they both have big *nalgas* and speak Spanish"), something died, or better put, Selena died a second death—the unique charm and spark of a South Texas superstar silenced and elided a second time on the silver screen.

---

iii. Enough Already . . .

Now, turn the page already, and dive into our twenty-first-century Latinx now!

—*William "Memo" Nericcio*

LATINX TV IN THE TWENTY-FIRST CENTURY

LATINX TVLANDIA

Moments to *Movement*

Frederick Luis Aldama

Televisual Industrial Complex

Today in Latinx TVLandia, much has changed *and* much has stayed the same from earlier epochs. Today, Latinxs seem to be more visible as shapers and agents of the televisual stories told and storyworlds built. We are more present in front of and behind TV camera oculi. However, given our massive demographic growth spurt of late, we're still far from the televisual presence we should be. We're at more than 19 percent of the U.S. population, yet we're still hovering below 3 percent representation in TV—and in all media combined. Today in the United States, Latinxs are the *majority* historically underrepresented ethnoracial group. Yet, we're still barely a blip on the media representational radar.

The 2020 Emmy Awards are a case in point. A quick scan of the nominee and awardee list reveals that today's *relative* abundance of Latinxs (writers, showrunners, directors, and actors, for instance) vitally shaping our televisual storyworld spaces were nowhere to be seen. One or two nominations went to Latinx hair design artists and a nod to the Latinx-passing Alexis Bledel. Otherwise, this was yet another Emmy ceremony where Latinxs walked away empty-handed. Afro-Latinx Jharrel Jerome's taking home a 2019 Emmy didn't give us the watershed we'd hoped for. With a few nods to our Black compadres, the shows that won the day were otherwise all Anglo cast, written, and helmed.

Latinxs' vital contribution to the shaping of a complex and rich televisual storyworld space continues to be willfully overlooked. We continue to be invisible as vitally creative shapers of televisual narratives, all while only ever *used* and *seen* as bodies: as the *braceros* brooming down sets, soaping down bathrooms, and changing out toilet rolls; and, as bloodthirsty criminals, bumbling buffoons, tempestuous lovers when in front of the camera. We are the conveniently invisible and the inconveniently hypervisible within this grand image-making machine of the Televisual Industrial Complex. And, of course, this Televisual Industrial Complex participates centrally in Vanessa Díaz's formulation of a Hollywood-Industrial Complex that manufactures "white, suburban, capitalistic, heteronormative family life as the norm"

(14)—all while fracturing—even obliterating—how we as Latinxs perceive, think, and feel about our*selves.*

I'm not the first to talk about this dual impulse in mainstream media that invisibilizes and hypervisibilizes Latinxs—with the end result of fracturing our sense of belonging and sense of self as Latinxs in the United States. The critical, interpretive work that digs into the manufacturing of race, gender, sexuality in this Televisual Industrial Complex is long, deep—and electrifyingly alive and au courant. In addition to Vanessa Díaz's groundbreaking work just mentioned, I think readily of the following scholars: Paul Alonso (*Satiric TV in the Americas*), Mary Beltrán (*Latina/o Stars in U.S. Eyes*), Isabel Molina-Guzmán (*Latinas and Latinos on TV*), Myra Mendible (*From Bananas to Buttocks*), Deborah Paredez (*Selenidad*), Angharad N. Valdivia (*Latina/os and the Media*), Frances Negrón-Muntaner (*Boricua Pop*), Clara Rodríguez (*Heroes, Lovers, and Others*), Christopher Chávez (*Reinventing the Latino Television Viewer*), Arlene Dávila (*Latinos, Inc.*), Arlene Dávila and Yeidy Rivero (coeditors, *Contemporary Latina/o Media*), Benjamin M. Han (*Beyond the Black and White TV*), Charles Ramírez Berg (*Latino Images in Film*), Frances Aparicio and Susana Chávez-Silverman (*Tropicalizations*), Domino Renee Perez and Rachel González-Martin (*Race and Cultural Practice in Popular Culture*), Richard T. Rodríguez (*Next of Kin*), Chon Noriega (*Shot in America*), Chon Noriega and Ana M. López (coeditors, *The Ethnic Eye*), Otto Santa Ana (*Juan in a Hundred*), Rosa-Linda Fregoso (*The Bronze Screen*), Camilla Fojas (*Border Bandits*), Tanya González and Eliza Rodriguez y Gibson (*Humor and Latino/a Camp in "Ugly Betty"*), Yeidy Rivero (*Tuning Out Blackness*), William Nericcio (*Tex[t]-Mex*), Priscilla Ovalle (*Dance and the Hollywood Latina*), and the work generally of Alisa Perren. And, with the recent publication of *Reel Latinxs* and *Talking #BrownTV*, I and my scholarly compadres Christopher González and William Nericcio have made some co-interpretive forays into this space as well. In each case, different questions are asked and a multiplicity of approaches and methods used. Taken as a whole, Latinx media scholars are generating concepts and knowledge that enrich deeply our understanding of all facets of how this Televisual Industrial Complex spins ideals of an aspirational Whiteness against a backdrop of undesirable Brownness. They also shine bright light on how Latinxs *sabo*tage and grind to a halt those cogs in the machine of this media industrial complex's spinning of a racist, sexist, and homophobic imaginary.

Latinx TVLandia: Moments to *Movement*

More than at any other time in TV history, today Latinx identities and experiences appear in all variety of storyworlds—and across all genres: sitcoms, comedy, action, romance, detective, and sci-fi, for instance. Today's TV that features Latinxs behind or in front of the camera explores anything and everything, including, for instance, intergenerational conflict; socioeconomic struggle; gender and sexual identity; ethnoracialization and racism; émigré identities and experiences; and so much more. Today's TV that features Latinxs (individual or collective) assumes all variety of formal shape and storytelling rhythm and sequencing, including flash-fictional webisodes, episodic chapters that form large seasonal story arcs, and the sequencing of self-contained storyworld episodes. And, whether on TV sets, computers, or smartphones, today's TV by and about Latinxs allows for many different styles and habits of consumption: from binge-watching entire seasons to carefully calibrated single-episode indulgences.

This is why I conceptualize today's TV by and about Latinxs as more of a *movement*. More than in earlier epochs, digital spaces and streaming platforms today have allowed for the making of Latinx televisual narratives that at once speak to Latinxs in all our rich and complex Latinoness *and* to non-Latinxs. There's this overwhelming sense of Latinx TVLandia today as seeking to provide rich nuance to the different ways we exist as Latinxs as variously informed by our Mexican, Dominican, Central American, Puerto Rican, and Cuban ancestral heritages. And, Latinx TVLandia is beginning to give careful nuance to regional, communal, and familial differences between and among U.S. Latinxs in ways that speak deeply to the conflicts, struggles, and achievements of the human condition. This is all happening in a more consistent and constant stream of televisually shaped narratives, and not as a series of disparate moments. Today's Latinx TVLandia is a *movement*.

In earlier epochs, the televisual representation of Latinxs came in fits and starts—as a series of skipping-rock *moments*. It skipped from Desi Arnaz's salsa and congo beats in *I Love Lucy* (1951–57), Speedy Gonzalez's exaggerated and malapropistic Spanish *arribas* (1953–55), and Latinx lover Manolito Montoya (Henry Darrow [born Enrique Tomás Delgado Jiménez]) in *High Chaparral* (1967) to the politically *woke* Francisco "Chico" Rodriguez (Freddie Prinze) in *Chico and the Man* (1974–78), motorbike-straddling and white-tooth-grinning Francis Llewellyn "Ponch" Poncherello (Erik Estrada) in *CHiPS* (1977–83), troublemaker Jewish-Latinx Juan Epstein (Robert Bruce Hegyes) in *Welcome Back, Kotter* (1979), PBS's fully bilingual *¿Qué Pasa, USA?* (1977–80), golf-playing WASPS vs. Down-and-Brown in *Condo* (1983), and assimilated high-school jock turned Latinx-woke college student A. C. Slater (Mario Lopez) in *Saved by the Bell* (1989–94). Yesteryear's skipping stones also carried us from *Miami Vice* (1984–89) with Jimmy Smits as Eddie Rivera (Sonny Crockett's first cop partner), Rosie Perez (choreographer), and J.Lo (dancer) of those famed Fly Girl intros and outros to *In Living Color* (1990–

94), and John Leguizamo and Luis Guzmán's teaming up to poke fun at Latinx and white America in *House of Buggin'* (1995). Of course, Latinxs do appear in earlier televisual storyworld spaces not mentioned. However, their Latinidad kept them hidden—closeted. I think readily of Lynda Carter (*Wonder Woman*), the Euro-*hispanified* Ricardo Montalbán (Mr. Roarke in *Fantasy Island*), and Madeleine Stowe (Annie Crane in *Little House on the Prairie*).

It's a fact that the proliferation of today's many streaming platforms have changed the game for Latinxs in front of and behind televisual oculi. In some cases we've seen Latinx-written, -produced, and -casted YouTube webisodes picked up, rebooted, and relaunched as full-season and multi-season stories. Think: *Gentefied*. First-time creators Linda Yvette Chavez and Marvin Lemus launched this as a web series; then, with the onboarding of America Ferrera as co-executive producer and Netflix's deep pockets, *Gentefied* (2020) was transformed into a high-gloss, ten-episode series. And, scratch a little and you'll see that many established network and cable TV channels have claimed some YouTube real estate: AMC with its *Walking Dead* webisodes, for instance. Indeed, this spin-off narrative gives full breathing room to Latinx protagonists and their stories. It can peel away from the main narrative with its elaborate and complex ensemble cast that typically sidelines Latinxs and clear a new space where the agent of the action is a Latina. I'm thinking of *Fear the Walking Dead: Passage* (2016), a mini-series that features Latina Gabi (Melissa Barrera, also in *Vida*) along with African American Sierra, who work as a team, surviving by killing white-men-turned-zombies in a subterranean U.S./Mexico borderland space. Think also of those webisode spin-offs from *The Flash* (2014–) that protagonize Latinx superhero Cisco Ramon ("Vibe"). In this show, Cisco functions more like the buffoon Brown sidekick. In the webisodes, he's smart, witty, and his own person.

As those clunky, tentacled cable boxes become more and more relics of our ancient televisual past, we're seeing the formation of a *movement* of Latinx-centered narratives shaped by the serialized, episodic format that has forever characterized TV storytelling. Keep in mind, that while we might not be sitting in front of big pieces of oak cabinetry and soaking up cathode rays today (as I did as a chavalito at my abuelita's), television storytelling hasn't changed much. Yes, we tend to see televisual narratives with greater numbers of characters and multi-threaded plots today that demand greater long-term (and short-term) memory work. Yes, the release of entire seasons in a single instant and the short-fiction bursts of webisodes may alter somewhat the use of the serialized storytelling shaping devices of the hook and recap as we move from one episode to another.

Serialized storytelling and the innovative technologies of its making and distribution are not new, of course. Indeed, with the birth of new mass media technologies (newspaper and magazine) in the nineteenth century, novelists like Charles Dickens, Eugène Sue, Alexandre Dumas, Gustave Flaubert, and Leo Tolstoy began using the serialized form to shape their narratives. They showed the world that it was possible to write and publish well-crafted novels in serial form. Think of Dickens publishing in installments his *Pickwick Papers* (1836–37), Sue his *Les Mystères de Paris* (1842–43), Dumas his *The Three Musketeers* (March–July 1844), Victor Hugo his *Les Misérables* (April and June of 1862), Flaubert his *Madame Bovary* (1856), Fyodor Dostoevsky his *Brothers Karamazov* (1879–80), and Tolstoy his *Anna Karenina* (1879–80). Along with greater control over income (newspaper owners paying by the word and installment), this was a period of tremendous narrative innovation, the most visible and long-lasting being the cliffhanger. The new technology opened up new ways of storytelling—and new ways to grow and reach a mass audience. (For more on the shaping devices of serialized narratives, see Sean O'Sullivan's "Six Elements of Serial Narrative," which identifies six key features: iteration, multiplicity, momentum, world-building, personnel, and design that shape any given serialized narrative's "rhythmic, compositional, and sequential relationship.")

The new technologies today allow for innovation behind and in front of the camera eye. It's a technology that's allowing more Latinx-created content. It's a technology that's allowing for the building of Latinx audiences. It's the *media* space of innovation today because it's attending to the Latinx building blocks that make up our reality by employing in increased numbers Latinx writers, showrunners, and actors in the shaping of televisual narratives. In this way, television narrative spaces have certainly taken first place over the silver-screen sibling, film.

White Oculi; or, Regressive Televisual Dross

I don't want to get ahead of myself here, nor forget that, while the quality of the Latinx TVLandia might be a huge improvement over what we had before, in the end we are still less than 3 percent of this televisual narrative space.

Today's technologies of production, creation, and dissemination have deep roots in serialized storytelling traditions and have helped transform and innovate televisual storytelling by and about Latinxs into a progressive TVLandia movement that reaches new and growing Latinx audiences with all variety of tastes. But, as with all movements, Latinx TVLandia *moves* against its targets of oppression and exploitation: that Televisual Industrial Complex with its White oculi that continue to destructively and denigratingly spin Latinxs as criminal, hypersexual, and buffoons.

Spinning Latinxs as part of the Latinx-threat master narrative comes in many different generic shapes and sizes. The most prominent: the border-crossing sociopathic narco. A contemporary exemplar is seen in *Ozark* (season 1, 2017), which constructs the Mexican kingpin Camino Del Rio (Esai Morales) as the ultimate threat to the entire existence of the upper-middle-class white Byrde family—and by metonymic association, a white U.S. North America. The narrative constructs the Latinx-threat narrative both in content *and* form. As the hooks move us from one episode to the next to complete the narrative arc of the first season, we see how the hook relies increasingly on Del Rio's slow, inexorable encroaching presence; the more the Byrdes slip up in their *cleaning* of dirty money, the closer Del Rio gets to them and the United States, ultimately crossing into and unleashing unthinkable levels of violence within the U.S. nation space. The backbone to the suspense device that hooks viewers (in form and content) spins yet again unreason (the south-of-border Latinx criminal) as threat to reason (the U.S.-based business-smart Byrdes). We see this same unreason versus reason master narrative in a show like *Breaking Bad* (2008–13)—and this even when the narco is U.S.-based and white (Walter White). In the end, the show's oculi heroize White for his genius smarts, denigrating all of the Latinxs, south-of-the-border narcos as well as Latino and Latina civilians. (For more on this, see Arturo J. Aldama's "Decolonizing Predatory Masculinities in *Breaking Bad* and *Mosquita y Mari*.")

White-oculi-created televisual narratives peddle the Latinx-threat narrative in other, less obvious ways. I think readily of how Latinas continue to be constructed as that criminal-next-door threat to the civilized order of things. Take the mamá, Harlee Santos (J.Lo), in *Shades of Blue* (2016–18), or queer Jackie Quiñones (Monica Raymund) in *Hightown* (2020–). Initially, the narratives frame both figures as hardworking law-and-order Latinas you might live next door to or see at the grocery store: the innocuous Latina next door. However, the narratives reveal in a subtextual, subterranean way uncivilized and uncivilizing dominant and domineering traits: Harlee as corrupt cop and Jackie as unreliable, self-destructive drug addict.

There are other subtle ways that the White oculi construct the Latinx-threat narrative. Think: flavor-of-the-month immigration narrative. Take season 10 of *Shameless* (2020). It continues to follow the ups and mostly downs of the Irish American-identified, working-poor Gallagher family. However, midway through season 10, Carl Gallagher's coworker and crush, Anne Gonzalez, has to move into the Gallagher residence; Anne along with her family and extended family are hiding from ICE. Within minutes of installing themselves in the house, Anne and her *extraordinarily* large family are seen cleaning and making tamales and heard offering advice about raising babies. When not making tamales and the like, they're watching telenovelas. Feeling pushed out of his own house, Frank tells a nameless Latina and his daughter Franny watching a telenovela: "This is why Brown countries always remain Third World, Franny. There's no depth to their storytelling." We're supposed to chuckle. We don't. We don't not only because the narrative spins all the stereotypes in the books about Latinxs—we clean, cook, and child-rear, preternaturally—but also because the White oculi shaping the narrative have just made clear that if working-poor white U.S. Americans open their house (and by extension country) to us, we'll take it over and push them out.

On the flipside, there are plenty of White-oculi-constructed narratives that contain and control Latinxs *already here* as acceptable by spinning images of the hypersexual *and* assimilated Latina. I think readily of the creating of a character like Gloria (Sofía Vergara) in *Modern Family*, whose linguistic bungles and references to crime-ridden Colombia are made safe through her aspirational and assimilatory attachment to white wealth: namely, Jay Pritchett (Ed O'Neill). On the other end of the class spectrum, I think of *United We Fall* (2020), which writes Jo Rodriguez (Cristina Vidal) as made safe through her identification as working class and assimilation to whiteness; not only in her marriage to Bill Ryan (Will Sasso) but also in the way language (Spanish) and Latinx culture (objects and references) appear minimally—as a safe and mild extra salsa spice. In *Station 19* it's the model minority (assimilated) narrative that makes the presence of the Latina safe. Andy Herrera (Jaina Lee Ortiz) saves people from burning buildings and takes care of her supposedly widowed papá, Pruitt Herrera (Miguel Sandoval), the fire chief at Station 19. While it's Andy's voice-over that launches and closes each episode—a voice with a slight Latinx accent and tonality—she's ultimately not the agent of the action nor of the narrative. Her "model minority" dedication and hard work dominate what could have been an interesting and complex narrative of the struggles of a Latina within a space filled with heterosexist and *machista* attitudes and behaviors. In contrast to *Station 19*, I think readily of how the narrative unfolds in *Jane the Virgin*, revealing to us that the male Latino voice-over narrator is *actually* the narrative construction of the protagonist, Jane Villanueva (Gina Rodriguez). The conceit of showing typing on the page at the beginning of each episode is actually Jane's typing of her novel. In this ekphrastic move, we learn that in actuality, all of the characters we meet are ventriloquizing Jane's words, thoughts, and actions. She's the supra-creator and uber-agent of the entire narrative that we are experiencing, and all this is informed deeply by her sense of self as a Latina.

The White oculi have made Latinxs safe in narrative form and formula, too. I think of those Cinderella narratives that shape the lives of Latina Betty Suarez in *Ugly Betty* or the Latino Daniel Garcia in *The Baker and the Beauty*. In both cases, the fairytale formula has Latinxs romance wealthy white characters, lifting them from their working-class life—and their Latinidad.

I also think here of superhero shows like *The Boys* (2020), which falls short less because of denigrative stereotyping and more for the near total failure of the writers to *see* Latinxs. It does write in the lesbian character, Elena (Nicola Correia-Damude)—but only as a very brief sideline to give more bisexual texture to an otherwise bland white superhero Queen Maeve (Dominique McElligott). However, in the two seasons thus far, you'd be hard pressed to spot a Latinx *anywhere* in the show's White-oculi-reconstructed streets of a contemporary urban U.S. America.

In other fantastical storytelling modes we see Latinidad also fall flat. I think of the 2018 *Charmed* reboot, with its hyped-up marketing proclamations of Afro-Latina inclusivity. In addition to casting only one of the sisters with a Latina actor (Melonie Díaz as Mel Vera) and the other two with non-Latinxs (Sarah Jeffrey and Madeleine Mantock), it comes up way short in its hyped-up Latinx content. It goes full throttle Celtic folklore and mysticism, sidestepping completely any Latinx *brujeria* traditions. And, it ultimately continues the mainstream televisual tradition of giving narrative primacy to Euro-white, male-protector figures by casting Rupert Evans as the "White-lighter" Harry Greenwood.

To be honest, I'm not even sure what to do with a narrative like *Penny Dreadful: City of Angels* (2020). Unlike *Charmed*, which gives with one hand (its hyped-up Latinx content marketing), then takes away with the other (non-Latinx casting, straight white protector figure, and Euro-mystic deliverables), *City of Angels* does put Latinxs (actors and roles) front and center in its fantastical storyworld space, but in ways that ultimately *contain* more than liberate. It opens and closes its ten-episode run with a jaundice-yellow-eyed Santa Muerte (Lorenza Izzo) and leather-clad demon sibling Magda (Natalie Dormer) having an epic argument about humankind. La Muerte's for humankind. Magda's against, dropping a few Hobbesian *homo homini lupus* lines on us like: "brother will kill brother" and "all mankind needs to be the monster he truly is, is being told he can." The story proper begins, and we're in a 1938 Los Angeles filled to brim with corrupt politicians, greedy capitalist developers, and a racist police force. One way or another, they work together to oppress, exploit, displace, expropriate L.A.'s Latinx communities. The narrative sees all of this mostly from the point of view of Santiago (Daniel Zovatto) as L.A.'s first Latinx detective. However, given the initial mystical framing of the narrative, all of this richly textured Latinx content and more—including the queering of zoot-suiter spaces with the introduction of the figure Rio (a transmogrified Magda)—is the result of fate and an inherent man-is-wolf-to-man messaging. That is, capitalist oppression and its racist institutional appendages are not of human doing. And, while the script clearly wants to Latinx-protagonize the narrative by giving Santiago the lion's share of space and time, it quickly slips into lazy cliché. The narrative catalyst: the brutal murder of wealthy Beverly Hills denizens, in a garish caricaturing of Día de los Muertos calavera face-paint makeup. At the sight of the murders, Tiago's partner remarks: "Is this some spic thing?" And, Santiago's mamá (Adriana Barraza) is characterized as a zealot worshiper of La Muerte. She's converted their ramshackle garage into a giant La Muerte altar, packed with hundreds of votive candles and B-horror flick paraphernalia. Not only is this somewhat anachronistic—Santa Muerte became popular as a saint to worship only in the late twentieth century, and mostly among narcos and the incarcerated—but when La Muerte finally does transubstantiate for the mamá, she speaks to her in English—and not, say, Spanish or even more appropriately, Nahuatl, as per her pre-Columbian, Aztec roots as Mictēcacihuātl, Queen of Mictlān.

In sum, no matter the genre, White-oculi-constructed televisual narratives demonstrate a serious lack of a will to style. By this I mean, the creator teams involved in the making of these shows bring a minimum degree of responsibility to their distillation and reconstruction of the ethnoracial building blocks that make up their storyworlds—and our reality.

Brown Oculi; or, TVLandia as *Movement*

Well done or not well done, televisual narratives by and about Latinxs are not contained by generic boundaries. Today, we see Latinxs in sitcoms, sci-fi, noir, soaps, rom-coms, food shows, drama, action, among others. Nor is LatinxTV a format. Latinxs appear in short-form webisodes, serialized big-arc narratives, self-contained yet braided narratives, encapsulated episodic narratives, and animated forms. This LatinxTV narrative landscape aims to reach a rapidly growing Latinx audience with its very varied tastes. Hence, my earlier identification of today's TVLandia as a movement. Indeed, in this section I turn to those shows that make up today's TVLandia that bring with their Brown oculi a great will to style in their reconstructions of all variety of Latinidades. Taken as a whole, we see how these shows *move* against those abovementioned careless and lazy White-oculi-constructed narratives.

Brown oculi work within all variety of televisual production and dissemination spaces: YouTube, cable, Vimeo, Amazon Prime, Hulu, Netflix, and network. They invite Latinxs to laugh, fear, and cry *with* their Latinx characters—all while also smuggling in decolonial modes of thinking, feeling, and behaving.

Today's Brown-oculi-created comedies shape narratives that ask us to laugh *with* the characters—and to wake us to our own internal modes of perceiving, acting, and thinking in the world. Take Erik Rivera's stand-up, which you can stream on YouTube and Amazon Prime. He pitches his lines and punch lines to Latinxs. And, he takes the stereotypes and turns them inside out:

> White people ask, where are you from, *from*. You're expected to have a story. I don't have one. So I just make one up, and the crazier the better: It was Cinco de Mayo. My mom hatched me out of a piñata, rolled me in a tortilla, then floated me across the border. (*Erik Rivera: I'm No Expert*)

We laugh, *really* laugh. We see clearly the microaggressions that we face daily. We also wake to our own internalized colonial thinking and practices. Erik Rivera is not alone. There are many other Brown-oculi-created shows with narrative designs that aim to trigger positive emotions and the expression of laughter. I think also of John Leguizamo's *Latin History for Morons* (Netflix 2018), *George Lopez* (2002–7), George Lopez's semi-autobiographical *Lopez* (2016–17), and *Mr. Iglesias* (Netflix 2019–). Each in their different ways and different platforms invite Latinx audiences to laugh *with* the characters and the punch lines that air our dirty, colonial-legacy laundry (whiteness-as-better, for instance) *and* that educate us about our rich cultural, social, historical contributions in the shaping of U.S. society today. While Leguizamo's gestures and punch-line delivery has us in stitches, his narrative asks us to think hard about serious questions: "What happened in the three thousand years between our great indigenous civilizations and us? How did we become so goddamn nonexistent?" He powerfully reminds, "Because if you don't see yourself represented outside of yourself, you just feel fucking invisible." Latinx writers like Peter Murrieta, Isaac Gonzalez, Luisa Leschin, Julia Ahumada Grob, and Chris Garcia give complex shape to the school-set sitcom *Mr. Iglesias* (2019–). In its self-contained episodic units, *Mr. Iglesias* drops Latinx viewers into a ragtag smart and quirky classroom space that's steeped in decolonial history and Latinx sociopolitical and cultural relearning. Through his use of humor and a call-and-response Socratic teaching approach, Gabriel "Fluffy" Iglesias not only deeply educates students like Marisol Fuentes, who works three jobs while going to school, but also us viewers. We, too, are invited to unlearn those school textbooks that white-washed U.S. history. We're invited to decolonize our minds—and this powerfully so through humor and laughter.

When we laugh, we learn—and deeply. When we're stressed, we don't learn. We know this from experience. We know this from neurobiology. Writers like Peter Murrieta and Cristela Alonzo know this well. In their respective shows—Peter's *Greetings from Tucson* (2002–3) and the eponymous *Cristela* (2014–15)—they use the humor of the sitcom form to reconstruct complexly layered Latinx family lives, and to poke fun at the everyday racism and sexism experienced by their Latinx audiences. In *Cristela* we laugh *with* intergenerational conflicts we recognize in our *familias*. We laugh with Cristela as she calls out her white boss's racism. We laugh with Cristela and feel seen and empowered. In *Greetings from Tucson* (2002–3), Murrieta invites us to step into the shoes of the mixed Latinx-Irish Taint family, especially those of teenaged son David (Pablo Santos). As the show unfolds, Murrieta invites us to laugh *with* David, all while revealing hard truths about the papá Joaquin's (Julio Oscar Mechoso) machista attitudes and actions. As we laugh with the characters, Murrieta's narrative asks that we delve deeply into the complexities of how race, class, and gender inform everyday Latinx life.

The Brown oculi are shaping narratives in *all* narrative spaces, including the building of Latinx kid, teen, and adult-aimed speculative storyworlds: sci-fi, superhero, and fantastical. In the K–12 speculative, superheroic storyworld narratives, I think of the pre-teen dynamic Black and Brown duo, teleporting and telekinetic superpowered Dion Warren (Ja'Siah Young) and wicked-smart, wheelchair-bound Esperanza Jimenez (Sammi Haney) in the WebTV series *Raising Dion* (2019–). I also think readily of Geoff Johns and his creative writer team (mostly women) re-creating from the print comic book Yolanda Montez (Yvette Monreal) as the teen Latina Wildcat II in *Stargirl* (2020–). As the *Stargirl* narrative unfolds, it sidesteps the White-oculi business-as-usual narrative where the Black and Brown characters only appear as sidekicks to spice up an otherwise dull Anglo A-lister superhero. (To wit: the Latinx and multiracial actors cast to play the Cushing family to give Smallville a slight chili-peppering of Brown in The CW's *Superman and Lois*.) Instead, Courtney/Stargirl's (Brec Bassinger) first recruit is the Latina Yolanda Montez. And, Courtney works hard to recruit her. She sees from the Blue Valley High School yearbook that Yolanda's superhero warrior material; like Montez in the print comic book, she's a medaled boxer. First meeting her at the lunch table for the misfits, loners, and unwanted, Courtney slowly befriends her over the first three episodes. In the fourth episode, the show's narrative gives Montez all of the breathing room, including an extended flashback that shows the traumatic moment when her wealthy Anglo boyfriend, Walker (Jake Austin), allows Montez's rival Cindy (Meg DeLacy) to get ahold of a sext pic of Montez that she then uses to publicly humiliate Montez. Word gets back to the Catholic *familia* Montez: a taciturn abuelita mostly seen around the kitchen and watching Spanish-language TV, stern papá, and a strict mamá. Her mamá, Maria (Kikéy Castillo), tells her, "You disgraced your family, and yourself!" To work out her anger and frustration, she goes to the school gym where she pulls out her gloves and hits the punching bag. However, the show doesn't drop Montez's narrative here. Also a loner and struggling with her own complex emotions (dead dad, stepdad, new superhero identity), Courtney gravitates to Montez. She hands Montez the Wildcat suit: "I can't do this alone!" As the narrative unfolds, Montez *claws* her way back to be a confident Latina—and a superhero in her own right as a new gen Latina Wildcat: "For months I've been afraid to listen to myself. To be me. I'm not going to do it anymore." Powerfully, too, in this Brown-oculi televisual reconstruction, Montez doesn't have superpowers as she does in the print comic. She's not of the superhero-manor born, with inherent ready-to-go superpowers. With the help of the Wildcat suit, she's a Latina who exercises her will to educate and train body and mind into a new mestiza, *nepantlera* warrior superhero.

Of course, there are many other Brown-oculi-constructed speculative narrative spaces that richly texture Latinx identities and experiences. I think readily of season 2 of *The Umbrella Academy* (2020) and the Latinx sibling, Diego Hargreeves (David Castañeda). Unlike season 1, which focused on the Anglo sibling Number 5, this second season's narrative arc gives much more narrative space to Diego. We get plenty of opportunity to see him in action: his martial arts and telekinetic object (mostly knives) superpowers. And the writers infuse him with depth and complexity of character: his singular drive to save John F. Kennedy from being assassinated. (The season takes Diego and his misfit siblings back to 1963.) In the storyworld, nobody understands his impassioned acts to save Kennedy. At one point he's committed to an insane asylum. Latinx viewers of the show, however, do understand. Kennedy was the first Catholic U.S. presidential nominee, and it was the Latinx "Viva Kennedy" voting campaign that won him the election in 1960. He remained a favorite among the Latinx community; so too did his brother, Bobby, who stood lock-armed with Cesar Chavez in the fight for Latinx civil rights. And, while it is not in the superhero genre per se, I'd be remiss not to mention the speculative *Los Espookys* (2019–). This show uses the shaping devices of the super-fantastical to take Latinx audiences into a Spanish-dominant, trans-hemispheric Americas storyworld (filmed in Chile and Los Angeles) that follows the adventures of a straight and queer goth ragtag team of paranormal ghost busters: Renaldo (Bernardo Velasco), Andrés (Julio Torres), Tati (Ana Fabrega), and Ursula (Cassandra Ciangherotti). It's Latinx hemispheric.

It's Latinx LGBTQ+. It's Latinx TVLandia at its decolonial best. (See Nicole Pizarro's chapter herein.)

I'd like to pay particular attention to the series *Doom Patrol* (2019–), where the wish-fulfillment fantasy formula of the superhero narrative seems at first blush to stop short when it comes to Latinx characterization. On a first viewing, I thought: White-oculi business as usual. We have a Latina actor, Diane Guerrero, *reinhabiting* the print original comic book's white misfit superhero character, Jane. Cool! But then, as the narrative unfolds, I began to scratch my *cabeza*, wondering if indeed this was the *right* white character for a Latina re-inhabitation. The character suffers a primal trauma that creates multiple personalities (and multiple superpowers). Again, my first thought was, are we ready for this given that we haven't had any Latina superheroes in the televisual space consistently and prominently; we had Jessica Alba as Max in *Dark Angel* and Rosario Dawson as Night Nurse/Claire Temple in the Netflix *Daredevil*, but with mostly a desert in between. And, I was a little baffled that in the pilot, all of the Anglo Doom teamsters got their backstory, but not our Latina-fied Jane. On reviewing and a second serious reflection, I realized that something more was happening. Yes, the show might be using a business-as-usual, White-oculi lensing to shape the story, but Diane Guerrero's incredible strength and range as an actor pushes against this. Guerrero's acting prowess allows her to breathe complexity into otherwise denigrative stereotypes. Indeed, that she gets her backstory only really in the second season also plays well into a Brown-oculi shaping of the narrative; Guerrero as Jane gets the lion's share of the season's narrative, taking us deeply into the complexities of her sixty-four personalities—and the subterranean space they inhabit; the show literalizes Jane's mind by locating the personalities in a physically material underground. That the second season gives so much story time to the development of this space allows Guerrero to add all sorts of layers into a character who suffered from a primal origin trauma. So with second thoughts, Guerrero very much at the helm steering the narrative depth and thrust of *Doom Patrol*, this is not business-as-usual victim narrative; this is not business-as-usual hypersexual and/or hot-headed Latina that we've come to expect of the Televisual Industrial Complex.

The Brown oculi that shape today's speculative TVLandia can and do take us into the space of the immigrant narrative. Unlike those White-oculi-constructed narratives mentioned above that use the émigré narrative to intensify viewer fears of Latinxs as "bad hombre" alien invaders of home and nation, a show like *Roswell, New Mexico* (2019–) uses the speculative to powerfully reinhabit the Latinx-threat narrative discourse. The show revolves around the two Latina protagonists, Liz (Jeanine Mason) and Rosa (Amber Midthunder), and their discovery of a network of aliens on Earth. Here, it reinhabits those erstwhile portrayals of the invading *alien* as dark and monstrous that are one way or another coded as the racial Other: the bad aliens in this show take the shape of Anglo U.S. Americans. And, the show gives breathing room to develop how the sisters handle fear and uncertainty about their widowed, working-class papá, Arturo Ortecho (Carlos Compean), and his life as an undocumented Latinx.

It's not just within the speculative narrative space that our Brown oculi complicate Latinx undocumented experiences. We see this in dramatic realist narrative spaces, too. I think of the *Party of Five* reboot (2020). The show immerses Latinx audiences in the tight-knit, claustrophobic storyworld space of the Latinx Acosta siblings: Emilio, Beto, Valentina, Lucia, and infant Rafael. The five siblings are not left alone because the parents were killed by a drunk driver as in the original show. Rather, it's that their parents Javier (Bruno Bichir) and Gloria (Fernanda Urrejola) are deported; up until the moment of their deportation, they had kept their undocumented status hidden from the children. The catalyst that launches the ten-episode narrative is their deportation; the constant reminders of the fragility of one's status and sense of belonging or not belonging as a U.S. citizen become the significant touchpoints in the development of the siblings. I think also of the America Ferrera coproduced and Latinx cocreated (Marvin Lemus and Linda Yvette Chávez) *Gentefied* (2020). In this near all-Latinx character-driven narrative, not only does the omnipresence of ICE weave its way throughout the story in an organic way, we see the many ways that we exist as Latinxs in the United States. There's the fierce, woke queer artist Ana Morales (Karrie Martin). The hipster chef Chris (Carlos Santos), who returns to East L.A. after having grown up in the dominant white space of Idaho. There's the Rumi and Dumas street-smart cholo, Erik (Joseph Julian Soria). There's the wise-beyond-her-age tween, Nayeli (Bianca Melgar). And, there's the elder romancings of Casimiro "Pop" Morales (Joaquín Cosío) and Lupe (Alma Martinez). However, it's one of the concluding images of the show that resonates long after we've flipped to another show: Casimiro arrested, handcuffed, and trapped like an animal in the back of an ICE van. *Gentefied* maps the full complexities of Latinx life: activism, intellectualism, art, education, and the paralysis that comes with living in fear of deportation—and actual deportation.

In addition to several characters and shows already mentioned—Ana in *Gentefied* and Lucia with her nascent queer desiring in *Party of Five*, who explores her own queer desires and bodily yearnings—there are other Brown-oculi-created shows in TVLandia that build storyworlds that respectfully weave into storylines LGBTQ+ Latinx identities and experiences—and this within and across all the genres. In the sitcom form, there's *One Day at a Time* (2017–), which richly characterizes Penelope Alvarez (Justina Machado) as smart and queer desiring. Importantly, it's not just her characterization at work here that makes a difference. The writers build many of the episodes around issues of sexuality and gender. For instance, in an episode in season 3 the story takes us into the territory of teen consent as well as how toxic masculinity generally and physical and sexual assault specifically traumatize Elena and her girlfriend, Syd. In this episode, too, the story wants us to not put the weight of decolonizing toxic behaviors on Elena. Rather, it places the burden on the male characters, including the little brother, Alex (Marcel Ruiz). He promises to unlearn behaviors and to *relearn* how to become a better Latino. I think also of season 1 of *13 Reasons Why* (2017), which fully fleshes out the Latinx queer character, Tony Padilla (Christian Navarro). He not only queers a 1950s straight, white James Dean look (hair coif and sartorial wear), but it ends up that he's the keeper of the secrets (the confessional tapes). It's the queer Latinx subject here who controls the flow and outcome of the story. There's also the more syrupy-sweet *Love, Victor* (2020–), which drops Latinx audiences into the life of teen Victor Salazar (Michael Cimino) and his struggles to come out to his conservative, religious Latinx parents and high school friends. Victor ultimately learns to confront his machista papá, Armando/Mando (James Martinez), and his mother's Catholic ideology. He finds the strength to *own* his queerness. And, aimed more at an adult Latinx viewership, there's GLAAD Media award-winning *Vida* (2018–19). With its all-Latinx creators and showrunners, this Brown-oculi-shaped narrative that follows the sisters Emma and Lyn Hernandez (Mishel Prada and Melissa Barrera, respectively) shines a remarkable light on the complex range of BIPOC LGBTQ+ identities and experiences in a quickly gentrifying Boyle Heights.

There are also shows that feature white and BIPOC ensemble casts that reconstruct in complex ways the Latinidad of queer Latinxs and Afro-Latinxs. I think of the high-glossy *L Word: Generation Q* (2019–), which surprises not only with its casting of Black and Asian trans actors, but also its complex representation of lesbian Latinx character Dani Nuñez (Iranian Latinx Arienne Mandi) and her fiancée, Dominican Afro-Latinx-identified Sophie Suarez (Rosanny Zayas). (As you'll see with Peyton Del Toro's chapter herein and her careful analysis of the original *L Word*, *Gen Q* is a radical departure from erstwhile Latinx queer representations, even in erstwhile queer safe televisual spaces.) With the latter Latinx character especially, the show represents her Afro-Latinidad in a natural and complexly layered way: she moves fluidly between English and Spanish, references Dominican food and culture, and discusses the pros and cons of her Afro-Latinx hair. The show *Claws* (2017–) includes among the five money-laundering manicurists the smart and fierce Afro-Latinx character Annalise "Quiet Ann" Zayas (Judy Reyes). She's college educated, queer, and embraces her Afro-Latinidad. In the Latinx-created and -produced show *Pose*, the cast of queer and trans Black and Brown characters struggle with a homophobic mainstream *and* their own internalized gender, race, and sexual traumas and phobias. And, of course, there's the much lauded dramedy *Orange Is the New Black* (2013–19), which, over the course of the huge arc of its multi-season narrative, eventually gives voice and agency to LGBTQ+ Latinas: revolutionary Dayanara Diaz (Dascha Polanco), bilingual, hyperliterate, and witty Maritza Ramos (Diane Guerrero), and Marisol "Flaca" Gonzales (Jackie Cruz).

As I wrap up this exploration of these Brown-oculi-created narratives today forming a TVLandia *movement*, I want to mention a few others that focus on Latinx kids and teens. There's Ernesto Javier Martínez and Adelina Anthony's short film *La Serenata* (2020), which focuses on a chavalito realizing, with the help of his loving parents, that it's okay to serenade another boy. In the Disney animation show *The Owl House* (2020–), the Latinx teen protagonist comes of age as a witch, Luz Noceda, and explores her relationship with Amity, including their going to the Grom (their world's version of prom) together and dancing together. Other Disney shows like *Diary of a Future President* (2020–) use the Brown oculi to create a noncondescending coming-of-age narrative of Elena (Tess Romero), as she learns to navigate her middle school as a Latina. And in Eddie Gonzalez's cocreated *On My Block* (2018–), Latinx audiences are invited to join a BIPOC crew of teens as they set out on an exciting (serious and fun) adventure that include quinceañeras, school dances, and sleuthing out buried money. And, while the narrative also takes Latinx audiences into the dangers of living in working-class urban cores in the United States for BIPOC youngsters, it neither slips into the teen-trauma porn of a *Euphoria*, the didacticism of an *East Los High*, nor the all-white space of a *Malcolm in the Middle*.

For the TVLandia *movement* to continue to gain force and power, our Brown oculi need to continue to work hard to create more complex narratives inclusive of LGBTQ+ *and* Afro-Latinx identities and experiences. As Nicole Pizarro powerfully reflects in her chapter in this volume, the TVLandia of her youth didn't include images of Latinxs like herself with "darker skin," "wide noses," and "kinky hair." Afro-Latinxs in TVLandia are as scarce today as they were yesterday. And we can't wait around for non-Latinxs to change the televisual order of things. We need to continue to mobilize around and forcefully support the creations of Latinx production companies like Zoe Saldana's BESE, as well as grassroots organizations such as The Latinx House, NALIP, and La Lista, with their creating of pipelines for new generations of Latinx talent: writers, producers, showrunners, directors, and actors. It's from these spaces and the creativity born of new technologies and disseminated from new distribution platforms that this

TVLandia movement will grow, reaching into and decolonizing the minds of our ever-expanding Latinx audiences.

I have organized *Latinx TV in the Twenty-First Century* into six main sections. The first section, "#Brown Laughter," focuses on Latinx TVLandia narratives that use the dominant shaping device of humor to carry messages that uphold or that subversively overturn a hetero-white status quo. I launch this section with Laura Fernández's "Laughing *at* or *with* Latinos?: Changing the Scope of the Camera's Narrative Gaze in Midwest-Based Comedies," which drops us into a TVLandia that uses humor to construct a "Latinx gaze" that straddles the "transgressive and the permissible." The use of the Latinx gaze to shape Midwest-set Latinx storyworlds in *Superstore* and the *Saturday Night Live* sketch "Diego Calls His Mom" appeals to Latinx audiences first and non-Latinx viewers second, turning those erstwhile "exoticizing" narratives of Latinxs back "onto white, mainstream culture." I follow with Melissa Castillo Planas's "Cristela Alonzo's Subversive Humor: Television, Nostalgia, and the New Latino American Dream." Here Planas examines how this Latina-created and -produced show uses the sitcom form to *trouble* the myth of the American Dream—especially for working-class Latinxs. I end this section with Yadira Gamez's "Humor as Subversion: Feminist Messages in *George Lopez*." Gamez walks us carefully through the way episodes of *George Lopez* walk a tightrope between mainstream and Latinx viewerships, creating a narrative that puts the spotlight on working-class Chicanx family life but dilutes its reconstructions of a Chicanx feminism.

The second section, "#BrownSuffering/#BrownWellness," brings together chapters that put the spotlight on an important yet much overlooked aspect of TVLandia: Latinx wellness narratives. I begin the section with Katlin Marisol Sweeney's "Peripheral Futurities of Multiculturalism: Suffering Latinas in the *Orange Is the New Black* Ensemble Cast." Sweeney carefully unpacks how over its six-year, multi-season stretch, *Orange Is the New Black* reconstructs its Brown and Black characters as only ever the suffering support system to the white protagonist, Piper. Formulating the concept of sustainable Latinx futurities, Sweeney carefully walks us through how the huge narrative arc of the entire show ultimately pushes to the side (peripheralizes) BIPOC futurities by prioritizing Piper's happy ending. To switch from a White-oculi televisual lens to a Brown one focused on Latinx wellness narratives, I follow Sweeney's chapter with the multi-authored "Latinxs in Prime Time: A Look at Mental Health Television Portrayals." José A. Muñoz, Anahi Reynoso-Franco, Lydia Perez-Palencia, and Sarai Tovar examine how the *One*

Day at a Time reboot clears new narrative space for the reconstruction of Latinx mental health issues. In order to demonstrate just how radical a space-clearing gesture *One Day at a Time* is, the authors first put under a micro-scope how a White-oculi-shaped TV landscape has portrayed Latinxs with mental health issues as "drug addicts, violent offenders, and sociopaths." As such, they show carefully how *One Day at a Time* disentangles itself from the larger Latinx-threat master narrative. I end this section with Danielle Alexis Orozco's "Inhala, Exhala: Latinas, Mental Health Journeys, and Accessible Shaping Devices in TV." Here Orozco brings a Chicanx, decolonial feminist lens to powerfully reveal how shows like *One Day at a Time*, *Jane the Virgin*, and *Undone* push against the Televisual Industrial Complex's spinning of a racist, sexist, and ableist imaginary, enabling audiences to more easily access stories that feature narratives centered on Latinx mental health.

The third section, "#StraightWhiteForms/BentBrownGenres," focuses on two bodies of scholarship: (1) Scholarship that unpacks how White-oculi-constructed forms and genres (mostly aimed at kids) continue to destructively essentialize Latinx identities, cultures, and experiences; (2) scholarship that looks to how televisual forms and genres that bring a great degree of a will to style in their narrative shaping construct rich and complex story-worlds. I launch this section with "Latinidad Through Dora the Explorer: Ignored Histories and Realities in Popular Children's Media." Here Cristina Rivera revises her once total celebration of the *Dora* animation series for bringing Spanish and Latinx culture into the TV sets of kids across the United States. After considering the *Dora* empire—kid and tween shows as well as its marketing and dolls—Rivera can only see *Dora* as stripping down to its most essentialist and denigrative forms Latinx culture, identity, and experience. Mathew Sandoval also interrogates televisual narratives shaped for children, this time focused on Disney's series *Elena of Avalor*. In his chapter "Unholy Holiday: Día de Muertos in Disney's *Elena of Avalor*," he breaks down how it strips the Latinx cultural tradition of Día de los Muertos of all of its richness. Instead, it peddles a Day of the Dead that upholds non-Latinx notions of mortality by mainstream-secularizing concepts of death. I follow these two incursions into White-oculi-shaped animated narrative spaces with a turn to genres such as the cop show and sci-fi. In "These Are Their Historias: Latinx Cops and Prosecutors in Police Shows," Mauricio Espinoza examines how genres of drama and comedy shape the few representations there are of Latinx cops. For Mauricio, while a drama such as *Law & Order: Special Victims Unit* does well in its creation of smart Latinx protagonists and reconstructs the complexities of straddling Latinx and mainstream (white) culture, it falls short when it comes to positive and progressive characterizations of Latinx politicians. And, according to Espinoza, a comedy like *Brooklyn Nine-Nine* uses humor to critique everyday workplace microaggressions directed at Latinxs and breaks new ground as a police procedural that places center-stage complex intersectional gender, race, sexuality, and class identities. I end this section with Carlos Gabriel Kelly González's chapter that takes us into the generic narrative space of sci-fi. In "¿Quien Manda in *Star Wars*? Disidentifying with the Bandido in *The Mandalorian*," Kelly combines a cocreative and *disidentification* approach with his concept of the "performance of *mando*" to show how *The Mandalorian* at once uses and abuses sci-fi and its use of the tropes of the western. Specifically, he unpacks how it at once inhabits the bandido stereotype and resists and challenges it.

The fourth section, "#BorderlandLatinxsReclaimed," includes scholarship that shows how today's TVLandia pushes back against the Televisual Industrial Complex's image making that has historically dehumanized undocumented Latinxs. The scholarship herein focuses on both nonfiction and fiction shows that lay bare the xenophobic images and practices that lead to raids and deportations—the fracturing of Latinx communities and the fanning of fear generally. I begin with "Undocumedia: Documentary Media and the Spectacle of Enforcement." Here Camilla Fojas examines how the Netflix series *Living Undocumented* (2019) turns inside out the "deserving" versus "nondeserving" migrant trope to construct an undocumedia narrative built out of eight testimonials that expose the violent ways that ICE has impacted people's lives. Fojas demonstrates how the series both offers a counternarrative to the many ICE deportation dramas made and how it ultimately acts as a cultural arm of the undocu activist movement that seeks to "unsettle, disrupt, and dismantle the entire border security complex." In "*Party of Five* Reboot: The Denaturalization of Undocumented Latinx Suffering," Stacey Alex analyzes how the 2020-released *Party of Five* show stands as an exemplary model of just what televisual storytelling (the writers worked directly with immigration consultants) can do to enrich viewers' understanding of the complexities of undocu status for Latinxs in the United States. For Alex, the power of doing one's homework for a willful reconstruction of dialogue, character, and plot makes for a Latinx televisual experience that "avoids using undocumented Latinx experiences only to showcase non-Latinx protagonists' qualities" and resists the "liberal privileging of DACA recipients and exceptionalism." I follow with Irma J. Zamora Fuerte's "Stories Valued, Bodies Excluded: Immigrant Narratives in *Jane the Virgin*, *On My Block*, and *Party of Five*." Zamora focuses on the televisual representation of unDACAmented immigrant narratives by focusing on the character arcs of Alba Villanueva, Olivia, and the Acostas. The arcs of these characters showcase the differences in gender and nationality that come with their respective immigrant experiences—as well as how the tendency to cast white-passing Latinxs as the characters we empathize with can and does exclude Indigenous and Black folks in immigrant narratives. In "Myth, Force, and the Burden of Prestige: *Narcos: Mexico* as Case Study," Ryan Rashotte digs deep into the show *Narcos: Mexico*, examining how it at once uses hyperviolence and a prestige TV production style to shape and solidify a grand narcos mythology. I end this section with "From Border 'Reality' to Narrative Possibilities in Latinx TV and FX's *The Bridge*." Here J. V. Miranda examines how a show like *The Bridge* challenges televisual constructions of the border as dangerous in contradistinction to a United States that is safe, stable, and secure. Moreover, in his formulation of the generative concept of the "borderland bridge," he shows how this borderland narrative gestures toward a *connected* space that spans "cultural, racial, and gender difference." However, ultimately the show comes up short in realizing a storyworld that's complex and celebratory of the "transnational, multi-racial, feminist, queer, and migratory."

With the fifth section, "#QueeringLatinxTV," I bring together scholarship that discusses and analyzes the televisual recreation of LGBTQ+ Latinx identities and experiences. I begin with Peyton Del Toro's "'Quiero que Vengas': Coming From, Out, and Into the Lesbian Latin(a) Lover." Here Del Toro examines how the original *The L Word* (2004–9) constructs the lesbian Latin(a) lover type as at once exotic *and* assimilated, safe in her sexual appeal to liberal, white audiences. However, Del Toro ultimately argues that even in this limited construction of the lesbian Latin(a) lover type, lesbian Latina viewers like herself can find self-empowerment by reframing such representations within a resistant, hemisexual, and new mestiza ontology. I follow with Héctor J. Pérez's chapter, "Cognitive Wealth and Serial Ingredients in *Vida*." Here Pérez leans into the advances in research developments in cognitive cultural studies (mental model) to enrich understanding of how the interepisodic narrative structure of *Vida* asks its viewers to construct a *gestaltic* whole from its various plotlines, which include the struggles and challenges of creating new models of kinship, LGBTQ+ desirings and identifications, as well as the threat of gentrification of working-class Latinx spaces. For Pérez, *Vida* clears new televisual narrative space for the creating of Latinx "knowledge as nourishment." I end this section with Lawrence La Fountain-Stokes's "Transloca(l) Poetics: Que(e)ring *Mucho, Mucho Amor: The Legend of Walter Mercado*." La Fountain-Stokes critically examines how in form (tarot-card-like intertitles enlivened with colorful animations) and content, Cristina Costantini and Kareem Tabsch's documentary "pinkwashes" (makes gay friendly) the life of Walter Mercado, a key figure in Puerto Rican and Latinx television. Costantini and Tabsch also don't problematize his white Latinx privilege nor his use of Yoruba/Lucumí practices. However, La Fountain also examines other queer recuperative televisual narratives of Mercado and his influence on new-gen queer performance artists. La Fountain-Stokes allow us to see Mercado more clearly as a *transloca*: a translocal bilingual and bicultural queer who appealed to a wide audience and has become a televisual "crucial referent for queer Latinx culture in Latin America and the United States."

The short yet conclusive and suggestive section "#StreamingBrown" includes scholarship that examines how today's streaming televisual spaces at once *constrain* and *liberate* TVLandia imaginaries. David Schmidt's "Beyond Narcos and Novelas: The Diverse World of Streaming in Latin America" analyzes the ever-proliferating Netflix-constructed shows that at once continue to reproduce the "narcos and novelas" tropes as well as hemispheric American streaming and production platforms that create a richer variety and more LGBTQ+- and Afro-Latinx-inclusive narratives within genres of fantasy, supernatural, and sci-fi, for instance. In "The Unstable Intersection of Witchcraft, Slavery and Representation in *Siempre bruja*," Nicole Pizarro at once celebrates Netflix's commitment to Afro-Latinx serialized storytelling and carefully unpacks how the *Siempre bruja* narrative denies real Afro-Latina agency. In the end, she demonstrates how the show relegates the Afro-Latina protagonist to "the *instersticios* of her own show," reproduces a "colorism" regarding Afro-Latinx representation, and whitewashes the horrors of slavery that bloodstain the real history of the hemispheric Americas. I end the volume with an interview with Peter Murrieta where he shares insights into his journey as an active shaper of Latinx TVLandia as writer, producer, and showrunner. Murrieta reminds us that while we've come a long way in the making of a rich and complex TVLandia, we still have more work to do and a long way still to travel.

Works Cited

Aldama, Arturo J. "Decolonizing Predatory Masculinities in *Breaking Bad* and *Mosquita y Mari*." *Decolonizing Latinx Masculinities*, edited by Frederick Luis Aldama and Arturo J. Aldama, U of Arizona P, 2020, pp. 117–30.

Díaz, Vanessa. *Manufacturing Celebrity: Latino Paparazzi and Women Reporters in Hollywood*. Duke UP, 2020.

O'Sullivan, Sean. "Six Elements of Serial Narrative." *Narrative*, vol. 27, no. 1, Jan. 2019, pp. 49–64.

PART I

#BrownLaughter

LAUGHING *AT* OR *WITH* LATINOS?

Changing the Scope of the Camera's Narrative Gaze in Midwest-Based Comedies

Laura Fernández

When considering the place of Latinx characters within Midwest-based television texts, it's clear that more contemporary television comedies set themselves apart from their predecessors by challenging the social boundaries of the majority-minority dichotomy. Given that comedy and humor are much more subjective than in dramatic series, the series I will analyze in this chapter, *Superstore*, demonstrates a form of agency that previously did not exist within Midwest-based dramas. By playing with the subjectivity of humor, the texts I will analyze work to set up a new perspective that manages to challenge the hegemonic gaze in a way that remains palatable to all viewers. These texts tease the audience to examine a world that is outside of their norms, and then allows for a cathartic release of that unease through laughter.

This deviation in the social norm is what I am calling the "Latinx gaze." It is a gaze that counters the "white gaze" by establishing an opposing perspective to the narrative gaze of the camera onto white culture. Where once a white audience was the presumed norm, now that same audience is meant to examine themselves from afar. In these texts, that Latinxs and Latinidad are present and visible is not questioned, but white assumptions about them are and become the subject of parody. Through my analysis of the sitcom *Superstore*, and a close reading of the *Saturday Night Live* sketch "Diego Calls His Mom," I propose a Latinx gaze: the established and assumed audience might still be predominantly white, but instead of their perspective being presented, an othered interpretation of mainstream culture is projected.

Defining the Gaze

Laura Mulvey established the idea of a "male gaze" as the active gaze that "projects its fantasy onto the female figure, which is styled accordingly. In their traditional exhibitionist role women are simultaneously looked at and displayed, with their appearance coded for strong visual and erotic impact" (436). In other words, the camera projects a "gaze" that is masculine in that it objectifies the female body in order to fulfill a male fantasy. The male gaze is that which utilizes the female body as an erotic spectacle. The woman, a passive figure in classic Hollywood, was meant only to inspire the male hero to act because "in herself the woman has not the slightest importance" (Mulvey 436). But despite this eroticism, Mulvey argues that the role of women in films is not purely one of pleasure; it is problematic as well, given that the female's role "also connotes something that the look continually circles around but disavows: her lack of a penis, implying a threat of castration and hence unpleasure. . . . Thus the woman as icon . . . always threatens to evoke the anxiety it originally signified" (438). Women in films had to play passive roles in order to relieve the male of his anxiety—as long as the woman is being objectified, she can pose no threat, "turning the represented figure itself into a fetish so that it becomes reassuring rather than dangerous" (438). While Mulvey was criticizing the role of women in Golden Age cinema, her arguments still hold true. The objectification of the female body is not limited to 1950s Hollywood, but persists to this day, most specifically in the case of the tropicalization of the Latina body as bold, colorful, and large-chested. For the purposes of this chapter, what is of relevance is how the camera's gaze has shifted—in part—from gender to race.

In defining "Latinx gaze," I borrow from the work of sociolinguists Nelson Flores and Jonathan Rosa, where they define the white gaze as a "perspective that privileges dominant white perspectives on the linguistic and cultural practices of racialized communities" (Flores and Rosa 150–51). This is not meant as an individual perspective, but instead is a "mode of perception that shapes our racialized society" (151). In other words, whiteness is the norm to which all national subjects should aspire. This white gaze moves into the field of film and television when diversity casting utilizes white perceptions of Latinidad to create "safe" images of the Other—in other words the stereotypes we are all familiar with (the spicy Latina—who is often poor and struggling to make ends meet—and the Latino gangbanger/Latin lover), characters who fail to "perform White middle class norms" (Flores and Rosa 151).

In contrast to this white gaze, I am identifying a Latinx gaze. In coming up with this concept, I question what happens when the white gaze is turned on itself. What happens when the "Othered" is no longer cause for humor/fear/discrimination? What is the Latinx perception of white culture? I find that a text is presenting a Latinx gaze when instead of presenting whiteness as the ideal norm, it highlights the cultural capital inherent in Latinx languages and communities. Though I use the term "Latinx" to define my understanding of this new turn in television, it is not necessarily limited to texts that are by/from/about Latinx characters. Such an understanding of television can be applied to a number of shows cataloging various other ethnic/racial groups, such as *Fresh Off the Boat*, which relates the experiences of Chinese Americans living in the United States, or *Black-ish* and its subsequent spin-offs, which highlight an affluent African American family's struggles to maintain their own racial and cultural identity against upper-middle-class (white) social pressures to assimilate. What ties all these series together is their ability to challenge the assumed "gaze" by presenting an alternative to the social order, just as the texts I will be analyzing manage to create.

The texts I have chosen to analyze for this chapter, while notable for all employing a Latinx gaze, all also fall into the same genre, comedy, which I argue is unique to a midwestern Latinx experience. While I would argue that the Latinx gaze is present in dramatic series such as *When They See Us* and *Vida*, both series are set in spaces that can be claimed as "Latinx"—New York and Boyle Heights, Los Angeles. When entering a space that is marked by whiteness, comedy becomes the medium for delivering an "acceptable" Latinx gaze. Before I can begin my analyses of those texts, I need to dive into what it is about the genre of comedy that allows it to become a space for the utilization of the Latinx gaze.

The Agency of the Laugh

As Jonathan Gray, Jeffrey P. Jones, and Ethan Thompson note, "satire can energize civic culture, engaging citizen-audiences . . . inspiring public political discussion, and drawing citizens enthusiastically into the realm of the political with deft and dazzling ease" (Gray et al. 4). Satire and parody, as Gray, Jones, and Thompson explain, are coded as subgenres of comedy, and so they primarily serve the purpose of providing humor to the audience. For some, humor is meant to be devoid of political, racial, or cultural commentary because it is a "zone of escape from real world problems that require pensive stroking of the chin, not laughter" (8). However, while some humor/comedy does not seek to challenge the established social order, it does provide a safe space for such challenges to occur. As Bakhtin notes, humor and laughter can empower the laugher (viewer/audience) precisely by subverting social norms: "laughter presents an element of victory . . . ; it also means the defeat of power, of earthly kings, of the earthly upper classes, of all that oppresses and restricts" (Bakhtin 92).

By empowering the viewer, comedy and humor provide a platform for change. In providing narrative critiques that push viewers to experience an emotional response, humor can call on viewers to question their social reality. As Simon Critchley illustrates, humor can have a redemptive power: "By showing us the folly of the world, humour . . . calls on us to face the folly of the world and change the situation in which we find ourselves" (17–18). The texts I am going to analyze can therefore promote a Latinx gaze because they call on the viewer to question what they know from within a safe space since humor is a genre that "encourages criticism and reflection about prevailing systems of power, and it can be a discursive tool used by both parties in a struggle between dominant and resistive forces" (Gray et al. 10).

In television, satire becomes the medium in which humor gains power. TV satire bridges the divide between politics and the general public since "contemporary satire TV offers viewers a means for playful engagement with politics" (Gray et al. 12). It is playful because it employs the ridiculous. That is not to say that satire is all light-hearted humor and fun. Satire programming, such as that which is the object of this study, "is always at least *potentially* transgressive" (Gray et al. 11). But that potentiality makes satire a safe space for social/political criticism—one viewer *may* be angered by the "humor," but another might simply find it amusing. Satirical humor is rarely straight-forward, allowing for myriad interpretations; and in order to fully "get" the joke, the viewer has to be willing to work for it: "Satire can be 'work,' and therefore it tends to require a level of sophistication that network television infrequently demands of audiences. . . . Satire demands a heightened state of awareness and mental participation in its audience" (15). Satire is therefore the perfect platform to employ the Latinx gaze, because it provides a means for audiences to "analyze and interrogate power and the realm of politics rather than remain simple subjects of it" (17), without fully expecting every audience member to be aware of its purpose. It is safe, because though the humor is accessible to all, its capacity to evoke social awareness and social criticism might not be as obvious.

As I will illustrate, what "Diego Calls His Mom" and *Superstore*, which I categorize as satirical texts, have in common is their ability to employ humor in order to produce an alternative for the American public. As Carl Scott Gutiérrez-Jones writes about the use of humor in Chicanx culture, humor allows writers to "draw upon everyday, readily accessible scenes, while also promoting a radical transvaluing of the images depicted" (Gutiérrez-Jones 118). The Latinx gaze is able to take shape because these two texts straddle the line between the transgressive and the permissible. Both "Diego Calls His Mom" and *Superstore* take the everyday microaggressions faced by Lat-inxs and other ethnoracial minorities and turn them back onto the white viewer—making them subject to questions and second-guessing, while at the same time allowing viewers to *laugh* at themselves. The sociopoliti-cal stakes are minimal when a joke can easily be laughed off or "misinter-preted." What makes them even more remarkable is that they are challeng-ing white hegemony while situated in the very center of "Americana"—the U.S. Midwest.

"Diego Calls His Mom": *SNL*'s Foray into the Latinx Immigrant Experience

SNL has been running for forty-five seasons now, and it was only in its forty-second season that the show hired its first full-time Latino writer, Julio Torres, and its first Latina cast member, Melissa Villaseñor (Villafañe). More often than not, when the *SNL* sketch includes a Latinx character, or alludes to Latinos in the United States, the Latinx character's linguistic incomprehensibility or "exoticness" becomes the running gag of the sketch. In order to understand what sets "Diego Calls His Mom" apart from its predecessors, this section will focus on these primary points of analysis: *what* makes the sketch in question funny and *who* is meant to be laughing? How is language being used—is Spanish the dominant language or English, and what type of Spanish is being promoted?

SNL'S HIGH NOTE: AN APPEAL TO LATINX VIEWERS

"Diego Calls His Mom" quickly became one of my favorite skits because, despite its simplicity, it manages to capture a very human moment that many Latin American immigrants can relate to: calling family members back home and telling them about one's new experiences with Anglo culture. I argue that by providing an alternative reading of American culture, the sketch presents a Latinx gaze. Instead of the immigrant being the objectified joke, midwestern (Anglo) culture becomes the subject of satire.

To sum up the sketch, "Diego Calls His Mom" features Diego (Lin-Manuel Miranda), a working-class immigrant who is calling his mother to tell her about his life in the United States. The skit takes place mainly in an isolated phone booth in the middle of a corn field, with Diego catching his mother up on what he has experienced of "American" culture while living in North Dakota. Though mainly in Spanish, the sketch also employs code-switching, mainly to highlight some of the more "exotic" U.S. attractions Diego has discovered. The skit is more of a quiet reflection on an immigrant's experience in the United States. The fact that it is mainly done in Spanish reflects a changing audience—one that might feel more at home with a Spanglish skit than an all-English one. This is one of the few *SNL* episodes I have seen "live" (as in while it was airing on television versus online), and I was pleasantly surprised with the skit. It was shown without subtitles despite airing in Spanish.[1]

The sketch begins with Diego walking into a lonely phone booth in the middle of nowhere, pulling out his calling card and dialing home. He then explains to his mother, in Spanish, some of his new experiences living in North Dakota, from "Marshmallow salad. No vegetales, marshmallows," to

Little Debbies, Walmarts, and 7-Elevens, and the carpeting everywhere: "Everything in América es carpeted." He tells his mother about his "bud" Preston, a high school quarterback with "baby blue eyes," and Preston's girlfriend, "Michelle o Becky o Sarah Beth o algo así"; and the new American phrases he has learned: "Hold your horses. These immigrants are coming to steal our jobs, but not like you though, you are different. Every kiss begins with Kay." The sketch then ends with Diego telling his mother that he hopes to see her soon; he says goodbye and asks for a "bendición"—a blessing—and hangs up. The sketch is simple but manages to portray the "American dream" from the perspective of the immigrant trying to achieve said dream.

The sketch is notable for its heavy use of Spanish. Diego begins and ends the conversation with his mother using only Spanish, but incorporates English to introduce cultural products or sayings only found in the United States. Diego's (one-sided) conversation moves between Spanish and English to show that he is proficient in both, yet he borrows English terms for words that are markedly "American." Diego practices code-switching, which Bonnie Urciuoli defines as "(the alternation of Spanish and English) . . . a complex mode of language use that integrates relations among those who do it and consolidates their identity" (5). In other words, as Diego describes his daily experiences to his mother, he can move fluidly between English and Spanish, and that ability helps him mark his identity as both an immigrant and a Latino. The switching between the two languages seems to come naturally to Diego and could also reflect his prior lack of knowledge of these items. By utilizing code-switching, the skit helps to normalize Spanglish, which Ed Morales defines as "a hybrid language, an informal code. . . . Spanglish is what we speak, but is also who we Latinos are, and how we act, and how we perceive the world" (3). Diego's role as an immigrant places him in the category of Latino, which means he is marked by his "otherness." As Urciuoli explains: "The generic white American is, in semiotic terms, unmarked while the non-normative, the racialized or ethnicized person, is marked" (17). Despite Diego's marked immigrant status, that is not the object of humor in the skit; the skit is funny because it makes the "unmarked" white culture the punch line.

The laugh track that goes with the sketch is used only when Diego remarks on American culture: the salad with zero vegetables, the mounds of yellow and orange food, carpeting in every house. When Diego is speaking only in Spanish, the laugh track is not present, making his conversation with his mother more meaningful, whereas the English bits are the subject of humor. In the sketch, Spanish is not funny, nor is the fact that he is calling home from a payphone in the middle of nowhere. The location of the payphone highlights Diego's isolation as a sole Latino in a primarily white environment. The audience is forced to view American culture from the perspective of the outsider, and forced to laugh at itself, because, let's face it, U.S. mainstream culture is just as "weird" as "foreign" cultures to someone not from the United States. In doing so, the sketch manages to conflate Urciuoli's "spheres of interaction," which are "sets of relations polarized by axes of social inequality. One's inner sphere is made of relations with people most equal to one; one's outer sphere is made of relations with people who have structural advantages over one" (Urciuoli 77). In the sketch, there is no clear divide between the inner and outer sphere because there is no one in a clear position of power. While Preston represents the stereotypical white guy, he works alongside Diego as a dishwasher, and the entire sketch can be understood as Diego critiquing strange Anglo ways. Preston may have structural advantages over Diego simply because of his whiteness, but in the sketch they are equals, just with different cultural values. When Preston's father remarks, "These immigrants are coming to steal our jobs, but not like you though, you are different," he is forced to acknowledge that maybe not all immigrants are evil. Is it condescending? Yes, but it serves as another example of Diego shaking his head at U.S. ideologies. The father may judge him for being an immigrant, but Diego is also judging the father's racist comments.

Another interesting component of the sketch is that the audience never hears the mother's side of the conversation. Diego rattles off a list of foods, places, and catchphrases to her, without stopping to explain himself, which goes to show the automatic and unconscious nature of his code-switching—Diego does not explain the items, because to him he is making perfect sense. The sketch made me nostalgic because I can recall similar situations when my mother would call her mother in Colombia (also using calling cards). As she described something that happened to her, she would slip in an English word here and there. She never caught herself doing so, and it was only when another member of my family heard her using English that we would remind her that my grandmother does not speak English. And so, for me, Diego's code-switching reflects reality. Sometimes bilingual speakers (myself included) cannot help ourselves. I know that when I am speaking Spanish to my mother, I often code-switch, sometimes as a "crutch" as Ana Zentella explains (98), but other times simply because "bilinguals sometimes are unaware of alternating between languages because it has become such an effortless way of speaking" (Zentella 99). And perhaps that is Diego's situation. The viewer is unaware of how long Diego has been in the United States. From the context it appears that he recently moved to North Dakota, but the audience has no way of knowing where he was before that; all we know is that life there is different from home.

While not one of *SNL*'s most glaringly political/in-your-face sketches, "Diego Calls His Mom" manages to make a political statement about the place of immigrants in this country. The sketch's use of Spanish highlights the importance of the language for the growing Latinx population in the United States. Moreover, by Diego using English only to describe American traditions, American culture from the perspective of an immigrant becomes the focal point. For once, it is not a heavy Spanish accent or Latinx culture that is the joke; instead, it is Anglo culture. The sketch helps to situate immigrants in a foreign country without focusing on the foreignness of the immigrant. By calling on this shared immigrant experience, "Diego Calls His Mom" illustrates a Latinx gaze by highlighting the changing landscape of U.S. society, one where immigrants should be viewed as part of the regular audience, where the Spanish language has just as much of a home on U.S. screens as English, and where the divide between immigrant and native is not as clear-cut as some think.

I argue that this sketch in particular is presenting a Latinx gaze through its ability to place white American culture as the center of the joke. The humor is compounded by the fact that a more "cultured," urban audience would find such situations foreign and exotic.[2] However, interestingly enough, when I have shown this sketch to students in various classes at Ohio State University, most (Anglo) students laugh as well at things that they agree are part of midwestern living. So yes, the sketch does take midwestern culture in general to be something to mock in comparison to life in the big city, but not to such an extreme that midwesterners cannot see the humor. It is transgressive, but only up to a point. The sketch is therefore able to present a Latinx gaze because its threat is minimal. While it is a positive step that the showrunners did not provide subtitles, it also means that for many non-Spanish speakers watching, those parts of the sketch are irrelevant. It is only when the Latinx gaze is present on a wider scale that I think it can begin to create a lasting impact, which is why I am now moving to the show *Superstore*. As an entire television series that continually promotes this gaze, it is one of the few examples of popular culture, especially midwestern-set popular culture, that manages to subvert social norms regarding white culture as *the* culture of the United States, and in particular of the Midwest.

The "American" Megamarket

Superstore is a sitcom television series that follows a group of employees working at Cloud 9, a fictional big-box store in St. Louis, Missouri. Cloud 9 is a fictional megamart, but it serves as a parody of Walmart, while the show in general is a satirical commentary on the consumerist practices of Americans in general. However, while the show employs satire, it would likely not fall into the category of "satire television," such as shows like *Saturday Night Live*,

Last Week Tonight, or *Full Frontal*—all series that harshly criticize American politics. Still, it manages to capture the Latinx gaze. As I will show, it is one of the few series that clearly employs a Latinx gaze, and one of the only series set in the Midwest that manages to criticize midwestern and Anglo ways of living without completely alienating its target audience. As of now, the series has been in production for five seasons, and has been renewed for a sixth. In that time frame, the show has covered a number of issues pertinent not just to Latinx audiences but all audiences: issues of race and racial appropriation, discrimination in the workplace, and the plight of undocumented immigrants living under the "U.S. deportability regime" (Maldonado et al. 321).

What sets *Superstore* apart is that it does not tend toward extremes. As Isabel Molina-Guzmán notes, the show is "gloriously basic and uncomplicated" (109). In comparison to shows that emerged during the "post-racial" Obama-era ideologies, argues Molina-Guzmán, comedies such as *Superstore* that have emerged in the Trump era are moving toward humor that is less racially and ethnically charged in order to provide audiences with a space to escape from recent political troubles. She notes that "the tone of many comedies provides audiences with a moment of escapism (from the widening wealth gap; state-sanctioned violence against black, brown, and queer people; and the 2015 campaign and 2016 election of Donald J. Trump) through the production of feel-good stories and characters" (113). While it is true that *Superstore* produces "feel-good stories," the show does delve into major issues such as cultural appropriation, Latinx identity and belonging, and most recently, in the show's fourth and fifth seasons, workplace detention raids by ICE.

The show's pilot episode introduces audiences to a number of different characters, each with "quirks" that highlight a number of different social identities across a number of races and ethnicities. Amy Dubanowski (later Sosa after she divorces her husband in the third season), played by America Ferrera, is introduced as the no-nonsense, yet caring floor supervisor of Cloud 9. Her foil (and later love interest) is Jonah Simms, played by Ben Feldman, who is the charismatic, happy-go-lucky character who is always trying to find the "fun" way to get through the days as a floor worker. Starting with the pilot, Jonah and Amy are put at odds when Jonah condescendingly admits to Amy, whose position as his supervisor is unknown to him, that he does in fact work in the store, despite appearances to the contrary—that yes, someone like him (white, young, good-looking) works in a place like Cloud 9. It is Jonah's arrogance and privilege that set him apart from his Cloud 9 colleagues, with Garret McNeill, played by Colton Dunn, revealing in the fourth episode of the second season that he keeps a list "of all the crazy white-person stuff" Jonah says, such as "I fenced in college . . . wearing boat shoes, BBC America, makes his own trail mix" ("Guns, Pills, and Birds"). Oftentimes Jonah attempts to humble-brag about his experiences in college and elsewhere, such as how he volunteered for Habitat for Humanity or spent a semester abroad, always to the annoyance of his fellow workers, who quickly shut him down and remind him to check his privilege.

The show is unique because although the characters are of various races and ethnicities, no one group is singled out or eliminated from a character's narrative. Often, misunderstandings regarding race and ethnicity become the focal point for the episode. Such is the case in the episode "Shots and Salsa," when store manager Glenn Sturgis, an extremely devout Christian played by Mark McKinney, who serves as the well-meaning but simple-minded, bordering on ignorant character of the group, asks Amy to promote the new Cloud 9 brand of salsa, Señor Salsa, because she has a "certain natural . . . spiciness." He had initially tasked the promoting of the product to Mateo, an undocumented Filipino worker played by Nico Santos, until he learned that Mateo was in fact Filipino and not Mexican like he had believed. When Amy refuses because she does not want to play into Glenn's stereotyping, she calls him out for picking the only other Latina worker, Carmen, to sell the product. He continues to pressure his employees of color to sell the product, noting later that the "Mexican hat" (a sombrero) "really pops on darker skin."

Amy confronts Carmen for agreeing to Glenn's idea, having noticed that Carmen had taken on a highly accented voice to sell the salsa. She exclaims to Jonah her frustration: "She is from Kansas City, why is she talking like Speedy Gonzalez." Carmen tells Amy that *she* chose that accent because, "Oh my God, people *love* it. [*Turns to customers*] Hola señorita, you want to make your day a *fiesta*?" and points out to Amy the larger number of customers she attracts by doing so. The exchange leads to a discussion between the two about cultural sensitivity:

> AMY: Yep, *some* people love it, and *some* people might find it offensive.
> CARMEN: Offensive? Like who?
> AMY: Oh, I don't know, maybe Latino people who would think you're exploiting your heritage and demeaning yourself.
> CARMEN: I don't know who made you the Latino police Amy, but I'm just trying to sell salsa.

When Carmen continues to speak in her accented voice to an elderly (white) customer, Amy angrily tells her to "Talk like a normal person!" prompting the customer to come to Carmen's defense. She tells Carmen, "You speak the language beautifully," and says to Amy, "Excuse me miss, but she is a normal person." Amy, and the rest of the Cloud 9 employees, are then subjected to an hour-long video training session about "racism," led by a blonde white woman. Garret remarks, "Thanks a lot guys. When I woke up this morning, I was *hoping* to learn about racism from a white lady." The session devolves into all the employees misunderstanding the point Amy was trying to make, with Glenn giving a final takeaway message: "Color blind is color kind." Amy's "punishment" for her allegedly racially insensitive remarks is to staff the Señor Salsa station. Dina, Amy's supervisor, sees the lackluster sales and prompts Amy to add a little "authenticity" to her pitch: "People are not going to buy salsa from you unless they think it's authentic! You gotta add some indigenousness, you know, put a little Vergara on!" Amy, again, is offended because Mexican and Latinx culture should not be exploited for financial gain, though she begins to doubt herself once Dina explains that all the proceeds benefit La Benevolencia Orphanage in Nogales, Mexico.

In light of needy children, Amy begins to play to customers' desires. One white customer asks slowly in English, "Is it similar to what you would eat in your village?" to which Amy responds in an accented English, "Sí, es muy auténtica. It is just like the salsa my mother would make in a bowl made from a giant rock." When the same woman asks (again in slowed-down English), "You must have enjoyed many fiestas growing up! Where are you from?" Amy is saved from lying when Mateo shows up as "Jose" her "brother" to explain they grew up in a small village near the Rio Grande. The woman looks around to her fellow customers and exclaims, "Oh, there's *two* of them!" as if to say, "Isn't that nice for them?" while at the same time implying that there had better not be more. The situation culminates with Amy and Mateo dancing along to "La Cucaracha" and Amy reminding the audience that while the dance was nice, there is so much more to Latinx culture: "We are so happy you liked our dance, but it is also important to remember that Latinos can be doctors and lawyers, and architects!" In light of the extremely confused faces of the customers, she remarks, "Never mind, I'm just playing, you should see the looks on your gringo faces!" To her shame, Amy is confronted once more by Carmen, who walks in at that moment on crutches, shakes her head at Amy and walks away, leaving Amy yelling "It's for charity!" while she finishes up another round of her dance.

The episode, like many others, evokes the Latinx gaze because it challenges a number of racialized discourses, while also poking fun at American expectations. What starts off as Amy's rejection of Glenn's overt typecasting becomes a nuanced discussion of cultural appropriation and who has the authority/power to perform culture. Carmen, who is judged by Amy for performing a "false" Latinidad, likewise judges Amy for claiming to be the voice of the "authentic" Latina. The situation is further complicated by the financial benefits in "selling" their authenticity—the performance sells salsa and in turn provides financial aid to needy children in Mexico. When Amy attempts to challenge the customers' assumptions of what Latinxs can achieve, in the face of their disbelief she has to go back to her song and dance, once again showing that it is the larger, mainstream audience that is too ignorant to understand the true Latinx experience in the United States.

Amy's ability to claim a Latinx identity is something she struggles with throughout the series, given that she is lighter-skinned and unable to speak fluent Spanish. In the third season, Amy briefly dates Alex, a Latinx beverage delivery guy, and faces another identity crisis when he jokingly states he is going to revoke her "Latina card" because she is willing to eat burritos made by "a burnout old white dude making money off Mexican food" ("Local Vendors Day"). In order to "prove" her Latinidad, Amy pretends to be able to understand his fast and heavily accented Dominican Spanish. When she finally admits to not being able to keep up, she defends herself by telling Alex, "My Spanish isn't that good! My parents never made me speak it in the house, and I really don't feel like I should be made to feel guilty about that, okay?" Alex sees that Amy is clearly upset by his constant joking about her Latinidad (and she had to spend the day being told by her non-Latinx coworkers how to "properly" date a Latino), and he backs off, letting her know it is no problem.

Moments like these are present throughout the series and allow for both the characters and the audience to reflect on what identity means to them and what it means to belong to a particular ethnic group. Amy's experience reflects that of many subsequent generations of Latinxs whose connection to the language declines as they become more distanced from their immigrant history (Lopez et al., "Hispanic Parents'"). The Pew Research Center has found that while many immigrant parents are likely to speak Spanish to their children, there is a general decline in Spanish use across generations (Lopez et al., "Latino Identity"). Amy's doubts in the episode reflect many of the doubts of Latinxs in their ability to "pass" as Latinx, not feeling Latinx "enough," and yet she refuses to allow any single definition of Latinidad to discredit her cultural identity.

Beyond questions of identity and cultural appropriation, the show also manages to tackle major political issues. Mateo is revealed to be undocumented, and in the fourth season he is apprehended by ICE during a worksite enforcement raid. Thankfully for Mateo, his immigration lawyer manages to get him out on bond, but not without Mateo having to spend a significant amount of time in the detention center. He tells his best friend/coworker Cheyenne (Nicole Bloom) the ugly truth of the conditions: "Girl, it's bad in here. It's cold and there aren't enough blankets. I mean, it's flat-out disgusting. And apparently this is one of the nicer places! The guards think all the undocumented are Latinos, so they just keep yelling at me in Spanish and I don't understand what they're saying. I just . . . I just want to go home" ("Cloud 9.0"). Mateo is assumed to be Latinx simply because of his name and his presence in the facility, demonstrating the lack of awareness of the immigration system about the people in custody.

This lack of awareness is tied to what Nicolas De Genova argues as the racialization of all "illegal" immigrants as "Mexican," where "'Mexican'-ness is always doubly produced at the conjunctures of race and space, as an 'illegal' transnationality, reracialized between whiteness and Blackness within the space of the U.S. nation-state" (De Genova, *Working* 9). Throughout the series, Mateo is terrified of people learning his undocumented status because it means he is in the "legally vulnerable condition of *deportability*—the possibility of deportation, the possibility of being removed from the *space* of the U.S. nation-state" (8). For the most part, Mateo provides a sarcastic commentary on the daily lives of his coworkers; many times he is seen gossiping with those around him without his documented status coming into question because, "On a day-to-day basis, their illegality may be irrelevant to most of their activities, only becoming an issue in certain contexts. . . . Much of the time they are undifferentiated from those around them, but suddenly . . . legal reality is superimposed on daily life" (De Genova, "Migrant" 422). While he does not always mention his status, Mateo is aware that in being labeled as "illegal," he is disposable, because an undocumented immigrant's value is in their disposable labor-power:

> It is *deportability,* and not deportation per se, that has historically rendered undocumented migrant labor a distinctly disposable commodity The very existence of the enforcement branches of the INS (and the Border Patrol, in particular) is premised upon the continued presence of migrants whose undocumented legal status has long been equated with the disposable (deportable), ultimately "temporary" character of the commodity that is their labor-power. (438)

Mateo understands that he can easily be replaced/disposed of, which is why he is constantly shown to be the hardest working employee at Cloud 9, often competing with others to prove himself the best.

Despite Mateo's hard work and dedication to Cloud 9, when gathering testimonials to aid in Mateo's defense, his lawyer explains to Amy that Mateo needs to be more than an "exceptional employee"; that is simply not enough for him to be released on bond. He explains that he is representing "a Pulitzer Prize winner, a heart surgeon that's a father of six, and a former Olympic athlete, and *those* people aren't guaranteed to get out on bond. So no, sorry, it's not enough" ("Testimonials"). The show, despite being a light-hearted comedy, is not willing to make light of Mateo's situation. Yes, he might be a great employee, and an integral part of Cloud 9 (and the show), but that does not mean he gets an easy "get out of jail free" card. His release comes about only as a result of his ex-boyfriend Jeff, a Cloud 9 regional manager, agreeing to testify that ICE was called in to break the store's attempts to unionize.

Superstore does not employ a character's Latinidad simply when it is convenient; and none of the characters of color in *Superstore* are divorced from their social realities. What also distinguishes *Superstore* from similar shows such as *Parks and Recreation* is that it is not couched in privilege—the narratives depicted are those of working-class individuals who are demeaned solely because of their employment. As I noted, in the show's pilot episode Jonah considers himself to be far above his fellow coworkers, and yet they are all working the same shifts and dealing with the same customers, who treat them all as inferior. In light of the COVID-19 pandemic, I am intrigued to see if in future episodes *Superstore* will make reference to the exploitation of big-box store workers to maintain the American way of life during a crisis. Regrettably, America Ferrera is stepping down from the show after the fifth season; though due to a halt in production because of the virus, she will be returning for the beginning episodes of the sixth season to wrap up her character's narrative arc (Schwartz 2020). Ferrera's departure is a loss not only for the show's narrative, but for the production team as well, given that Ferrera served as executive producer for the show since its inception. It will be interesting to see how the show adapts its perspective. Without any major Latinx characters or producers left, can it still present an authentic alternative perspective?

Conclusion

The texts analyzed give me hope for the future of Latinx bodies in the mainstream media. With the creation of more and more shows featuring Latinx characters and Latinx plotlines, I look forward to seeing how my conceptualization of the Latinx gaze, where the camera turns the exoticizing narrative onto white, mainstream culture, can be understood in those shows. In proposing a Latinx gaze, I am highlighting the potential in popular culture to subvert the racialized rhetoric of U.S. political discourse. By presenting an image of America in which the gaze (and laughter) is turned on the white viewer, texts that employ the Latinx gaze are managing to dive into the unspoken, taboo topic of race while straddling the lines of comedy and the unfamiliar.

Saturday Night Live has had a longer history of exoticizing its Latinx hosts than honoring them, though as I argue, "Diego Calls His Mom" is an excellent example of the Latinx gaze in practice. The skit questions the very whiteness of *SNL*'s audience by making Spanish the main language of the sketch and by employing a number of visual cues (such as the calling card) that are more familiar to immigrant families. *Superstore* manages to encapsulate working-class America while also emphasizing the inherent diversity of that sector of society. Instead of downplaying a character's ethnic or racial identity, those aspects come up time and time again as relevant plot points, whether that be Amy's fears of losing her Latinx identity or Mateo's status as an undocumented immigrant. The show relies on humor in order to present major issues in a seemingly nonthreatening manner. It relies on its feel-good nature to slip in a new perspective on American culture and force a new form of understanding about otherness—that it is not necessarily the immigrant or the person of color whose customs are strange and exotic and worthy of ridicule. By encouraging audiences to laugh at the mainstream culture, the show encourages audiences to laugh at themselves.

The texts discussed in this chapter force an almost uncomfortable humor on their viewers—it creates a sense of the uncanny by focusing the mirror back on the white viewer. Beyond creating a sense of anxiety within the mainstream audience, by projecting a reality that is not expected, the Latinx gaze also questions who is meant to be the intended audience, for once not expecting it to be a white viewer, as in "Diego Calls His Mom." I chose to focus only on shows set in the Midwest in order to question the political rhetoric that continues to isolate Latinx voices. By claiming a midwestern Latinx presence in popular culture, I seek to challenge racialized discourses that whitewash an increasingly Brown sector of America. It is my hope that one day this analysis can be applied to noncomedic texts also set in the Midwest.

Notes

1. The online version of the sketch also does not provide translations for the Spanish utilized. When subtitles are included, it merely states "Speaking in foreign language" when Diego is speaking in Spanish.
2. It cannot be forgotten that *SNL* is satirizing midwestern life in general, from the perspective of New York City writers and dwellers.

Works Cited

Bakhtin, Mikhail. *Rabelais and His World*. Translated by Helene Iswolsky, Indiana UP, 1984.
"Cloud 9.0." *Superstore*, created by Justin Spitzer, performances by Nico Santos, America Ferrera, Ben Feldman, and Mark McKinney, season 5, episode 1, Spitzer Holding Company and NBC, 2019.
Critchley, Simon. *On Humour*. Routledge, 2011.

De Genova, Nicholas P. "Migrant 'Illegality' and Deportability in Everyday Life." *Annual Review of Anthropology*, vol. 31, no. 1, 2002, pp. 419–47.

De Genova, Nicholas P. *Working the Boundaries: Race, Space, and "Illegality" in Mexican Chicago.* Duke UP, 2007.

"Diego Calls His Mom." *YouTube*, uploaded by Saturday Night Live, 18 Feb. 2017, www.youtube.com /watch?v=Fid_gQEShSg.

Flores, Nelson, and Jonathan Rosa. "Undoing Appropriateness: Raciolinguistic Ideologies and Language Diversity in Education." *Harvard Educational Review*, vol. 85, no. 2, 2015, pp. 149–71.

Gray, Jonathan, et al. "The State of Satire, the Satire of State." *Satire TV: Politics and Comedy in the Post-network Era*, edited by Jonathan Gray, Jeffrey P. Jones, and Ethan Thompson, New York UP, 2009, pp. 3–6.

"Guns, Pills, and Birds." *Superstore*, created by Justin Spitzer, performances by America Ferrera, Ben Feldman, and Colton Dunn, season 2, episode 4, Spitzer Holding Company and NBC, 2016.

Gutiérrez-Jones, Carl Scott. "Humor, Literacy, and Trauma in Chicano Culture." *Comparative Literature Studies*, vol. 40, no. 2, 2003, pp. 112–26.

"Local Vendors Day." *Superstore*, created by Justin Spitzer, performances by America Ferrera, Ben Feldman, and Mark McKinney, season 3, episode 18, Spitzer Holding Company and NBC, 2018.

Lopez, Mark Hugo, et al. "Latino Identity Declines Across Generations as Immigrant Ties Weaken." *Pew Research Center*, Pew Research Center, 20 Dec. 2017, www.pewresearch.org/hispanic/2017 /12/20/hispanic-identity-fades-across-generations-as-immigrant-connections-fall-away/.

Lopez, Mark Hugo, et al. "Hispanic Parents' Spanish Use with Children Falls as Generations Pass." *Pew Research Center*, Pew Research Center, 2 Apr. 2018, www.pewresearch.org/fact-tank/2018 /04/02/most-hispanic-parents-speak-spanish-to-their-children-but-this-is-less-the-case-in-later -immigrant-generations/.

Maldonado, Marta Maria, et al. "Latin@ Immobilities and Altermobilities Within the U.S. Deportability Regime." *Annals of the American Association of Geographers*, vol. 106, no. 2, 2016, pp. 321–29.

Molina-Guzmán, Isabel. *Latinas and Latinos on TV: Colorblind Comedy in the Post-racial Network Era.* U of Arizona P, 2018.

Morales, Ed. *Living in Spanglish*. St. Martin's Press, 2002.

Mulvey, Laura. "Visual Pleasure and Narrative Cinema." *Feminisms: An Anthology of Literary Theory and Criticism*, edited by Robyn R. Warhol and Diane Price Herndl, Rutgers UP, 1997, pp. 432–42.

Schwartz, Ryan. "Superstore Sets Up America Ferrera's Exit in Penultimate Season 5 Episode; Ben Feldman Teases Finale Cliffhanger." *TVLine*, 3 Apr. 2020, tvline.com/2020/04/02/superstore-amy -exit-explained-america-ferrera-leaving-season-5/.

"Shots and Salsa." *Superstore*, created by Justin Spitzer, performances by America Ferrera, Ben Feldman, and Mark McKinney, season 1, episode 3, Spitzer Holding Company and NBC, 2015.

"Testimonials." *Superstore*, created by Justin Spitzer, performances by Nico Santos, America Ferrera, Ben Feldman, and Mark McKinney, season 5, episode 2, Spitzer Holding Company and NBC, 2019.

Urciuoli, Bonnie. *Exposing Prejudice: Puerto Rican Experiences of Language, Race, and Class.* Westview Press, 1996.

Villafañe, Veronica. "SNL Starts New Season with Debut of First Latina Cast Member, Latino Writer and Lin-Manuel Miranda." *Forbes*, 30 Sept. 2016, www.forbes.com/sites/veronicavillafane/2016 /09/30/snl-starts-new-season-with-debut-of-first-latina-cast-member-latino-writer-and-lin -manuel-miranda/#36a588b77ccc.

Zentella, Ana Celia. *Growing Up Bilingual: Puerto Rican Children in New York.* Blackwell, 1997.

CRISTELA ALONZO'S SUBVERSIVE HUMOR

Television, Nostalgia, and the New Latino American Dream

Melissa Castillo Planas

About a third of the way through the 2014–15 run of the sitcom *Cristela*, the title character, played by comedian Cristela Alonzo, has a seemingly small argument with her family: whether or not she can take her nephew to see the play *West Side Story*. The problem is not that the play deploys problematic stereotypes of Latinos, but apparently because her family does not see the necessity of theater. As the always crotchety matriarch of the family puts it, "I did not come here so my children could be snobs" ("Enter Singing"). Yet, the realities of the family's aversion to theater go deeper. Father Felix is concerned that theater is something he cannot provide his son, Henry. On the other hand, for Cristela these types of opportunities represent her version of the American dream. The American dream for Cristela is about each generation having more opportunities than the last, including access to cultural offerings. It is not about a rags-to-riches aspiration, but rather a striving for a middle-class professionalism that Anglo-Americans often take for granted. And that includes occasional trips to the theater. In order to afford her dream of becoming a lawyer, she lives in cramped quarters with her sister, Daniela (Maria Canals-Barrera), her long-suffering brother-in-law, Felix (Carlos Ponce), and their two young kids (Isabella Day and Jacob Guenther), and a traditional Mexican mother, Natalia (Terri Hoyos), while Felix's cousin and coworker Alberto (comedian Gabriel Iglesias) drops in to shamelessly to profess his undying love for Cristela and provide further comedic relief.

Alonzo's character, Cristela Hernandez, is a protagonist not often explored on television. The show, about a young, ambitious Latina striving to achieve her piece of the American dream through entry into the field of law, has similarities to ABC's *Ugly Betty*, whose main character aspires to run her own magazine, but is otherwise unique for its time in a television landscape with few Latina protagonists (Bush 506) or Latina protagonists who are often only used for their sex appeal (Castillo-Garsow). The pilot introduces Cristela, a young woman with a quick sense of humor, entering her sixth year at law school after juggling taking care of her mom during an illness and working multiple jobs to pay her own way. Cristela wants to become a lawyer, but her traditional Mexican American family doesn't quite understand the time commitment or financial sacrifices.

Cristela was the first program to be created, written, and produced by a Latina: stand-up comedian Cristela Alonzo. Significantly, in that season ABC released two new sitcoms: *Black-ish* (2014–) and *Cristela* (2014–15). Moreover, along with John Ridley's anthology drama *American Crime* (2015–17) and *Fresh Off the Boat* (2015), the first Asian American-focused show since the notorious 1994 cancellation of Margaret Cho's *All American Girl*, both premiering midseason, ABC's slate of 2014–15 offerings indicated a purposeful shift toward inclusion (Acham). This does not overshadow, however, the ways in which Latinxs have been marginalized in English-language television, from characters, to writers, to producers. In "Latina/os on TV! A Proud (and Ongoing) Struggle over Representation and Authorship," Mary Beltrán comments: "In the 2000s, narrative series more often attempted to include Latina/o characters and to portray them in a multidimensional light. Diverse ensemble cast shows, a programming trend in this decade, often featured one or a few Latino/a character or characters among its ensemble and sporadically focused on these characters."[1] Furthermore, according to Beltrán:

> The most recent study looking at these questions, by Frances Negron Muntaner and other researchers at Columbia University in 2014, found that the gap between our numbers in the general population and in television has, in fact, grown. While Latina/os comprised 17 percent of the population in 2013, there were no Latino or Latina lead characters in the top prime time television series that year. When they are part of the television landscape, characters such as Betty Suarez of *Ugly Betty* thus have the unenviable (and ultimately impossible) task of standing in for the vast diversity of Latina/os. (Beltrán 24)

This lack of diversity is even more stark when considering other creative positions on TV, such as writers, directors, and producers. Few Latinx were in any sort of creative position prior to the 1990s, and from 2010 through 2013 Latinx still composed only 1 percent of employed producers, 2 percent of writers, none of the showrunners, and 4 percent of directors in television (Beltrán 23). Thus, 2014 and *Cristela* represented an important direction for Latinx representation in English-language television as a show not only centered on a Latina but written and produced by one as well.

Cristela is groundbreaking in many other ways. Cristela's striving (even against her own family) for something more and different from what her poor upbringing would allow her to expect is at the center of the year-long run of this comedic sitcom, which often revolves around arguments with her often unsupportive realist family about her more middle-class aspirations. Thus, while the main character Cristela represents a somewhat traditional version of the American dream, conversations with her family as well as with non-Latinx characters on the show demonstrate the way in which the American dream is not monolithic. Instead, some characters see the American dream as accessible mostly only to white people, while others see it as completely inaccessible to those of Mexican descent. In this way, *Cristela*, despite having a lighthearted family tone and style nostalgic of sitcoms of another generation, nevertheless enters into a very real debate about the realities of the American dream for working-class Mexican Americans. In the end, the negotiated American dream that is presented is a more holistic one, based more in familial success than an individual achievement.

Cristela Alonzo's American Dream

Cristela Alonzo grew up outside McAllen, Texas, in the sort of poverty that many can hardly imagine. It included squatting in a deserted diner and sharing a bed with her mother until she graduated from high school (Alonzo 8, 17). From these origins, she grew into one of the most popular comedians on the college circuit, appeared on Conan O'Brien's late show, starred in her own eponymous sitcom, did voices for Disney, and starred in a 2017 Netflix special, *Lower Classy*. Alonzo details her childhood and career in her 2019 memoir, *Music to My Ears: A Mixtape Memoir of Growing Up and Standing Up*. She also details her version of the American dream.

For Cristela Alonzo, following her dreams was something that her immigrant mother never had the opportunity to do (Alonzo 6). As she writes in the dedication of her memoir, "People like me get to live out their dream because of people like you who have sacrificed their own dreams in order to let their future generations have a chance at life" (v). Although this dedication may sound superficially like a fairly standard version of the American dream, it isn't. Not only does it recognize that some in society don't have the opportunity to pursue or even think of an American dream, Alonzo complicates this dream further by grounding her story in family: past generations sacrifice for future generations. It is the community that supports its members, not an individual who succeeds because of extraordinary virtue or talent.

This is a lesson that Cristela Alonzo takes to heart. Over and over again in her memoir she recounts being faced with the opportunity to pursue her dream or to support her family, and in every instance she chooses to support her family, especially when it comes to her mother. When her mother became ill, Cristela not only returned from Los Angeles, where she was pursuing a performance career, but moved in with her mother and sister to be a caretaker until the end of her mother's life (Alonzo 147–48). This is such a significant moment in Cristela's life and artistic formation that she based her show *Cristela* on this period. As she explains: "The sitcom *Cristela* I had on network TV for a year was based on this time in my life when I had to move in with my sister and help take care of her kids and my mother. I originally wanted to share this part of my life to show that so many of us had to live this kind of life whether against our wishes or not. It was just something you had to do as a member of the family" (Alonzo 149). Yet, for many it is not. In the traditional American dream narrative there is no footnote that says you will chase success unless your family needs you. In the conventional American dream, one pursues individual riches and fame, no matter the consequences. It is for this reason that presidential candidate and then president Donald Trump portrayed himself as a self-made man when in fact he came from a wealthy family.

Moreover, for Cristela, success is in the shape of the dream and her pursuit of it, not necessarily in any sort of specific monetary accomplishment or fame. According to Alonzo, "The best chance you have at being successful is being honest about your story. I always tell people, if you're in the business because you think you're going to be famous or rich, don't do it. You're already setting yourself up for failure. When someone says that they want to be rich, or famous, how much fame is enough and how much money is enough?" (Balderas). Thus, it should come as no surprise that Cristela Alonzo has over and over again in her career turned down roles and opportunities that would bring greater fame or money in order to engage in other projects that she found more fulfilling, such as community work (Alonzo 233). For example, after her show was canceled, she was offered the opportunity to cohost the popular television show *The View* as well as develop another show, and in both instances she turned down the offers (Alonzo 233–34). Although she did a stand-up special in 2017, she stayed silent on that front as well for two years until the release of her memoir. Again this was purposeful. As Alonzo explains:

> After my first stand-up special was released, I decided to take a break from stand-up. I also didn't feel like it was time for me to do anything related to the entertainment industry. The 2016 election had just passed and a lot of people in my community weren't doing well. There were feelings of fear and sadness. I didn't feel right trying to make a living at the time because, overall, I wanted to make sure everyone was okay. Instead of working, I decided to spend my time going across the country and checking in to see how different parts of my community were doing. I had no idea

how the dust would settle and I figured that my top priority was to make sure I did everything I could so that people knew we were going to be okay. (237)

Thus, rather than continue in the field of entertainment, Alonzo joined organizations working on issues of poverty, immigration, and healthcare. As a result of her choices, today Alonzo is not rich, nor is she particularly famous outside certain circles; however, that is not her version of the American dream. She is comfortable, and her family is comfortable, which for her means not having to do any work she doesn't want to do, being able to take her family on vacation to Hawaii, and having healthcare (Alonzo 282, 285).

Cristela Hernandez's American Dream

Alonzo's path toward the American dream is significant because it represents the journey of a family rather than just an individual. For this reason, although her show is called *Cristela*, it is really a show about a family struggling with and arguing about the American dream. This comes across strongly in the pilot, which introduces Cristela, a sixth-year law student, and her family (consisting of her sister, Daniela; brother-in-law, Felix; their children Izzy and Henry; and mother, Natalia), who all live together in Daniela and Felix's modest Dallas, Texas, house. Cristela is up for an unpaid internship at a law firm, which creates tension in the household because her mother and sister don't understand why she would be working for free, while Felix is concerned that Cristela is "never going to leave" ("Pilot"). Amid this lighthearted tension, in just the first few minutes a number of important factors of Cristela's life are revealed. She is in her sixth year of law school (usually a three-year full-time program) and living with her sister and brother-in-law because she is paying her own way and had to drop out several times to care for her mother. Nevertheless, her family doesn't understand the long process to professional achievement, nor the social capital of an unpaid internship, nor the sacrifices that living together requires. They want her to follow Daniela's route and settle down and have a family. As critic Alyssa Rosenberg describes:

> The episode strikes a nice balance. Daniela and Cristela's other relatives are not hostile to achievement in any way, and "Cristela" does not try to paint them as adherents of some sort of nebulous culture of poverty. Instead, they have real and pressing financial needs, and they are packed together in a house too small for all of them, ratcheting up family tensions. The family's need for immediate relief is real and understandable. (Rosenberg)

Thus, what is at stake here are two different versions of the American dream: Cristela's more naive view that hard work can raise her or anyone out of poverty versus her family's immediate needs to survive and their view that life is not, in fact, fair for everyone. Not all jobs are meant to be dream jobs, but rather work as a means to an end—putting food on the table and a house over their head.

Here Doug Bush's assessment rings true to a great extent: "ABC's *Cristela* (2014–2015) presents a quintessential American dream narrative, and we are invited to cheer for the legal intern protagonist because she is hardworking, well-educated and makes sacrifices to get ahead" (505). However, I disagree that these sacrifices reflect some sort of assimilation; rather, they reflect what is developed in the series as a more holistic view of the American dream. This version of the dream is less individualistic and more rooted in family. While Bush argues that Cristela submits and conforms to the norms of a white establishment, I argue instead that Alonzo overwhelmingly employs a subversive humor to address the realities of racism in the workplace and the way in which Latinx immigrants negotiate and come to terms with their own understanding of the American dream narrative. While she begins the series following her boss Trent's directives and laughing self-consciously at his racist jokes, throughout the series she also stands up to him in important ways that include choosing family over career. Thus, there are certain sacrifices she is unwilling to make, and those choices are based more on familial needs than any desire to assimilate. For example, in episode 16, Cristela chooses to attend her nephew Henry's confirmation rather than serve as a token person of color for her boss, who is experiencing a public relations debacle that includes charges of racism ("Confirmation").

The quintessential American dream narrative of individual success is also implicitly highly gendered, and always focused more on the accomplishments of heterosexual white men, to the detriment of white women, whose traditional role was to support ambitious husbands and nurture their children. This gendered aspect dovetails uncomfortably with one aspect of the family-oriented Latinx stereotype, and *Cristela* does not shy away from this uncomfortable narrative. One of the family's major concerns about Cristela is her failure to date. In episode 2, for example, her sister registers her on a dating website, while her mother, married at seventeen, warns her of the danger of being a spinster ("Soul Mates"). Meanwhile in episode 12, Daniela exerts pressure on Cristela to lose weight in order to "find a man" ("Hypertension"). Here again, the two versions of the American dream conflict and put pressure on the way gender defines these goals. While Daniela wants Cristela to have a life like hers with a husband and children, Cristela is focused on her career and doesn't see Daniela's career as a call center manager as significant.

Here Alonzo crystalizes the familiar conflict with profound simplicity when she asks her sister, "How do you think it makes me feel when you and Ama criticize my life every day?"

Despite Cristela's seemingly naive view of the American dream, she nevertheless recognizes that it is different for not just women but all people of color. In a heart to heart with her niece Izzy in episode 11, she notes, "I'm the first one in the family to go to college and in that world we have to work twice as hard and be twice as good to get as far as everyone else" ("Dead Arm"). Significantly, this understanding that the American dream is not equal for all is a reflection of the history of the American dream itself. As Jim Cullen writes in *The American Dream: A Short History of an Idea That Shaped a Nation*, the idea of an American dream has never been monolithic. Nevertheless, as the book also shows, for the majority of its history that dream has been limited to white males and most recently is associated with the emergence of Hollywood and the culture of celebrity. Again, none of these apply to Cristela's story.

Conversations about gender and ethnicity come together in episode 15 when niece Izzy has the opportunity to get into the gifted and talented program at her school ("Gifted and Talented"). Cristela helps Izzy study and really wants her to get in because she herself didn't get into the program when she was in school and feels it will help Izzy have an "easier route" to success. Meanwhile, Natalia frets about men not liking women who are too smart and Izzy surpassing her brother, Henry, who did not gain entrance into the program. As it turns out, Natalia doesn't want Izzy to grow up to be like Cristela, since although Cristela is smart, she is currently working for no pay and has no husband. Moreover, Natalia reveals that Cristela did get into the program as a child but Natalia tore up the letter. As Natalia explains, "We are not supposed to aim so high because the higher you aim the farther you fall." For Natalia, the American dream is not for people of color, especially not for women, who should understand and accept their place in society.

This conflict is played out over and over again in the Hernandez household, but it is also resolved into a negotiated American dream in which individual achievement is allowed and at times even celebrated, though never at the expense of the family. On reflection, Natalia helps Izzy study for a retake of her exam so she can "aim high" like her aunt. Overall, although the family does not understand Cristela's journey toward professional success and even makes fun of it, they generally come around and support her. This becomes especially clear in episode 21 when Daniela loses her job and Natalia goes into "village mode," looking for any way to save money, including postponing Cristela's $320 bar exam so they can save the money and she can take a job at a salon instead ("Village Mode"). In this case, Cristela agrees, yet again, to put her family's needs first over her individual ones. It is only when her white male coworker comes to her house and intervenes that Cristela stands up for herself. She has to learn to become more individualistic from someone who has never considered putting family above self. When Cristela argues, "My family needs me to look out for them," Josh responds, "Who's looking out for you?" Having been raised in an immigrant household and close family, Cristela never imagined her American dream deviating from support for her family. But in many ways it must. Finally standing up to her mother, she says, "Ama, this is not about survival anymore. You're not in your village. You survived. You're here. Now shut up and enjoy this great country that you brought us to and watch your daughter succeed." Although Cristela stands up to her always crotchety and intimidating mother, she does so in a way that indicates that the American dream is for both of them—not just her. They negotiate an American dream that both of them can accept—one where Cristela reaches professional status at the same time that she stays connected and rooted in *familia*.

While *Cristela* tackled numerous issues, including sexism in the Latinx community, class, bullying, weight, and anti-Mexican racism, at the show's core, Cristela Alonzo, through the character of Cristela Hernandez, is exploring what the American dream means for not just her but her family. Moreover, a big part of this exploration is the acknowledgment by Cristela that there is a way to negotiate the American dream so as to incorporate a mixed-status family centered by women of color. According to Alonzo:

> You know, one of the big things I want to do with this show is I want to give Latino kids a chance to know that if I can do it, they can do it. When I was a kid, I really loved TV, but I really didn't have anybody who looked like me that I could look up to. I want to be able to tell people like me that if they really want to do something, they can absolutely do it if they're willing to work towards it. The chance is there. We're living in a time where anything is possible. I'm living proof of that, and that's what the show is about. (Holtz)

Again, while these comments seem to point toward a traditional view of the American dream, Alonzo's memoir and show demonstrate the ways in which she negotiated her dreams to incorporate her family.

The End of the Dream

Cristela premiered on Friday, October 10, 2014, with over 6.6 million viewers, making it #1 in its time slot. By its April 17, 2015, final, it had dropped in popularity, while still maintaining a high of 4.7 million viewers (Terrero). Overall the show received generally positive reviews as well as endorsements from Latinx organizations like the National Hispanic Leadership Association.[2] Nevertheless, the show was canceled after a single season. According to Alonzo, this was due to a lack of proper publicity as well as lack of a regular time slot. As she wrote on her blog after the cancellation: "It was a multi-cam sitcom that SOMETIMES aired on Friday nights. I say sometimes because a lot of times we were preempted for more important things like an Easter egg hunt happening in real time. Kidding. In reality, we were preempted for other things like a documentary on a parade and some other things I can't remember. I think one night was a show about Christmas lights?" (Rodriguez). Still her memoir reveals another side to this American dream—one of constant battles with writers over the creation of authentic Latinx characters. According to Alonzo:

> One day, I was in the writers' room and one of the writers had mouthed off at me because he didn't like a note I gave. I took a moment to explain to him that this show had MY name on it, not his. If this was the only chance I got, I had to try to make the best of it because once the show was canceled, he could move on and write on another show. I, on the other hand, would have to answer questions about this show for years to come. That was why I wanted things done a certain way. For me, this show was not about churning out stories for the sake of filling the time slot. For me, this show was about making sure that people who connected with the show knew that it was trying to be as authentic as I was in real life. (231)

What this quotation reveals is the conflict between Alonzo's attempt to portray *her* life, in a way that felt authentic to her experience, and the way her show was often received as needing to represent *all* Latinos.

Again this goes back to the paucity of Latinx characters on TV. If there were numerous Latinx shows, there would be no need to have authenticity debates. As Mary Beltrán elucidates:

> There are also ongoing debates regarding whether a focus on "positive" images should be sought by advocates lobbying for television narratives and characters that will be empowering for Latina/os. The fear of stereotyping arguably has had a chilling effect on Latina/o representation on network and cable television. Images of middle-class Latina/os in professional positions

have typically been viewed by advocates as more desirable than presenting Latina/os as working class, in manual labor jobs, or as not fluent in English. Given the fact that a third of U.S. Latina/os are currently first-generation immigrants and that many Latina/o families still struggle with issues of socioeconomic disadvantage, it's useful to consider what it means to push to never see these images on television.... Has focus on the eradication of stereotypes had the indirect consequence of encouraging television producers to only depict Latina/o characters as completely assimilated to American mainstream culture and to erase Latina/o communities altogether? (Beltrán 32)

In many ways, these were the debates that occurred on the set of *Cristela*. For Alonzo, everything about the show was a fight. The family, for example, was portrayed as much more middle class than her family, while the idea to name the show after her didn't represent the family focus of the show (Alonzo 220). Nevertheless, the show was still groundbreaking in many important ways, most of all in its portrayal of a different type of American dream, negotiated in family needs.

In many ways, *Cristela* paved the way for shows like *One Day at a Time*, now in its fourth season. Still, the similarities between *Cristela* and *One Day at a Time* mean that television is still slow to evolve in its portrayal of Latinx characters. As Alonzo points out:

I think that right now, we're doing better than we have, which I think we should acknowledge, but I think there's so much work left to do. My show was a family sitcom. *One Day at a Time*...is a family sitcom. I would like to see us grow, where it doesn't have to be family-based. . . . Now we need to work on evolving the narrative to where we actually don't show the same thing over and over again, and we actually show other facets of our personalities. (Balderas)

In many ways, shows like *Gentefied*, *Vida*, and *East Los High* partially fill that void. Yet they are all set in the same area of Los Angeles, continuing the narrative that Latinx live in only certain areas, limiting the TV experiences.

In 2017, Cristela Alonzo returned to standup with her Netflix special *Lower Classy*. In it she spoke warmly about the show *Cristela* to loud cheers and shouts of "bring it back." In that special she describes the inspiration for the show:

I loved that show. That show . . . That show was really about a part of my life where I'd moved in with my sister, I helped take care of her kids and my mom, and it was very important for me to do that show. You might notice, in my stand-up, I talk a lot about my mom. And for me . . . if you saw the show, she was this very crotchety old woman. She hated everyone, you know? But, like, if she made fun of you, that meant she loved you. You know what I mean? And for me, my mom was always the star of my show. I talk a lot about my mom because I feel like when we talk about immigrants . . . we never really give them a heart or a soul. And I wanted people to know the story of my mom and know that she was a real person and she was like that, and that she went through a lot so that I could be here tonight. That's why I do it. And, you know, for some people, my experience isn't their Latino experience. And I get that, you know? I just wanted to show mine. I wanted to show my life, you know? The show wasn't called Every Latino in the World. It was called *Cristela*. And for me, I wanted to show a mom like that because you ever notice that the moms on TV, they're never like that? They're always kind of the same. They're always very happy. They never get mad. My mom used to get mad, you know?

Significantly, even though sitcoms tend to emphasize stereotypes of middle-class values, Alonzo again broke the mold with the character of her mother, who was also not the stereotype of the long-suffering immigrant but rather a unique character with vibrancy and complexity. Although in many ways its multi-camera operation complete with a laugh track was nostalgic of a past era in television, in building a new sort of family show, *Cristela* in many ways paved the way for the Latinx television we see today.

In 2019, Cristela returned to stand-up to promote her memoir, *Music to My Ears: A Mixtape Memoir of Growing Up and Standing Up*. I had the pleasure of seeing one show of her *Affordable Care Act* tour in New York City on October 8, 2019. During the show she emphasized her journey over the previous three years after the 2016 election, during which she left stand-up to pursue advocacy work and write her memoir. Discussing the work she's done with activist Dolores Huerta, Alonzo lamented, "She's never gotten the attention she deserves because she's a Mexican woman." I wondered if she was talking about herself as well. Still, cheers from the full crowd at Carolines on Broadway made it clear that many were just waiting for what was next.

Notes

1. Beltrán elaborates: "Popular series that did so included *Lost* (2004–2010), *Desperate Housewives* (2004–2012), *Modern Family* (2009–), *CSI: Miami* (2002–2012), and *Grey's Anatomy* (2005–), to the benefit of actors such as Jorge Reyes on *Lost*, Eva Longoria on *Desperate Housewives*, Sofia Vergara on *Modern Family*, and Adam Rodriguez on *CSI: Miami*. Another, more troubling trend was the resurgence of Latino criminal roles in popular dramas, for example on *Breaking Bad* (2008–2013) and *Weeds* (Showtime, 2008–2012), which featured Latino characters as frightening thugs, drug dealers, and hit men" (29–30).

2. According to June Jennings, "All in all, 'Cristela' defies the narrow stereotypes that have plagued Latina characters for decades. Cristela is neither a 'spicy' temptress with a temper nor a near-mute housecleaner (not that there is anything wrong with doing housework or being comfortable with one's sexuality). Cristela is outspoken, loves watching football (and not just because of Tony Romo) and cracks jokes about her weight. She is juggling student loans, racial microaggressions in the workplace and trying to please her no-nonsense immigrant mother. Cristela is—for lack of better words—an actual person. 'Cristela' (both the show and the character) has a lot of potential and I will definitely be tuning in next week to see how she fares."

Works Cited

Acham, Christine. "Black-Ish: Kenya Barris on Representing Blackness in the Age of Black Lives Matter." *Film Quarterly*, vol. 71, no. 3, spring 2018, pp. 48–57.

Alonzo, Cristela. *Music to My Ears: A Mixtape Memoir of Growing Up and Standing Up*. Atria Books, 2019.

Balderas, Kristen. "Cristela Alonzo: Why the Comedian Wants the Latino Narrative to Evolve." *Philadelphia Inquirer*, 9 Oct. 2019, inquirer.com/celebrity/cristela-alonso-stand-up-mixtape-memoir-philadelphia-helium-20191010.html.

Beltrán, Mary. "Latina/os on TV! A Proud (and Ongoing) Struggle Over Representation and Authorship." *The Routledge Companion to Latina/o Popular Culture*, edited by Frederick Luis Aldama, Routledge, 2017, pp. 23–33.

Bush, Doug P. "The Cost of Citizenship: Assimilation and Survival in Cristela." *Latino Studies* vol. 17, 2019, pp. 505–21.

Castillo-Garsow, Melissa. "What Not to Love About Latinas on TV." *In America* (CNN Blog), 22 Nov. 2011, cnn.com/2011/11/22/us/the-sadly-sexy-legacy-of-latinas-on-tv/index.html.

"Confirmation." *Cristela*, created by Cristela Alonzo and Kevin Hench, directed by Robbie Countryman, written by Kay Cannon, season 1, episode 16, ABC, Mar. 2015.

Cullen, Jim. *The American Dream: A Short History of an Idea That Shaped a Nation*. Oxford UP, 2003.

"Dead Arm." *Cristela*, created by Cristela Alonzo and Kevin Hench, directed by Gail Mancuso, written by Peter Murrieta, season 1, episode 11, ABC, 16 Jan. 2015.

"Enter Singing." *Cristela*, created by Cristela Alonzo and Kevin Hench, directed by Gail Mancuso, written by Dana Gould, season 1, episode 7, ABC, 21 Nov. 2014.

"Gifted and Talented." *Cristela*, created by Cristela Alonzo and Kevin Hench, directed by Robbie Countryman, written by Kevin Hench, season 1, episode 15, ABC, 27 Feb. 2015.

Holtz, Natalie. "If It's Not a Longshot, It's Not Alonzo." *Latino Leaders Magazine*, Oct./Nov. 2014, pp. 70–71.

"Hypertension." *Cristela*, created by Cristela Alonzo and Kevin Hench, directed by Gail Mancuso, written by Pat Bullard, season 1, episode 12, ABC, 30 Jan. 2015.

Jennings, June. "Review: 'Cristela' Is Revolutionary yet Relatable." *Student Life*, studlife.com/cadenza/tv-cadenza/2014/10/12/review-cristela-is-revolutionary-yet-relatable/.

Lower Classy. Directed by Marcus Raboy, written by Cristela Alonzo, Netflix, 24 Jan. 2017. Netflix app.

"Pilot." *Cristela*, created by Cristela Alonzo and Kevin Hench, directed by John Pasquin, written by Cristela Alonzo and Kevin Hench, season 1, episode 1, ABC, 10 Oct. 2014.

Rodriguez, Priscilla. "Cristela Alonzo Reacts to Cancellation of 'Cristela' in Long Letter to Fans." *Latina.com*, 12 May 2015.

Rosenberg, Alyssa. "'Jane the Virgin' and 'Cristela' Cast Sharp Eyes on the Quest for a Better Life." *Washington Post*, 14 Oct. 2014.

"Soul Mates." *Cristela*, created by Cristela Alonzo and Kevin Hench, directed by Gerry Cohen, written by Cristela Alonzo and Kevin Hench, season 1, episode 2, ABC, 17 Oct. 2014.

Terrero, Nina. "Cristela Alonzo Writes Blog About Show Cancellation: I'm 'Angry.'" *EW.com*, 12 May 2015, https://ew.com/article/2015/05/12/cristela-alonzo-blog/.

"Village Mode." *Cristela*, created by Cristela Alonzo and Kevin Hench, directed by Bob Koherr, written by Pat Bullard and Peter Murrieta, season 1, episode 21, ABC, 10 Apr. 2015.

Cristela Alonzo's Subversive Humor

55

HUMOR AS SUBVERSION

Feminist Messages in *George Lopez*

Yadira Gamez

It's a bird! It's a plane! Superman? No, it's a Latinx on primetime television. As one of the few Latinx-led television shows on a prime-time network, *George Lopez* has had a significant cultural impact. At its conception in 2002, there had been only two long-running and successful shows with Latinx leads, *I Love Lucy* and *Chico and the Man* (Schneider, "Slayer" A1). *George Lopez* was frequently hailed as playing an important role in combating Latinx stereotypes in popular media (Schneider, "Slayer" A1; Schneider, "Latinxs Get Leverage" 17; Lopez and Keteyian 115; Fernandez). Therefore, it should come as no surprise that academic research on *George Lopez* has focused on Latinx representation and how the show deals with stereotypes. While research on stereotypes and representation is valuable, research on *George Lopez* has failed to shift in order to accommodate the growth of the Latinx studies field.

In this chapter, I will discuss how humor was used in *George Lopez* as a subversive method to interact with Latinx issues such as feminism. *George Lopez*'s position as a groundbreaking show of its kind meant it had to resonate with mainstream audiences *and* Latinx audiences in order to stay on the air. This led to it representing a middle-of-the-road feminism that melds Chicana and American middle-class feminism. The two types of feminism diverge when discussing the value of women's work, as shown in the three episodes I analyze: "George's Grand Slam," "Charity," and "George Says I Do . . . More in This Marriage." The three episodes all deal with feminism, but they are disjointed when examined together because they do not convey a consistent message. The concern with ratings and the show's position on a prime-time network significantly impacted the content *George Lopez* put out, but the episodes are consistent in their dependence on humor to connect with audiences.

The central role humor would play in *George Lopez* was evident from its conception. The show ran for five seasons, from 2002 to 2007, but work on the project began in 2000. It should be noted that *George Lopez* came to be because a white woman had a dream. Sandra Bullock decided to address the lack of diversity found on television because she "was tired of everything being whitewashed on TV" (Lopez and Keteyian 101). Her work began when she traveled to several stand-up comedy performances and discovered George Lopez. While Lopez was worried that a network would not agree to do a show depicting a non-stereotypical Latinx family in America, Bullock was not. The actress famously told him, "Let me worry about the network … you just worry about being funny" (Lopez and Keteyian 103). Through her contacts, Bullock was able to secure a contract with Warner Brothers and ABC. Bullock's connections would not only get the show going, but also keep it in motion. Without her contributions, *George Lopez* would not have been able to succeed on its own, and without *George Lopez*, the dearth of diversity on prime-time television may have continued to this day.

While diversity is a hot button issue today, at the conception of *George Lopez* diversity was just beginning to permeate fields such as television. In the early 2000s, 12.5 percent of the American population was Latinx, but Latinxs made up only 3.9 percent of prime-time television (Mastro and Behm-Morawitz 110). In other words, there were very few Latinx-centered shows on television that featured both Latinx people and issues. When Latinx characters were depicted, they were often cast in a revolving set of stereotypes. This was the scene *George Lopez* was trying to enter, and it is important to note how the show was different from others at the time. Not only did Lopez and other Latinx actors star in the show, but they also had creative control in the writing room and received production credits (Calvo). The Latinx characters were given central and recurring roles instead of occupying the supporting role that provided comedic relief, such as Fez in *That 70's Show*. Their Latinx identity is also unambiguous and embraced during advertising and filming, but more importantly the show is not engaging in the tokenism that was rampant in the industry. Instead, *George Lopez* tries and succeeds in dispelling some of the stereotypes that permeated the mainstream through such characters as Speedy Gonzalez. The limited Latinx representation made every Latinx representation the standard by which mainstream America came to understand the group (Aldama and González 25). *George Lopez* changed that.

It is not a coincidence that Bullock purposefully went out in search of comedians to build a show. Ethnic and gender minorities such as Bill Cosby and Roseanne Barr had already proven they could make the jump from stand-up to sitcom as well as white men. Social minorities have used humor strategically because humor "is always subversive, and always responds to cultural imperatives" (McIntire-Strasburg 8). In other words, minorities have recognized stand-up comedy as a safe space from which to critique the social and cultural norms that place them in marginalized positions. Since humor is subversive by nature, mainstream audiences often laugh before they begin to unpack why a joke is funny. In order to interact with and truly understand a joke, one must have foundational knowledge about the way society operates. This fact makes comedy a perfect tool for social critique. In fact, Latinx comedians are well known for using comedy in order to "exploit stereotypes created by whites to amuse, but at the same time call attention to the real problems" the community faces (McIntire-Strasburg 6). Comedy is the perfect genre in which to insert a minority voice because society has many stereotypes about Latinx people. When diversity expands on television, existing stereotypes about Latinxs can be recognized and then modified to show the heterogeneity of the group.

In order for a show like *George Lopez* to succeed, it had to find a balance: between making Latinx audiences feel represented and appealing to a mainstream audience. Previous Latinx-centered shows had not succeeded because they had a problem maintaining the attention of a mainstream audience (Markert 150). For this reason, humor had to be used subversively in order to comment on Latinx culture. Kant, one of the most popular philosophers used in humor studies, says "laughter is an affect resulting from the sudden transformation of a heightened expectation into nothing" (116). When Kant wrote this in *Critique of Judgement*, he was certainly not thinking about *George Lopez*, yet the show draws heavily on his statement about incongruity being at the core of humor. Kant explains that agreement and belief in a concept is not necessary in order to produce humor, which means that the humor used in *George Lopez* could appeal to all audiences. Specifically, the show relies on the heightened expectations of mainstream and Latinx audiences.

Audiences might have expected *George Lopez* to replicate the stereotypical portrayals of Latinx people on TV up to that time. In describing his eleven theses of stereotypes, Charles Ramírez Berg states, "repetition tends to normalize stereotypes" (18). The constant and consistent repetition of Latinx stereotypes in media normalize these prejudiced viewpoints. Ramírez Berg's thesis is backed by psychology's cultivation theory, which states that long-term exposure to stereotypes can lead to a stable perception of those being stereotyped (Mastro and Behm-Morawitz 124–25). Consumption of media such as TV can keep stereotypes alive in the minds of audiences; so the repeated casting of Latinx actors into stereotypical roles can be harmful to the group as a whole. The most prominent six stereotypes for Latinxs are: el bandido, the harlot, the male buffoon, Latin lover, female clown, and dark lady (Ramírez Berg 66). All six of these representations hit on the idea of the Latinx as excess: excessively sexual, excessively criminal, or excessively stupid. The repeated presentation of these stereotypes leads mainstream audiences to expect this excessive behavior whenever Latinxs appear on the screen. This can greatly limit the types of roles Latinx actors are given. *George Lopez* sets up scenes in which an audience expects the stereotype but then does not have that expectation met. *George Lopez* is setting up an expectation and dissolving it into nothing, thus provoking a natural human reaction to laugh away the moment, just as described by Kant. In this humorous moment lies *George Lopez*'s ability to critique the media space that has placed Latinxs in an ethnic minority box that limits their media representation.

The ethnicity of the characters is treated as adjacent instead of central in *George Lopez*. In fact, one of the most important features of the show is not the characters' ethnicity but their social class. The show begins with George being promoted to manager at Powers Aviation. Having the show represent a middle-class family was a groundbreaking decision because the stereotype is that most Latinx families are working class. Thanks to the Chicano Movement, the chances of Latinx families moving out of the working class into the professional class was a great possibility. In fact, due to the increase of educational opportunities for Latinx people, more and more Latinxs were entering professional fields and managerial positions (Román 14). The aspiration of moving up in social class is often depicted, but rarely are non-working-class Latinx families shown on prime-time television. This move allows for the show to de-emphasize the family's Latinidad and become what George Lopez calls just a show about an American family (Schneider, "Slayer"). George's new social class generates the show's humor as he figures out his new position in society. Through his discoveries, he often makes the working-class characters and women the butt of his jokes.

George, the person and character, has a working-class background that ties him to his Latinx culture, but in his new middle-class life the most interesting interactions he has are with white characters. White people are frequently cast as points of disruption for George, and his interactions with them are always revealing. For example, in "George's Grand Slam" (season 4, episode 19), the show directly addresses the difference between mainstream American middle-class feminism and Chicana feminism for the first and only time in the series using a white body. The scene begins in the living room with George's daughter Carmen (Masiela Lusha) and her friend Kenzie (Hilary Duff) practicing their poetry. When George and Carmen's boyfriend, Jason (Bryan Fisher), enter the room, the girls are displaced to the kitchen so the men can enjoy the game. Jason says he is hungry and is going to the kitchen to make a sandwich. George reaches out a hand to indicate he should sit back down and instructs Carmen to make the sandwich instead. Carmen, stepping into the gendered expectations placed on Latinas within families, agrees. Kenzie immediately yells out "¡Órale!" and proceeds to explain to Carmen that her father is being "sexist" since "he is only asking because she is a girl." Carmen is shocked and agrees with Kenzie's assertion, which leads to a confrontation between George and Kenzie. The interaction between a Latinx patriarch and an underaged white woman is unusual for the show.

Except for Carmen's boyfriend, Jason, the Lopez family limits their intercultural interactions. While *George Lopez* is known as being a positive portrayal of a Latinx family, it rarely allows for Latinx people on the show to interact with their white peers. The lack of interaction with white people, when they make up a majority of the population, removes them from cultural inclusion (Mastro and Behm-Morawitz 125). Therefore, the fact that the scene depicts a culture clash in regard to feminism is even more powerful.

Latinx culture is patriarchal, but this does not mean feminism does not thrive within the culture. Specifically, Latinxs have their own brand of feminism known as Chicana feminism, developed for and by Latinx women. The show sets up a stark dynamic by having a white woman come into a Latinx home and call the traditional family dynamic sexist. Kenzie is cast in the role of the white hero who gifts Carmen with her knowledge of sexism. The "white hero is the sun around which the film narrative revolves, and the rationale of a typical Hollywood story is to illustrate how moral, resourceful, brave, intelligent—in a word, superior—he is" (Ramírez Berg 67). The designation "white hero" can aptly be applied to Kenzie in this episode because she is the central figure via her role as catalyst. The fact that she is played by a pop star heightens her pay-attention-to-me status. Her temporary existence on the show should give members of the Lopez family a sense of immediacy when they interact with her. When Kenzie talks about feminism, she is speaking from a historically white kind of feminism that excludes the experience of women of color (Lorde). To ridicule the type of feminism Kenzie is selling, the writers have her talk abstractly about the patriarchy in relation to poetry as she argues with George. This is an effective method of highlighting her pseudo-intelligence, which George later teases her for. Kenzie's abstract observations alienate her from the audience and make them question whether this white hero is one who should be listened to at all. The fact is, Kenzie is disruptive to the Latinx family dynamic when she enters and says the word "sexism," a word that had not directly entered the home in any other episodes. To soften the seriousness of her claim, Kenzie aligns herself with Carmen and Latinx women through her use of Spanish language. Now it is not George versus Kenzie, but George versus a feminist female alliance. While Kenzie may believe that her actions are righting a wrong that Carmen does not know has been committed against her, what Kenzie is really doing is critiquing the idea of what it means to be a *mujer* in Latinx culture.

Women in Latinx cultures are known as mujeres, and the label comes with strict gender expectations. A mujer is not just a woman. The term is used as a weapon against female bodies because it connotes being supportive as their primary role. A supportive mujer is meant to make every facet of a man's life easier so he can focus on having cultural and economic impacts outside of the home (Retter 77). Latinx households are dominated by this tradition, but as a white woman Kenzie does not have access to this experience. On the other hand, Carmen as a Latinx woman has frequently been exposed to the tradition, whether she recognizes it or not. Carmen's immediate compliance with George's request indicates that she is aware of how the supportive mujer is to behave, even if she cannot directly verbalize the tradition. George, as a manager at a factory, is simultaneously making a cultural and economic impact by showcasing the ability of a Latinx man to be in a managerial position. His economic achievement is so great that his wife, Angie (Constance Marie), can afford to be a stay-at-home mom and Carmen can attend private school. Women are not expected to have a cultural and economic impact. Therefore, they must play a secondary role in the home to allow the men they are connected to, by marriage or blood, to succeed.

By showcasing the interaction and difference between the Latinx patriarchy and American middle-class feminism, the show is openly inviting audiences to be critical of how events unfold. George's last line to Kenzie is, "I'm betting you have a forest under there," which is accompanied by George looking under his armpits, a laugh track, and the camera zooming out to include Jason's look of surprise. George's last words to Kenzie are initially shocking, and George's bulging eyes, body language, and the laugh track invite the audience to laugh along with him as he ridicules Kenzie. Recalling Kant's explanation of humor, the scene is funny because the audience's expectation is that George will not understand the complex argument Kenzie is making. This expectation falls flat, as George's response reveals that he understands feminism and its nuances more than Kenzie or a general audience would give him credit for. Feminism as an idea is alive in Latinx homes, but it is not understood in the same terms as American middle-class feminism. Even its name is alienating to Latinx audiences, since being American and middle class are often associated with whiteness. On first glance, it might seem that George is ridiculing the idea of feminism and expelling that American idea from his home. Yet, the rhetoric he chooses to use about feminists having hairy armpits is rooted in the suffragette movement. Suffragettes were often labeled as being unfeminine for wanting the right to vote. A common insult at the time was to imply that suffragettes had hairy armpits like a man because wanting to vote was a masculine desire. The invocation of feminist history is purposeful as it calls to mind how the movement was originally focused on equality for white women. Kenzie's hippie-inspired outfit also recalls the feminist movement of the 1960s, which emphasized the natural woman. George's humor masks his statement about the difference between white middle-class feminism and Chicana feminism. By employing this language, George is not critiquing feminism, but rather the specific not-inclusive-to-women-of-color feminism that Kenzie is liberally applying and upholding as the one and only kind of feminism.

The order to make a man a sandwich is a common trope used in American society to denote the service role women play. When employed in *George Lopez*, the scene is more complicated than Kenzie can understand. While she is right to recognize the actions as possibly sexist, the scene needed to play out more to truly be labeled as such. If Carmen refused the request and George demanded compliance on the basis of gender, this could be sexism. But Carmen being asked to make the sandwich for her father and boyfriend is not inherently sexist. As the scene unfolds, George says, "Carmen, please don't make me beg—what I'd really like is some chorizo and egg" in an attempt to ridicule Carmen's poetry and lack of compliance. Now the scene could be understood as sexist since he places little value on Carmen's work, but the additional back and forth was needed so that Kenzie doesn't seem to be jumping the gun. Carmen did not need a white hero to identify sexism for her. As the rest of the episode plays out, we see Carmen identifying the behavior and confronting her father for it. Latina women are more than capable of being feminists on their own even if it looks different from American middle-class feminism.

While Chicana feminism is brought up in *George Lopez*, it is not a central preoccupation of the show. Ten episodes of *George Lopez* directly address themes related to feminism, such as female sexuality and agency, gender expectations, and female body expectations. But these themes were meant to be embodied by the female characters of the show. Carmen has ongoing storylines that deal with her sexuality, agency, and the gendered way in which she is treated in comparison to her younger brother, Max (Luis Armand Garcia). Angie occupies the role of stay-at-home mom and business owner to demonstrate the various roles women can occupy in society. Benny (Belita Morena), George's mom, is used as a foil to Angie to show different generational understandings of womanhood, gender expectations, and female agency. The show's lack of commitment to feminist themes is disappointing, but in line with the way Chicana feminism is received by mainstream media. The value of feminism is still debated today, and "if white women's knowledges were ignored and, therefore, subjugated historically in Western academia, Chicana feminism (feminism proposed by Mexican-American women in the United States) was triply 'buried,' 'disguised,' and 'disqualified'" (Lugo 95). Chicana feminism is not something mainstream society is well versed in. This is not a judgment on mainstream Americans; many Latinx women themselves are not familiar with Chicana feminism. By tackling the subject on a prime-time show in a subversive manner, *George Lopez* is addressing the issue while simultaneously staying relevant to non-Latinx audiences.

Much of the feminist theory addressed in *George Lopez* is talked about in a general manner in order to remain relevant to all women. The idea of being a supportive mujer may be unique to Latinx culture, but many women can relate to it. This was especially true at the time of the show's original airing because the value of women's work was a popular topic in the media. Being a supportive mujer is essential to the functions of Latinx culture, regardless of the physical, emotional, mental, or monetary sacrifice it requires. In other words, "the female is supposed to be first and foremost a self-sacrificing wife and mother" (Gowan and Treviño 1081). Chicana feminists such as Pilar Melero use the term *madresposa* to indicate the way the roles of mother and wife are often intertwined and inform each other. *Madresposa* also indicates that the role is effective in tying "women down to others as caregivers, constraining them, and curtailing their personhood" (Melero 17). To be a supportive mujer via the role of madresposa is all encompassing. In this role one is constantly in the service of others, with no pause button. Women are madresposas twenty-four hours a day, seven days a week. While the madresposa role may have previously been viewed as restrictive, Chicana feminism sees the role as a place of power.

The idea of being a supportive mujer is passed down via the women in Latinx families. Angie has successfully embodied the role of madresposa in the Lopez family. And when she slacks off, she is sure to hear of her failure from her family. This is evidenced in the episode "Charity" (season 2, episode 10). At this point in the show, Angie is still a stay-at-home mom. She decides to do charity work because she has extra time on her hands and wants to feel needed. Angie takes on several charity ventures, and what was supposed to be an activity done in her free time turns into the only thing she has time for. The climax of the episode takes place in the kitchen, a traditionally female space, where Angie is preparing meals for Meals on Wheels. George tries to eat the food and pouts when Angie explains the food is not for him. A Meals on Wheels coordinator proceeds to ask Angie if she can also deliver meals and, eager to please, Angie agrees. While Angie is busy trying to pack everything up, the kids enter the scene and demand she fulfill her motherly duties. These include hemming Carmen's pants for school and helping Max find his misplaced backpack. Overwhelmed, Angie asks George for help with the kids. When the camera pans to him, he is seen eating a chicken leg from the Meals on Wheels food, before mumbling, "Listen to your mother." George's lack of contribution enrages Angie. She explains that she does not understand what the problem is since George encouraged her to use her free time to do charity work. George puts down the chicken leg and looks directly at Angie and yells, "But I didn't encourage you to do so much you couldn't do anything else." The "anything else" are her duties of wife and mother. Because of her charity work, Angie is neglecting the children and, more importantly to George, him. She neglected her wifely duty of companionship when she refused to watch a movie with him. Angie is not fulfilling George's physical or emotional needs because all of her time is being used to give to people outside of the home. Therefore, Angie has failed in her role of madresposa and forgotten her cultural obligation.

Mainstream American audiences relate to Angie's search for fulfillment outside the home at the cost of her Latinx identity as madresposa. Her primary concern should be the children and husband who make up the home she is in charge of. By spending energy on charity work, Angie has failed to live up to her culture's expectations. Angie resists her role, by exploding in the kitchen at her family with, "A week ago, you guys didn't need me for anything! But as soon as I find something I want to do, you're helpless!" In her statement, Angie is aligning her role of madresposa with a loss of autonomy. A direct translation of *madresposa* is motherwife. While in English and in American middle-class feminism the motherwife role leaves no room for the woman herself, the role does not function the same in Latinx culture. When Max fails an exam that she was too busy to help him study for, Angie realizes that her role as madresposa gives her the space to practice charity at home for her own family and that in itself is powerful. In Latinx culture, motherhood is deemed sacred because "it redeems woman from the original sin of being born and grants their life justification of being" (Rosario Castellanos, qtd. in Melero). The role of mother has value beyond its traditional gender value. Motherhood has a cultural value because to be a supportive mujer approaches the ideal of the Virgen de Guadalupe. By realigning Angie with her role of madresposa, the show is allowing her to find power from inside the home. Chicana feminism does not mandate that women leave the home to establish their personhood. The home can be an extension of a woman's personhood. Nuances of Latinx culture presented in this episode can appeal to a mainstream audience because they are so close to the traditional values of an American audience, but in reality the show emphasizes the need to take an intersectional approach to feminism.

George Lopez's need to appeal to mainstream audiences in order to stay on the air led to inconsistencies in the show's treatment of feminism. Each episode of *George Lopez* is its own container of information; the episodes do not cohere as a whole. This can be seen in the episode "George Says I Do . . . More in This Marriage" (season 5, episode 10). The episode revolves around the idea of women's work and its value in a middle-class home. While "Charity" showcased the value of motherhood and its restrictive expectations in Latinx culture, "George Says" seemingly undoes this idea entirely. The episode centers on George and Angie having a competition about who does more work around the house. George initiates this competition because he believes that Angie does not contribute to the household nearly as much as he does. Specifically, he muses, "I don't know what else she does [besides making George a chore list], but apparently [George uses a feminine voice and includes hand gestures] it's just so exhausting." By trivializing Angie's role as madresposa, he is also seemingly trivializing Chicana feminism, which directs women to find power in this role. His argument is that his job at the factory is harder than any work Angie does at the home. The language he uses is parallel to language used in "Charity." The ending of "Charity" takes a stance in favor of work done in the domestic sphere when George tells Angie that by deciding to be the stay-at-home parent, she "picked the harder job." Having a "harder job" implies that the work Angie does as a madresposa is important just as Latinx culture dictates. Yet, three seasons later George is found complaining about Angie's insignificant contributions to the home. At the end of "George Says," George, with advice from Angie's father, Victor (Emiliano Díez), decides to let Angie win, because it is more important to have Angie happy in the marriage than it is to be right. While George lets Angie win, he ultimately cannot stand losing and confesses that he is the true winner. Angie does not believe him and instead smiles at him and says, "Get busy, Mrs. Lopez." Angie's words are not just said to be humorous. Instead, they underscore the fact that now George will occupy the role of madresposa and again learn its value. George having to learn this lesson emphasizes the fact that the show is not consistent in the way it interacts with and represents feminism.

While *George Lopez* was known as being groundbreaking, it shows a mixed representation and understanding of Chicana and American middle-class feminism. Much of its reception focused on its representation of Latinx people. In showcasing a middle-class Latinx family on prime-time television, the show portrayed something that already existed. There was much hope that this positive portrayal of a Latinx family would begin the process of undoing the stereotypes that the mainstream media had cultivated about Latinx people. In a 2002 article in the *New York Times*, Mireya Navarro hailed the show as "a refreshing contrast to the usual portrayal of Latinxs in film and television as recent immigrants, victims or criminals." The Latinx community had finally gotten the different representations it had craved. And the positive sentiments came not just from people outside the show, but also within the walls of the show itself. One of the executive producers of the show, Bruce Helford, was quoted as saying, "To get this far is a cultural milestone. . . . I hope we get to be remembered as a show that changed the way Hispanic families are viewed. We've kicked out the stereotypes" (Schneider, "Slayer" A1). The show was positively received and was successful at capturing the attention of Latinx and non-Latinx audiences.

While the cultural impact of *George Lopez* on Latinx representation in America was significant, it is important to recognize how it failed to consider the unique issues Latinas face and the influence of American middle-class feminism. There could be several reasons for this, but the two most prominent are as follows. The first is that the show is loosely based on George Lopez's life; so many of the storylines are centered on him and his experiences. He had difficult relationships with the women in his life and an unstable childhood, which may have guided his selection of the themes the show would cover. The decision to de-center the family's ethnicity to appeal to a mainstream audience helped with ratings but significantly restricted the content the show could present. The episodes that deal with specifically ethnic issues are cleverly coded as class issues. American middle-class feminism generally excludes the experience of woman of color and also women of lower social economic classes (Lorde). Which means it was quite difficult to focus episodes on feminism without alienating a mainstream audience. The need to stay on air to be representative of Latinx people was greater than the cause of feminism. The second reason is that representation is the first step in giving an oppressed group a firm foundation from which it can grow. Since *George Lopez* was the first of its kind, it had to do the groundwork of combating stereotypes before it could take up other issues. While the show was not consistent with its messages, it did attempt to center and comment on Latinx issues. The limitations placed on the show because it was on a major network meant that its content was regulated a lot more than with modern-day Latinx-centered shows featured on streaming networks, such as *One Day at a Time* and *Diary of a Future President*, which tackle nuanced feminist issues. In fact, streaming services such as Netflix, Hulu, Amazon Prime, and Disney+ are changing the viewing habits of the population and leave room for more diverse content (Aldama and González 5). More scholarly work needs to be done on *George Lopez*, so that its contributions beyond representation can be better understood by the community.

Works Cited

Aldama, Frederick Luis, and Christopher González. "Laughing Matters." *Reel Latinxs: Representation in U.S. Film and TV*, U of Arizona P, 2019, pp. 75–90.

Calvo, Dana. "George Lopez." *Washington Post*, 14 Apr. 2002, www.washingtonpost.com/archive/life style/tv/2002/04/14/george-lopez/a227e5f2-ec9b-495c-9159-2549c6ca1c1b/.

"Charity." *George Lopez*, created by Bruce Helford, George Lopez, and Robert Borden, directed by Barnet Kelman, written by Dailyn Rodriguez and Jim Hope, season 2, episode 10, ABC, 4 Dec. 2005, Warner Bros.

Fernandez, Maria Elena. "George Lopez Lashes Out at ABC." *Los Angeles Times*, 15 May 2007, www .latimes.com/archives/la-xpm-2007-may-15-et-lopez15-story.html.

"George Says I Do . . . More in This Marriage." *George Lopez*, created by Bruce Helford, George Lopez, and Robert Borden, directed by Joe Regalbuto, written by Kathy Fischer, season 5, episode 10, ABC, 7 Dec. 2005, Warner Bros.

"George's Grand Slam." *George Lopez*, created by Bruce Helford, George Lopez, and Robert Borden, directed by Victor Gonzalez, written by Valentina Garza, season 4, episode 19, ABC, 8 Mar. 2005, Warner Bros.

Gowan, Mary, and Melanie Treviño. "An Examination of Gender Differences in Mexican-American Attitudes Toward Family and Career Roles." *Sex Roles*, vol. 38, no. 11–12, 1998, pp. 1079–1093.

Kant, Immanuel. *Critique of Judgement*. Oxford UP, 2000.

Lopez, George, and Armen Keteyian. *Why You Crying? My Long, Hard Look at Life, Love, and Laughter*. Simon & Schuster, 2004.

Lorde, Audre. "The Master's Tools Will Never Dismantle the Master's House." *Sister Outside: Essays and Speeches*, Crossing Press, 2007, pp. 110–14.

Lugo, Alejandro. "Genders Matter: Women, Men and the Production of Feminist Knowledge." *Disciplines on the Line: Feminist Research on Spanish, Latin American, and U.S. Latina Women*, edited by Anne J. Cruz, Rosilie Hernández-Pecoraro, and Joyce Tolliver, Juan de la Cuesta, 2003, pp. 79–100.

Markert, John. "*The George Lopez Show*: The Same Old Hispano?" *Bilingual Review*, vol. 28, no. 2, 2004, pp. 148–65.

Mastro, Dana E., and Elizabeth Behm-Morawitz. "Latinx Representation on Primetime Television." *Journalism and Mass Communication Quarterly*, vol. 82, no. 1, 2005, pp. 110–30, www.research gate.net/publication/242200851_Latino_Representation_on_Primetime_Television.

McIntire-Strasburg, Janice. "Introduction: Humor Is Serious Business." *Studies in American Humor*, vol. 3, no. 13, 2005, pp. 3–10.

Melero, Pilar. "Introduction: Motherhood as a Feminist Discursive Space." *Mythological Constructs of Mexican Femininity*, Palgrave Macmillan, 2005, pp. 1–34.

Navarro, Mireya. "A Life So Sad He Had to Be Funny: George Lopez Mines a Rich Vein of Gloom with an All-Latino Sitcom." *New York Times*, 27 Nov. 2002, www.nytimes.com/2002/11/27/arts/life-so -sad-he-had-be-funny-george-lopez-mines-rich-vein-gloom-with-all-latino.html.

Ramírez Berg, Charles. *Latinx Images in Film: Stereotypes, Subversion, and Resistance*. University of Texas Press, 2002.

Retter, Yolanda. "Chicana Feminism." *Encyclopedia of Feminist Theories*, Taylor & Francis, 2000, pp. 76–79.

Román, Elda María. "Jesus, When Did You Become So Bourgeois, Huh? Status Panic in Chicana/o Cultural Production." *Aztlán: A Journal of Chicano Studies*, vol. 38, no. 2, fall 2013, pp. 11–40.

Schneider, Michael. "Latinxs Get Leverage: Hispanic Demo Power Hasn't Translated on the Screen." *Daily Variety*, vol. 391, no. 7, 2003, pp. 17.

Schneider, Michael. "Slayer of Stereotypes." *Daily Variety*, vol. 290, no. 64, 26 Mar. 2006, pp. A1, A14, variety.com/2006/scene/features/slayer-of-stereotypes-1117940523/.

PART II

#BrownSuffering/#BrownWellness

PERIPHERAL FUTURITIES OF MULTICULTURALISM

Suffering Latinas in the *Orange Is the New Black* Ensemble Cast

Katlin Marisol Sweeney

With seven seasons airing concurrently on streaming platforms, multiple "breakout" stars, and mainstream visibility for incarcerated women in an otherwise male-dominated genre, the Netflix Originals series *Orange Is the New Black* (*OITNB*) (2013–19) has become one of the most recognizable examples of fictional U.S. prison media in the twenty-first century.[1] The series follows affluent, bisexual, white woman protagonist Piper Chapman as she serves out her sentence for drug-trafficking crimes in the fictional women's prison Litchfield Penitentiary.[2] Both scholars and writers for the popular press have thoroughly examined the extent to which Piper is an effective focalizer in a series set in a U.S. women's prison where Black and Latina women are incarcerated at disproportionately higher rates than their white counterparts.[3] The majority of discourse on *OITNB* extends Piper's privileged position by concentrating on how her narrative offers a point of entry or "open door" into the U.S. prison industrial complex for viewers who may otherwise be emotionally and geographically removed from it (Terry). When Black and Latina characters are mentioned in this discourse (if at all), it is typically in the context of a generalized embrace of *OITNB*'s "veritable binder full of talented women of all identities" (Berman), or of how the ensemble storytelling format "allows [the viewer] to feel empathy for the people we're taught to have no sympathy toward" (Morast). Indeed, it is crucial to underscore the regularity with which *OITNB*'s diverse cast and ensemble storytelling format are lauded as key components of what makes the series "the biggest TV drama trendsetter since *The Sopranos*" (VanDerWerff) and "the most important TV show of the decade" (Berman).

Although buzzwords like diversity and representation are foregrounded in this discourse, what is both minimized and overlooked is how *OITNB* relegates Black and Latina characters to a status that I identify as the white, cisgender, heterosexual, able-bodied protagonist's "suffering support system." This figure appears in the narrative to supplement the white protagonist's storyline; rather than provide the comedic relief associated with tropes such as the gay best friend, this character's function is to endure substantial pain and/or violation representative of structural oppression. In doing so, this character undergoes a process of dehumanization, during which they experience harm so that the protagonist—and the viewer who identifies with this protagonist—can be exposed to the larger issue that this violation signifies. That is, the narrative will temporarily shift from the events of the protagonist's storyline to focus on the suffering support system figure by emphasizing their ethnoracial identity, gender, disability, and/or socioeconomic position as the target of individual or state violence. The suffering support system figure will move to the narrative forefront only when their painful experiences can advance or add complexity to the white protagonist's personal growth and storyline. Therefore, this portrayal of suffering is not presented to develop the suffering support system character; it occurs at their expense, despite the narrative possibilities of representing this violation to call for the abolition of systems that subject women of color, queer folx, and disabled folx to ongoing states of precarity.

In *OITNB*, Black and Latina characters function as suffering support system figures to the white protagonist through plot twists in multi-episode and season story arcs in which their hopes for a sustainable future are reduced to peripheral futurities that ultimately prioritize Piper's happy ending. I employ the term "peripheral futurity" here to characterize instances in which a Black or Latina suffering support system figure is promised the fulfillment of their individuated desires—a better future—so long as she accepts a marginalized position in the narrative that prioritizes the advancement of one or multiple white woman characters. If this character of color fails to abide by the rules of the periphery—to never encroach on the central position of the white character or protagonist—they are subjected to expulsion in the form of utter destruction or forced removal from the narrative.

Throughout the series, *OITNB*'s plot twists consistently depend on a dramatic reveal in which Black and Latina inmates who have transformed from background characters to antiheroes or main characters undergo significant pain—sometimes even death—while the white protagonist benefits in some way, often by becoming more socially aware. The impact of these plot twists relies on momentum built across multi-episode or season story arcs, during which a viable narrative possibility has been presented for a Black or Latina character to achieve an individuated "happy ending" they have longed for and worked toward. The plot twist occurs once the happy ending has become most palpable for the Black or Latina character, thus producing the maximal degree of pain and disappointment for her when this happy ending is revoked. It also generates the most "shock" possible for the white protagonist—and by extension, the intended white viewer—as they watch a woman of color suffer and ideally develop a newfound sense of empathy for her in the process. The interconnectedness between Piper, Black women, and Latina women is always implied by *OITNB*'s narrative structure, which Ashley Ray-Harris describes as being "perpetually filtered through a white lens."[4] The show's plot twists are designed as opportunities for "consciousness raising" for the white protagonist and viewer, in which they become increasingly aware of how women of color are what Lisa Marie Cacho defines as "permanently criminalized people" that the law deems "ineligible for personhood" (6). However, this process makes incarcerated Black and Latina characters expendable and further dehumanizes them for white consumption by forcing them to undergo significant pain and suffering to visualize the complex forms of oppression they endure due to their criminalization, racialization, and hypersexualization. Even as the narrative temporarily shifts perspective to characters of color throughout the series, the narrative possibilities made available to Black and Latina women are never fully divorced from how, according to *OITNB*'s showrunner, executive producer, and writers, the show's overarching focus is how prison affects Piper.[5] The narrative emphasizes Piper and the viewer's "time" spent in Litchfield (whether serving out a sentence or watching a season of *OITNB*) as temporary, followed by a guaranteed happy ending beyond the prison—unlike that of the incarcerated women of color they come into contact with, for whom a future beyond the prison industrial complex is implied as impossible.

Critical approaches to *OITNB*, and by extension ensemble cast narratives designed around a white protagonist, must refrain from perpetuating the white centrality of the series, even when problematizing how the production team and narrative privilege these characters. Though some attention to the white protagonist is necessary to articulate how the series is designed around her development, *OITNB* scholarship largely contributes to the marginalization of Black and Latina characters enacted by the series by failing to analyze their storylines and characterization at length. In my discussion of *OITNB*'s ensemble storytelling format, diverse casting, as well as the public and scholarly discourse that attend to these elements, I offer a new conceptual framework for how to recognize and engage with the limitations of the suffering support system status and peripheral futurities imposed on Latina characters in contemporary televisual storytelling. More specifically, in this chapter I look to prison media as a mainstay of U.S. popular culture that normalizes the existence of, and violence enacted by, the carceral state. I demonstrate how prison media makes Black and Latinx characters hypervisible though restricts their narrative and sociopolitical advancement by portraying them as "criminals" in and outside of the physical prison space. I then transition to a discussion of how prison media like *OITNB* should be read in tandem with other contemporary, white-led ensemble narratives that rely on a semblance of multiculturalism to distract from how it does little to intervene in the racist, xenophobic, and exploitative treatment of Black, Indigenous, Arab, Latinx, and Asian people in the United States.

Through my close readings, I model how critical engagements with prison media and white-led ensemble narratives must interrogate the ways in which "diverse" representation is made palatable for white audiences, often at the expense of nuanced storytelling and humane treatment for characters like the Black and Latina women of *OITNB*. In this chapter, I consider how *OITNB*'s dramatic plot twists visualize the paradox of hypervisibility and marginalization for Black and Latina suffering support system characters, though I limit my examples to instances in which Latina characters take on this status. This is for two reasons. First, it is beyond the scope of this chapter to adequately address the extent to which the series has relied on graphically depicting the murder, pain and suffering, and/or violation of Black female characters like Poussey Washington (Samira Wiley), Yvonne "Vee" Parker (Lorraine Toussaint), Tasha "Taystee" Jefferson (Danielle Brooks), Suzanne "Crazy Eyes" Warren (Uzo Aduba), and Cindy "Black Cindy" Hayes (Adrienne C. Moore) to position itself in solidarity with the Black Lives Matter movement. Second, scenes such as Poussey's death have garnered critical attention for how the show enacts symbolic violence on Black women through its recurring, on-screen depictions of violence against them. However, until the season 6 storyline on deportation and Immigration and Customs Enforcement (ICE), little has been written on how Latina women have consistently endured symbolic violence throughout the series as well.

In this chapter, I focus on instances in which dramatic plot twists involve Latina characters enduring substantial pain and/or violation as they realize that a happy ending gradually made plausible by the narrative has been revoked. In doing so, I aim to open up readings of the show's portrayals of women of color characters that push back against the suggestion made by some critics and scholars that *OITNB*'s diverse cast and ensemble storytelling format are satisfactory evidence that women of color are "equal" to Piper in the narrative. Through my analysis, I identify three types of plot twists regularly used in the series—the dramatic demise, the season finale montage, and the open ending—and briefly examine scenes that exemplify how Latina characters are subjected to an ongoing state of precarity exacerbated by how their narratives orbit around Piper. I consider how *OITNB*'s exploitation of Latina characters in these plot twists often masquerades as moments of parity between ensemble characters of color and the white protagonist, which I argue are always designed as white-facing illusions.[6] I use "white-facing" here to describe instances in which the presence of Black and/or Latina characters on-screen evades mainstream criticism by appeasing twenty-first-century neoliberalism and multiculturalism through offering "more" diverse representation, regardless of quality. Simultaneously, the script and camera angles used to narrativize these characters verbally and visually reinforce white audiences' expectations of what an "authentic" Black and/or Latina experience should look like by relying on stereotypes and by reenacting the harm caused by systems that profit off of their pain.

In this chapter, I demonstrate how the Latina characters temporarily foregrounded in *OITNB*'s dramatic plot twists experience a peripheral futurity that is a condition of their suffering support system status. This peripheral futurity reveals how the diverse casting and ensemble storytelling format that the series is celebrated for distracts from the problems associated with its routine, graphic depictions of violence against incarcerated women of color. To demonstrate the issues with *OITNB*'s approach to representing women of color in prison, I consider plot twists involving three characters—Dominican American inmate Maria Ruiz (Jessica Pimentel), Dominican inmate Blanca Flores (Laura Gómez), and Salvadoran detainee Karla Córdova (Karina Arroyave). In doing so, I contend that the Latina characters' suffering and their constant juxtaposition to Piper are white-facing illusions that reinforce white supremacy by implying that their bodies and narratives can and should be expended to effectively convey a critique of structural racism and oppression. *OITNB*'s ensemble storytelling format mirrors the structure of the prison industrial complex it purports to critique by capitalizing on the brutalization of incarcerated Black and Latina women to sustain itself. Notably, Lisa Marie Cacho argues that "criminalized populations and the places where they live *form the foundation* of the U.S. legal system, which situates them as both the object and target of law, never its authors or addressees" (5). Similarly, Black and Latina characters and their stories compose the diverse, ensemble foundation of the *OITNB* storyworld; they are perpetually targeted and criminalized within the narrative, never in control of it as protagonists. Though the series exposes the innerworkings of the prison system by representing it on-screen, I argue that these portrayals ultimately affirm what Angela Davis argues is prison media's legacy of rendering the prison hypervisible while refraining from questioning its existence (18–19). As I will demonstrate here, *OITNB*'s trend of exploiting Latina characters' pain in dramatic plot twists makes visible their suffering within the U.S. prison industrial complex, while failing to offer them sustainable futures beyond the prison or periphery.

Prison Media's Limited Representation

OITNB's exploitation of Latina characters to supplement Piper's narrative builds on prison media's legacy of profiting from depicting the "realities" of prison and the particularities of individual inmates' experiences on-screen for mainstream consumption. As Joey Mogul, Andrea Ritchie, and Kay Whitlock assert in the introduction to their 2011 study of queer criminalization, "crime has become a national obsession in America" (xi). Television shows developed around the premise of offering viewers an inside look at what a prison is "really like" and the people who are imprisoned within them have experienced long-term success in maintaining audience interest. Prison media permeates television screens and Internet streaming services across the globe. It delivers images of both real and fictional worlds in which harm is enacted on incarcerated people at the hands of the authority figures who operate these facilities. Angela Davis posits in her seminal work *Are Prisons Obsolete?* (2003) that "the way we consume media images of the prison, even as the realities of imprisonment are hidden from almost all who have not had the misfortune of doing time" directly impacts why the prison industrial complex has been normalized as a permanent feature of U.S. life (17–18). Some series based in the United States allow viewers to "see inside" the prison system by following the daily lives of incarcerated people in jails and prisons across the nation, whether in single, stand-alone segments, as in the case of the docuseries *This Is Life with Lisa Ling* (2014–), or in sustained, weekly engagements, like the reality show-esque docuseries *Lockup* (2005–17). Other reality prison shows declare themselves to be taking a risk in entering the prison to make a positive impact on the prison population, as in the case of *60 Days In* (2016–), in which security agents go "undercover" in maximum security prisons to find institutional problems and presumably correct them. Some prison reality shows like *Beyond Scared Straight* (2011–) show juveniles deemed at risk of incarceration taken into various prisons to be verbally and physically "roughed up" by adult inmates to give them a sort of "reality check" about what prison life is like. These examples, particularly those that focus on incarcerated women, emphasize what Camilla Fojas describes as "stories [that] are cautionary, often meant to put wayward girls back on the right social track" (101–2). In this way, prison media is designed to act as both entertainment and warning to the viewer. As they safely—and willingly—consume these images from the comfort of their own home, viewers may accept and internalize racist or classist attitudes about criminality, personhood, and punishment.

Like reality prison media, fictional films and television dramas in the genre typically offer viewers escapist and/or graphic portrayals of the familiar yet concealed space of the prison. As Frederick Luis Aldama underscores in *Brown on Brown* (2005), media depictions of prison often function as a "microcosm" of the larger system though vary in messaging, as "some films reveal the machinations of control, while others simply reproduce for the comfortable, middle-class audience the blueprint for social control that allows the moviegoer to breathe a sigh of relief" (123). Among these repro-ductions are stereotypes and one-dimensional representations of vulnerable and criminalized populations that ultimately center whiteness as normal, valuable, and law-abiding. In *Queer (In)justice* (2011), Mogul, Ritchie, and Whitlock associate prison media's recurring portrayal of incarcerated Black folx, lesbians, and queer folx as aggressive, predatory, and violent with their ongoing criminalization and hypersexualization in real life (105). Relatedly, Fojas contends that when prison media takes an interest in portraying the prison system and incarcerated characters, the narrative "largely glosses its systemic violence and connection to larger patterns of surveillance and the policing of the impoverished, the racialized, migrants, and trans/queers" (101). It is crucial here to recall Angela Davis's argument that prison media's legacy is in making the prison hypervisible without putting forth an aboli-tionist critique. In keeping with Davis, prison media's enduring presence in twenty-first-century televisual storytelling reflects how contemporary stu-dios and networks are among "the many corporations that have acquired an investment in the expansion of the prison system" (83–84). Additionally, prison media's success with audiences reveals how media functions as an in-tegral arm of the prison industrial complex that extends its reach beyond the physical prison space. As Michelle Alexander explains in her seminal work *The New Jim Crow* (2012), mass incarceration must be understood as "a sys-tem that locks people not only behind actual bars in actual prisons, but also behind virtual bars and virtual walls—walls that are invisible to the naked eye but function nearly as effectively as Jim Crow laws once did at locking people of color into a permanent second-class citizenship" (12–13). And as Cacho proposes, the enforcement of socio-legal categories that portray some groups as law-abiding and permanently criminalize others—regardless of behavior or choices—ensures that these categories will go largely unchallenged by the general public and will preserve an enduring state of precarity for people of color (18).

These readings attest that media depictions of the prison and incarcer-ated people may be mistaken by viewers as automatically subversive or crit-ical by nature of their visibility, when in actuality many fail to interrogate the existence of the prison industrial complex. Importantly, the narrative's focalizer(s) may determine if the viewer will see marginalized and/or incar-cerated characters as human like the detectives, police officers, and correc-tional officers that enforce their sustained state of precarity. Some fictional prison dramas grant viewers varying degrees of insight into the struggles and desires of inmates living within the prison walls, such as *Oz* (1997–2003) and *Prison Break* (2005–17), which focus on incarcerated men, and *Bad Girls* (1999–2006) and *Wentworth* (2013–), which focus on incarcerated women.

Other dramas focus less on populations and individuals vulnerable to punitive measures issued by the U.S. prison industrial complex and more on the figures who enforce these laws, such as *Law & Order* (1990–2010), *NCIS* (2003–), *Criminal Minds* (2005–), *Blue Bloods* (2010–), and *Shades of Blue* (2016–18). Television serials like these are typically focalized through one or multiple members of the fleet of detectives working to keep "crimes" off of the streets of their respective cities. While viewers may gain some insight into the backstory or motivations for the antagonist of an episode or season, oftentimes the limited development of these figures is exclusively reserved for a narrative arc that ultimately serves the character development of the detective force as opposed to the one-dimensional "criminal."

Importantly, a study of the ongoing criminalization of Latinxs and Afro-Latinxs must also account for how xenophobia informs this state of precarity. Prison media's portrayals of incarcerated Black and Latinx characters are often constrained by what Leo R. Chavez conceptualizes to be the "Latino threat narrative" that shapes public discourse, in which "Latinos are unwilling or incapable of integrating, of becoming part of the national community" and instead operate as "an invading force from south of the border that is bent on reconquering land that was formerly theirs (the U.S. Southwest) and destroying the American way of life" (3). According to Chavez, the media effectively transforms Latinxs into dehumanized objects and media spectacles, both of which consolidate U.S.-born Latinxs and immigrant Latino/a/xs into an "Othered" group of "perpetual foreigners" regardless of citizenship status or their contributions to society (6–7). Similarly, Patrisia Macías-Rojas underscores that Mexican, Central American, and Latin American immigrants are portrayed as "threatening" to the United States in the following ways:

> Political actors and the media or other institutions construct
> migration as a criminal threat by associating immigrants with
> smuggling, trafficking, and terrorism; as an economic threat to
> employment, wages, and welfare; as a social threat to national
> culture and identity; and as a political threat to existing power
> structures enacted through elections and other forms of political
> participations. (20)

The existence of the Latino threat narrative and criminalized immigration emphasize why media portrayals of incarcerated Black and/or Latinx people can enact harm by presenting images that normalize this xenophobic and racist messaging to mainstream U.S. audiences.

Although *OITNB* emerged in the 2010s as the most recognizable—and celebrated—example of fictional prison media, its critiques of the prison industrial complex are limited and occur at the expense of women of color. It is a prime example of how, according to Jillian M. Báez, "contemporary Latina/o media representation presents a paradox" in which Latinxs are "more visible than ever" as "a mainstay in mainstream media" yet remain constrained by stereotypes and marginalization, both in these representations and in their daily lives (137). In *OITNB*, incarcerated Black and Latina women are visible throughout every season and are developed through flash-backstories and present-day interactions with correctional officers, the members of their group, and white characters who maintain the status quo. Indeed, Jane Caputi argues that given its setting and main characters, "*OITNB* does represent women regularly erased in the mass media, as well as stereotypically demonized and denigrated," though what gets overlooked is how its "diversity also must be recognized as a reflection of the disproportionate overrepresentation of marginalized women" in the prison industrial complex (1131). Similarly, Christina Belcher contends that *OITNB* adopts a "multiculturalist approach" to its portrayals of women of color in prison, in which it "eschews overt racism by representing a diversity of bodies and cultures, but the structural racism that lands a skewed sample of black and Hispanic women in prison is ultimately left without much interrogation" (494). That is, for women of color not to be highly visible on-screen in a television series set in a U.S. women's prison would be to misrepresent the population that the series sets out to represent. However, the diversity that the show is associated with is insufficient proof of the series offering a substantial social commentary on or even abolitionist critique of the prison industrial complex. Rather, it demonstrates more opportunities made available to actors and actresses of color, while the characters they play remain tethered to familiar stereotypes that enforce the Latino threat narrative and the criminalization of Mexican, Central American, and Latin American immigrants and constrain U.S. Latinx storytelling.

White Centrality in *OITNB* Discourse

Since 2013, the U.S. popular press and television industry have embraced *OITNB* for its diverse casting and ensemble storytelling format, often crediting them as key components in making the show's exploration of contemporary, "real" issues more compelling to watch. How *OITNB* fared in critics' reviews and during awards seasons throughout the 2010s reveals the interconnected praise and exploitation of the characters of color that compose much of the ensemble and that seemingly differentiate the series from other prison media. The ensemble's diversity and size of thirty to forty cast members per season have been recognized in articles and awards for "revolutionizing" televisual storytelling. That a character of color is guaranteed to experience substantial suffering and violation to garner more screen time in *OITNB* is routinely overlooked, if not normalized, as a requisite for telling stories about incarcerated women of color. From 2014 to 2019, *OITNB* was recognized for achievements in writing, directing, casting, editing, and acting. It is a five-time SAG Award winner (including three consecutive wins for Outstanding Performance by an Ensemble in a Comedy Series from 2015 to 2017), a four-time Emmy Award winner (including an Emmy for casting), and the recipient of a total of twenty Emmy nominations, six Golden Globes nominations, and eight SAG Awards nominations. Though these industry accolades do not equate to audience reception or popularity, they are an industry metric of success that can impact an individual performer's future opportunities and a studio or network's interest in continuing to produce a program. Additionally, these accolades reflect what Roxane Gay posited in 2014 to be the "overwhelmingly positive" reaction to the series that encourages viewers to "be *grateful* diverse actors finally have more opportunity to practice their craft, despite the fact that *Orange Is the New Black* is diverse in the shallowest, most tokenistic ways" (252). That is, characters of color in the ensemble are foregrounded as important to the narrative given that they provide the diversity that the series is recognized and rewarded for, but as Gay contends, the series' problematic approach to diversity can be understood by how women of color function as "planets orbiting Piper's sun" (252). This is also evident in promotional materials and cast appearances on red carpets and talk shows, as the actress who portrays Piper, Taylor Schilling, is physically centered or foregrounded at all times, with *OITNB*'s actresses of color standing or sitting around her.[7]

Indeed, consistent across popular press publications, discourse on the series during awards season, and cast and crew interviews is the suggestion that *OITNB*'s wide range of diversity is what sets it apart from other programs of the decade. During its run, *OITNB* was praised by many writers in the popular press for casting "a diverse set of women" and featuring them "at the forefront" of the narrative, for using trending news headlines as "depressing inspiration" for scripts, and for developing a "story that isn't Piper's alone" but is in fact "a patchwork of intriguing personalities constantly at odds."[8] *OITNB*'s use of an ensemble cast format to feature characters and storylines often marginalized or entirely erased in mainstream media prompted the *Guardian* to call its success with audiences "revolutionary" among women-led television series and *Rolling Stone* to characterize the series as "brilliantly subversive" and "one of the most forward-thinking and revolutionary shows on television."[9] Relatedly, many critics consider *OITNB*'s diversity in the context of it being one of the first Netflix Originals and a key component in Netflix's growth throughout the decade, as Cindy Holland, Netflix's vice president of content acquisition, confirmed it to be the most-watched original series on the platform.[10] Some critics have contended that the series should be recognized as a watershed moment in television for helping to usher in the streaming era, or for the ways its scripts "anatomized the limited scope of white compassion."[11] Others have argued that the series should be remembered for its complication of stereotypes of Black and Brown people in "groundbreaking" ways, for its many characters that make the series relatable and "all things" to its viewers, or for its ability "to trick viewers into watching a series about black and brown women, most of them poor, by using an upper-middle-class white blonde as bait."[12]

These reviews and awards demonstrate how mainstream celebratory embraces of *OITNB*'s storylines and ensemble cast situate diverse representation and social commentary on "taboo" topics as the show's major contributions to the cultural milieu. Indeed, many scholars who have written about the series echo elements of this positive interpretation by reading the series as one that "raises awareness" about social issues (Terry), subverts conventions of the women in prison genre (Schwan; Symes; Martínez García and Aguado-Peláez), complicates power dynamics and stereotypes (Aguado-Peláez and Martínez García; Fernández-Morales and Menéndez-Menéndez; McKeown and Parry; Eguskiza-Sesumaga), and undoes Piper's centrality as her white privilege is examined (Sullivan Barak; Rakes; Demers). Others contend that the show gestures at critique but ultimately fails to provide sustained, nuanced critiques or subversive representations of labor and pleasure (Pramaggiore), elderly women (Silverman and Ryalls), incarcerated women of color (Caputi; DeCarvahlo and Cox; Kim; O'Sullivan, "Who Is Always"), and the prison industrial complex (Enck and Morrissey; Smith; Belcher; Fojas). Indeed, a fair number of scholars have taken at least some issue with the show's portrayals of incarceration and social justice; that this scholarship extends the centrality of Piper visible across *OITNB*'s narrative, promotional materials, and cast appearances has been largely ignored. That is, when critiquing the series' shortcomings, a conventional approach in *OITNB* discourse is to analyze the issues associated with Piper's storylines, making only marginal mention of specific instances in which women of color are harmed or limited by the protagonist.

It bears mentioning that this trend is in part a by-product of *OITNB* showrunner Jenji Kohan's now-infamous interview with *NPR*. In this 2013 interview to promote the series, Kohan characterizes Piper as her "Trojan horse" through which she could convince networks typically uninterested in "really fascinating tales of black women and Latino women and old women and criminals" to buy a show about incarcerated women in the United States.[13] By successfully pitching a story about Piper, Kohan could "then expand [her] world and tell all those other stories" of the "other" women incarcerated in the prison. Her characterization of Piper in the interview as "this sort of fish out of water" in Litchfield, one who can successfully generate "buy-in" from potential networks—and by extension, from potential viewers—reflects what Shannon O'Sullivan identifies as the convention of using white characters as "the legitimating lens" through which women of color's stories are told (401). More specifically, she argues that the issues present in Kohan's comments do not isolate *OITNB* as a special case but are in fact representative of "the seemingly invisible predominance of white supremacist logic in television productions . . . that Kohan does not seem to challenge or question" (402). Based on Kohan's comments and O'Sullivan's reading, *OITNB*'s narrative structure can be understood as reflective of industry conventions in its normalization of white supremacist ideologies, particularly through effective integration of characters of color into the narrative without ever actually decentering whiteness.

Kohan's pitch aligns the viewer with the network by suggesting that both entities must *first* invest in "the girl next door, the cool blonde," before they can *also* invest in women of color. She implies that support for women of color is impossible without first being supportive of white women. Her pitch demonstrates how the show is designed with a white viewer in mind, one who is middle or upper class (unlike the criminalized poor and working-class women in the series) and who can securely identify with Piper on the basis that they too feel like a "fish out of water" in the context of the U.S. prison system. Kohan's suggestion that Piper's centrality is nonnegotiable and that women of color must always depend on a white lead interfaces with an observation made by Isabel Molina-Guzmán regarding the increase of characters of color in twenty-first-century television comedies: "The visual and comedic existence of ethnic and racial minority actors on TV rarely challenges dominant ethnic and racial values and is never portrayed as explicitly threatening to whiteness, white privilege, and the norms of white civility" (*Latinas and Latinos* 10). Indeed, as Mohadesa Najumi argues, the series presents Piper as a naive "WASP protagonist who appropriates WoC [women of color] stories for television audiences," while Black and Latina women are portrayed as hypersexual, loud, and aggressive. Like many other television serials and series of the decade that feature multicultural ensemble casts, *OITNB* is credited as being transgressive and "groundbreaking" on the basis that it consistently shows characters of color on-screen. However, as Molina-Guzmán's and Najumi's findings reveal, the show's diversity is designed to uplift whiteness rather than distract or detract from it. And as the show's plot twists reveal, Black and Latina characters who threaten to move beyond their suffering support system status will be forced back into the periphery or expelled entirely.

Kohan's statements support my assertion that *OITNB* can and should be read as white-facing programming even as its reception by the popular press, television industry, and the academy reveals how its diverse casting and ensemble storytelling format have been read as proof of the show's commitment to social justice and multicultural representation. The ensemble storytelling format that *OITNB* is built on, and that is conducive to temporarily foregrounding characters of color in the narrative, is representative of how television networks, studios, and streaming platforms in the 2010s have attempted to pacify demands for more nuanced representation of Black folx, Indigenous folx, people of color, disabled folx, and queer folx. They do so—to varying effect—by adding "diverse" characters to an ensemble cast designed around a "quirky" or "cool" white lead, as in the case of *The Office* (2005–13), *Glee* (2009–15), *Parks and Recreation* (2009–15), *New Girl* (2011–18), *Brooklyn Nine-Nine* (2013–), *Young & Hungry* (2014–18), and *Riverdale* (2017–). The approach that shows like *OITNB* take in placing characters of color in a story about a white lead is demonstrative of what Molina-Guzmán identifies as how "neoliberal multiculturalism manages the contradictions of ethnic and racial life in the United States by producing the appearance of equity" (*Latinas and Latinos* 114). While there are an increasing number of characters of color on-screen in ensemble cast series, their storylines often remain constrained by one-dimensional stereotypes, hipster racism, and secondary positions to white leads (9–10). Fojas reads the limitations imposed on characters of color in series like *OITNB* as a convention of "the storyform of capitalism" that emerged on television screens after the 2007 economic "freefall" (5). According to Fojas, cardinal to these mainstream tales is "a simple return to normalcy or even reform" for characters who started out as the hegemonic elite and whose status has been temporarily rescinded because of economic crisis, while "for those at the bottom of the economic order, this outcome means only more violence" (9–10). That is, the narrative is built around white characters like Piper temporarily falling from their elite position and learning through their interactions with characters who populate these spaces—such as prison or the lower classes—how to ascend back to the top. This relationship exposes how "racialized characters are ancillary but useful; their histories and social worlds are exploited and extracted as resources" for white elite protagonists who have temporarily hit "rock bottom" but will eventually profit in some way from the lessons they learn while there (17). Akin to their marginalization in society and capitalism, characters of color exist at the periphery of the fallen white elite's narrative until an opportune moment in which their experiences and suffering transform into stepping stools on which the elite return to the economic and social top.

In *OITNB*, the resource extracted from incarcerated Latina characters is their suffering in dramatic plot twists, which—through viewing this suffering and developing empathy—Piper and the viewer can both eventually profit from their time spent at "rock bottom" (i.e., within the prison system). That is, both Piper and the viewer are positioned to emerge from the prison better off, whereas the women of color who populate the prison as suffering support system figures are restricted to extended sentences in Litchfield for dramatic effect, or have dismal prospects for a sustainable future on the outside. There are three types of plot twists regularly involving Latina characters: the dramatic demise, the season finale montage, and the open ending. In each case, one or multiple Latina characters endure substantial violation and suffering as they learn that a future outcome once deemed plausible by the narrative has been revoked. They uphold *OITNB*'s ensemble storytelling format, which relies on what Héctor J. Pérez characterizes as "the multiplot structure of the twist" in which "the convergence of different plots becomes the key narrative strategy for provoking surprise" (65). Pérez argues that for this surprise to be effective, viewers must first "construct the belief" that a specific character cannot be expended because of their role in a particular storyline (62). Once this belief is established, the viewer will then experience a heightened degree of surprise if this character is in fact expelled from the narrative. *OITNB* also relies on one of the crucial narrative elements in serial storytelling, which Sean O'Sullivan identifies as momentum, or "the dynamic storytelling relationship between one serial episode and another—in particular, that part of the story that explicitly demands that we keep watching or reading" (55). Though O'Sullivan underscores that cliff-hangers are one of the best-known examples of this strategy in televisual storytelling, Frederick Luis Aldama notes in his analysis of emerging frontiers in Latinx storytelling that streaming, and the availability of a full season at once, has changed viewing habits so that "the cliffhanger device is no longer needed to keep us interested, freeing writers and showrunners to create bigger story arcs" (Aldama, "I Want"). *OITNB* indeed reimagines the cliff-hanger convention given that the full season is available all at once on Netflix; it is its dramatic plot twists involving Black and Latina characters that function as the momentum that O'Sullivan outlines as being a crucial component of narrative storytelling. Without it, the series' tracking of Piper's time in prison would be limited in scope, and the ensemble storytelling approach it is celebrated for would not be possible.

OITNB's Latina Characters as Suffering Support System Figures

Since the first season of *OITNB*, Latinas consistently appeared on-screen, often as adversaries to Piper, to correctional officers, and to incarcerated white supremacists. Though their numbers fluctuate throughout the series, their group is primarily recognized as the following characters: Gloria Mendoza (Selenis Leyva), Aleida Diaz (Elizabeth Rodriguez), Dayanara "Daya" Diaz (Dascha Polanco), Blanca Flores (Laura Gómez), Maria Ruiz (Jessica Pimentel), Marisol "Flaca" Gonzales (Jackie Cruz), and Maritza Ramos (Diane Guerrero). Some pop culture critics propose that the range of Latina characters and experiences represented in *OITNB* resist one-dimensional storytelling, while others argue that the series fails to meaningfully develop the Latina characters beyond "flattened stereotypes for the white American gaze, devoid of any historical or cultural context."[14] I argue that the Latinas' narratives follow a mutual pattern of peripheral futurity in which Latina characters who reject their marginal position in the narrative—or threaten the centrality of Piper as protagonist/hero—endure substantial harm or are expelled from the narrative. Latina characters are restricted to ensemble roles in the background, occasionally gaining more screen time through their suffering support system status when their bodies and/or narratives can be exploited to support Piper's return to the top. This restriction underscores how, according to Molina-Guzmán, it is "through the media's commodification of gendered constructions of Latinidad—usually grounded in racialized representations of ethnicity—Latina bodies are disciplined into docility" (*Dangerous Curves* 11). That is, *OITNB* relies on a model of discipline in which Latinas are hypervisible yet are not permitted to surpass the white protagonist or to step outside of the bounds of a specific gendered and racialized model of Latinaness that is safe for U.S. audiences to consume.

Their relationship to Piper depends on their subjugation and dehumanization as suffering support system figures, which can be understood through what Cacho describes as how "human value is made legible in relation to the deviant, the non-American, the nonnormative, the pathologized, and the recalcitrant—the legally repudiated 'others' of human value in the United States" (18). The impacts of these plot twists can be understood in part through what Robyn Warhol argues to be a narrative's ability to "leave real effects—in the form of feelings—on readers' bodies, [with these] narratives also tak[ing] up 'real' time in the lives of audiences who have to 'make space' in their days for reading or for viewing" (72). That is, the viewer's "time spent" watching *OITNB* functions similarly to Piper's sentence in that both figures undergo various emotions as they engage with the prison industrial complex and witness incarcerated women of color experience heightened degrees of pain and suffering. However, the plot twists function to amplify the intensity of suffering for a character of color so that the viewer and Piper can experience the most possible shock. These plot twists advance Piper's larger narrative by putting forth a sustained view of the Latina character(s) in a state of disappointment and suffering to expose how the prison industrial complex treats criminalized populations (i.e., people of color, immigrants, and queer folx) worse than law-abiding populations (i.e., the white elite and white people more generally, though class status can impact this). In doing so, the series tethers these two kinds of portrayals to each other to ultimately produce white-facing content that periodically explores the exploitation of criminalized populations before returning to the centered narrative of the white elite who is only temporarily at rock bottom with the criminalized.

In considering the dramatic demise, the season finale montage, and the open-ending montage plot twists involving Maria Ruiz, Blanca Flores, and Karla Córdova throughout the show's seven-season run, it is evident how the series punishes and/or expels the Latina suffering support system characters who threaten Piper's centrality in the narrative. Each of these characters moves to the foreground when the prospect of their ideal future appears to become plausible, with release from prison or detention being the most common theme. However, the dramatic plot twist is built on the disintegration of this promised future, thus leaving the viewer—and often Piper—to watch or be shocked as the Latina character endures a prolonged state of suffering to visualize how they are routinely exploited by the prison system. Throughout the series, the treatment of the Latinas in Litchfield is a combination of racist, xenophobic, and sexist attitudes and actions that range from heightened surveillance to group exclusion to a higher likelihood of time added to their sentences for "infractions" that the white women are not penalized for. In the first few seasons as the Latinas begin to grow in number and develop more influence over Litchfield, what becomes clear is that the poor conditions they face in the prison are the direct result of Piper's discussions with the correctional officers (COs). Beginning in season 3 and continuing through season 4, the Latinas become involved in inmate organizing efforts to demand better conditions in the prison and to demand a fair wage and benefits from the business that Piper starts. To stifle these organizing efforts, Piper quickly shuts out more Latinas—specifically the Dominicans—from joining her business and fires Flaca when she becomes the leader of the employee strike. This prompts Maria to become a strong business competitor and rival to Piper's interest, which leads to Piper suggesting to the head CO that the Dominicans are forming a gang and are responsible for graffiti on the walls and are safety risks in Litchfield.

Importantly, it is at this point that Maria shifts from background character to antihero main character and begins to threaten Piper's centrality in the prison and the narrative. It is also at this point that she begins to endure the first type of plot twist on a routine basis—the dramatic demise—which can be recognized as instances in which her gradual rise to the "top" of the prison hierarchy falls apart as she is punished by COs, Piper, and her peers for developing an excess of confidence in herself as a leader and organizer. As a result, she is forced back into a peripheral, submissive role to Piper as protagonist. In a season 4 plot twist, because of the "intel" from Piper to the COs, Maria gets time added to her sentence and is labeled a major gang leader. For the rest of the season, Maria and the Latinas are subjected to racial profiling in the hallways and frisked under the racist and sexist likelihood that their "ample" Latina bodies make it easier for them to hide contraband in their clothing. Piper also receives permission from the head CO to form a "community protection" taskforce to act as the "antibodies" that keep the prison morally and physically "clean" by preventing the spread of "'miscreant activity . . . any malfeasance'" (S4 E5: "We'll Always Have Baltimore"). This task force turns into a forum for white supremacists in Litchfield to congregate and form a white power unit. The white supremacists are not treated as a prison gang like the Dominicans are; instead, their surveillance of the prison (specifically of Black and Latina inmates) is condoned by the COs and led by Piper. The conditions for the Latinas continue to worsen until they gain control of the prison in the season 4 finale and maintain it throughout season 5. However, all of the Latinas are brutalized in seasons 6 and 7 as they are forced into the background of Piper's narrative.

The tension that develops between Piper and Maria throughout season 4 over their rival business enterprises threatens to displace Piper as *OITNB*'s protagonist in that Maria replaces her as the "hero outsider" that viewers can root for. Piper's centrality in the narrative is initially asserted by her narrativization as a likable, accidental "Alice in Wonderland" in Litchfield, but her unlikability inflates as her ego and greed become more obvious.[15] Her control over other inmates and *OITNB* in general falters as Maria rises to prominence. While Maria is presented as Piper's antagonist, her rationale for control reflects a desperation and fear that differs from Piper's self-interest. By gaining control of the prison, she can protect the Latinas from the racist and xenophobic violence inflicted on them by the COs and the white supremacists. Maria's leadership is initially attractive to the Latinas because it is group-oriented, even as her reckless decision-making and rage drive her to seek revenge on those who have hurt them, including branding Piper's arm with a swastika so that her white skin bears a "marking" of gang affiliation, just as Maria's brown skin has been racialized to be by the COs (S4 E7: "It Sounded Nicer in My Head"). The legibility of Maria's desire for control in comparison to the individualism and selfishness of Piper's leadership generates the possibility that viewers will have compassion for Maria and the Latinas and resent Piper for helping to create the circumstances that endanger them and other Black and Latina inmates in Litchfield. Maria's anger and frustration with the time added to her sentence, the racial profiling of the Latinas, and the COs' willingness to believe Piper's racialized "intel" that every Dominican in Litchfield is gang-affiliated mark her rage as one that viewers can potentially identify with in a way that they cannot with Piper's anger over other inmates encroaching on her business monopoly.

However, because Maria's rivalry with Piper largely contributes to Piper's displacement as the central figure of the show, her narrativization temporarily throws off the balance of the periphery. That is, by season 4 she no longer passively stays in the background of Piper's story, only to appear in the foreground when Piper needs a Black or Latina character's suffering to witness so that she can "learn" from and be better for it. Instead, Maria rejects her status as Piper's suffering support system by demanding centricity in the dominant storyline. By branding Piper's arm and leading the prison takeover, Maria is successful in temporarily gaining this centricity. After both of these events, Piper's confidence is shaken, and she drifts toward the background to avoid more confrontation with the other inmates—all of whom hate her for how she has acted. While this destabilization of Piper as the "hero outsider" briefly opens up more narrative space for Black and Latina characters at the center— not the margins—of *OITNB*'s plot, this possibility is quickly prevented from flourishing. Throughout season 6, Maria is effectively punished for having transgressed the laws of the periphery and is forcibly returned to the background. When the guards regain control of the prison, the inmate population, in an attempt to avoid punishment falling on them, overwhelmingly uses Maria as their scapegoat as having been the only organizer of the riots. Maria's narrativization is dominated by isolation, sadness, and regret, particularly in relationship to Piper. Maria is shown feeling remorseful for having wronged Piper, and the validity of her anger is effectively delegitimized. Her narrative is reinstated as a peripheral futurity by suggesting that only through making amends with Piper and helping her get what she wants—a kickball league for Litchfield—will she find peace. This continues through season 7 as Maria's storyline is reduced to her attending a group to work through her seemingly irrational "aggression" toward other inmates.

The other Latinas in Litchfield face similar fates of being reinstated within the realm of peripheral futurities despite their temporary advancement toward the possibility of a future during the prison takeover. Their hopes that they can successfully negotiate for fairer treatment in Litchfield, that they can survive on the outside, and that they will be reunited with their families are destroyed. At the same time, Piper is released from the prison in the season 6 finale, presumably as someone who has learned her lesson, while her release is juxtaposed with a false release for Dominican inmate Blanca (S6 E13: "Be Free"). This finale functions as a key example of the second type of plot twist involving Latina characters in the series: the season finale montage. This plot twist capitalizes on the multiplot structure of the twist as outlined by Pérez in two ways: by building momentum throughout the episode for Blanca and Piper to experience an unexpected, rare happy ending, only for this happy ending to be revoked in the final montage at Blanca's expense. Notably, the season 6 finale's emphasis on the connection between Blanca and Piper builds on an existing storyline. Their narratives have been intertwined throughout the series, particularly in seasons 3 and 4 when the Latina cast members evolved from background characters to an organized group with influence over the prison's inner workings. Their past interactions have been shaped by Piper's white privilege, racism, and abuse of power, all of which have enacted individual and institutional harm on the Latina and Black inmates. Following the Latina takeover of Litchfield in seasons 4 and 5, Blanca emerges as a key leader of the protests that take place against the COs and, much like Maria, is forced back into a peripheral position following her rise within the prison hierarchy. However, in her season 6 storyline, Blanca is featured prominently in a season finale montage in a manner that extends the state of suffering visible in a dramatic demise plot twist.

The season 6 finale opens with Blanca and Piper learning that they have been approved for early release from Litchfield Penitentiary the following day. Blanca and Piper's respective anticipation of and preparation for their release is explored periodically in the episode as *OITNB*'s format of ensemble cast storytelling weaves together the narratives of multiple characters that coalesce in the larger story arc of the season. For most of the eighty-five-minute episode, Blanca and Piper's narratives focus on how the news of their release transforms their hopes for the future into a complex reality within reach. The episode visualizes a sense of solidarity and possible equality between Blanca and Piper by placing them in the same situation in three scenes. The first two scenes build up the viewer's expectations that these characters, despite their ethnoracial and socioeconomic differences, are mutually experiencing a plot twist that affords them their desired happy ending. In the final scene, however, Blanca's storyline undergoes a second plot twist, one that is representative of how there is ultimately no parity between her and Piper and any implication of such is a white-facing illusion.

In the season 6 finale, the final scene is structured as a four-minute montage; the outcomes of multiple characters' storylines are revealed as the Weyes Blood song "Be Free" plays over minimal character dialogue. The montage opens with a long tracking shot of Blanca, Piper, and trans, Black American inmate Sophia Burset being processed for release, with the lyric "false dreams and promises" timed to match the pacing of this shot. This line reflects a poignant moment in which the song's narrator recognizes that a future she expected with a loved one is impossible. This line subtly warns of the plot twist that the viewer does not expect for Blanca, as the episode has led them to expect a joint release by juxtaposing Blanca's enthusiasm to be released and reunited with her boyfriend, Diablo, with Piper's hesitation to be released and separated from her incarcerated wife, Alex. The montage extends this momentum through long tracking shots that place the characters side by side to show Blanca's subtle, hopeful expressions beside Piper's wistful demeanor. These shots are disrupted by quick, alternating point-of-view shots as the women line up for departure but are ushered down separate hallways. The camera then cuts to a gradual tracking shot of an administrator from the private company that owns Litchfield as she announces that they will begin operating immigration detention centers.

Following this reveal, the camera cuts to a final, close-up tracking shot of Blanca under a gray sky, sobbing as she and everyone that was in her line (all of whom are Latinas) are handcuffed by ICE agents and taken into custody. This is followed by a brief close-up shot of Diablo smiling and standing beneath a bright blue sky as he waits with other families for his loved one to be released. The camera then switches to brief, alternating point-of-view shots as Sophia reunites with her wife and as Piper happily embraces her brother, Hal. A second and final close-up shot of Diablo shows his concern and confusion before the camera quickly cuts to Hal joking with Piper that they should leave before the prison administrators "change their minds." This joke emphasizes the disparity visualized between Piper and Blanca in this montage, as Blanca's final moment in the episode is a gray exterior shot that represents how this "joke" to her white counterpart is a racialized plot twist in her narrative. It functions in stark contrast with Piper's final exterior shot, in which she smiles and is backlit by sunshine as she pauses to happily look back at the prison through a chain-link fence. This moment is further intensified when she drives away with Hal and their car passes a van bringing Black American inmate Tasha "Taystee" Jefferson back to Litchfield after being given a life sentence in her court hearing.

This montage exemplifies how in all seven seasons of *OITNB*, the writers build momentum for the white protagonist—and by extension, the viewer—by seemingly offering Black and Latina characters a chance at achieving the futures they hope for beyond the prison. These opportunities, which are initially presented as multi-episode or season-long story arcs, are gradually revealed to be plot twists that heighten the dramatic effects of a scene at the expense of women of color. That is, this season finale montage, as well as the momentum that builds throughout the episode, implies that Blanca and Piper have finally achieved parity by presenting a false promise of a future for both women beyond the prison. Although this scene, and the focus on ICE and detention in season 7, may be read as an indictment of the prison industrial complex and the financial investment in detention centers, the concentration on drawing out Blanca's pain and the pain of other women in the detention center is an example of how the series relies on putting forth graphic images of Latina women in pain to up the stakes of the season's trajectory.

Among the numerous examples of exploited Latinas suffering in season 7, the open-ending plot twist endured by Salvadoran detainee Karla is among the most horrific. A convention of *OITNB*'s exploration of Litchfield's expansion into privatization and ownership of immigration detention centers is its open-ending plot twists, during which vulnerable, criminalized characters, who are all women of color, undocumented, and/or migrants, are gradually expelled from the narrative and from the United States. In this plot twist, the series attempts to visualize the invisibility and erasure of these populations within the U.S. legal system and nation by ending their individual storylines with dramatic, agonizing open endings that are often visualized through long shots or fading into nothing. In the case of Karla, she is introduced in season 7 as a detainee in the Litchfield detention center who unwillingly guides Blanca through the process of advocating for herself against deportation and seeking asylum under the Convention Against Torture act. Her knowledge of the U.S. legal system and confidence in advocating for herself quickly position her as a character whom the viewer can root for and focus on other than Piper. However, much like with Maria and Blanca, Karla is forced back into the background as she becomes more and more central to the storyline. She and Blanca become part of the Latina group as the incarcerated Latina population takes over kitchen duties in the detention center; this newly formed group that offers moments of reprieve is quickly fractured as Karla learns that her request for asylum has been denied and she will be deported. With their help, Karla is able to sneak a call to her children, who have been placed into the foster care system due to her detention. In an emotional exchange, Karla tells her children that she will "have to be away for a little while, but [she's] coming back" at a time that she is uncertain of (S6 E13: "Here's Where We Get Off"). Toward the end of the episode, she is shown back in El Salvador after being deported. She is walking with a group in the middle of a desert to attempt to reenter the United States on foot. She falls and injures her leg, which prevents her from continuing on the journey with the rest of the group. The man leading the group carries her for a brief period of time before leaving her in the dirt and making a hurried promise to return for her when he is able, though the expansiveness and heat of the desert imply that this is yet another false promise for futurity made to a Latina in the series. The final image of Karla shows her screaming in the desert as the camera pans out and moves upward to show how much farther the group has to go before they make it to their destination and visualizes how unlikely it is that she will survive.

Though there is no graphic violence perpetuated against Karla on camera, the image of her that the viewer is left with—of her screaming—implies the violence that she will fade into memory and into the distance as she becomes one of many asylum seekers who dies while trying to reach the United States by foot. That is, this open ending, which is juxtaposed with final happy scenes for Piper, is meant to intensify the disparity between the temporarily "fallen" white elite and the permanently criminalized, vulnerable populations whose stories and bodies are ultimately invisible within the scope of the prison industrial complex, global capitalism, and xenophobic U.S. policies. Though this open ending may be read as a graphic attempt to humanize the criminalized, it instead exposes how the series makes the storylines of Latina characters disposable as they function as suffering support system characters who are expelled when they refuse to accept a peripheral position. Within the scope of global capitalism, the prison industrial complex, and *OITNB*'s narrative, the labor, bodies, and suffering of Latina women are exploited until they are no longer deemed useful.

It is worth noting that *OITNB*'s portrayals of the disparity between criminalized and law-abiding characters are constructed to represent the starkly "real" conditions in which different groups of women endure the effects of the carceral state. These portrayals may be mistaken for parity between the Latina characters and the white protagonist, when in actuality the Latina narratives are used to add complexity and drama to Piper's time in prison. My reading of this false parity aligns with Ashley Ray-Harris's assessment that *OITNB* offers "beautiful, moving character drama [for] the white characters" throughout its seven seasons, while simultaneously putting forth "'topic of the week' political drama" in which "the show uses its characters of colors' arbitrary suffering to unfurl it, because headlines demand that they suffer in these ways" (VanDerWerff and Ray-Harris). That is, the show normalizes the suffering of Latina characters on the basis that telling their stories—telling the stories of criminalized populations like women of color, immigrants, and queer folx—requires that they must be shown in a state of suffering that resembles how their death, suffering, and exploitation is represented in news media. In this way, *OITNB* marginalizes happy endings and sustainable futures for Latina characters under the guise of showing the effects of mass incarceration for what it "really" is—much like the promise advertised by many reality prison shows. *OITNB*, in adopting much of the same approach as reality prison shows, fails to provide an abolitionist critique of the system and instead perpetuates the same exploitation of incarcerated Black and Latina women by forcing these characters to suffer for "edutainment" purposes (i.e., educational entertainment). That is, *OITNB* fails to imagine alternatives or futures for women of color in the series beyond criminalization and incarceration; instead, it accepts these options as unavailable and prioritizes instead what white women can learn about themselves by recognizing the possibilities afforded to them through privilege. Latina characters like Maria and Blanca are effectively left behind, even as they experience short periods of joyfulness, once they serve out their usefulness as stepping stools that helped Piper to get where she is going. Characters like Karla are disposed of in season finales after their hopes for release, relationships, and personal development are advertised as a possibility for them, only for these hopes to then be revealed as a false promise that results in more violence, like deportation and a presumed death.

Notes

1. I use "prison media" as an umbrella term to refer to genres that represent incarcerated people and the U.S. prison industrial complex in mainstream U.S. popular culture, including but not limited to: television and print news media, documentary film and podcasts, women in prison literature, scripted prison dramas, Hollywood film, and scripted prison "reality" shows.

2. The series is inspired by Piper Kerman's 2010 memoir *Orange Is the New Black: My Year in a Women's Prison*. Notably, Kerman has served as a consultant to the Netflix series for all seven seasons and appears briefly in the series finale. While it is beyond the scope of this project, it is important to note that many *OITNB* scholars have chosen to integrate elements of Kerman's memoir into their study of the series given its contributions to the "women in prison" genre in literature alongside television and film. See Smith, Kalogeropoulos Householder and Trier-Bieniek, and Fojas.

3. See The Sentencing Project's fact sheet on "Incarcerated Women and Girls" and Sawyer and Wagner.

4. See VanDerWerff and Ashley Ray-Harris.

5. See Strause.

6. My characterization of these scenes/scripts as white-facing is influenced by Paloma Martinez-Cruz's study of white-facing Mexican food restaurants in the Midwest in *Food Fight! Millennial Mestizaje Meets the Culinary Marketplace*. She argues that these establishments cater to white consumers by performing a type of "culinary brownface" in which they serve an Americanized replica of Mexican food consisting of familiar ingredients and market it as "authentic," both of which will be palatable to the white consumer. Television series like *OITNB* perpetuate a comparable colorblind replica of Black and/or Latina experience to appeal to white consumers who buy into the notion that being aware of structural racism is sufficient to be effectively "post-race."

7. Key examples of this convention include the *OITNB* cast's 2015 interview on *Good Morning America*, Jessica Derschowitz and Dalene Rovenstine's *Entertainment Weekly* feature "Binge Orange Is the New Black," and "Orange Is the New Black: The Farewell Show."

8. See Matlow; McFarland, "Seeing Ourselves"; and Derschowitz and Rovenstine.

9. See Bernstein and Selliger.

10. See Chi.

11. See Poniewozik and Nussbaum.

12. See Maxwell; Lawson; and McFarland, "'Orange Is the New Black' Ends Justly."

13. See Gross.

14. See Betancourt and Estévez-Cruz.

15. See Strause.

Works Cited

Aguado-Peláez, Delicia, and Patricia Martínez Garcia. "Otro arquetipo femenino es posible: Interseccionalidad en *Orange Is the New Black*." *Miguel Hernández Communication Journal*, vol. 6, 2015, pp. 261–80.

Aldama, Frederick Luis. *Brown on Brown: Chicano/a Representations of Gender, Sexuality, and Ethnicity*. U of Texas P, 2005.

Aldama, Frederick Luis. "I Want My Incredible Shrinking Screen: Latinx Storytelling in the Age of Our Planetary Lockdown." *LatinxSpaces*, 20 Apr. 2020, www.latinxspaces.com/latinx-film/i-want-my-incredible-shrinking-screen-latinx-televisual-storytelling-in-the-age-of-our-planetary-lockdown.

Alexander, Michelle. *The New Jim Crow: Mass Incarceration in the Age of Colorblindness*. 2nd ed., New Press, 2012.

Báez, Jillian M. *In Search of Belonging: Latinas, Media, and Citizenship*. U of Illinois P, 2018.

Belcher, Christine. "There Is No Such Thing as a Post-racial Prison: Neoliberal Multiculturalism and the White Savior Complex on *Orange Is the New Black*." *Television & New Media*, vol. 17, no. 6, 2016, pp. 491–503.

Berman, Judy. "Forget *Game of Thrones*. *Orange Is the New Black* Is the Most Important TV Show of the Decade." *Time*, 22 July 2019, time.com/5631804/orange-is-the-new-black-season-7-legacy/.

Bernstein, Arielle. "What Women Want: How *Orange Is the New Black* Changed Female Narratives." *Guardian*, 25 July 2019, theguardian.com/tv-and-radio/2019/jul/25/orange-is-the-new-black-season-seven-female-narratives.

Betancourt, Manuel. "The Most Radical Thing About 'Orange Is the New Black' Is Its Latina Characters." *Mic*, 15 June 2016, www.mic.com/articles/146318/the-most-radical-thing-about-orange-is-the-new-black-is-its-latina-characters.

Cacho, Lisa Marie. *Social Death: Racialized Rightlessness and the Criminalization of the Unprotected*. New York UP, 2012.

Caputi, Jane. "The Color Orange? Social Justice Issues in the First Season of *Orange Is the New Black*." *Journal of Popular Culture*, vol. 48, no. 6, 2015, pp. 1130–50.

Chavez, Leo R. *The Latino Threat: Constructing Immigrants, Citizens, and the Nation*. 2nd ed., Stanford UP, 2008.

Chi, Paul. "How *Orange Is the New Black* Changed TV for Good." *Vanity Fair*, 26 July 2019, vanityfair.com/hollywood/2019/07/orange-is-the-new-black-season-7-premiere.

Davis, Angela Y. *Are Prisons Obsolete?* Seven Stories Press, 2003.

DeCarvalho, Lauren J., and Nicole B. Cox. "Extended 'Visiting Hours': Deconstructing Identity in Netflix's Promotional Campaigns for *Orange Is the New Black*." *Television & New Media*, vol. 17, no. 6, 2016, pp. 504–19.

Demers, Jason. "Is a Trojan Horse an Empty Signifier? The Televisual Politics of *Orange Is the New Black*." *Canadian Review of American Studies*, vol. 47, no. 3, 2017, pp. 403–22.

Derschowitz, Jessica, and Dalene Rovenstine. "Binge Orange Is the New Black." *Entertainment Weekly*, Summer 2017, pp. 1–19.

Eguskiza-Sesumaga, Leyre. "Diversidad entre rejas: Estereotipos e identidad de género en la ficción televisiva *Orange Is the New Black*." *Comunicación y Medios*, vol. 37, 2018, pp. 79–92.

Enck, Suzanne M., and Megan E. Morrissey. "If *Orange Is the New Black*, I Must Be ColorBlind: Comic Framings of Post-racism in the Prison-Industrial Complex." *Critical Studies in Media Communication*, vol. 32, no. 5, 2015, pp. 303–17.

Estévez-Cruz, Mechi. "How 'OITNB' Season Four Failed the Dominican Community." *Remezcla*, 3 July 2016, remezcla.com/features/culture/oitnb-season-four-dominican-stereotypes/.

Fernández-Morales, Marta, and María Isabel Menéndez-Menéndez. "'When in Rome, Use What You've Got': A Discussion of Female Agency Through *Orange Is the New Black*." *Television & New Media*, vol. 17, no. 6, 2016, pp. 534–46.

Fojas, Camilla. *Zombies, Migrants, and Queers: Race and Crisis Capitalism in Pop Culture*. U of Illinois P, 2017.

Gay, Roxane. "When Less Is More." *Bad Feminist*, Harper Perennial, 2014, pp. 250–53.

"Getting to Know the Ladies of Litchfield." *ABC News*, 18 June 2015, youtube.com/watch?v=Nzgal LAQGq0.

Gross, Terry. "'Orange' Creator Jenji Kohan: 'Piper Was My Trojan Horse.'" *NPR*, 13 Aug. 2013, npr .org/transcripts/211639989?storyId=211639989.

"Incarcerated Women and Girls." *The Sentencing Project*, 6 June 2019, www.sentencingproject.org /publications/incarcerated-women-and-girls.

Kalogeropoulos Householder, April, and Adrienne Trier-Bieniek. *Feminist Perspectives on "Orange Is the New Black": Thirteen Critical Essays*. McFarland & Co., 2016.

Kim, Minjeong. "'You Don't Look Full . . . Asia': The Invisible and Ambiguous Bodies of Chang and Soso." *Feminist Perspectives on "Orange Is the New Black": Thirteen Critical Essays*, edited by April Kalogeropoulos Householder and Adrienne Trier-Bieniek, McFarland & Co., 2016, pp. 61–76.

Lawson, Richard. "*Orange Is the New Black* Season 2 Is Bigger, Better, and Bursting with Life." *Vanity Fair*, 6 June 2014, www.vanityfair.com/hollywood/2014/06/orange-is-the-new-black-season-2 -review.

Macías-Rojas, Patrisia. *From Deportation to Prison: The Politics of Immigration Enforcement in Post-Civil Rights America*. New York UP, 2016.

Martinez-Cruz, Paloma. *Food Fight! Millennial Mestizaje Meets the Culinary Marketplace*. U of Arizona P, 2019.

Martínez Garcia, Patricia, and Delicia Aguado-Peláez. "La reapropiación de los cuerpos de las mujeres en la ficción televisiva: Análisis de *Orange Is the New Black*." *Investigaciones Feministas*, vol. 8, no. 2, 2017, pp. 401–13.

Matlow, Orli. "7 Ways 'Orange Is the New Black' Has Changed Society Since the Season 1 Premiere." *Bustle*, 11 June 2015, www.bustle.com/articles/89491-7-ways-orange-is-the-new-black -has-changed-society-since-the-season-1-premiere.

Maxwell, Zerlina. "9 Ways 'Orange Is the New Black' Shatters Racial and Gender Stereotypes." *Mic*, 7 July 2014, www.mic.com/articles/91477/9-ways-orange-is-the-new-black-shatters-racial-and -gender-stereotypes.

McFarland, Melanie. "'Orange Is the New Black' Ends Justly, Asking: Where Do We Go from Here?" *Salon*, 25 July 2019, www.salon.com/2019/07/25/orange-is-the-new-black-ends-justly-asking -where-do-we-go-from-here/.

McFarland, Melanie. "Seeing Ourselves in 'Orange Is the New Black.'" *Salon*, 18 June 2017, www.salon .com/2017/06/18/seeing-ourselves-in-orange-is-the-new-black/.

McKeown, Janet K. L., and Diana C. Parry. "Women's Leisure as Political Practice: A Feminist Analysis of *Orange Is the New Black*." *Leisure Sciences*, vol. 39, no. 6, 2017, pp. 492–505.

Mogul, Joey L., et al. *Queer (In)justice: The Criminalization of LGBT People in the United States*. Beacon, 2011.

Molina-Guzmán, Isabel. *Dangerous Curves: Latina Bodies in the Media*. New York UP, 2010.

Molina-Guzmán, Isabel. *Latinas and Latinos on TV: Colorblind Comedy in the Post-racial Network Era*. U of Arizona P, 2018.

Morast, Robert. "'Orange Is the New Black' Final Season Leaves a Heartfelt Legacy." *Datebook*, 30 July 2019, datebook.sfchronicle.com/movies-tv/orange-is-the-new-black-final-season-leaves-a-heartfelt-legacy.

Najumi, Mohadesa. "A Critical Analysis of *Orange Is the New Black*." *Feminist Wire*, 28 Aug. 2013, thefeministwire.com/2013/08/a-critical-analysis-of-orange-is-the-new-black-the-appropriation-of-women-of-color/.

Nussbaum, Emily. "Empathy and 'Orange Is the New Black.'" *New Yorker*, 11 July 2016, www.newyorker.com/magazine/2016/07/11/empathy-and-orange-is-the-new-black.

"Orange Is the New Black | The Farewell Show | Netflix." *Netflix*, 26 July 2019, www.youtube.com/watch?v=ikogYVL1wvU.

O'Sullivan, Sean. "Six Elements of Serial Narrative." *Narrative*, vol. 27, no. 1, 2019, pp. 49–64.

O'Sullivan, Shannon. "Who Is Always Already Criminalized? An Intersectional Analysis of Criminality on *Orange Is the New Black*." *Journal of American Culture*, vol. 39, no. 4, 2016, pp. 401–12.

Pérez, Héctor J. "The Plot Twist in TV Serial Narratives." *Projections*, vol. 14, no. 1, 2020, pp. 58–74.

Poniewozik, James. "'Orange Is the New Black' Taught Us What Netflix Was For." 17 July 2019, www.nytimes.com/2019/07/17/arts/television/orange-is-the-new-black-final-season.html.

Pramaggiore, Maria. "From Screwdriver to Dildo: Retooling Women's Work in *Orange Is the New Black*." *Television & New Media*, vol. 17, no. 6, 2016, pp. 547–60.

Rakes, H. "Piper Chapman's Flexible Accommodation of Difference." *Feminist Perspectives on "Orange Is the New Black": Thirteen Critical Essays*, edited by April Kalogeropoulos Householder and Adrienne Trier-Bieniek, McFarland & Co., 2016, pp. 194–209.

Sawyer, Wendy, and Peter Wagner. "Mass Incarceration: The Whole Pie 2020." *Prison Policy Initiative*, 24 Mar. 2020, www.prisonpolicy.org/reports/pie2020.html.

Schwan, Anne. "Postfeminism Meets the Women in Prison Genre: Privilege and Spectatorship in *Orange Is the New Black*." *Television & New Media*, vol. 17, no. 6, 2016, pp. 473–90.

Selliger, Mark. "How 'Orange Is the New Black' Revolutionized TV: Inside the New Issue." *Rolling Stone*, 3 June 2015, www.rollingstone.com/tv/tv-news/how-orange-is-the-new-black-revolutionized-tv-inside-the-new-issue-37678/.

Silverman, Rachel E., and Emily D. Ryalls. "'Everything Is Different the Second Time Around': The Stigma of Temporality on *Orange Is the New Black*." *Television & New Media*, vol. 17, no. 6, 2016, pp. 520–33.

Smith, Anna Marie. "*Orange* Is the Same White." *New Political Science*, vol. 37, no. 2, 2015, pp. 276–80.

Strause, Jackie. "'OITNB': How Every Inmate's Season 6 Journey Ended." *Hollywood Reporter*, 30 July 2017, www.hollywoodreporter.com/live-feed/orange-is-new-black-season-6-finale-explained-interview-1130502.

Sullivan Barak, Katie. "Jenji Kohan's Trojan Horse: Subversive Uses of Whiteness." *Feminist Perspectives on "Orange Is the New Black": Thirteen Critical Essays*, edited by April Kalogeropoulos Householder and Adrienne Trier-Bieniek, McFarland & Co., 2016, pp. 45–60.

Symes, Katerina. "*Orange Is the New Black*: The Popularization of Lesbian Sexuality and Heterosexual Modes of Viewing." *Feminist Media Studies*, vol. 17, no. 1, 2016, pp. 29–41.

Terry, April. "Surveying Issues That Arise in Women's Prisons: A Content Critique of *Orange Is the New Black*." *Sociology Compass*, vol. 10, no. 7, 2016, pp. 553–66.

VanDerWerff, Emily. "Why *Orange Is the New Black* Deserves Even More Respect Than It Already Gets." *Vox*, 5 Dec. 2016, www.vox.com/culture/2016/12/5/13821692/orange-is-the-new-black-netflix-review-oitnb-sopranos.

VanDerWerff, Emily, and Ashley Ray-Harris. "*Orange Is the New Black* Celebrated Diverse Women. It Also Exploited Their Stories." *Vox*, 7 Aug. 2019, www.vox.com/2019/8/7/20754146/orange-is-the-new-black-diversity-final-season-review.

Warhol, Robyn. *Having a Good Cry: Effeminate Feelings and Pop-Culture Forms*. Ohio State UP, 2003.

LATINXS IN PRIME TIME

A Look at Mental Health Television Portrayals

José A. Muñoz, Anahi Reynoso-Franco, Lydia Perez-Palencia, Sarai Tovar

This essay explores how television builds reality and socializes the public about mental health and Latinx populations.[1] The stigmas associated with mental health problems are attributable in part to the ways in which they are portrayed in popular culture. The audience tends to be left unaware of many of the realities of mental health issues. Popular culture has become one of the main sources of information on mental health and treatment that is accessible to the general audience. An audience that is exposed to popular culture content in which mental illness is depicted, either in its manifest or latent form, may come away with inaccurate conceptions of people with mental illness and how these conditions are treated (Stout et al. 554). Similarly, when Latinxs appear on the small screen, their depictions are usually limited and stereotypical and often include misinformation about the Latinx community. A focused examination of how television shows portray Latinxs with mental health problems indicates that these depictions reinforce stereotypes of Latinxs as drug addicts, violent offenders, and sociopaths. Elizabeth Monk-Turner and associates found that Latinx characters are often disrespected, portrayed as despicable, and display limited acculturation skills (110). Research has also found that if Latinxs are exposed to negative and stereotypical images of their community on TV, it can impact their sense of self-worth (Shafer and Rivadeneyra 5; Martinez and Ramasubramanian 221–22).

The stereotypes perpetuated by popular culture contribute to the stigmatization of everyday health issues, and the media industry uses them as a way to make Latinxs look more menacing. Consequently, people with mental health problems are viewed as dangerous, socially inferior outcasts from society (Goodwin and Tajjudin 386; Stuart 100; Stout et al. 543). John Goodwin and Izzat Tajjudin state that although mental health depictions may have an entertainment value, the inaccuracies are stigmatizing and expose the audience to misinformation (386). The authors argue that the "the negative portrayal of mental ill-health within popular media results in public confusion and the fostering of false beliefs. This can lead to stigma, described as a combination of ignorance, prejudices, and discrimination and a serious problem for those experiencing mental ill-health" (386).

Popular culture portrayals also reinforce the message that mental health problems are untreatable and can manifest in violence. The contexts in which the audience sees these problems include forced isolation, subjects being committed to mental health institutions, and various other misrepresentations of their treatment (Goodwin and Tajjudin 386). Television programming often depicts mental hospitals as prisons for patients, and the settings convey a feeling of being trapped and hopeless. The repetitive nature of these scenarios sends a negative message about seeking treatment or being open about mental health conditions. These popular culture portrayals may deter people with mental illness from acknowledging their illness and seeking treatment (Stout et al. 544).

We can combine the above arguments with what Steven Bender writes, when he highlights that "popular songs, movies, television shows, news media, and advertising campaigns, when they portray Latina/os, invariably draw on this store of stereotypical conceptions" (12). Thus, popular culture recklessly misrepresents mental health problems by ignoring medical accuracy, instead prioritizing common beliefs and reinforcing stereotypes. As Leo Chavez writes, "the Latino Threat Narrative is pervasive even when not explicitly mentioned. It is the cultural dark matter filling space with taken-for-granted 'truths' in debates over immigration on radio and TV talk shows, in newspaper editorials, and on Internet blogs" (4). Building on this work, Jason Ruiz states that the media do "not passively represent Latinos in the United States but actively shape public perceptions of that population either as a nonfactor in American life or as a distinct threat to the US body politic" (45). Additionally, there is a wealth of works exploring how popular culture contributes to the development of stereotypes about Latinx populations and the attitudes toward Latinxs as outgroup members (Aldama and Nericcio 21; Bender 12; Mastro and Behm-Morawitz 111; Ramírez Berg 39). A combination of negative stereotypes and the stigma of mental illness creates a detrimental view of mental health problems overlaid onto a Latinx body. What can we learn from an examination of a small pool of Latinx character roles and stories on the small screen?

Latinxs and Mental Health in Prime Time

Within popular culture settings and spaces, Latinx characters are often imbued with violent tendencies, threatening qualities, prior traumas, or are witnesses to violence (Ruiz 40). Chavez writes that "media spectacles" portray Latinxs as objects, as if they were illegitimate members of the society and therefore not worthy of full citizenship (Chavez 4). Writing about immigrant lives, Chavez states that "media spectacles transform immigrants' lives into virtual lives, which are typically devoid of the nuances and subtleties of real lived lives. . . . It is in this sense that the media spectacle transforms a 'worldview'—that is, a taken-for-granted understanding of the world—into an objective force, one that is taken as 'truth'" (6).

That "truth" is that Latinxs are to be viewed as "erratic," "unpredictable," and "emotional" beings. These mediated stereotypes, according to Charles Ramírez Berg, provide a "concrete depiction of the other" (39). He writes further that "a mediated stereotype, then, operates by gathering a specific set of negative traits and assembling them into a particular image" (39). These traits cannot be applied to a single character; they are distributed across different portrayals (39). When these stereotypes are used by the cultural production industry, we can observe mental health issues serving as a vehicle to reinforce the menacing, disturbed, and traumatized characteristics found within Latinx character portrayals. This fits with scholarship that explores the ways in which Latinx characters and the cultures they represent are portrayed as pathological (Ramírez Berg 39). Finally, we see the industry make these deliberate associations between violence and mental health problems, which include prisoners (Jackson and Gordy

Table 1 Latinos, Mental Health, and Television Characters

Media	Title	Actor	Character	Racial/Ethnic Identity of Actor
Amazon series	*Homecoming* (2018–)	Stephan James	Walter	Jamaican/ Canadian
CBS series	*Blue Bloods* (2010–)	Omar Maskati	Hector	Asian Indian/ Puerto Rican
NBC series	*Law & Order: SVU* (1999–)	Jessica Camacho	Gloria	American
CBS series	*Criminal Minds* (2005–)	Aubrey Plaza	Cat	Puerto Rican
CBS series	*Criminal Minds* (2005–)	Andre Royo	Armando	Black/Cuban
Netflix series	*One Day at a Time* (2017–)	Justina Machado	Penelope	Puerto Rican
Netflix series	*One Day at a Time* (2017–)	Isabella Gomez	Elena	Colombian
Netflix series	*One Day at a Time* (2017–)	Judy Reyes	Ramona	Dominican
Netflix series	*On My Block* (2018–)	Jason Genao	Ruby	Dominican
AMC series	*Fear the Walking Dead* (2015–)	Ruben Blades	Daniel	Panamanian
Netflix series	*Orange Is the New Black* (2013–19)	Jessica Pimentel	Maria	Dominican
Hulu	*East Los High* (2013–17)	Carlito Olivero	Eddie	Puerto Rican/ Mexican
AMC series	*Breaking Bad* (2008–13)	Raymond Cruz	Tuco	Mexican
AMC series	*Better Call Saul* (2015–)	Raymond Cruz	Tuco	Mexican

97; Terry 557), veterans (Papayanis 112), and individuals dislocated from community (Stuart 100).

Given the previous scholarship summarized above, this chapter utilizes a purposive selection of television shows selected using a Google search, an IMDb (Internet movie database) search, published works that explore Latinx television portrayals, and researcher knowledge.

The popular culture portrayals were found between the summer of 2019 and spring 2020. The content selected includes television shows that feature Latinx characters, Latinx actors playing non-Latinx characters, and non-Latinx actors portraying Latinxs. We examined our selected content for the ways in which the characters were portrayed with mental health issues in a U.S.-based setting. The following sections include an exploration of the various themes related to violence and analysis of Latinx character portrayals that involve stereotypical portrayals of mental health problems. This is followed by discussion of an authentic portrayal of Latinx mental health issues on the *One Day at a Time* (*ODAAT*) series. This show is explored by applying Karp's (12–13) model for understanding depressive "career moments" and our conclusions.

Traumas

Among the various depictions of trauma that we find in popular culture are a number of cases depicting postpartum depression (PPD) (Farrell 20; Garcia-Hallett 97; Tropp 77–91). Scholarship on *Orange Is the New Black* (*OITNB*) explores the mental health portrayals in the show (Jackson and Gordy 97–110; Terry 5557–58). Garcia-Hallett explores PPD and examines the early onset of depression and feelings of emptiness that emerge among incarcerated women when newborns are taken away (97). Terry's work describes the lack of authenticity of mental health portrayals in *OITNB* (557). This builds on what is known about incarcerated women and other prison populations and the mental health symptoms and disorders exhibited by them (Vogel et al. 630). This issue is depicted in *OITNB* when actress Jessica Pimentel's character, Maria Ruiz, experiences PPD after her baby is taken away because of her status as an inmate. We hear the feelings of emptiness and loneliness in the following statement made by the character about her baby: "She's gonna be okay. I'm not freaking out because she needs me, I'm freaking out because I need her" (Garcia-Hallett 108). The character must cope with the trauma of having her baby taken away and not being able to parent (Farrell 20–21). It is not inconsequential that Maria is played by an Afro-Latina and that actress Pimentel is provided this modest space to portray PPD.

Alena Papayanis states that popular images of veterans reflect the cultural and political attitude toward a nation's current conflicts, resilient cultural stereotypes and tropes about being a warrior, and the current medical understanding of war-related illnesses—war trauma in particular (112). Post-traumatic stress disorder (PTSD) is one of the vehicles used when exploring this experience. Papayanis's overview examines the sense of alienation, detachment, diminished interest in social life, and delusions seen in popular culture content about the "veteran problem." In the television series *One Day at a Time* (*ODAAT*), Justina Machado's portrayal of an Afghanistan War veteran who suffers from PTSD explores, through multiple episodes, the stages of anxiety, isolation, and disengagement from her life and family. What is unique about this role is that Machado has a leading role and provides the exploration of mental health in a Latina body. In the scene excerpted below, Penelope is confronted by her friend Schneider (Todd Grinnell) about the fact that she is not doing well mentally. The scene from "Hello Penelope" is prompted by a recording of her thinking out loud that reveals she is in great despair. We witness Schneider respond in the following way:

> SCHNEIDER: (sighing) You need to go back on your meds Pen.
> PENELOPE: (exasperated) . . . Don't wanna be on a drug for the rest of my life! I should not have to need it!

Figure 5.1 *One Day at a Time* episode "Hello Penelope," 2018.

The scene ends with Penelope accepting that she needs to go back on her meds. In several episodes of the same series, the Judy Reyes character Ramona plays the part of a veteran and lesbian who is a member of Penelope's therapy group. In the episode "Pride and Prejudice," Ramona reveals her feelings of isolation and anxiety and having to deal with "combat stuff." What the audience witnesses in *ODAAT* is not only the positive effect of group therapy but that this space provided is for female vets.

The stories of young Latinxs and their mental health issues are explored as well in the show *East Los High*. We look at issues related to detention centers, deportation, and gang violence. The character of Eddie (Carlito Olivero) expresses several emotions related to his mistreatment in an immigration detention center. In the episode "Orange Is the New Brown," Eddie is thrown in isolation as punishment for challenging the guards about the health of another inmate.

This experience in the detention center is referenced three episodes later in the opening scene of "Eddie's Got a Heart-On," where the audience views a blurred flashback of Eddie's placement in a cramped space with other men. The voice-over in this scene adds the following refrain: "This is my country! Eddie Ramirez! *(sound of a door slamming)* . . . I am your master! Do you understand! When I tell you to get back in line . . . ! Do you understand! This is my country; you are just a parasite!" The scene ends with Eddie coming out of this fugue state while waiting to rehearse a dance performance. In the episode that follows ("We Got Obamacare!"), we see some exploration of Eddie's feelings and their connection to being detained. However, unlike in *ODAAT*, there is little exploration other than showcasing Eddie experiencing

Figure 5.2 *East Los High* episode "Orange Is the New Brown," 2016.

symptoms of PTSD and the source of his illness. Another illustration of youth and trauma comes from the character Ruby (Jason Genao) in *On My Block*. In this case, the trauma is associated with gang violence. Ruby was shot at Olivia's (Ronni Hawk) quinceañera, and in the aftermath exhibits depression and anger about the incident. We see him scream his feelings at the Santo gang leader Spooky (Julio Macias), venting about how his gang is the reason why he got shot. During the episode, Spooky essentially "mentors" Ruby through his experience and helps him place what occurred in a larger context. In a classic television resolution of problems, by the end of the episode Ruby comes to understand what he is feeling.

The aforementioned explorations of PTSD in this section are quite different from what is found in *Fear the Walking Dead*, where the character of Daniel Salazar (portrayed by Ruben Blades) suffers from what seems to be PTSD. His condition stems from witnessing the killing of people in his village as a child. He was also forced to become a child soldier in the Salvadoran Army, where he became a skilled torturer and assassin serving in a CIA-backed death squad. Salazar can regularly be seen entering dreamlike states that haunt him, which Papayanis explores in her discussion of "flashbacks" as a construct associated with PTSD symptoms beginning after the Vietnam War era (117–18). The audience witnesses that there is little help for someone experiencing PTSD symptoms in an apocalyptic setting, and we observe Salazar becoming more disengaged over time from the group he is accompanying.

"Unpredictable"

The characters in the "unpredictable" category fit Ramírez Berg's description of unstable, pathological, or "simple minded sociopaths" (39). Latinxs with mental health issues are often seen in crime dramas. For example, the *Criminal Minds* series has multiple examples of this plot device. In the episode "Catching Out," the team goes on the trail of a transient, drug-addicted former farmworker who murders people living next to the train line. The character Armando, portrayed by Andre Royo, is observed spending time in the homes of his victims, living out his fantasy of having his own home. The portrayal of Armando as a serial killer is different from that seen in other crime dramas. In "Poisoned Motive," an episode of *Law & Order: SVU*, Gloria (Jessica Camacho) goes on a killing spree after her emotions and depressive feelings come to a breaking point. We learn that she sought a discharge from the military after learning her mother was diagnosed with cancer and needed to care for her. Gloria's father loses his police pension after the system learns that he took on extra work to pay for cancer treatment. This leads to the loss of their family home and sends Gloria spiraling out of control. Finally, in the *Blue Bloods* episode "Bitter End," the character of Hector (Omar Maskati) is a mentally challenged resident of the Bitter End public housing project. Hector is introduced in a scene where he is being bullied and laughed at by gang members. In a later episode ("This Way Out"), Hector attempts to assassinate Mayor Carter Poole (David Ramsey) at a town hall meeting. We learn that Hector was manipulated into carrying out the assassination attempt. In a tone and body language reminiscent of Dustin Hoffman's performance in *Rain Man*, Hector states what he was told when he was given the gun to shoot the mayor: "It ain't real Hector, it just for fun man, like Grand Theft Auto Vice City." Here the character's mental handicap explains his use of violence, which varies from what occurs in the *Criminal Minds* and *Law & Order: SVU* episodes.

A different degree of unpredictability is performed by Raymond Cruz as "Tuco," a character in the *Breaking Bad* and *Better Call Saul* series. This character encapsulates much of what Ramírez Berg frames as the "el bandido" character, whose portrayals tend to be pathological and encompass the actions that

> reveal psychology in the Hollywood narrative; accordingly, el bandido's behavior unveils a warped worldview squarely at odds with what is considered normal human behavior. Based on his actions, el bandido is at the very least a simpleminded sociopath, though from decades of experience with his various screen incarnations, we gather that he is also maladjusted and unstable, alcoholic and sadistic, and a sexual psychopath. (39)

Tuco is portrayed as a drug-addicted and hyperviolent criminal. The character is given negative and aggressive tendencies, which are shown as innate personal attributes. As Ruiz states, the Tuco character "embodies a vision of out-of-control machismo that has long haunted representations of Latino men on film and television" (27). Going further, Ruiz writes that the Tuco character is not merely Mexican or Mexican American; he is hyper-Mexican, a trope that frequently frames the Latino threat narrative (49). Tuco's emotions are portrayed as uncontrollable and unpredictable. The audience is shown this early in the *Breaking Bad* series when the character beats one of his lieutenants to death for merely stepping out of line at a drug buy. A greater sadism is shown in the *Better Call Saul* episode "Mijo," where Tuco takes the main character, Saul, and two skateboarders who tried to scam his grandmother into the desert to be tortured and executed. We learn that part of his motivation for this act is his paranoia about the possibility that

Figure 5.3 *Breaking Bad* episode "A No-Rough-Stuff-Type Deal," 2008.

these three are law enforcement agents out to get him. Tuco walks through the multiple ways of executing the two skateboarders for disrespecting his grandmother. After he decides instead to break one leg each, we watch as he revels and appears giddy at the amount of pain he has inflicted. He is relieved because he has accomplished his duty of protecting his vulnerable grandmother, while also reinforcing his violent domination over others.

Non-Latinx Characters and Non-Latinx Actors

In this section we examine how mental illness qualities are tagged onto non-Latinx characters played by Latinx actors, as well as Latinx characters played by non-Latinx actors. This casting choice creates a situation wherein the Latinx body again is the subject of danger and menace, reinforced by stereotypes about mental health. An example of this occurs in the *Criminal Minds* series, where Aubrey Plaza's character Cat Adams is a "psychopathic" serial killer who was sexually abused by her father and stepfather. The protagonists of the Behavioral Analysis Unit eventually arrest her and she is put in solitary confinement, which triggers further mental instability. In television programming one finds non-Latinx actors portraying Latinx characters. These performances can be described as lazy attempts to portray Latinx identities through "brownface," following the tradition of Hollywood's use of non-Latinxs for Latinx characters (Aldama and Nericcio 39–42). However, in the cases examined here, Spanish and non-white actors are cast as Latinxs. For example, what would seem to be a Cuban American character named Walter Cruz, played by Stephan James in the first and second seasons of the series *Homecoming*, experiences a mental breakdown associated with PTSD. The character's Latinx identity is not explored, perhaps due to the fact that James is actually Canadian and the son of Jamaican immigrant parents. The audience learns that Walter Cruz has Haitian ancestry from observing dialogue between his mother and aunt. It is conceivable that someone of Haitian ancestry might also have a Latinx background in a Florida community. However, this is not explored in the show, and most members of the audience may not question such a gap in the character's development. The Latinx identity of this character is not central to the role. That issue aside, we do have an Afro-Latinx character as a protagonist (although not played by an actor with that ethnic identity). The portrayal of Walter Cruz in *Homecoming*, like that of the character Penelope in *ODAAT*, is a substantive and thoughtful look at PTSD-like experiences. These shows do not resort to the use of fictitious character aggression to portray a person experiencing PTSD.

Authentic Portrayal? *One Day at a Time*

We have looked at several stereotypical, incomplete, and damaging portrayals of mental health, leaving open the question: what is an authentic portrayal of mental health problems?[2] Through the Penelope character, *ODAAT* does substantively and thoughtfully explore depression/PTSD. The series walks the audience through a series of Penelope's decisions, including her decision to stop taking her medication, which eventually launches her into a depressive episode. The audience is socialized into recognizing potential signs of depression, the acknowledgement of the ailment, and its treatment. The truncated, episodic format of TV makes it difficult to model the incipient and long-term processes of living with depression. However, *ODAAT* does explore what David Karp describes as the "career moments" (see table 2) in the process of defining oneself as depressed (12). Karp describes several stages of a depressive career as follows:

> (a) A period of inchoate feelings during which they lacked the vocabulary to label their experience as depression. (b) a phase during which they conclude that "something is really wrong with me," (c) a crisis state that thrusts them into a world of therapeutic experts, (d) a stage of coming to grips with an illness identity, during which they theorize about the cause(s) of their difficulty,

José A. Muñoz, Anahi Reynoso-Franco, Lydia Perez-Palencia, Sarai Tovar and (e) a stage during which they either surrender to an illness identity or define depression as a condition that they can get past. Each of these career moments assumes and requires redefinitions of the self. (Karp 12–13)

As Karp explains, these career moments include inchoate feelings that are difficult to define, but include feelings of marginalization, being uncomfortable, and being scared (13). In *ODAAT*, Penelope is introduced to the audience as someone dealing with a mental health issue. We observe Penelope talking to her landlord Schneider about how the antidepressant pills her boss prescribed ended up in the trash. She states, "He doesn't even know what he is talking about! I don't need them!" We can see Penelope struggling with her feelings and not ready to accept that she needs medication. This processing of feelings goes further with her boss, Dr. Berkowitz (Stephen Tobolowsky). In this scene they discuss the pills Berkowitz has prescribed:

> PENELOPE: Well . . . it's just a lot of pressure and sometimes . . .
>   I don't know.
> DR. BERKOWITZ: Do you ever take those . . . ?
> PENELOPE: No, no I threw them right in the trash. It's fine!
>   There's just a lot going on right now.

Figure 5.4 *One Day at a Time* episode "This Is It," 2018.

DR. BERKOWITZ: But it's more than that, right? You were
    talking about nightmares?
PENELOPE: I know what I said.

Given that *ODAAT* episodes run thirty minutes, the show quickly moves the Penelope character through the stage of depression that, according to Karp, generally takes the longest amount of time to unfold (12–13). Karp explains that his interviewees' understanding of their depression is "centered on the structural conditions of their lives rather than the structure of themselves" (15). The focus of interpretation is on the situation rather than the self. In the interactions described earlier, Penelope is struggling with the definition of what she is experiencing and requires a shift toward recognizing her problem as internal (Karp 15).

The next stage in Karp's model has to do with recognizing that there is something "wrong" (15–16). Seeking treatment is coupled with weighing the costs of telling others in your social circle. In the series the viewer can observe why Penelope does not want to tell her family, specifically her mom, Lydia (Rita Moreno). We see that Lydia is bothered by the idea that her daughter is taking "drugs." The audience is shown Penelope's decision not to tell her family about her group therapy sessions, and her avoiding telling her love interest about the antidepressants she is taking. Some of Penelope's concerns are justified, given that Lydia at one point refers to the group therapy session as a "cuckoo party." In this stage we see that once Penelope has come to terms with the idea that something is wrong with her, she struggles with whether or not to make her condition public (Karp 16). One of the reasons to not make a mental health problem public is the worry that those around you are not capable of understanding.

At the crisis stage Karp describes, the person enters the world of hospitals, talking to medical experts, and taking medication (19–20). The person also confronts a diagnosis of depression. In *ODAAT*, Penelope stops taking her medications because she feels that she doesn't need them anymore. The result is that she becomes agitated, stressed, disengaged, and eventually has a depressive episode. In one scene the Lydia character struggles to understand what is happening with her daughter. At this point in the series Penelope decides that she is someone who will have a lifelong illness and accepts this new identity (Karp 24). This is followed by the stage of coming to grips with the illness and defining one's unique situation for oneself (Karp 22–23). In a revealing exchange between Penelope and her therapist, we learn that her problem is likely hereditary and may have started around puberty, meaning that her family should know. Penelope becomes defensive and asks to keep her kids out of it: "I'm their mom and I don't want them worrying about things they don't need to worry about. . . . I don't bring stress. . . . I take away

Table 2 Application of Karp's Model to Penelope's Mental Illness Career

"(a) Period of inchoate feelings during which they lacked the vocabulary to label their experience as depression" (Karp 12)	Penelope debates her problem with her boss and landlord. Struggles with defining her feelings.
"(b) Something is really wrong with me" (Karp 13)	Penelope does not want to talk to her family and friends about depression. Hides the fact that she is taking medication and going to therapy.
"(c) Crisis stage that thrusts them into a world of therapeutic experts" (Karp 13)	Penelope stops taking medication, which launches her into a depressive episode. Receives more treatment from a therapist.
"(d) [Come] to grips with an illness identity . . . [and] theorize about the cause(s) for their difficulty" (Karp 13)	With the help of her therapist, Penelope explores what she is feeling and why she continues to battle with being defined as depressive.
"(e) Either surrender to an illness identity or define depression as a condition that they can get past" (Karp 13)	Penelope explains her illness to her children. Her mother comes to the understanding that medication and therapy is what Penelope needs to feel better.

stress." The audience observes the weight Penelope is trying to shoulder, with multiple concerns about her family and career goals.

The last stage involves reconciling the fact that while depression can be overcome, it is a lifelong condition. Penelope has not told her children that she has depression and anxiety. She feels the weight of the whole family on her shoulders and states that her children need to believe that they're being raised by a "stable person." Eventually she tells her children about her anxiety. In this episode, Elena (Isabella Gomez), Penelope's daughter, experiences an anxiety attack while applying to college, especially because of her inability to afford attending Yale University. She does not understand what is happening to her. This scene is part of a longer exploration of depression, and it provokes Penelope to open up to her family about her own mental illness.

Conclusion

Television provides a limited window into the Latinx experience in the United States, as all the research on this topic has shown. When Latinxs are portrayed on television, the depictions are often stereotypical and mis-informed, and Latinx identity and culture do not surface in these television portrayals.[3] Within this narrow pool of depictions, the television industry uses mental health as a device for incorporating Latinxs in the television plots. Most of the cases presented here are about mental health issues linked to some form of physical violence. Mental health problems are added to a role in which the Latinx character is written as aggressive or violent, the victim of violence, or has witnessed violence. Therefore, we associate Latinxs with the performance of violent acts. The constant negative messaging about Latinxs renders this community appropriate for exclusion, as members are portrayed as "unwilling or incapable of integrating" (Chavez 3). This is despite the fact that no link has been found between migration and crime (Sampson 29). The character types explored above involve portrayals of erratic behavior, trauma, and experiences with PTSD-like episodes.

The standard for presenting mental health and its pain is met to some extent in the *ODAAT* series. In its characters and plot lines, the show delivers complexity, thoughtfulness, and potential socializing effects for understanding mental health in Latinx communities. *ODAAT* uses different people, settings, and interactions that allow the viewer to recognize illnesses such as depression. The show also provides an idea of how therapy can operate. In the episode "One Lie at a Time," we see that Penelope hides the fact that she is going to attend a therapy session with other female veterans. She lets them think she is going on a date.

In the next scene we observe the comical monopolization of the therapy session by Penelope, who tells her stories of being away in combat conditions and what life is like after one reintegrates into society. The session ends with Penelope fighting back tears and stating, "It just feels so good to let it all out with you ladies. . . . Thank you for having me."

ODAAT is the only show that locates the type of Latinx pain described in this chapter and that can educate the general viewership about Latinx mental health issues and experiences. The amount of airtime, in terms of episodes and content, demonstrates that the show's creators are committed to the topic of mental health. This unique exploration of mental health was

Figure 5.5 *One Day at a Time* episode "One Lie at a Time," 2017.

accomplished over the course of several episodes and multiple seasons. The show can serve as a model for other programs to address mental health or other health issues. It can serve as a teaching tool for undergraduates and graduate students interested in mental health issues. Finally, *ODAAT* provides a model for the Latinx community to follow, to connect to culturally, and to use to work past the stigmatization of mental health conditions found within this population.

Notes

1. Muñoz and Reynoso-Franco contributed equally to the paper and their names are listed alphabetically.
2. There are of course other mediums that explore Latina mental health issues. See Raquel Cepeda's *Some Girls* documentary (somegirlsdoc.com/).
3. The entire third season of the television series *Insecure* was about understanding depression. theundefeated.com/features/insecure-hbo-third-season-issa-rae-was-about-depression/.

Works Cited

Aldama, Frederick Luis, and William Anthony Nericcio. *Talking #browntv: Latinas and Latinos on the Screen.* Ohio State UP, 2019.

"Anxiety." *One Day at a Time*, created by Gloria Calderon Kellett and Mike Royce, directed by Kimberly McCullough, written by Janine Brito, season 3, episode 9, Netflix, 8 Feb. 2019.

Bender, Steven. *Greasers and Gringos: Latinos, Law, and the American Imagination.* New York UP, 2003.

"Catching Out." *Criminal Minds*, created by Jeff Davis, directed by Charles Haid, written by Jeff Davis and Oanh Ly, season 4, episode 5, CBS, 29 Oct. 2008.

"Chapter Ten." *On My Block*, created by Lauren Iungerich, Eddie Gonzalez, and Jeremy Haft, directed by Lauren Iungerich, written by Lauren Iungerich, season 1, episode 10, Netflix, 16 Mar. 2018.

"Chapter Twelve." *On My Block*, created by Lauren Iungerich, Eddie Gonzalez, and Jeremy Haft, directed by Lauren Iungerich, written by Eddie Gonzalez and Jeremy Haft, season 2, episode 2, Netflix, 29 Mar. 2019.

Chavez, Leo R. *The Latino Threat: Constructing Immigrants, Citizens, and the Nation.* 2nd ed., Stanford UP, 2013.

"Don't Make Me Come Back There." *Orange Is the New Black*, created by Jenji Kohan, directed by Uta Briesewitz, written by Sara Hess, season 3, episode 12, Netflix, 11 June 2015.

"Entropy." *Criminal Minds*, created by Jeff Davis, directed by Heather Cappiello, written by Jeff Davis and Breen Frazer, season 11, episode 11, CBS, 13 Jan. 2016.

Farrell, Ashley. "A Critical Analysis of Violence as a Symptom of Mental Illness in *Orange Is the New Black*." *Verso: An Undergraduate Journal of Literary Criticism*, vol. 9, 2018, pp. 17–22.

Garcia-Hallett, Janet. "Pregnancy and Postpartum Life Behind Bars: What's Present and What's Missing in *Orange Is the New Black*." *Caged Women*, edited by Shirley A. Jackson and Laurie L. Gordy, Routledge, 2018, pp. 97–110.

Goodwin, John, and Izzat Tajjudin. "'What Do You Think I Am? Crazy?': The Joker and Stigmatizing Representations of Mental Ill-Health." *Journal of Popular Culture*, vol. 49, no. 2, 2016, pp. 385–402.

"Hello, Penelope." *One Day at a Time*, created by Gloria Calderon Kellett and Mike Royce, directed by Phill Lewis, written by Michelle Badillo and Caroline Levich, season 2, episode 9, Netflix, 26 Jan. 2018.

Horowitz, Eli, and Micah Bloomberg, creator. *Homecoming*, seasons 1–2, Amazon Prime Video, 2018–2020.

Jackson, Shirley A., and Laurie L. Gordy, editors. *Caged Women: Incarceration, Representation, and Media*. Routledge, 2018.

Karp, David A. "Living with Depression: Illness and Identity Turning Points." *Qualitative Health Research*, vol. 4, no. 1, 1994, pp. 6–30.

Martinez, Amanda R., and Srividya Ramasubramanian. "Latino Audiences, Racial/Ethnic Identification, and Responses to Stereotypical Comedy." *Mass Communication and Society*, vol. 18, no. 2, 2015, pp. 209–29.

Mastro, Dana E., and Elizabeth Behm-Morawitz. "Latino Representation on Primetime Television." *Journalism and Mass Communication Quarterly*, vol. 82, no. 1, 2005, pp. 110–30.

"Mijo." *Better Call Saul*, created by Vince Gilligan and Peter Gould, directed by Michelle MacLaren, season 1, episode 2, AMC, 9 Feb. 2015.

Monk-Turner, Elizabeth, et al. "The Portrayal of Racial Minorities on Prime Time Television: A Replication of the Mastro and Greenberg Study a Decade Later." *Studies in Popular Culture*, vol. 32, no. 2, 2010, pp. 101–14.

"One Lie at a Time." *One Day at a Time*, created by Gloria Calderon Kellett and Mike Royce, directed by Phill Lewis, written by Debby Wolfe, season 1, episode 8, Netflix, 6 Jan. 2017.

Papayanis, Alena. 2012. "'The Veteran Problem': Examining Contemporary Constructions of Returning Veterans." *Mental Illness in Popular Media: Essays on the Representation of Disorders*, edited by Lawrence C. Rubin, McFarland & Co., 2014, pp. 111–28.

"Poisoned Motive." *Law & Order: SVU*, created by Dick Wolf, directed by Arthur W. Forney, written by Julie Martin and Ed Zuckerman, season 14, episode 22, NBC, 8 May 2013.

"Pride and Prejudice." *One Day at a Time*, created by Gloria Calderon Kellett and Mike Royce, directed by Linda Mendoza, written by Sebastian Jones and Andy Roth, season 1, episode 11, Netflix, 6 Jan. 2017.

Ramírez Berg, Charles. *Latino Images in Film: Stereotypes, Subversion, Resistance*. U of Texas P, 2002.

Ruiz, Jason. "Dark Matters: Vince Gilligan's *Breaking Bad*, Suburban Crime Dramas, and Latinidad in the Golden Age of Cable Television." *Aztlan: A Journal of Chicano Studies*, vol. 40, no. 1, 2015, pp. 37–62.

Sampson, Robert J. "Rethinking Crime and Immigration." *Contexts*, vol. 7, no. 1, 2008, pp. 28–33.

Shafer, Jessie, and Rocío Rivadeneyra. "The Impact of Televised Stereotypes on the State Self-Esteem of Latino/a Emerging Adults: The Moderating Role of Ethnic-Racial Identity." *Emerging Adulthood*, 5 May 2020, pp. 1–7.

"Shiva." *Fear the Walking Dead*, created by Robert Kirkman and Dave Erickson, directed by Andrew Bernstein, written by David Wiener, season 2, episode 7, AMC, 22 May 2016.

Stout, Patricia A., et al. "Images of Mental Illness in the Media: Identifying Gaps in the Research." *Schizophrenia Bulletin*, vol. 30, no. 3, 2004, pp. 543–61.

Stuart, Heather. "Media Portrayal of Mental Illness and Its Treatments." *CNS Drugs*, vol. 20, no. 2, 2006, pp. 99–106.

Terry, April. "Surveying Issues That Arise in Women's Prisons: A Content Critique of *Orange Is the New Black*." *Sociology Compass*, vol. 10, no. 7, 2016, pp. 553–66.

"This Is It." *One Day at a Time*, created by Gloria Calderon Kellett and Mike Royce, directed by Pamela Fryman, written by Gloria Calderon Kellett and Mike Royce, season 1, episode 1, Netflix, 6 Jan. 2017.

Tropp, Laura. "Off Their Rockers: Representation of Postpartum Depression." *Mental Illness in Popular Media: Essays on the Representation of Disorders*, edited by Lawrence C. Rubin, McFarland & Co., 2012, pp. 77–91.

Vogel, Matt, et al. "Mental Illness and the Criminal Justice System." *Sociology Compass*, vol. 8, no. 6, 2014, pp. 627–38.

"We Have Obamacare!" *East Los High*, created by Carlos Portugal and Kathleen Bedoya, directed by Carlos Reza, written by Robin M. Henry and Nick Najera, season 4, episode 5, Hulu, 15 July 2016.

INHALA, EXHALA

Latinas, Mental Health Journeys, and Accessible Shaping Devices in TV

Danielle Alexis Orozco

In this essay, I explore how several of today's TV shows represent the heterogeneity of mental health conditions and disability status in Latinx communities. The shows I examine represent the mental health journeys of Latinas by using accessible shaping devices to portray (and in some cases, even embrace) both Western and non-Western traditions of treatment, healing, and mindfulness—teaching audiences about the different forms that self-care and health care can take. In many ways, this chapter responds to and builds on the scholarship presented in the preceding chapter, "Latinxs in Prime Time: A Look at Mental Health Television Portrayals." I, too, analyze *One Day at a Time* (*ODAAT*), and extend my examination of televisual representations of Latinas and mental health to The CW's *Jane the Virgin* (*JTV*) and Amazon Prime Video's *Undone*.

In my examination of these shows, I also demonstrate how mental health continues to be a topic of stigmatization and erasure in the Latinx community. Indeed, this resonates deeply with my own experiences. As beliefs and cultural values change, mental health can be understood as simultaneously communal and personal—and, while my personal journeys with mental health began a long time ago, it was only within the last few years that I decided to undergo a diagnosis process as an adult. I still remember getting my results on an early spring day. The rainwater outside was sticky, hanging humid in the air, but still a little chilly, as if at any moment, a midwestern winter could enter stage left. I was sitting in my 2001 Buick Century with the windshield wipers on, holding a packet of paper detailing the results of a mental health assessment I'd spent the last few weeks participating in. I had just been diagnosed with adult attention-deficit/hyperactivity disorder (ADHD) and generalized anxiety disorder, and was crying because I was experiencing *all* the feelings—happy, distressed, and relieved.

So, what was I to do with this information? Well, I did what I usually do when I'm stressed out. I went home, ate something, lit a candle, and watched TV. And, what I found surprised me, as I came to realize mental health conditions like anxiety were being represented on television shows like *JTV* (2014–19), *ODAAT* (2017–), and *Undone* (2019). *Wait,* I thought. *Shows that center working-class Latinas and their families are portraying discussions about mental health? And, they've all been released on accessible streaming platforms within the space of a year? Amazing!!*

Why had I been so touched by this information? After all, it's not like there isn't Latina representation in twenty-first-century media. Ultimately, it was the intersectionality drawing me in—or, the idea that not only were the protagonists of these shows Latina (in both performance and in real life), but the show's creative team chose to explore these Latinas' journeys *with* their mental health—an especially big deal when in Latinx communities mental health can still be stigmatized. I know from my own experiences that if I'm navigating something difficult, the unofficial motto has been *"con ganas,"* as I am gently pressed to move forward.

Though such statements are filled with *cariños*, they also buy into a neo-liberal vision of "pulling oneself up by one's bootstraps" in order to succeed. Moreover, such thinking can divorce mind and body, as we learn to ignore that our feelings are embodied. With more media narratives representing Latinx mental health, I remain hopeful *"con ganas"* can change into something that embraces and celebrates difference and neurodivergence, as opposed to shaming or repressing them.

Specifically, the historic representation of Latinas hasn't always featured complex and multidimensional characters like *JTV*'s Jane Gloriana Villanueva (performed by Gina Rodriguez), *ODAAT*'s Penelope Alvarez (fulfilled by Justina Machado), and *Undone*'s Alma Winograd-Díaz (represented by Rosa Salazar). Optically, shows like *JTV, ODAAT,* and *Undone* seem to disrupt traditional conventions of visual media regarding hero representation, as Latinas are the protagonists of these stories rather than cis-het white men. Still, I would be remiss if I didn't mention a key caveat here: as Latina/o media scholars like Angharad N. Valdivia suggest, Latinx inclusion doesn't necessarily mean radical shifts in status quo (92).

I will analyze these three shows with the help of Latinx media studies, decolonial women-of-color feminism, and pleasure politics. This exploration interrogates how each of these shows (appearing on U.S. mainstream media platforms) represent the personal journey of a Latina with her mental health. When I have seen shows about mental health and/or about disability status, the central protagonist has typically been middle class and white. However, these three shows are explicit in their conversations about mental health conditions like anxiety, depression, PTSD, ADHD, and schizophrenia—especially as they pertain to working-class Latinas and their extended kinship, family, and communities.

By looking at what Frederick Luis Aldama calls "blueprints," I will analyze the varying shaping devices and unique techniques each show implements in representing complex mental health conditions for Latinas and Latinxs.[1] With more exposure, these shows allow audiences to consider how mental health for Latinxs can continue to be represented across serial mediums.

As the work of Latinx media scholars has helped me understand the representation of Latinas in popular visual media, Aldama's curated work also encourages me—as an analytical critic and eager audience member—to *cocreate* the visual texts I consume in order to make that which is *new*.[2] In other words, although the creators of a text may provide predetermined material for an audience, I have the ability to read my own experiences into texts to create *new* meaning. Pretty powerful stuff, right?

Moreover, one of the ways I make *new* is through the lens of decolonial feminists like Gloria Anzaldúa and Emma Pérez, along with the insightful practices of pleasure activists, such as adrienne maree brown, Sonya Renee Taylor, and Leah Lakshmi Piepzna-Samarasinha. While Anzaldúa's "Coyolxauhqui process" emphasizes healing through fragmentation, Taylor's work situates bodies not as inherently fragmented but as already and always whole.[3]

As brown's work asks readers to take pleasure in the bodies we occupy and to fill our interpersonal encounters with joy, Piepzna-Samarasinha's *Care Work* reminds us about the importance of empathy, "emotional labor, femme emotional labor, access, and crip skills, and science" through the implementation of "disability justice" (19). Disability justice, as defined by Piepzna-Samarasinha, is a framework underscoring that "all bodies are unique and essential . . . all bodies have strengths and needs that must be met. We know we are powerful not despite the complexities of our bodies, but because of them" (19). In this framework, differences make us strong and access needs are nothing to be ashamed of.

Before I move any further into scene analysis from *JTV*, *ODDAT*, and *Undone*, I want to reel things back to provide a brief overview of historical and current representations of Latinas in popular visual media. In twentieth-century cinema and television, Latinas were usually relegated to flat secondary or tertiary characters whose main purpose was to provide contrast when compared to central protagonists. The hero of each story was usually a "white, handsome, middle-aged, upper-middle class, heterosexual, Protestant, Anglo-Saxon, male" (Ramírez Berg 67).

Working in tandem with landmark scholars like Chon Noriega, Ana López, Mary Beltrán, Angharad Valdivia, Clara Rodríguez, and many others who have critically founded the field of media studies as it specifically pertains to Latinidad, Charles Ramírez Berg outlined three flat stereotypes that have existed for Latinas in terms of cinematic representation. They include the promiscuous Harlot, the buffoonish Female Clown, and the mysterious Dark Lady.

As the Harlot is typically hot-tempered, driven by her sexual temptations (which usually manifest as lustful encounters), the Female Clown is a comic device to be ridiculed and mocked; she is seen as ditzy and frivolous when compared with white counterparts (Ramírez Berg 70–75). Lastly, the Dark Lady is "virginal, inscrutable, aristocratic—and erotically appealing precisely because of these characteristics. Her cool distance is what makes her fascinating to Anglo males" (76). In all these cases, the Latina is seen as the ethnic and sexual Other.

Such tropes also focus primarily on the body of the Latina. As Myra Mendible and Isabel Molina-Guzmán have discussed in their work, the Latina performer—who operates within capitalist modes of production—is seen as simultaneously dangerous yet containable because her body is perceived to be a tradable media commodity. Building on López's claim that each of the above female characters (or a combination of these tropes) represents a sexual threat to—or deviation from—notions of white femininity, Valdivia calls the phenomenon "the Latina threat" (98). Yet, as Valdivia posits, stereotypes are not exclusive to Latinas and Latinxs; in fact, they are shorthands for the Hollywood industry.

Nevertheless, stereotypes have done and still can do harm. While film scholars such as Ramírez Berg, Rodríguez, and Rosa Linda Fregoso detail how Latina performers and cinematic creators can be sites of subversion, variations of the stereotypical "hot-blooded" and "voluptuous" Latina still appear in contemporary media. Valdivia believes the issue is not with the use of stereotypes, but with reducing "a particular group to a small number of stereotypes serv[ing] to marginalize or demonize a group of the population. Stereotypes, like myths, arise within a particular historical and social context, yet they endure long past their origin" (80). Because of the long-standing influence stereotypes have, representations can have "real, life-and-death, implications" (71), especially if Latinxs are demonized to the point of dehumanization.

For a moment, consider how the world continues to see ICE agents cage young Latinx children in detention centers around the United States, even in the midst of an ongoing global pandemic. This image continues the U.S. legacy where those who are perceived to be different are locked up. Consider U.S. mental health asylums in the twentieth century, Japanese/Japanese Americans placed in internment camps during World War II, or Mexican/Mexican Americans who were deported during the Great Depression.

While such efforts suggest an annihilation of the individual and their body through able-bodied ethnic and racial cleansing measures via detainment, Valdivia also addresses the problem of symbolic annihilation existing in popular media. Symbolic annihilation is when "groups of people are underrepresented, and furthermore, sensationalized, victimized, or ridiculed," thus triggering "political, health, and educational results" (Valdivia 71). In other words, underrepresentation and misrepresentation can result in grave consequences for the real-life experiences of Latinx folks, especially for Latinas who can experience the intersections of racial, ethnic, national, class, sexual, gender, and ableist discrimination.

Even if Latinxs are one of the largest ethnic groups in the United States, it still matters who has creative and financial control of visual media projects. When it comes to mainstream media, representation "speaks to power, not of numbers" (Valdivia 70). Combined with the "virtual absence of Latina/os throughout most of US history in the mainstream press" and the fact that many Latinxs continue to experience discrimination due to perceived differences as the Other, we've had "lack of access to the fruits of a democracy" (Valdivia 71). Discrimination, predicated on damages of -isms, limits social, political, and economic possibilities for Latinxs.

Today, complex and fair inclusion is something the entertainment industry can certainly strive toward, though there is no easy way to address historical erasure, the trauma of discrimination, and the continued marginalization of Latinxs both in and outside of the industry. Television—through its relative accessibility and powers of *cocreation*—can provide a window of reckoning as it asks U.S. audiences to become familiar with more complex representations of Latinxs. This is especially true if, as Valdivia notes, audiences "use mainstream media to make decisions about ethnic minorities" in the absence of personal experience (24). We aren't just the disgruntled bandido criminal or the silly yet sexy maid. We are more than stereotypes.

Despite how I can be considered relatively able-bodied to some, I consider myself neurodivergent—specifically during moments of intense anxiety. Panic attacks are often debilitating and physically painful for me, and while I recognize that it's important to make distinctions between mental health and disability so as not to contribute to the erasure of disability status, I am interested in what it means for humanities scholars to consider what a braid between the two means—especially given recent studies in epigenetics.[4] Such research suggests that for those who have and continue to experience trauma (including prejudicial violence), this trauma can literally appear in our *freakin' genes*.

As a queer, femme, working-class, neurodivergent person of color like myself, it can be difficult to provide hard separations when it comes to where my mind ends and my body begins; but, if I not only believe but embody Taylor's declaration that "your body is the body it is" (23), then I don't have to divorce my mind from my body; I can love them—separately and jointly—for their difference.

JTV, *ODAAT*, and *Undone* seek to represent the complex discussions of mental health and disability status in Latinx communities. Moreover, these conversations are made accessible through the wide distribution of the shows via popular streaming platforms like Netflix and Amazon Prime. Such conversations about mental health are relatively new, and while the shows (and/or critics writing about the serials) may reinforce ableist logic at times, they may also try to circumvent such beliefs by providing diverse shaping devices—including monologues and flashbacks.

Perhaps such a belief is hopefully naive; however, I do feel that taken together, these shows can begin not only a discourse about Latinx representation, but also some robust conversations about the relation between Latinxs and their mental health. In a sense, television industries should model Emma Pérez's central claim in *The Decolonial Imaginary*; if there is a need to write Chicanas into history, then TV must write the potential mental health journeys of Latinas and Latinxs into television.

Jane the Virgin

Inhala, exhala . . . these are the words Jane from *JTV* uses as a mantra to periodically assuage her rising anxiety levels throughout the telenovela-inspired series. As the series develops, we learn more about Jane, but what we ascertain immediately is that she is a working-class Latina who aspires to become a famous writer. She works at the Marbella resort hotel in Miami, Florida, and while exploring romance as a young Venezuelan American woman in her twenties, she also lives under the same roof as her free-spirited mother and religious grandmother. Already, we see a diverse cast of multigenerational characters.

The show's drama begins almost immediately when Jane—who has never had sex—becomes pregnant. We quickly learn this is because Jane has been accidently and artificially inseminated with the handsome Marbella owner's baby . . . I know, right? True telenovela content! The hotel owner's name is Rafael Solano, and together they decide they will co-parent the child, whom they name Mateo.

In addition to co-parentship, the two also entertain an on-again, off-again romance, with Jane harboring feelings for both her baby-daddy and her first true love, Miami police officer Michael Cordero—whom she was seriously dating at the time of her accidental insemination. Think, "entanglement," as Jada Pinkett Smith would say . . . As romantic affiliations fluctuate throughout the series, Jane's family supports her and helps raise Mateo—signaling a support network.

What catches my attention is not only the types of content the show chooses to feature (which include sociopolitical topics like immigration, voting, and medical-care access), but also the unique shaping devices used to represent such important issues. Specifically, the technique of the extra-diegetic narrator—in addition to flashbacks, flash-forwards, and shifting perspectives between characters—is one of the primary devices the show uses to define mental health conditions as well as to disseminate information about possible therapeutic strategies. Taken together, these strategies seem to de-stigmatize and normalize varying experiences with mental health, specifically Western modes of wellness for Latinxs.

The extra-diegetic narrator of *JTV* is actually Jane's grown-up son, Mateo. The series is essentially a flashback in which he details the events of his family's life, with a focus on Jane's romances. The narrator provides us with all the details we need to know—as the viewer—by framing the beginning and ending of each episode through recaps and summaries. He also provides some humorously snarky commentary throughout each episode.

Even though the voice of the narrator/Mateo can't be heard by the characters in the storyworld of *JTV*, this doesn't mean his voice isn't influential. Indeed, we as audience members are pulled into the story through his continuous interjections in the form of exclamations or questions; in a way, the narrator/Mateo breaks down the fourth wall for the viewer, making his relay of information noteworthy, especially when it's about mental health. While the narrator/Mateo frames *JTV*'s storyworld, Jane remains the center of the show.

Nevertheless, across seasons 3 through 5, the show explores several mental health conditions, including anxiety, panic attacks, trauma, PTSD, and ADHD, affecting several different characters. Specifically, in season 3, the narrator/Mateo provides viewers with flashbacks about Jane's distress after Michael—whom she marries—suddenly dies. Viewers bear witness to Jane's anxiety and PTSD through the help of the narrator/Mateo, who flashes us back to when Jane sees a therapist to cope with Michael's death. In addition, for the remainder of the series, we see Mateo's experiences before, during, and after he is diagnosed with ADHD, as well as the uncertainty Jane and Rafael feel about his diagnosis.

We first see Jane wrestle with her debilitating anxiety in chapter 55, which is set three years after Michael's death. The episode provides a montage of flashbacks detailing how Jane's family helps her cope with her grief while raising Mateo, who is still a toddler. She even experiences performance anxiety before a reading of her new book, which is about her love story with Michael. Afraid she won't be able to read her work without bursting into tears, Rafael coaxes her back onto the stage. Even if Jane's character is a nervous little ball of energy (like me, ha), her anxiety peaks after the sudden loss of Michael.

In chapter 56, the narrator's voice begins the episode, framing Jane's feelings for us. Over a white screen, the narrator states sympathetically, "after Michael, there were times when reality felt overwhelming . . . well, let's have Jane tell us." Here, the narrator momentarily relinquishes his storytelling duties so Jane can assume power of voice in recounting her feelings. The scene quickly fades into an image of Jane sitting on a couch. Text appears on the screen as if being typed out (which is a common motif in the show) and is superimposed over the image of Jane. The text reads: "One Month After Michael's Death." Here, the narrator provides us with a sense of time, and we understand as viewers that based on the chronology of the show, this is a flashback.

Jane's demeanor is one of devastation. Wearing a light blue hoodie, she sits amid yellow-accented pillows on a beige couch, cuddling a gray blanket. The hoodie and blanket are cool-toned, setting a gloomy mood for the scene. However, the yellow and warm accents of this mise-en-scène suggest Jane may be in a safe space. As the scene continues, we see how Jane is with her therapist, explaining her feelings within the last month. We are brought into their conversation in medias res: "And my heart is racing, I'm sweating, and everything looks and sounds far away. It's like I'm dying." Jane seems to not only be expressing her feelings but confusion over what they mean. Here, dialogue helps convey hurt and pain.

However, her therapist is there to assist and assure her. She tells Jane gently, "Yeah, that's definitely a panic attack. . . . I can give you some tools." At this, Jane straightens her shoulders as she perks a little, saying, "Yes, please, yes." This scene demonstrates how Jane is not only *not* averse to Western mental health tools like therapy, but willing to embrace new, unfamiliar psychological concepts.

In other words, she isn't suspicious about what therapy can do for her. You may ask, Well, why should she be? Again, mental health can be a stigmatized topic in Latinx communities.[5] For characters like Lydia (who is portrayed by Rita Moreno) in *ODAAT*, the church is supposed to be your therapy. This is coupled with the fact that typically, therapy is *freakin' expensive* and time intensive, especially if commuting is involved (thus, this can make access to therapy difficult for working-class folx). Language barriers can further prevent Latinxs from seeking resources they want and need.

As a result, the exchange between Jane and her therapist takes on new meaning. As we watch this scene, we listen along to what Jane's therapist recommends for her. After receiving positive affirmation from Jane, she states, "First, take a deep breath, put your hand over your heart, and give yourself a reality check. Remind yourself you are not dying, and this is just a physical sensation that will pass. Then go through a checklist to figure out the trigger. HALT." As the therapist lays out this plan, Jane listens carefully, nodding her head slowly and breathing deeply—her therapist's recommendations have become her (and the audience's) main focus.

Here, the narrator/Mateo inserts himself again as the therapist continues, asking Jane if in these moments she is "hungry, angry, lonely, or tired?" The narrator/Mateo superimposes the acronym "H A L T" on-screen, proceeding to provide the words "Hungry? Angry? Lonely? and Tired?" next to each disembodied letter. Given that Jane can't see the suspended words, it's clear this information is meant not only for her but also the audience.

On hearing the list her therapist just described, Jane throws her hands up in the air—clutching a tissue in one hand as her voice breaks in response. "Usually all four," she says. The therapist nods empathically and tells Jane: "Try to figure out which is strongest, and then keep breathing. . . . When the panic attack passes, address the underlying trigger." After Jane agrees to try, the narrator/Mateo sweeps us further into the narrative as the scene fades into a white screen reading "89 sessions later." Again, Jane's willingness "to try" here is significant, especially when I have seen how Latinxs in my own community can be "understandably" skeptical about Western practices like therapy.

This transition tells us not only about Jane's mental health but that of the narrator/Mateo. The scene fades into a future session between Jane and her therapist, where Jane decides she is ready to stop therapy. The narrator's

Figure 6.1 Jane's therapist recommends HALT. The narrator/Mateo provides superimposed text on-screen to help us visualize the process.

extra-diegetic voice interjects with, "Ah, the awkward therapy breakup. Who hasn't been there?" With such a comment, the narrator/Mateo normalizes the process of both beginning and ending therapy, while also making light of a potentially awkward moment through humor.

We're also cued into the idea that the narrator—like Jane—has been in therapy. When Jane's therapist congratulates her, saying this means they've made "real progress," the narrator's voice interrupts the scene, saying, "Hmmm, mine was much more awkward." At this point in the series, it hasn't been revealed the narrator is indeed Mateo. When I rewatched this scene after the conclusion of the show, such a comment demonstrated to me how the Villanueva family—at some point—formulates a lineage of therapy, a new tradition, if you will.

And, it seems Jane learns a lot from her therapist—a fact the narrator/Mateo highlights. When Jane tells her therapist, "You have been so helpful. . . . And I will take everything I learned with me," the narrator's voice adds, "Which she did, for the record. . . . Especially that deep breathing technique." As we see later in the episode, Jane does use deep breathing when she experiences a panic attack while she is with a young Mateo.

After going through her checklist, she openly discusses her panic attack with Mateo. She reveals to him how she was triggered into overwhelming feelings, and together they agree it would be best if she "use her words" next time (a technique Jane and Rafael use to help Mateo express himself in difficult moments). This tender moment between them suggests tough yet intergenerational conversations can and should happen—especially when children are young. Representations like this help normalize not only effective coping strategies for stress, but how "teachable moments" can help us learn to express our feelings in healthy, affirming ways.

In all honesty, I still use HALT when I'm feeling crappy and/or overwhelmed, and because I've found success with it, I've shared it with my loved ones. Ultimately, this episode demonstrates how the show makes therapy techniques accessible for general audiences—*how cool is that?* Viewers not only see a representation of therapy and tools, but also intergenerational conversations take place about mental health, so stigmas about it can change or, better yet, be lessened so neurodivergence is not, in the words of Lydia from *ODAAT*, "a great family shame."

Such acceptance of therapy reminds me of Sonya Renee Taylor's work with radical self-love. In *The Body Is Not an Apology*, she states, "There are times when our unflinching honesty, vulnerability, and empathy will create a transformative portal, an opening to a completely new way of living." In the scenes I have described, we can see how Jane is honest about her feelings and her panic attack symptoms, and ultimately we see her impart what she learned to her son; however, her son also teaches her. Such moments not only revolutionize the way Latinxs can think about mental health but can create new ways of existing in the world—all through TV.

As the series continues, the show tackles other important topics related to depression, trauma, PTSD, and ADHD. Rafael is on medication for depression, and his two daughters are in therapy. Through a series of parent-teacher conferences and doctors' appointments, it's determined Mateo has ADHD (and, the narrator/Mateo helpfully spells out the acronym at the moment of his diagnosis).

In addition, Jane delivers a heartfelt monologue at the beginning of season 5; it's worth noting that Rodriguez's delivery was given heaps of critical praise. This monologue occurs after Michael shockingly comes back from the dead, due to the whims of supervillain and Miami crime boss Sin Rostro.

The shaping device of the monologue is atypical for a prime-time television show like *JTV* . . . yet, such a move attests to how the show hasn't been shy in representing the challenges trauma and PTSD can present. Jane's words and actions, in addition to Gina Rodriguez's performance, hold undivided attention because the scene feels so *damn* real. This monologue expresses the raw emotion of Jane's character—and sometimes, we need to see characters like Jane fall apart so they can come back together again (kind of like Anzaldúa's "Coyolxauhqui process"). Even if *JTV* situations are influenced by the exaggerated drama of telenovelas, moments like this monologue can ground us—as viewers—especially if and *when* we need to take a beat to ask ourselves, *"Am I okay?"*

Figure 6.2 Jane and Rafael receive the results of Mateo's assessment, when he has been diagnosed with ADHD. The narrator/Mateo spells out the acronym on-screen for us.

Toward the end of the series, Jane ends up revisiting her therapist after learning Sin Rostro has escaped from prison. Thrust into the past and unable to cope with the present (even though she has tried yoga and prayer), Jane is encouraged by Rafael to seek professional help. In reconnecting with her therapist, Jane—and we, as the audience—learn new strategies like the emotional freedom technique (EFT).[6] We learn about this tool in much the same way we learned about HALT with the help of the narrator/Mateo.

Other notable episodes include chapters 89–93, where Jane and Rafael experience Mateo's diagnosis process and deliberate how they can best help Mateo navigate his ADHD. However, since such a process is relatively new to them, Jane and Rafael struggle with what his diagnosis means. Though some critics like Jay Rattray have called their efforts to help Mateo cope with his ADHD as ableist, I choose to see their conversations as grounded in empathy.

If Jane and Rafael make misguided steps along the way (at one point, Jane tries to get an unwilling Mateo into exercise), it's only because they're trying their best to work through different learning strategies for Mateo. This, in my experience, is part of the diagnosis process, as both children and adults learn what works best for them and what doesn't—and strategies can change from moment to moment. And as children with ADHD mature, learning techniques may have to change in order to adapt to their specific interests, needs, and lifestyles. Nevertheless, as Jane and Rafael help Mateo cultivate "his normal" (to use Jane's words), such a statement suggests Mateo's difference and neurodivergence are nothing to be ashamed of.

Figure 6.3 Jane and Rafael lovingly embrace Mateo, who is expressing frustration about his ADHD in this moment.

Such discourse reminds me of Piepzna-Samarasinha's *Care Work*. Piepzna-Samarasinha states that within a disability justice framework, folx are "not left behind; we are beloved, kindred, needed" (22). As mentioned before, Jane learns from Mateo too, even amid a panic attack. Piepzna-Samarasinha writes that in disability justice, we "learn to care for each other when everyone is sick, tired, crazy, and brilliant. And neither is possible without the other" (24). In this light, I choose to read the actions of Rafael and Jane as doing the loving and sometimes messy yet necessary work of disability justice. Because after all, what isn't messy?

Personally, as someone who has ADHD, it's empowering to see Mateo's diagnosis process. Witnessing how the family is supportive of Mateo's mental health has been validating for me—and reveals that the process of discovering which learning practices work best will not always be "perfect," because perfection doesn't exist anyway.

Holistically, *JTV* seems to normalize conversations and practices surrounding mental health instead of shunning or stigmatizing them, even as actor Gina Rodriguez has navigated her own mental health challenges. Moreover, through its shaping devices, the show seems to make mental health a top priority as it creatively represents tools like meditation, therapy, deep breathing, self-check-ins, and EFT. The show's seriality allows for these techniques to be repeated as each of the series' other characters also navigate their own unique mental health experiences. With Jane's acceptance and embracing of therapy, she utilizes the lessons she learns in her life and shares this knowledge with her family and viewers.

The narrator/Mateo makes sure of this by framing Jane's experiences for us, and by inserting himself into the storyworld, even if as an extra-diegetic voice. Keywords on screen like "HALT," "ADHD," and "EFT" can help the viewer identify, research, and even finds ways to practice self-care and healthcare in ways I haven't seen previously in television shows.

One Day at a Time

"Hello, Penelope" is the name of episode 9 in season 2 of *ODAAT*, where Penelope finds herself in a mental health crisis. Unlike *JTV*, *ODAAT* is a sitcom—a reboot of the American TV series from the 1970s bearing the same name. However, this version features a Cuban American family living in an apartment in Echo Park, Los Angeles. The heads of the household include Penelope, who is a nurse, military veteran, and single mother, and her "wonderfully" dramatic mother, Lydia, who has a delicious flair for the spotlight.

Together, the two raise Penelope's teenage kids, Alex—a too-cool-for-school kiddo obsessed with designer sneakers—and Elena, a woke Generation

Z baby who explores her queerness and lesbian sexuality through the show's duration. As in the original TV series, the family is "besties with the superintendent of their building," Schneider, who just so happens to be "a trust-fund hipster" (Smith). Together, the characters of the show work through "issues that are timely, relevant, and important" (Smith). The sitcom blueprint—with its tender balance of humor and pathos—allows for the show to pack some punch in addressing sensitive topics. Furthermore, *ODAAT* has received copious critical praise for its representation of mental health within Latinx communities.

After all, why shouldn't it? *ODAAT* includes a complex portrayal of how difficult conversations about mental health can unfold in Latinx families. Chelsea Candelario states that "the writers portray struggles with mental health . . . to provoke more dialogue about the taboo subject. . . . Cultural factors like religious beliefs, family dynamics, and generational divides can make it difficult to talk openly about mental illness—and might influence how families interact, cope, and ask for help." Indeed, the show highlights these struggles immediately in the pilot episode, as well as in "Hello, Penelope" and "Anxiety" (season 3, episode 9).

In the pilot episode, Penelope resists taking antidepressants. Although she struggles with her recent separation from her husband (also a veteran with PTSD) and starting a new life with her kids and mother, she fears what Lydia may say about medication.

Furthermore, in a conversation with friend and boss, Dr. Berkowitz, she reveals the pressure she feels at home. When he asks her if she has filled the prescription he ordered, she shakes her head vehemently: "No, no, I threw them right into the trash. It's fine." When he tries to convince her to take them (because of recurring nightmares due to her PTSD), she jokingly states, "As a nurse, I would totally recommend it, but as a Cuban, I suffer in silence."

Figure 6.4 In *ODAAT*, Penelope finds support in her group therapy.

Following her dismissive remark, a laugh track sounds off (a hallmark of the sitcom genre).

However, as a Latina, I know such a statement isn't far from the truth.[7] Penelope not only wrestles with her mother's disdain, but with herself about whether to take medication. This dilemma continues into future episodes, as Penelope eventually begins to take her medication and attend group therapy, where a diverse crew of femme veterans provide support for one another.

Tensions arise again in "Hello, Penelope," as we see Penelope stop taking her medication. Various factors contribute to this decision, including her shame and embarrassment over needing medication, and the fact that she doesn't want her boyfriend Max to know how she manages her mental health. These factors are coupled with Lydia's often insensitive remarks. In the episode, she refers to Penelope's need for medication as "humiliating," cites her group therapy as a "cuckoo party," and even suggests they stop their medications together, so they can make room for lipstick in the bathroom's medicine cabinet. Lastly, Penelope stops taking her medication because, as she states, she is feeling "freakin' fantastic."

Despite some initial reservations, Penelope stops her medication and discontinues group therapy. In her last meeting, she states that her metaphorical toolbox of mindfulness strategies has been closed and placed under her bed. Even when the group's facilitator, Pam, expresses excitement over Penelope's joy, she continues to teach about mindfulness strategies the group can use when feeling overwhelmed.[8]

When Pam suggests the power of recording one's thoughts so one can play them back for perspective, Penelope scoffs: "Like: Hello, Penelope, it's me. Penelope? . . . That sounds stupid." Penelope's friend Ramona, played by Judy Reyes, seconds that thought: "Yeah, that sounds stupid, Pam." A laugh track accompanies their skeptical giggles, even as the therapist gently insists that recordings—like meditation, exercise, and service—can be tools for working through panic attacks, depression, and anxiety.

Although Lydia is excited about these changes in her daughter, we see how Penelope's anxiety and depression return full force. We recognize how Penelope is momentarily without her toolbox. Within the storyworld, Schneider first recognizes this when he checks in with her about her stress levels. When she tells him she has gone off her meds, he asks if she thinks this is "really a DIY situation." Feeling frustrated, Penelope lashes out, causing him to leave.

From there, Penelope spirals. After her tense exchange with Schneider, she retreats to her bedroom where she spends the better part of a week bedridden, holed up in her dark room where she either sleeps or watches TV. Lydia makes a *sopa de fideo* for Penelope and tries to give her some *vaporu*, but Penelope waves her away.[9]

Distressed she can't help her daughter in ways she knows, Lydia goes to confession. Her priest advises: "Señora, taking on someone else's suffering is not possible. . . . I mean, you can't know and fix everything, including your daughter. You can only be there for her while she fixes herself." While I don't really like the idea of "fixing" anyone or anything (since the idea of "fixing" requires a subject be broken), Anzaldúa's "Coyolxauhqui process" allows for a more generous reading, if fragmentation is ultimately understood as part of healing. At the end of their exchange, Lydia sobs, telling the priest she will try, in much the same way Jane in *JTV* initially accepts her therapist's advice in coping with Michael's death.

Meanwhile, there is a fade back to Penelope in her dimly lit bedroom where a spotlight haloes over her. As the center of the frame, she sits upright against a sea of dark and baby blue pillows. Similar to *JTV*, the mise-en-scène adds to the scene's cool tone. In the background, her alarm clock reads 3:18—meaning it's early morning and she hasn't been able to sleep. Penelope looks down at her phone, and we hear a click.

She speaks aloud. Audiences quickly recognize that she has opened her toolbox to use Pam's recording technique. She says tiredly, "Hello, Penelope. It's me, Penelope." However, this time there is no laugh track; its absence sets a more serious tone. She sighs, "This is so stupid," and we assume she continues to record. There is a fade to the interior of Schneider's apartment, where we hear a knock. On answering the door, Schneider encounters a remorseful Penelope, who wants to share her recording with him. When she starts the recording, we are taken back to the scene in Penelope's room through another fade.

In the next scene, Penelope delivers a powerful monologue of feelings. Her voice breaks as she speaks, and she breathes hard through her words: "It literally feels like the weight of my life is sitting on my chest. . . . And then I see those kids. . . . those beautiful kids . . . and I'm so tired."

She exhales deeply, runs a hand through her hair, and bites her nails before continuing: "Maybe I'm too tired to be what they need. . . . I want so badly for them to grow up and live full, happy lives. But I can't teach them how to do that because I don't know how to do that myself. I'm failing them. I'm failing them. They deserve so much better than me." Here, Penelope's character exhibits anxious behaviors through deep sighs and nail-biting, as well as doubting how she raises her kids, shedding light on how difficult single parenting can be.

She continues, detailing her frustration when people tell her, "Be happy. You have a great life." She recounts how comments like this make her "feel like garbage." She sighs, and the scene fades back to the interior of Schneider's apartment, where Penelope is visibly shaken by her words.

She reassures Schneider she doesn't want to commit suicide, but she still feels overwhelmed; moreover, she explicitly concludes that the woman she hears "is not okay." This identification proves essential and can teach viewers about the necessity of self-check-ins.

Luckily, Penelope has support from those closest to her. In this moment, the support comes from Schneider. After some back-and-forth where Penelope and Schneider discuss the benefits and drawbacks of medication, Schneider tells her about his addiction, saying, "There's something I want that I can't have for the rest of my life. And there's something you don't want . . . that you have to have for the rest of yours." Afterward, they hug and Penelope returns to her family's apartment, where a worried Lydia has been waiting up for her. Now, it's Lydia's turn to be supportive, as she practices the techniques recommended to her by her priest.

First, Penelope tells her mom she is going back to therapy and getting back on medication. Expecting disapproval, she huffs, "My Cuban brain should be able to fight off the crazy like a matador in a bullfight or whatever." Instead of arguing with her, Lydia calmly agrees, stating, "Okay. You do what you need to do to fix yourself. And I will be here for you."

This is a reversal of Lydia's previous behavior where she openly scoffed at therapy and medication. After Penelope embraces her mother, the scene fades again and we see how she discusses her mental health with her boyfriend Max in an open, honest, and vulnerable way—a conversation ending with acceptance, and also with an appreciation of her presence in his life.

Figure 6.5 Penelope's mother, Lydia, embraces her and offers her emotional support after a tough week.

Figure 6.6 The show represents Penelope's panic attacks in black and white. Here, Penelope texts Schneider for support. Their messages appear on-screen so we can follow and learn from their conversation.

While the conversations that take place between Penelope, Schneider, and Max are all significant because viewers can see that Penelope has a network of support, the moment between Lydia and Penelope is perhaps even more critical because it's intergenerational. Here, their embrace symbolizes a *mezcla* of cultural perspectives where traditions of medication and therapy coexist with religious empathy.[10]

Taken together, this multigenerational and diverse family have all kinds of adventures and tackle their experiences with mental health together. The show never seems to shy away from representing experiences with mental health; as such, intergenerational conversations and support continue. As Penelope's anxiety is explored in the episode entitled "Anxiety," we also learn that Elena has been experiencing panic attacks. In this episode, Pam reveals that having anxiety and depression does not make you an "unstable person."

Whenever Penelope or Elena experience panic, the color of their world drains, leaving the storyworld in a swath of monochrome. Even if folx, especially Latinxs, experience panic differently, the show's creators attempt to represent how panic manifests specifically for Penelope and Elena. Recognizing Elena's distress, Penelope sits Elena down and comforts her while Alex watches, learning skills he can use to support his sister in a following episode.

Here, *ODAAT*'s storyworld models intergenerational conversations similarly to *JTV*'s interactions between Jane and Mateo. After Penelope calms Elena, Penelope explains that Elena has just experienced a panic attack and defines anxiety, while also revealing that she too experiences them. We, the audience, listen carefully to Penelope. She tells her kids that anxiety and depression "have nothing to do with happiness; it's a chemical imbalance, and it runs in our family. And it's nothing to be ashamed of. Even though I'm ashamed of it . . . but that's something I'm trying to end with me."

This reminds me of Taylor's work, where she cites the damages of body shaming. Of the pervasiveness of body-shaming, she writes, "body shame is a fantastically crappy inheritance" (7). She continues: "On some cellular level, we know our bodies are not something we should apologize for. After all, they are the only way we get to experience this ridiculous and radiant life" (17). The show seems to embody notions of radical self-love, as Penelope teaches her kids to not be ashamed of or to apologize for their embodied feelings, because after all, our bodies and our minds *do feel*.

Creative decisions such as the show's choice of cinematography (scene coloration), implementation of monologues, careful construction of mise-en-scène, and shifting character perspectives all help frame representations of mental health conditions like PTSD, anxiety, and depression. Character humor—performed through the cast—along with sitcom laugh tracks (or the absence of them) can also help viewers visualize how Latinxs can work through their own personal mental health journeys. Despite Penelope's initial ambivalence about her "toolkit," we see her embrace medication and therapy and pass down such knowledge to her kids. Together, the shaping devices of *ODAAT* allow viewers to deeply reflect on the varied and complex manifestations of mental health in Latinx communities in our contemporary society—and just how loving and difficult these conversations can be.

Undone

Try, not try . . . these are the words Alma uses throughout the psychedelic animated indie series *Undone*, as she develops a mysterious and potentially shamanistic ability to move through dimensions of space and time after a major car crash. The show centers on Alma Winograd-Díaz and her Mexican American family, who live in San Antonio, Texas.

Alma is a restless biracial young woman with Jewish heritage who works at a day care center. She is one of the first animated Latina characters I've seen represent disability status (she has a hearing implant), and she is also one of the first Latina characters I've seen experience psychosis, or "altered perspectives." Moreover, the show's ambiguous nature (especially its open-ended conclusion) leaves open the possibility that she may have schizophrenia—which we discover runs in her family.[11]

Additionally, the show has been lauded for its creative animation style of rotoscoping, which helps create a hallucinogenic experience for the characters of the storyworld and viewers alike. Kayla Cobb notes that it is "the first series to be animated almost entirely by rotoscoping," which seems to "lend *Undone* an otherworldly air, forcing the series to straddle between reality and animation." Leah Harris calls the show a "magical, mystical, trippy, masterpiece," while Steven Scaife writes that the rotoscoping gives the show "an appropriately in-between feel," which helps to metaphorize Alma's "state of mind." In effect, rotoscoping makes Alma's "experiences of altered states accessible to the viewer" (Harris).

Critics vary in how they discuss the representation of Alma's mental health. Several critical reviews frame *Undone* in terms of *mental illness* instead of *mental health.* Such decisions inspire me to ask why there is a willingness to attach words like *mental health* to shows like *JTV* and *ODAAT,* while there's been a tendency for critics to associate *Undone* with *illness*— since "illness" can carry stigmatized connotations.

This is not to disparage or discount how the Western medical community typically labels mental health conditions—rather, this is my curiosity about the practices of naming, as language describing mental health and disability status changes and will continue to change.

Of the series, Scaife writes, "Whether due to schizophrenia or because she's some sort of time wizard, the point is that Alma isn't in total control." On the other hand, critics like Emily Van DerWerff, Megan Shea, Samantha Rollins, and Leah Harris—along with the work of Piepzna-Samarasinha and adrienne maree brown—can offer more nuanced readings of Alma's subjectivity, as I will cover momentarily.

The plot of the show follows Alma before and after a devastating car accident. When she awakens from a coma, she begins to see apparitions of her dead father, Jacob. He asks for her help in solving his murder, which happened twenty years prior. As he explains, the car accident awakens an ability in her to become invested in multiple realities simultaneously. Alma is aware schizophrenia runs in her family and seems to be both devastated and resigned to this fact. Yet, she is also excited at the possibility of having completely new, mind-bending, and unique experiences of space and time.

To me, Alma is anything but atypical. Like many, she experiences boredom. The shaping devices of monologue and montage help further characterize her within the pilot's first moments, as the show opens with her voice-over narration. There is no initial small talk in this introduction. She divulges: "I'm so bored of living. I wake up every morning in the same bed with the same person. I shower, brush my teeth, get dressed. . . . And I eat the same breakfast, and then take the same commute to work. I'm twenty-eight years old and I'm terrified this is all there is." During the monologue, a montage of her performing her daily routine flashes before our eyes.

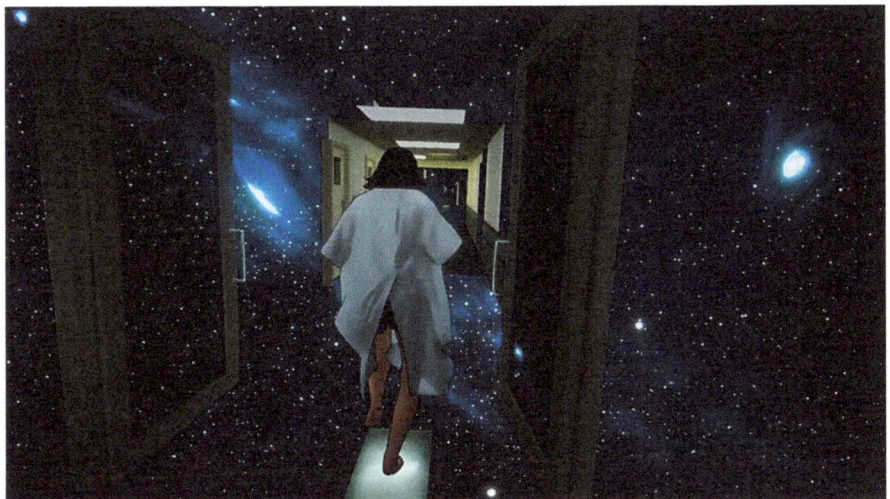

Figure 6.7 *Undone*'s Alma discovers she can move through space and time after a traumatic car accident. Here, she runs down a hospital corridor set in outer space.

The montage foreshadows her coming abilities. She stays in the same place—front and center of the frame—yet everything blurs around her as she wakes up, showers, brushes her teeth, dresses, inserts her hearing device, eats breakfast, and commutes to work. From just these opening scenes, we're not only given insight into Alma's subjectivity and personality but propelled through space and time with her. That is, the montage technique helps scaffold what journeys we will take with Alma within her storyworld.

When Alma's sense of reality is altered after her accident, the show uses the televisual techniques of flashbacks and flash-forwards to signal changes in space and time—and rotoscoping animation allows for fluid changes in setting, achronological dialogue, and flexible mise-en-scène.

In the beginning of *Undone*, Alma's monologue reveals her deepest feelings and anxieties. After her monologue, the viewer is transplanted into a bar. The monologue has been given to Alma's sister Becca, who sits next to her. Becca, who is giddy about her sudden engagement to her boyfriend, seems to wave away Alma's concerns when Alma recalls that their maternal grandmother was about their age when "she ended up on lithium, getting shock treatments, and shoving a broom handle through the television set."

In a conversation tinged with ableism, they reflect on their grandmother. Becca casually scoffs, "Getting married isn't what made her crazy. She just had a bad brain." Alma shoots back, "Yes, but if you know you have a broken brain, then why would you put someone else through that?"

The ideas of being "defective" or "broken" appear here and are similar to the ideas of "fixing" that appear in *ODAAT*. Although Alma may buy into

Figure 6.8 Alma and her sister, Becca, experience the world differently. Rotoscoping helps highlight their differences in dreamlike ways.

an ableist narrative about "brokenness," it's still clear the sisters understand mental health differently. Where Becca is dismissive, Alma is skeptical—signaling her questions regarding what it means to be fulfilled.

Such sisterly tensions erupt in the first episode's conclusion, where Becca reveals her discomfort with the label of "brokenness." When Alma tries to convince her sister they're broken, she tells Alma, "I'm not broken, Alma . . . and I wish that you would stop telling me what you think is best for me because I'm not you. . . . You are so insanely self-involved. You don't even know all the things that are wrong with you." Here, Becca uses harmful language to *other* her sister, believing Alma to be inherently different—and in a negative way.

This exchange propels the story forward. After this conversation, Alma begins to experience visions of her deceased father, Jacob. Right before her accident, his mirage appears on the roadside. Distracted by his sudden reappearance, she gets into a car crash and wakes up in the hospital two weeks later with a concussion and memory loss.

This is also when Alma begins to discover her abilities to move through space and time more fluidly. For the rest of the series, she experiences reality differently than others around her (Becca, her boyfriend Sam, and her mother Camila) as Jacob trains her to time travel.

Jacob becomes a mentor to her and uses his research experience with theoretical physics and quantum entanglement to help her navigate these new realities. In a conversation where the two sit inside a three-dimensional form of a get-well card Sam created for Alma while she was in the hospital, Jacob explains how acquiring her new abilities is comparable to when she could hear for the first time after receiving her implant, and how her brain needed time to process and make meaning from new sounds. Ultimately, Jacob describes her abilities to traverse different realities as a "new way of hearing."

Episode 5, "Alone in This (You Have Me)," explores more of Alma's past and how indigeneity may influence her abilities. In flashbacks, we see Alma when she is first diagnosed with hearing loss. On attending a school specializing in teaching children with hearing loss, Alma finds love and joy with friends and learns new ways to explore her senses.

In one key scene, her music teacher and a group of young children sit in a circle and play on different musical instruments. While a tender music score composed of strings accompanies the scene, the sounds of the storyworld are reduced. The teacher smiles, signing in ASL, "Imagine [this music] moving through your neighbor's body. It's moving through all our bodies, connecting us." Relishing in the vibrations, a young Alma gets up to dance gleefully in the center of the circle—and as she does this, her child's body morphs into her adult body. Suddenly, she is standing in a shallow pit called El Baño del Rey, a place Alma visited with her family when she was a child.

Through reduced sounds in this scene, viewers can experience the joy the young children have with vibration. This scene reminds me of Taylor's work on radical self-love, as the young children take joy in their bodies and abilities before they are socialized to be ashamed of them (6–7).

Moreover, while this transition signals a shift in space, the abrupt replacement of Alma does not necessarily signal a shift in time. As the teacher

Figure 6.9 Alma and Jacob sit inside a greeting card as Jacob explains to her what her newfound abilities mean.

and children gradually disappear, sound returns (with the whoosh of rattles permeating the scene) and Alma morphs into her older self.

While Jacob stands over the pit and looks down at Alma below, she signs to him in ASL—telling her father she doesn't want to leave such a tender moment yet. It's as if young Alma and present Alma have collided; previously, we have not seen Alma use ASL as an adult, but in this moment she uses it to express her feelings. This is an example of how the show cleverly blends past and present so we can travel with Alma on her mind-bending journeys.

While the series continues exploring the idea that Alma's newfound abilities may come from Indigenous roots, the show also portrays how the people in Alma's life become increasingly worried about her. Alma's boss, Tunde, believes she isn't the best judge of her emotional recovery after her accident; Camila pressures Alma to take an antipsychotic medication; lastly, Sam is initially supportive of Alma's visions, though he eventually withdraws his support.

Again, several critics have commented on the ambiguity of the series. Rollins from *Bustle* writes: "It's never clear if Alma really does have powers propelling her toward completing an extraordinary mission, or if this visually dazzling animated series is simply the manifestation of symptoms of her mental illness. Perhaps, *Undone* seems to posit, it depends on which way you choose to look at it. . . . You're right there in the moment with Alma, figuring it out."

Even if the show, for Rollins, represents a "mental break and mental illness . . . you can also call it incredible healing, or the potential for healing" due to its engrossing viewing experience, mash-up of genres (mystery, existential drama, with a drizzle of comedy, often due to Alma's quirky remarks), and its commentary on non-Western Indigenous traditions, where in "some cultures . . . hallucinations are considered powerful and valuable visions, not signs of life-threatening madness."

Yet, Harris from PEERS (Community Mental Health Empowerment) is careful not to label Alma's altered perspectives as simply "illness." She writes that "a remarkable aspect of 'Undone' is that it doesn't seek to reduce the experiences of 'mental illness' to simple explanation. The show does not reduce Alma's experience to purely biological explanations, hinting at cultural and spiritual ones as well. . . . Plotlines guide Alma close to exploring her own Mexican ancestral heritage as a source of healing and strength."

As critics suggest, *Undone* also doesn't veer too much into cultural appropriation. Harris believes that unlike other narratives, *Undone* "doesn't fall glibly into the 'mental illness is a superpower' stereotype . . . glossing over the suffering that can be associated with altered states." This is because the show's writers do not shy away from Alma's early loss and trauma (Harris). For Harris, *Undone* "captures the complicated reality of navigating altered states and voice-hearing in a world that often doesn't understand these experiences."

Lastly, VanDerWerff from *Vox* explains how, typically, fiction narratives that wander into the "illness vs. superpower" territory can be dangerous. This is because they "can inadvertently create the sense that a character should avoid seeking treatment for their mental illness to help sustain whatever their superpowers are."

Indeed, Piepzna-Samarasinha discusses this tension in *Care Work*, stating that disability justice is about "looking at how Indigenous and Black and brown traditions value sick and disabled folks (not as magical cripples but as people of difference whose bodyspirits have valuable smarts), and how in BIPOC communities being sick or disabled can just be 'life'" (22). In disability justice, Indigenous forms of knowledge are not fetishized as superheroic, but as ways of life.

Indeed, I choose to believe the show circumvents major cultural appropriation by creating ambiguity about Alma's mental health. In addition to including the pain and trauma Alma navigates, the show also takes care to highlight when Alma experiences pleasure, and the rotoscoping animation helps us move along with Alma as she explores the possibility of making representations of space and time *new*.

Even if an unresolved tension in *Undone* exists between Western and non-Western Indigenous cultural beliefs about mental health and notions of wellness, *Undone*'s shaping devices—especially its use of rotoscoping—suggest we may not have to choose between them. We can gap-fill the show's outcome based not only on the information of the show's storyworld, but through *cocreation*, as we bring in our own perspectives regarding what it means to be well and what it means to be different.

Conclusion

This chapter has been heavily influenced by the social justice work of decolonial women-of color feminists, pleasure activists, and disability justice advocates. To return briefly to the historical representations of Latinas (so I can highlight—one last time—how *JTV*, *ODAAT*, and *Undone* shake things up), Emma Pérez has written that, typically, "voices of women from the past, voices of Chicanas, Mexicans, and Indias, are utterances which are still minimized, spurned, even scorned. . . . We are spoken about, spoken for, and ultimately encoded as whining, hysterical, irrational, or passive women who cannot know what is good for us, who cannot know how to express or authorize our own narratives. But we will. And we do" (xv). Such a statement can still apply to contemporary representation of Latinas. At times, stereotypes of the Harlot, the Female Clown, and the Dark Lady abound; but, every once in a while, Latinas are represented as having more complex perspectives and stories in visual media. Of transformative justice, brown writes, "we need to find the roots of the harm, together, and make the harm impossible in the future. I believe that the roots of most harm are systemic, and we must be willing to disrupt vicious systems that have been normalized" (11).

With representations like *JTV*'s Jane, *ODAAT*'s Penelope, and *Undone*'s Alma, we can see more clearly how, within the Hollywood industry, there has been a lack of representation of Latinas, Latinxs, and mental health. The shows disrupt these racist, sexist, and ableist systems of power so that audiences can more easily access stories that specifically feature narratives centered on Latinx mental health.

More complex representation of cultural groups like Latinas and Latinxs leads me to think of Taylor, and how these shows seem to move toward depictions of radical self-love. Of this process, Taylor writes, "Radical self-love demands that we see ourselves and others in the fullness of our complexities and intersections and that we work to create space for those intersections" (9). Indeed, these shows create space for such intersections, as we follow each of the show's protagonists through their multifaceted journeys with mental health.

If shows can organize in the name of movements like radical self-love, pleasure activism, and disability justice, then the world can reimagine how systems of power and support reside in the very bodies we occupy. Awareness of our own embodiment allows us to make empathetic connections around not only what we need, but what others need.

When we choose embodiment, then we can, as Pérez claims, "[challenge] power relations to decolonize notions of otherness to move into a liberatory realm" (110). When we can decolonize not only our media but our minds and bodies, then we can move into a new healing consciousness that privileges empathetic relationships with the self—a consciousness where such sentiments "can serve to free us and not obstruct, stifle, and limit our identities" (124).

As shows like *JTV, ODAAT,* and *Undone* feature Latinas at the heart of each narrative, these shows also operate within different genres, using shaping devices to portray humorous and pathos-packed representations of mental health. In fact, such shows can also activate conversations about mental health within the Latinx community.

Televisual shaping devices like monologues, montages, mise-en-scènes, and flashbacks provide insight into the perspectives of Jane, Penelope, and Alma. Through the shows' seriality, we're given access to their inner-most thoughts, which is important because it contests the erasure of conversations about mental health in Latinx communities.

Although all of these Latina characters think—at some inevitable point in the series—they are going "crazy," it becomes clear (through shaping devices) they just have different ways of understanding the world around them.

In addition, these shows center on Latinas who are in multigenerational families and extended communities, and we can see how love and heartbreak inform these fictional discourses of mental health.

In these shows, mental health is personal and also communal. While Penelope and Jane use the coping tools they've learned in therapy to help their children, Alma chooses to lean away from medication so she can learn more about Nahuatl forms of wellness, and her father assists in this cultivation of knowledge.

When taken together, these shows highlight how conflicts may exist between Western mental health traditions (medication and therapy) and non-Western Indigenous beliefs. Jane and Rafael struggle with Mateo's ADHD diagnosis, and Penelope is skeptical about prescription medication and group therapy even though she is a nurse; cultural stigmas seem to factor into their reservations. Conversely, Alma is resistant to Western practices of medicine, deciding to pursue Indigenous forms of knowledge instead.

In my own communities, I have seen a similar skepticism about medication and therapy. Unfortunately, I've also seen skepticism about Indigenous practices and spirituality; but, I've also seen acceptances of both Western and Indigenous traditions of wellness—which raises the question: what does "wellness" mean, and according to whom?

These shows initiate dialogue about Latina characters who experience their mental health in unique ways, with each show's shaping devices allowing for complex representations. These shows can be helpful for anyone and everyone to see, but especially for Latinas and Latinx folks to see themselves represented in such nuanced and *real* ways.

So, what does it mean for me as a Latina to see complex and different representations of mental health in each of these shows? Because, let's face it—I can't pretend to be a disembodied person who is experiencing this televisual content in an objective, dispassionate way.

When I'm able to turn on the TV and see parts of myself reflected in the characters on-screen, it creates in me a sense of identification and pride as I come to understand I'm not alone, and that once again mental health is nothing to be ashamed to talk about. If we can continue to do the work of Pérez's decolonial imaginary, then we can imagine more stories that disrupt conventional stereotypes of Latinxs in order to make *new*.

In some ways, this chapter is entirely personal and has been difficult for me to write, especially since much of it has been triggering. Yet much of it has also been fulfilling. While I can identify with these shows, I have also learned from them.

To be clear, I'm not saying these shows are without flaws; what I want to say is that these particular televisual representations can provide future creators and audiences with even more innovative ways to envision mental health in Latinx communities.

Finally, these television serials show me the multitudinous ways we can exist as Latinxs—in all our happy, distressed, and relieved manifestations. Echoing Taylor's claim that "your body is the body it is" (23), I also believe that through embodiment "your mind is the mind it is." We don't have to separate the mind and body; it's okay that I think, feel, and work differently. And, it's okay that you think, feel, and work differently too.

Notes

1. For more information on cinematic blueprints, see Aldama's *Mex-Ciné*. I use "Latinas" to refer to femmes-of-color, while Latinx aims to be inclusive of nonbinary folx. I also see "folx" as a term that specifically indicates the inclusion of marginalized people. See Courtney for more info.

2. See *Latinx Superheroes in Mainstream Comics*, where Aldama writes that shaping devices like gap-filling help audiences *cocreate* texts to make *new* experiences.

3. The "Coyolxauhqui process" is the idea that we must first fall apart in order to bring ourselves back together.

4. Findings in epigenetics suggest that trauma from our ancestors is passed down into our own genes. See Jaye; Curry; and Henriques.

5. See "Latinx/Hispanic Communities and Mental Health," published by *Mental Health America*.

6. This technique is, as Jane's therapist describes, "a self-soothing tool based in acupuncture."

7. See "Latinx/Hispanic Communities and Mental Health," published by *Mental Health America*.

8. See Smith's passage on Mackenzie Phillips, since her role as the "woman who runs the support group is . . . a nod not only to the original series, but to Phillips's own famous struggles with addiction and mental illness" (Smith).

9. Some believe VapoRub is a cure-all for ailments. Its minty yet spicy freshness awakens the soul, to be sure.

10. See Smith, who says that "neither perspective is discounted, and the generations are able and willing to learn from one another."

11. For essays on *Undone*'s ambiguous ending, see Meslow; Radulovic; and Saraiya.

Works Cited

Aldama, Frederick Luis. *Latinx Superheroes in Mainstream Comics*. U of Arizona P, 2017.

Aldama, Frederick Luis. *Mex-Cine: Mexican Filmmaking, Production, and Consumption in the Twenty-First Century*. U of Michigan P, 2013.

"Alone in This (You Have Me)." *Undone*, created by Raphael Bob-Waksberg, Kate Purdy, and Hisko Hulsing, season 1, episode 5, Amazon Prime Video, 13 Sept. 2019.

Danielle Alexis Orozco

"Anxiety." *One Day at a Time*, created by Gloria Calderon Kellett and Mike Royce, written by Janine Brito, season 3, episode 9, Sony Pictures Television, Feb. 2019.

Anzaldúa, Gloria. *Light in the Dark / Luz en lo oscuro: Rewriting Identity, Spirituality, Reality*, edited by AnaLouise Keating, Duke UP, 2015.

Beltrán, Mary C. *Latina/o Stars in U.S. Eyes: The Making and Meanings of Film and TV Stardom*. U of Illinois P, 2009.

brown, adrienne maree. *Pleasure Activism: The Politics of Feeling Good*. AK Press, 2019.

Candelario, Chelsea. "How 'One Day at a Time' Perfectly Summarizes How the Latinx Community Deals with Mental Health." *Mashable*, 23 Mar. 2018, mashable.com/2018/03/23/one-day-at-a-time-summarizes-mental-health-latinx-community/.

"Chapter Fifty-Five." *Jane the Virgin*, created by Jennie Snyder Urman, written by Paul Sciarrotti and Jennie Snyder Urman, season 3, episode 11, The CW, Feb. 2017.

"Chapter Fifty-Six." *Jane the Virgin*, created by Jennie Snyder Urman, written by Valentina Garza, season 3, episode 12, The CW, Feb. 2017.

Cobb, Kayla. "'Undone' Is a Heartbreakingly Gorgeous Look at Mental Illness." *Decider*, 10 Sept. 2019, decider.com/2019/09/10/undone-review-prime-video/.

Courtney. "What Does the Term 'Folx' Mean?—For Folx Sake." *For Folx Sake Podcast*, 9 Sept. 2019.

"The Crash." *Undone*, created by Raphael Bob-Waksberg, Kate Purdy, and Hisko Hulsing, season 1, episode 1, Amazon Prime Video, Sept. 2019.

Curry, Andrew. "Parents' Emotional Trauma May Change Their Children's Biology. Studies in Mice Show How." *Science*, 18 July 2019, www.sciencemag.org/news/2019/07/parents-emotional-trauma-may-change-their-children-s-biology-studies-mice-show-how.

Fregoso, Rosa Linda. *MeXicana Encounters: The Making of Social Identities on the Borderlands*. U of California P, 2003.

Harris, Leah. "Undone." *PEERS: Envisioning and Engaging in Recovery Services*, Community Mental Health Empowerment: #WeArePeers, 8 Oct. 2019, https://peersnet.org/2019/10/08/undone/.

"Hello, Penelope." *One Day at a Time*, created by Gloria Calderon Kellett and Mike Royce, written by Michelle Badillo and Caroline Levich, season 2, episode 9, Netflix, Jan. 2018.

Henriques, Martha. "Can the Legacy of Trauma Be Passed Down the Generations?" *BBC Future*, 26 Mar. 2019, www.bbc.com/future/article/20190326-what-is-epigenetics.

"The Hospital." *Undone*, created by Raphael Bob-Waksberg, Kate Purdy, and Hisko Hulsing, season 1, episode 2, Amazon Prime Video, Sept. 2019.

Jaye, Lola. "Why Race Matters When It Comes to Mental Health." *BBC Future*, 11 Aug. 2020, www.bbc.com/future/article/20200804-black-lives-matter-protests-race-mental-health-therapy.

"Latinx/Hispanic Communities and Mental Health." *Mental Health America*, www.mhanational.org/issues/latinxhispanic-communities-and-mental-health.

Mendible, Myra. *From Bananas to Buttocks: The Latina Body in Popular Film and Culture*. U of Texas P, 2007.

Meslow, Scott. "Rosa Salazar Has No Answers About *Undone* and Likes It That Way." *Vulture*, 1 Oct. 2019, www.vulture.com/2019/10/rosa-salazar-undone-interview-ending.html.

Noriega, Chon A. *Chicanos and Film: Representations and Resistance*. U of Minnesota P, 1992.

Noriega, Chon A., and Ana M. López, editors. *The Ethnic Eye: Latino Media Arts*. U of Minnesota P, 1996.

Pérez, Emma. *The Decolonial Imaginary: Writing Chicanas into History*. Indiana UP, 1999.

Piepzna-Samarasinha, Leah Lakshmi. *Care Work: Dreaming Disability Justice*. 3rd ed., Arsenal Pulp Press, 2018.

Radulovic, Petrana. "Making Sense of *Undone*'s Ending." *Polygon*, 18 Sept. 2019, www.polygon.com/2019/9/17/20870764/undone-amazon-prime-ending-explained.

Ramírez Berg, Charles. *Stereotypes, Subversion, and Resistance*. 7th ed., U of Texas P, 2015.

Rattray, Jay Tee. "The Ableism of *Jane the Virgin*." *Medium*, 6 Jan. 2020, medium.com/@MsJayTeeRattray/the-ableism-of-jane-the-virgin-b8ca28b35087.

Rodríguez, Clara E. *Heroes, Lovers, and Others: The Story of Latinos in Hollywood*. Oxford UP, 2008.

Rollins, Samantha. "How the Creator of 'Undone' Turned Her Mental Break into a Healing TV Series." *Bustle*, 17 Sept. 2019, www.bustle.com/p/how-undone-creator-kate-purdy-re-contextualized-her-mental-illness-with-gorgeous-animation-18756072.

Saraiya, Sonia. "The Creators of Amazon's *Undone* on the Show's Philosophy, That Ambiguous Ending, and a Potential Season Two." *Vanity Fair*, 30 Oct. 2019, www.vanityfair.com/hollywood/2019/10/undone-kate-purdy-raphael-bob-waksberg-interview.

Scaife, Steven. "Review: *Undone* Is a Rich, Complicated Character Piece About Mental Illness." *Slant Magazine*, 14 Mar. 2020, www.slantmagazine.com/tv/review-undone-is-a-rich-complicated-character-piece-about-mental-illness/.

Shea, Megan. "'Undone' and Why Complex Depictions of Mental Illnesses Matter." *Flip Screen*, 28 Oct. 2019, https://flipscreened.com/2019/10/28/undone-and-why-complex-depictions-of-mental-illnesses-matter/.

Smith, Cat. "*One Day at a Time*: Anxiety, Depression, PTSD, and a Whole Lotta Love." *25YL*, 24 May 2019, 25yearslatersite.com/2019/05/24/one-day-at-a-time-anxiety-depression-ptsd-and-a-whole-lotta-love/.

Taylor, Sonya Renee. *The Body Is Not an Apology: The Power of Radical Self-Love*. Berrett-Koehler, 2018.

"This Is It." *One Day at a Time*, created and written by Gloria Calderon Kellett and Mike Royce, season 1, episode 1, Netflix, Jan. 2017.

Valdivia, Angharad N. *Latina/os and the Media*. Polity Press, 2010.

VanDerWerff, Emily. "You've Never Seen Anything Quite Like Amazon's *Undone*. We Mean That Literally." *Vox*, 13 Sept. 2019, www.vox.com/culture/2019/9/13/20863500/undone-review-amazon-rosa-salazar-recap.

Wang, Jessica. "Gina Rodriguez Just Got Candid About Advocating for Her Mental Health." *Bustle*, 17 June 2019, www.bustle.com/p/gina-rodriguez-stopped-filming-jane-the-virgin-to-focus-on-her-mental-health-video-18012470.

PART III

#StraightWhiteForms/BentBrownGenres

LATINIDAD THROUGH *DORA THE EXPLORER*

Ignored Histories and Realities in Popular Children's Media

Where to Begin: Dora the Explorer Then and Now

This essay started with the intention of revising a conference paper in which I argued that Dora (the iconic character of Nickelodeon's popular children's show *Dora the Explorer*) was a Latina superhero in children's media. However, as I sat down to rework and add to the paper for this volume, I realized how much had changed over the preceding three years. The stakes that I originally presented on—the Latinx community finally having a positive Latina figure in popular media—weren't "fitting" into the current climate and conversations about race and police brutality. Unable to ignore this context and considering that racial disparities in the United States are now more apparent due to the global pandemic of 2020, I returned to my original question: Is representation for the sake of representation worth it?

Dora the Explorer (2000–2019) was, and still is, a milestone for popular children's media. The show was developed as an educational and interactive television experience for preschool-aged children on the Nickelodeon (a multimedia children's television network) programming segment Nick Jr. It also provided a holistically "good" impression of a Latinx character in popular media. The animated series follows a cute, doe-eyed Brown girl with big brown eyes and brown hair in a pixie cut with bangs—as seen in the image.

Each episode consists of a challenge or goal that Dora must complete with the help of her audience, following in the tradition of the pedagogical elements found within *Sesame Street* and *Blue's Clues*. The show's main accomplishment, however, was giving U.S. audiences—children and the adults watching alongside—a positive role model who was Brown.

Dora the Explorer originally aired in 2000, six years after the infamous California Proposition 187, supported by Republican governor Pete Wilson and approved by voters. The proposition was "designed to restrict the influx of Hispanic and Latino immigrants across the Mexican border," taking away government aid for basic human needs (such as education) and requiring government workers, such as law enforcement and teachers, to report suspected undocumented persons in the state (Lee et al. 431).

Figure 7.1 Nickelodeon's Nick Jr. *Dora the Explorer* ad

Dora the Explorer thus provides insight on the generalization of Latinx folk living in the United States and the influence of this constructed identity on assumptions about not belonging. Given the findings of a 2001 study published in the *Hispanic Journal of Behavioral Science* that "prejudice and racism" against Mexicans played a part in the "endorsement of Proposition 187," it is evident that not much has changed. The authors stated, "Prejudice toward people of Hispanic decent may be rooted in gut-level affective reactions derived from childhood socialization, the belief that Hispanics undermine cherished American values, or both" (431). Dora, as a Latina animated figure who occasionally uses Spanish vocabulary, marked a starting point in establishing a positive Latinx representation for U.S. audiences that would hopefully aid in countering outdated beliefs about those coming from south of the border. Yet, based on a statement from Dan Martinsen, a Nickelodeon spokesman, who told ABCNews.com that "[Dora] was developed to be pan-Latina to represent the diversity of Latino cultures," there are still unquestioned tropes in the media regarding Latinx backgrounds. Her character's appearance on the largest preschool programming segment on television was not only being used to educate audiences about the diverse cultures that make up the Latinx identity but was also erasing the history of colonialization (from both Spain and U.S. American settlement) that displaced and continues to marginalize Brown people. In other words, Dora's presence in mainstream media does not take into account things like the U.S. acquisition of Mexican land (from Arizona, California, Texas, Nevada, New Mexico, and Utah) and the incredible injustice of laws like Proposition 187.

When Dora first aired, she was a new sort of Brown figure who demonstrated agency in her exploration and mystery-solving talent, a popular figure who spoke Spanish and aimed to "do good" for others. Before Dora, the celebrated non-white-presenting characters of children's television were often animals, such as in *Franklin* (1997–2006), *Little Bear* (1995–2003), and *Blue's Clues* (1996–2020) and creatures from a fantasy world, such as in

Allegra's Window (1994–98), *Maggie and the Ferocious Beasts* (1998–), and *Maisy* (1999–2008). Nickelodeon did, however, produce and air a few shows with a diverse cast, such as Bill Cosby's *Little Bill* (1994–98) and *Gullah Gullah Island* (1994–98) (murphytv). Yet, Latinx characters were mostly absent—until Dora. Airing on Nick Jr. over the course of nineteen years, *Dora the Explorer* became a marker of true success for diversifying children's television. As a visibly Brown character on prime-time TV, she became a hero for children of color, yet as mentioned, one who also belittles the real implications of being Latinx in the United States.

In this chapter, I focus on the holistic production of *Dora the Explorer* and its sequel, *Dora and Friends: Into the City*. Through Dora's success as a Latina figure, I also question what mainstream media allows in terms of Latinx representation. And because her Latina configuration brings in a vast amount of revenue and is so well known, I will highlight several places she appears off the network—for profit and for political discourse. Ultimately, by looking at her configuration as a pan-Latina who is now a global sensation, I evaluate the impact of her presence in popular children's television and its impacts on immigrant stereotypes and what legacy this fictional character might leave on maturing youth in the United States.

Dora in a Pre-Pandemic World

In 2019, Ebony Elizabeth Thomas pointed out the absence of color in the identities of characters in children's and young adult publications and their adaptations to film. Writing from her own experiences as a Black woman growing up and reading all the staple fantasy titles, she remembered feeling the inconsistency between the characters in those works and who she was and the way the stories made her align with characters who were vastly different (1–2). She writes: "When people of color seek passageways into the fantastic, we have often discovered that the doors are barred. Even the very act of dreaming of worlds-that-never-were can be challenging when the known world does not provide many liberating spaces" (2). And today, this absence means more than ever—#BLM, #TVSoWhite.

Television is so embedded in childhood culture today and provides a way for children to consume imaginative spaces before they can read, which is why equal representation matters in these spaces. Dora was originally conceived as a young, white character—until the creators realized that of the eighty prime-time characters who were under the age of eighteen, none were Latinx (Cereijido and Llamoca). It is safe to say that not all people are seen equally. "This problem of representation has created discord in the collective imagination," and there are undoubtedly "implications for young people who aren't mirrored in those texts" (Thomas 3–4). For Thomas, this disparity causes what she calls the "imagination gap," or a lack of authentic representation of the diverse population who are consumers of literature for young people (4–5).

In *Dora*, the scripted pauses continually encourage the audience to participate in solving puzzles, learning Spanish vocabulary, and keeping children engaged through repetition (Banet-Weiser 165). Therefore, *Dora the Explorer* is not only seen as a milestone for Latinx representation, but also *the* incorporation of positive participation in Latinx culture. This success, however, doesn't mean that she has had an easy path as a primary Latina character on screen. The show stopped airing in 2019—one year shy of its twentieth anniversary. Celebrating the twenty-year success of her character and Latinx presence on television during a time when people of color are taking to the streets, demanding equality, would have been a positive and productive thing to do. This oversight signals the still corporate control of her identity and the network's failure to participate in immigrant and immigration political discourse.

In a 2019 interview with the creators of Dora, on the occasion of the new live-action film *Dora the Explorer and the Lost City of Gold*, Antonia Cereijido and Janice Llamoca produced a thorough history of the show and how it came to be what it is. Since the show's creators were not Latinx, they hired a consulting team in order to produce a more "authentic" and reliable representation of Latinx culture. The aim was to make her a "cross cultural problem solver" (Cortez, qtd. in Cereijido and Llamoca), with her superpower being that she is bilingual. The show has since been translated into twenty-five languages and airs all over the world (Cereijido and Llamoca). Yet, instead of clarifying where exactly Dora is supposed to be from, the transnational visibility of her pan-Latinidad depicts the vast array of cultures that make up the meaning of Latinx, but at the same time is an erasure of the history that created the political and public need for such an amalgamation. While *Dora the Explorer* fundamentally changed children's television in favor of non-white representation, it continued to profit from and marginalize the Latinx community.

This failing was extended with the release of the show's sequel. In *Dora and Friends: Into the City*, her character, performance, and image play off of a more "girlie-girl" culture, encapsulated in the image of Dora standing in a shimmering glow. This refiguration emulates the princess franchise that has been exceptionally profitable for Disney. Dora's capacity to enter a position of princess girlhood culture enables her to bring Latinahood to a popular position on the market, but according to the American Psychological Association, "the girlie-girl culture's emphasis on beauty and play-sexiness can increase girls' vulnerability to the pitfalls that most concern parents: depression, eat-

Figure 7.2 Dora's preteen image from *Dora and Friends: Into the City*

ing disorders, distorted body image, risky sexual behavior" (Orenstein 6). In this second iteration of her character, she is ultimately a disempowered consumable Latina object, used for the "best interest" of the dominant, white culture/society. But Dora can be so much more.

The new show not only made Dora look and feel older, but it was also quite different from the original *Dora the Explorer*. In a *Los Angeles Times* article, Sandra L. Calvert, director of the Children's Digital Media Center at Georgetown University, stated, "Kids become so attached and develop intense relationships with characters when they're young. . . . And then they outgrow them. . . . Older Dora could allow for a longer-lasting relationship. It'll be interesting to see how long kids will stick with her now." According to the article, there was a good intention of positively influencing young viewers, in creating a show "dealing with themes such as community service and friendship skills" (Villareal). Yet, even if this older Dora was created to maintain a positive Latina member in children's popular media, Nickelodeon had no qualms releasing a complete new line of Dora merchandise and keeping her pan-Latinidad identity.

In 2009, before the release of the new show, Mattel and Nickelodeon partnered up and announced the upcoming release of a middle-school, preteen-aged Dora doll (Villarreal). Her revamped character spawned a slew of comments from parents that have even made it onto the official "Dora's Explorer Girls" Fandom.com website, the concern being that she was going to be "a fashion icon or shopaholic." Yet, once her older version doll was released, it didn't take long for Dora fans to fall in love with this new iteration. Later that year this new version of Dora was animated into a holiday special, *Dora's Christmas Carol Adventure.* Along with the tween version of Dora, Nickelodeon introduced four other preteen girls, naming the quintuplet the Explorer Girls. *Dora and Friends*, however, didn't run nearly as long as the original show, with only four seasons (airing dates of August 18, 2014–February 5, 2017).

Even though *Dora and Friends* didn't make it as long as the original series, it too has a colonizing impulse beneath the façade of representation. A 2014 *Los Angeles Times* article reports that *Dora* brought in $13 billion in retail sales and still averaged 1.4 million viewers back then—fourteen years after its original release and one year after the last episode of *Dora and Friends* aired (Villarreal). The billions her image generates raise the question: what defines Dora's popularity for children's television?

Carlos Cortés, a professor at the University of California, Riverside, and a member of the Nickelodeon consulting team for the show, has discussed his motivations for having Dora come from an indeterminate Latinx background. His argument was that making Dora a pan-Latina would allow more children to relate to her (Cereijido and Llamoca). However, her ambiguity prompted a critique of Latinx representation in mainstream culture. In "*Dora The Explorer*, Constructing 'Latinidades' and the Politics of Global Citizenship," Nicole M. Guidotti-Hernández calls attention to the other implications of making Dora pan-Latina.

> The show encodes a monolithic, consumer-ready Latino identity that is accessible to members of the dominant culture.... Herein lies the problem: when the viewers cannot distinguish or decode specific national histories and cultural practices of different Latin Americans and Latino/as within the show, Dora distorts Latino/a identity, making it seem that there is one singular, authentic Latino/a culture. Such single, "authentic" representation appeals to essentialist racial, cultural, and physical traits instead of presenting cultural practices and racial identities as fluid, differentiating depending upon region. (214–15)

And, I would argue, such representation adds to the missing dialogues of U.S. Latinidad—one where Latinxs are born and raised in the United States—and the problematic immigration laws that allow children to be taken from their parents and locked in cages. While Cortés's argument is logical, appealing to all Latinx backgrounds in this way can also result in misunderstandings about Latinidad and its primary definition—being of a multifaceted yet interdependent colonized subjectivity.

One example of how the show erases the plurality in defining Latinidad is in the *Dora and Friends* episode titled "Dance Party." In the episode, Dora and her friends are getting ready for a dance party in which all the profits will be donated to the local dance studio. Dora says she has made up her own dance, which is "basically salsa, with a little mamba." Pablo points out she has "a little bit of samba in there too." Here Dora's dance highlights her ambiguous cultural background while at the same time teaching U.S. audiences various forms of Latinx dance styles. Yet, what remains is the production of one Latinidad and the erasure of the histories of these styles of dance and the places from which they originate. This example is just one of many blendings that most audiences accept without question, which is perhaps the biggest flaw of her character's conception.

Subversive Pan-Latinidad: Superpower or Flaw?

Considering Dora as a colonized subject brings up several aspects of her character that at first appear helpful but on closer consideration leads to the erasure of colonial subjectivity, which is ultimately harmful to the Latinx identity and experience in the United States. Her Brown presence on mainstream television and bilingual pedagogical use represent an attempt to create a subversive Latinx figure, but in the end she becomes another hegemonic condition for Latinx folk that continues to ignore history. If we challenge the notion of Latinidad presented in its white hegemonic containment, our attempt to reclaim individual Latinx identities will never overcome the dominant discourses of marginalization. However, in children's literary scholarship, the child is already understood as a colonized figure. Could Dora's figuration as child and the Latinx colonized subjectivity that makes up her character challenge the way we see Latinx identities on TV?

To begin addressing the subjectivity of the colonized, let's consider what it means to be no longer colonized. In "Radical Bilingualism in North African Literature," Samia Mehrez defines decolonization as

> never simply the physical ousting of the colonial presence. . . . Rather, decolonization has been, and continues to be, an active confrontation with a hegemonic system of thought and hence a process of historical and cultural liberation. . . . [It] becomes the contestation of all dominant forms and structures whether they be linguistic, discursive, or ideological. Moreover, decolonization comes to be understood as an act of exorcism for both the colonized and the colonizer. For both parties it must be a process of liberation: from dependency, in the case of the colonized, and from imperialist racist perceptions, representations, and institutions which unfortunately, remain with us till this very day, in the case of the colonizer. (258)

That is, decolonization is more than the removal of objective force on a nation, person, or cultural framework. Instead, it becomes a space that must be actively worked toward by both colonized and colonizer. If we think of Nickelodeon (or Viacom) as the colonizer because it profits from, controls who Dora is, and when she is on TV, the colonizer thus seems to not consider the restrictive quality of her character.

In Perry Nodelman's foundational work *The Hidden Adult*, he argues that children's literature is a colonizing force and connects colonial subjectivity to the child as a social construction. This idea not only speaks to the duplicity of hegemonic discourse on Dora's characterization as a pan-Latina, but it also opens up a dialogue for the improvement of representation through children's literature and media. In the book, he argues that childhood/adolescence is an "othered" position, predetermined and always already defined by society, as can be seen in children's literature. Defining literature for young people means to acknowledge the separate, outside space of childhood where literatures for child audiences get created (3).

The fact that adults are the main purchasers of texts for young people suggests that producers are concerned with what adults want their children consuming in the form of literature. Nodelman finds that because of this dynamic, children's literature becomes more like popular literature and "not so much what children read as what producers hope children will read" (4). However, as he goes on to point out, this phenomenon also implies that children need adults and "things done for them by adults" (4), which also means that "the intended audiences of the texts are defined by [children's] presumed inability to produce such books or make decisions about purchases of books for themselves" (5). Nodelman recognizes the child state as being un-able, in-capable, and lesser than the adult, a relationship that aligns with marginalized communities and the racist, self-entitled, right-wing rhetoric surrounding immigrants. Just as literature for young people "invite[s] child readers to mimic . . . the childhood that adults imagine for them" (186), immigrant minority groups may find their only way to (somewhat) exist in dominant social circles is to mirror the behaviors of those who make up these right-wing spaces. This relationship also mirrors that between the Latinx community and U.S. white hegemonic society, especially in the way that Nodelman utilizes Homi Bhabha's idea of "discourse of mimicry" to identify the colonized subject as being "constructed around *ambivalence*" (186–87). Dora's need to be pan-Latina suggests the ambivalence Bhabha refers. The need to create a "less authentic" and individual identity to mirror the image of Latinidad that white audiences require releases her from a position that identifies the wounds inflected on the Latinx body/figure historically and presently.

Returning to Mehrez's ideas about the process of decolonialization, *Dora the Explorer* becomes both a subversive attempt to normalize Latinidad in U.S. American culture and a structure that maintains the colonized status. Here, I find Mehrez's idea of "radical bilingualism" significant. She defines this term as a "literary production [that] challenges its own indigenous, conventional models as well as the dominant structures and institutions of the colonizer" (259). She goes on to suggest that this term redefines "postcolonial bilingualism" by challenging what "national literatures" fundamentally mean.

> It is this radical bilingualism that will allow us to speak of a subversive poetics: a poetics that seeks to create a new literary space for the bilingual, postcolonial writer. . . . By doing so, this subversive poetics not only challenges our conventions of reading and writing, but it also questions the structuring of institutions of learning and disciplinary boundaries. (260)

Because *Dora the Explorer* and *Dora and Friends* follow an educational programing agenda, I find that the Latinx figure here, as an indefinable identity in general and in the show (mentioned above in Guidotti-Hernández's article), merges all Latinx cultures owing to Western requirements of pedagogical programing. Arguably, because the programing itself is already marked white—through those who produce and manufacture it—its methods of educating children are too. What it demonstrates, then, is that in order for Latinidad to emerge in popular media, it must shed historical and individual cultures.

Conversations about the pedagogical policing of language and experience are nothing new. In her "How to Tame a Wild Tongue," Gloria Anzaldúa discusses an ideological divide within the non-Standard American English or othered dialect. She writes, "I remember being caught speaking Spanish at recess. . . . I remember being sent to the corner of the classroom for 'talking back' to the Anglo teacher when all I was trying to do was tell her how to pronounce my name. 'If you want to be American, speak "American." If you don't like it, go back to Mexico where you belong'" (34). Anzaldúa's memories touch on the lasting implications of racialized judgments determined by how one languages. Dora's educational value conveyed in Standard American English suggests that "the ways we judge language form some of the steel bars around our students and ourselves—we too maintain white supremacy, even as we fight against it in other ways. We ain't just internally colonized, we're internally jailed" (Inoue 3). *Dora*'s success as a prime-time children's television program suggests that her character is a hero for normalizing the Spanish language. But clearly, in maintaining the ESL Latinx identity as that of not belonging, the show creators missed a valuable opportunity to reformulate the way accents are always "othered."

Yet, viewed through the frame of "radical bilingualism," *Dora* also performs a subversive role in the way it attempts to reform Latinx identity by replacing negative stereotypes with a kind and attentive child. Guidotti-Hernández's feminist reading of her character reveals how Dora breaks the traditional mold of Latinx representation on television. Her character is subversive in being a positive representation of Brown bodies on the screen. Guidotti-Hernández highlights a significant quality about Dora: she is not connected to "women's work" and "domesticity" (214). Instead, the *explorer* part of Dora's character unconsciously connects her Latina subjectivity to its historical identity and also reclaims it through her role as a female leader explorer. While Spanish exploration led to the colonization of Latin countries, *Dora* departs from "the 'original' script of colonizer" and challenges any notion of inscribed gendered, cultural assumptions (226). Nodelman points out that children's literature has always contained and reinforced gender assumptions; it is a "particularly important aspect of the colonizing work of children's literature—so much so that a defining characteristic of children's literature is that it intends to teach what it means for girls to be girls and boys to be boys" (173). Dora's disruption of these traditional gender roles not only draws in all gendered child viewers, but it also challenges the gender division constantly reinforced in children's literature and media.

But before we can completely praise *Dora* creators for this subversive and impactful, gender role-disrupting Latinx character, let us not forget the sequel. *Dora and Friends* returns to gender stereotypes. The tween version of Dora that first emerged on store shelves as a doll completely ignored her character's segue from dominant gendered norms and recolonized the progressive role she played for child audiences. The original Dora Links doll was released with a computer program that allowed the owner to control physical traits, such as hair length and eye color. The commercial aired with the following message to consumers (conveyed in a conversational narrative):

> Dora's grown up, as you can see. "Meet Dora Links, the girl who's on the screen and on the scene." She's got a love of friends and style and mystery. "Let's go online." She's a doll that connects to your computer. "Are you ready for a disguise." Changes here, make changes there. "Change her jewelry, her eye color, her growing hair." "This is just my style!" Dora Links, she's the link to her life. "Dora Links comes with this. Other dolls and accessories sold separately. Ask your parents to go online." (Mattel Shop)

Watching her hair grow and eyes change from brown to blue is uncanny and also an erasure of her power as a completely Brown representation of Latinidad. It places agency in the hands of non-Latinx children to reclassify the physical aspects of the Brown and regulate which traits are allowed into spaces of popular culture.

Dora Reaches Politics

Dora has had a significant presence on the screen and on the shelves. However, her image doesn't end there. In 2010, she made headlines with a picture of her with a beaten face and a prisoner place card that read "Dora the Explorer; Illegal Border Crossing; Resisting Arrest" (see figure 7.3). The image was intended to bring awareness to a bill passed in Arizona that allowed police to ask anyone for their immigration status paperwork (BBC News). In other words, law enforcement was given the green light to racially profile people of color. The core of the article reads:

> For almost a decade, the doe-eyed cartoon heroine has been one of the most prominent Hispanic characters on children's television in the US. Her TV show has spawned a global empire, with her smiling face appearing on everything from lunch boxes to computer games. But as the controversy over illegal immigration has intensified, Dora has been drawn into the political debate. Most of the websites that have appropriated her image assume she is a migrant from Mexico. . . . But Nickelodeon has declined to comment on her background, and her place of birth and citizenship have never been made clear. ("Is Dora the Explorer")

Here the configuration of Latinidad seems to be working as a binary. In one sense, Dora's popularity provides a visual representation of the abuse that immigrants and people of color endure. In another sense, she embodies the

Figure 7.3 Dora meme depicting the potential danger of Arizona's SB 1070 and HB 2162 laws

figuration of a child, whom society deems must always be protected but clearly isn't if read as too Brown. The child is "a ubiquitous fixture in public life. Daily, even hourly, one is confronted with images of children posed to capture the consuming gaze" (Cook 1). Since it is clear that Dora's Brownness in popular children's media is significantly familiar for U.S. audiences, this image imparts dominant assumptions of noncitizenship merely because she is Brown and speaks Spanish.

However, her use for making political statements regarding illegal immigrants doesn't end there. Nine years later a teacher in Ohio used this same image next to a picture of a convicted felon in order to "illustrate his lesson on voting eligibility" (Thebault). The meme he shared with his students depicted Dora as an illegal immigrant and suggested that her status was the same as that of a convicted felon (Thebault). Putting the two images side by side is not only incredibly offensive—Dora's image (shown above) for "resisting arrest" and "illegal border crossing" on the right, an image of a white male in an orange prison suit on the left—but it highlights the teacher's sense of entitlement, one where he felt he could use Dora's image without considering her characterization and what she stands for holistically. Given her ambiguous Latinx heritage and her U.S. American English accent, who's to say this fictional character is not a U.S. citizen?

This meme is not just a problematic image for the reasons stated above; it also conveys incorrect information about Latinx communities. First, according to the U.S. Census Bureau in 2019, Latinx polled in at 18.5 percent, which is the highest percentage of a minority group in the United States ("U.S. Census Bureau"). Yet *legal* immigrants who are not yet citizens are also not allowed to vote. Therefore, this image and its use in this example demonstrate that the figuration of Latinidad is marked as not belonging and also the same as a criminal. The teacher was ultimately told not to do it again; but even if he and other teachers learn from this example, the scar remains. "Scholars like Jamie Naidoo remind us, there is not a child in the United States who will not be interacting with Latinos on playgrounds and in classrooms. The building blocks of today's US reality are Latino" (Aldama 4). But images like Dora as felon will create a consensus that members of the largest minority in the United States aren't part of the country they live and work in.

Conclusion

My first publication on *Dora the Explorer* was in 2016. Back then I wrote about Dora setting the course for positive Latinx figures on screen. Yet, what now stands out to me is that her character is used for profit for a non-Latinx community, hidden under the guise of being "for the better good." But Dora isn't the only Latina figure to be marketed. In the introduction to *From Banana to Buttocks*, "Embodying Latinidad," Myra Mendible takes up the embodiment of Latinas (female identifying) bodies in the United States and problematizes how these bodies are literally manufactured for consumption. "Mediated through various forms of visual representation and discourse, 'the Latina body' functions within a social and cultural taxonomy that registers but an echo of the clamor, complexity, and variety of women who embody Latina identities" (1). Therefore, U.S. society ascribes imagined taxonomy to Brown identity in general and, at the same time, the Latina body is a constructed site of otherness that popular children's media hasn't shown interest in getting right through its most popular Latina figure.

Ultimately, even though Dora arguably takes control of the narrative, giving the original show an anti-colonial feel, her dialogue with children is appropriated through a prescribed Western bilingualism. The subversive power she holds through reclaiming the historically colonizing Brown figure and limiting gender roles in children's literature is not enough to excuse the larger commodification of the Brown "other" and a lack of knowledge of what Latinx folk are going through today. The problem ultimately lies in the amalgamation of all Latinidades within a white colonial frame that erases immigrant struggles. What could be more telling than the gradual but perceptible whitening of Dora's skin with Mattel's Dora Links Doll? The doll, like the show, is ultimately a watered-down, whitewashed version of Latinidad aimed to generate profit.

Works Cited

Aldama, Frederick Luis. "Introduction: The Heart and Art of Latino/a Young People's Fiction." *Latino/a Children's and Young Adult Writers on the Art of Storytelling*, by Aldama, U of Pittsburgh P, 2018, pp. 3–25.

Anzaldúa, Gloria. "How to Tame a Wild Tongue." *Borderlands. La Frontera*, by Anzaldúa, Aunt Lute Books, 1999, pp. 53–64.

Banet-Weiser, Sarah. *Kids Rule! Nickelodeon and Consumer Citizenship*. Duke UP, 2007.

Cereijido, Antonia, and Janice Llamoca. "The Breakdown: The Legacy of 'Dora The Explorer.'" *Latino USA*, 14 Aug. 2019, www.latinousa.org/2019/08/14/doratheexplorer/.

Cook, Daniel Thomas. *The Commodification of Childhood: The Children's Clothing Industry and the Rise of the Child Consumer*. Duke UP, 2004.

"Dance Party." *Dora and Friends: Into the City*, created by Chris Gifford and Valerie Walsh Valdes, written by Jorge Aguirre, Dana Chan, and Chris Gifford, season 1, episode 5, Nickelodeon, 4 Sept. 2014.

"Dora's Explorer Girls." *Dora the Explorer Wiki*, Fandom TV, dora.fandom.com/wiki/Dora%27s _Explorer_Girls.

Friedman, Emily. "Is Dora The Explorer an Illegal Immigrant?" *ABC News*, 21 May 2010, abcnews.go .com/Entertainment/Media/dora-explorer-labeled-illegal-immigrant/story?id=10711944.

Guidotti-Hernández, Nicole M. "*Dora The Explorer*, Constructing 'Latinidades,' and the Politics of Global Citizenship." *Latino Studies*, vol. 5, no. 2, 1 July 2007, pp. 209–32, doi:10.1057/palgrave .lst.8600254.

"Is Dora the Explorer an Illegal Immigrant?" *BBC News*, 21 May 2010, news.bbc.co.uk/2/hi/americas/8698065.stm.

Inoue, Asao B. "How Do We Language So People Stop Killing Each Other, Or What Do We Do About White Language Supremacy?" Conference on College Composition and Communication, Annual Convention, 14 Mar. 2019, tinyurl.com/4C19ChairAddress.

Lee, Yueh-Ting, et al. "Attitudes Toward 'Illegal' Immigration into the United States: California Proposition 187." *Hispanic Journal of Behavioral Sciences*, vol. 23, no. 4, 2001, p. 430–43.

Mattel Shop. "Dora Links Commercial." *YouTube*, 14 Oct. 2009, www.youtube.com/watch?v=mbcohDeCOJ8.

Mehrez, Samia. "Radical Bilingualism in North African Literature." *The Bounds of Race: Perspectives on Hegemony and Resistance*, edited by Dominick LaCapra, Cornell UP, 1991, pp. 255–77.

Mendible, Myra. "Introduction: Embodying Latinidad: An Overview." *From Bananas to Buttocks: The Latina Body in Popular Film and Culture*, edited by Mendible, U of Texas P, 2007, pp. 1–28.

Murphytv. "Nick Jr Shows." *IMDb*, 1 Apr. 2020, www.imdb.com/list/ls092562062/?sort=release_date,asc.

Nodelman, Perry. *The Hidden Adult: Defining Children's Literature*. Johns Hopkins UP, 2008.

Orenstein, Peggy. *Cinderella Ate My Daughter: Dispatches from the Front Lines of the New Girlie-Girl Culture*. HarperCollins, 2013.

Thebault, Reis. "Teacher Uses a Meme of Dora the Explorer as an Illegal Border Crosser in a Lesson About Voting." *Washington Post*, 16 Nov. 2019, www.washingtonpost.com/education/2019/11/16/teacher-uses-meme-dora-explorer-an-illegal-border-crosser-lesson-about-voting/.

Thomas, Ebony Elizabeth. "Introduction: The Dark Fantastic: Race and the Imagination Gap." *Dark Fantastic: Race and the Imagination from Harry Potter to the Hunger Games*, by Thomas, New York UP, 2019, pp. 1–14.

"U.S. Census Bureau QuickFacts: United States." *Census Bureau QuickFacts*, U.S. Census Bureau, 2019, www.census.gov/quickfacts/fact/table/US/PST045219.

Villarreal, Yvonne. "Dora the Explorer Is Growing Up and Getting a Spinoff Series." *Los Angeles Times*, 18 Aug. 2014, www.latimes.com/entertainment/tv/la-et-st-aging-dora-20140818-story.html.

UNHOLY HOLIDAY

Día de Muertos in Disney's *Elena of Avalor*

Mathew Sandoval

Television representation—of our stories, our bodies, our skin, our lives, our experiences, our aesthetics, our dreams—matters. TV representation of our holidays *also* matters. This is as true of scripted and reality Latinx television as it is for animated Latinx television. In this chapter, I focus my analytical sights on Disney's *Elena of Avalor* (2016–20)—a show that has chosen to reconstruct the Día de Muertos/Day of the Dead holiday for a primarily non-Latinx audience.

I'm interested in analyzing representations of Día de Muertos in animated television series specifically because illustrated, animated, cartoon, and comic depictions of this cultural tradition and its related iconography are the mediums responsible for the growing popularity of the holiday over the past century. From the political lithographs of Jose Guadalupe Posada in the early twentieth century, to Javier Hernandez's comic *El Muerto: The Aztec Zombie* in the late 1990s, to Jorge Gutierrez's animated film *The Book of Life* or Pixar's *Coco* in the twenty-first century, it has been the hand-drawn or computer-generated illustration that has advanced the global recognition of this holiday, to the point where Día de los Muertos is now an "Intangible Cultural Heritage of Humanity" protected by UNESCO (United Nations Educational, Scientific, and Cultural Organization). Furthermore, animated television tends to be aimed at children, whose developing minds use these images, stories, and ideas to make sense of the world, not merely to be entertained. Thus, animated representations of Día de Muertos on television are knowingly or unknowingly responsible for teaching children about the holiday. This raises a number of critical questions. How exactly is Día de Muertos depicted in animated television? What might audiences understand or misunderstand about Día de Muertos based on these representations? And how do these mass media Día representations affect the way that Día de Muertos is celebrated in the real world?

In this essay I examine the *Elena of Avalor* episode "A Day to Remember" (season 1, episode 9) to unpack Disney's visual and narrative choices made to reconstruct Día de Muertos for a non-Latinx audience. Indeed, this episode's release was a milestone in U.S. animated TV production. It was the first animation narrative focused on Día de Muertos, introducing vast numbers of young viewers to this holiday. Furthermore, this was Disney's first attempt to represent Día de Muertos after it famously and stupidly attempted to trademark "Día de los Muertos" in 2013 in order to secure the name and merchandising rights for a Day of the Dead film then in pre-production, which became their 2017 global sensation *Coco*. In short, there was a lot at stake for Latinx representation in this princess-themed afternoon cartoon.

All things considered, the "A Day to Remember" episode of *Elena* successfully showcases the holiday's vibrant festive qualities and the feelings of joy and togetherness that accompany it. However, as I argue below, the episode ultimately presents Día de Muertos as a secular cultural festival in which the central component of death, as well as the holiday's sacred and religious character, are completely disguised or disappeared. The result is that one of the most sacred and venerated aspects of our *cultura* is represented to audiences as little more than a colorful, but meaningful, party.

Día de Muertos

Día de Muertos, otherwise known as Día de los Muertos, Día de Difuntos, or Day of the Dead in English, is an annual holiday that takes place over a series of days centered on November 1 and 2. It's dedicated to honoring, remembering, and celebrating the dead. This can mean honoring a particular family member or loved one who has recently died, honoring all family and loved ones who have died, honoring one's ancestors, as well as honoring the universal dead more generally. It's commonly understood to be a distinctly Mexican holiday, but due to immigration patterns and cultural diffusion it is celebrated in the United States, as well as parts of Central and South America.

Día de Muertos is a syncretic holiday, meaning it's a mixture of (at least) two separate spiritual traditions—in this case between pre-Columbian Indigenous spirituality and Spanish Catholicism. The holiday has its roots in pre-Columbian Mesoamerica, most notably among the Nahuatl (Aztec) culture, although it's likely that a similar holiday existed among earlier Mesoamerican cultures such as the Olmec, Teotihuacan, and Toltec civilizations. The Nahuatl held annual Feasts for the Dead in the ninth and tenth months of their calendar year. These ritual feasts featured weeks of elaborate ceremonies, games of competition, banquets of food and alcohol, symbolic commemorations for the deceased, spectacles of ritual sacrifice, as well as dancing and general revelry.[1] This Indigenous series of holy days was syncretized with Catholic traditions during Spain's brutal colonization of the Americas in the sixteenth and seventeenth centuries, when hundreds of millions were forced to renounce their religion and adopt Catholicism. However, numerous Indigenous communities in Central Mexico chose to disguise their religion rather than abandon it, which resulted in a blending of the Nahuatl Feasts for the Dead with the Catholic holy days of All Saints Day (November 1 of the Catholic liturgical calendar) and All Souls' Day (November 2), creating a hybrid holiday that satisfied Catholic religious observation while remaining in many ways fundamentally and distinctly Indigenous in orientation.[2]

This multiday celebration traditionally centers on the *ofrenda*, an altar for the dead, who are honored and remembered through ceremonial and symbolic objects such as marigold flowers, candles, photographs, *papel picado*, food and drink, and meaningful personal items. Far from a mere personal or familial observance, Día de Muertos is usually accompanied by a large public celebration, ranging from a community event of a couple hundred to tens of thousands of celebrants who gather in cemeteries, plazas, civic centers, or museums and other cultural institutions. These celebrations typically feature ceremonies, music, dance, festive attire, and the omnipresent imagery of death in the form of skeletons and sugar skulls.

Elena of Avalor

The computer-animated series *Elena of Avalor* premiered on the Disney Channel in July 2016 to overwhelming success, garnering 4.2 million viewers with the first episode (Umstead). It's a coming-of-age tale about sixteen-year-old Elena Castillo Flores, a princess in the magical kingdom of Avalor. The story begins with an evil witch, Shuriki, who casts a magic spell on Elena, trapping her inside an amulet. Shuriki then kills Elena's parents, the king and queen of Avalor, and begins her dark reign of the kingdom. Forty-one years later, Elena magically escapes the amulet, ousts the evil witch, and ascends to the vacant throne. The rest of the series follows Elena on her many adventures as she learns how to rule her newly inherited kingdom as a princess training to be queen. She assumes her leadership with the advice and help of her grandparents, her younger sister, her friends, and her spirit guide, Zuzo. After three successful seasons, *Elena of Avalor* drew to a close in August 2020.

Elena is perhaps most notable for being Disney's first Latina princess. After decades and decades of a "whites only" Disney princess club and the subsequent multicultural shift of the 1990s and 2000s, Disney finally introduced a princess with Latin roots. Elena has no specific Latinx identity in terms of ethnicity, race, or nationality, because she's from the make-believe (but Latin-inspired) kingdom of Avalor. In a way that is equal parts fascinating and potentially problematic, Elena is a composite of diverse Latinx identities and cultures. Disney would have us believe that in this thin, almond-skinned body resides all of Latinidad, or at least all the aspects of Latinidad that are worthy of inclusion in their magical universe. On the other hand, Elena is also a kind of wish fulfillment for those of us invested in Latinx identity, insofar as we imagine ourselves having some unifying umbrella identity that contains a dizzying diversity that spans three continents, dozens of nation-states, a variety of races, hundreds of different languages, and an immeasurable number of cultures. Elena, as a Latina princess, is as fascinating and potentially problematic as the very notion that a Latinx identity actually exists. In that respect, she's the accurate embodiment of our messy notions of Latinidad. Turns out Disney got us right.

For all the potential critiques of the show, which are truly outside the scope of this essay, Disney did make legitimate attempts to infuse *Elena of Avalor* with Latinidad. Mexican American, Emmy-nominated screenwriter Silvia Olivas served as head writer and producer on the show. The main characters were voiced by an all-Latinx cast of actors. Much of the production crew were Latinx. *Elena of Avalor*'s theme song is sung by Guatemalan singer-songwriter Gaby Moreno. Each episode of the show features musical traditions and genres from across Latin America—salsa, mariachi, merengue, banda, and bossa nova, to name but a few. Elena's costumes were designed by Brazilian fashion designer Layana Aguilar. Many of the plot devices used in the show's seventy-seven episodes incorporate elements of mythology and folklore drawn from across Latin America. Additionally, Disney was savvy enough to bring a number of cultural consultants into production, including Marcela Davison Avilés, founder of the Chapultepec Group and cofounder of the international Latino arts initiative Camino Arts, and Diane Rodriguez, associate artistic director of Center Theatre Group and cofounder of the theater ensemble Latins Anonymous (McLennan). In terms of cultural representation, the producers worked intentionally and respectfully at multiple levels to, in their words, "get it right" (McDermott).

There is, perhaps, an unfair burden placed on Disney's first Latina princess series, which is that the show has to educate its primarily non-Latinx audience about Latinx culture. *Elena of Avalor* regularly has to engage in a kind of cultural translation. Elements and aspects of Latinx culture are explained to the audience in terms they can understand or with a sense of familiarity that makes them legible and intelligible. This is especially true in season 1 of the series. Por ejemplo, there are episodes explaining Carnival, quinceañera, and the various Latin American customs performed for Navidad. For American audiences more attuned to visions of a "white Christmas" or "Sweet 16" birthday on their television screens, these episodes provide a diverse cultural experience. Very rarely, though, do these episodes function exclusively to explain the particular Latin American cultural tradition. More often than not they serve as narrative vehicles to advance a plot in which Elena has to solve some kind of problem that helps her friends and family, unifies the people of Avalor, or defends her kingdom from outside harm. However, the show often goes to great lengths to explain to the audience elements that might be foreign to them.

This is especially true in the episode "A Day to Remember," in which the holiday Día de Muertos gets culturally translated for the audience. But how exactly does Disney represent and characterize Día de Muertos in this episode? What is Disney explaining to the audience about Día de Muertos? What understandings of the holiday might the audience walk away with? And how does Disney's version of Día de Muertos compare to the actual Día de Muertos celebrated in Mexico and the United States? In short, insofar as Disney is translating an aspect of Latinx culture to a diverse but primarily non-Latinx audience, what is it that's actually being translated, and what gets lost in translation?

Death Euphemisms

Día de los Muertos may seem like a weird or morbid holiday to those unfamiliar with its meaning, history, or symbolism. The overwhelming spectacle of skulls and skeletons often makes people judge the holiday as grotesque and gothic at best, or nefarious and demonic at worst. There's no doubt such castigations of our cultura are related to the broader demonization of Latinx people in the United States more generally, but it's also true that the idea of celebrating death is off-putting to those unacquainted with the holiday. This context of cultural ignorance is the backdrop from which Disney has to bring Día de los Muertos into relief. The result is a representation of the holiday that is more or less sanitized of death.

In "A Day to Remember" Disney attempts to make Día de los Muertos less exotic and morbid for its audience by actually refusing to have the words "death," "dead," or "dying" uttered anywhere in the episode. This is an oddly phenomenal achievement given that the episode's central topic and plot concern death. Save for the Spanish palabra "muertos" that gets spoken when a character names the holiday Día de los Muertos, the word "death" never makes an appearance. The episode's writers instead opt to utilize a whole slew of euphemisms. These include such classics as "passed away," "gone," "no longer here," and "not with us anymore." It's as if Día de los Muertos contains too much death, and thus requires the show's creators to use all number of circumlocutions to tame it and moderate its excess.

There's no way around it: to understand Día de los Muertos one has to face death. Employing euphemisms actually prevents a full reckoning with the reality of death. This is especially true for children who compose the show's primary audience. To be fair, discussing death with children of any age can be quite difficult. In the U.S. context this is made all the more difficult because, as research has shown, death and dying constitute a taboo subject filled with an onslaught of fear and anxiety.[3] By and large the United States has a culture of grief and death avoidance. When discussing death with children (if it's discussed at all), adults will often default to using rhetoric they believe is more socially acceptable, in which case the objective moves from explaining death to children to protecting them from the reality of death. However, for decades developmental psychologists and child educators in the United States have made it clear that euphemisms and abstract terms ("gone on," "gone somewhere better," "left us," "passed away") have little meaning for children, and obscure and confound far more than they clarify. Indeed, as Dr. Clarissa Willis states explicitly in her guidelines for adults on how to talk with children about death, "Avoid euphemisms; they are confusing and misleading" (Willis 223). Yet despite such clinical advice, Disney has made a ninety-year habit of relying on euphemisms for death rather than naming it squarely, and that is definitely the case in the "A Day to Remember" episode of *Elena of Avalor*.

When Disney isn't using linguistic substitutions to avoid death in "A Day to Remember," it's using conceptual substitutions. Rather than making the holiday about death and the deceased, they opt to make it about love. Early in the episode Elena explains Día de los Muertos in the form of a musical. She sings an upbeat poppy merengue titled "Festival of Love" that's accompanied by a stylish spectacle of ensemble choreography. In the song she describes many of the traditional cultural practices associated with Día de los Muertos—visiting graveyards, decorating altars, lighting candles, making special food, and festive behavior—while also relating to the audience her love of the holiday. Characters come together with Elena to sing the chorus: "This is the day we all await. This is the day we celebrate. The festival of love! The festival of love!," which gets repeated a dozen times in the span of a nearly two-minute song. What gets conveyed through this musical number is that the holiday is primarily, even exclusively, about love. Disney would have the audience believe that Día de los Muertos isn't actually about death at all.

But why? Why the conceptual substitution? In part it may be an extension of the logic that goes into Disney's reliance on euphemisms—it's a way to protect children from the reality of death. But transforming Día de los Muertos from a holiday about death to a "festival of love" may also be Disney's strategy for protecting the holiday from ridicule and condemnation by non-Mexican/Chicanx/Latinx audiences who might think it macabre. Thus, Disney may have erred on the side of caution in "A Day to Remember." Making the holiday about love (because love = "good") and downplaying death (because death = "bad") ultimately makes the holiday safe, familiar, acceptable, and appealing to an audience unacquainted with the holiday. But Disney's conceptual substitution comes at an expense; it kills death, the central core of the holiday. I'm not suggesting that Día de Muertos isn't also about love. But nearly every holiday is, at least in some way, about love. There's nothing unique about that. That death is Día de Muertos' focal point and raison d'être is ultimately what makes it different from other holidays. Death is what gives this holiday its identity, no matter how much Disney would like to bury that fact in a grave of euphemisms and conceptual substitutions.

In many ways this is on-brand for Disney. They have a history of evading direct dealings with death. In the last two decades a variety of scholars have investigated the way that death operates in Disney productions, and they've generated measurable conclusions. The first large-scale research was conducted by professors Meredith Cox, Erin Garrett, and James A. Graham in the early 2000s. In their study they performed content analysis on popular Disney animations from 1937 to 1999 in order to examine the potential influence on children's concepts of death. This initial study accumulated a wealth of data. The researchers found that instances of "explicit death," in which the audience sees a character dying or dead on screen, was roughly equal to the number of instances of "implicit death," in which the audience has to assume a death has taken place because a character doesn't appear again, has encountered something that would presumably result in death, or it's left unsaid (explicit, 48 percent; implicit, 43 percent). A similar, updated study was published in 2018 by professors James A. Graham, Hope Yuhas, and Jessica A. Roman using Disney animated productions from the twenty-first century. Their findings were different, however. Their research showed that there was a much higher prevalence of implicit death in Disney's most recent productions. Implicit death constituted 80 percent of all Disney deaths, while explicit deaths constituted only 20 percent. In other words, almost counterintuitively, Disney has recently gotten more conservative in its representations of death. They have opted to deal with death through on-screen innuendo and implication, rather than dealing with death plainly and unequivocally. Whether it's a reliance on euphemisms or implicit death, Disney isn't doing child audiences any favors by being evasive and/or protective. These narrative strategies aren't helping viewers come to a fuller understanding of death. Neither are they helping viewers come to a fuller and proper understanding of Día de los Muertos in the "A Day to Remember" episode of *Elena*. This holiday is nothing if not an honest, unblinking, unadulterated encounter with death.

As a Chicano who celebrates Día de Muertos, teaches Día de Muertos in the classroom, and conducts fieldwork on celebrations throughout California and the Southwest, I can say with confidence that the holiday is an opportunity for us to deal squarely with death. On this holiday death is death, muerte is muerte. It's not something else. Our language and attitude about death's essence, magnitude, and meaning may be poetic, but never euphemistic. No amount of linguistic sleight of hand will save us from the bone-hard reality that everyone we know and love on this earth will die, as we too will die. The holiday's profoundness is located in the unique opportunity to confront death face-to-face, skull-to-skull, so as not to shrink from it or be scared by it. On Día de Muertos the enormity of death is brought down to a relatable human level. We don't skirt or sidestep it. Instead, we swaddle death in color, decorate it with delicate and dazzling beauty, disseminate its omnipresence everywhere from our graveyards to our living rooms, and amplify it until it's larger than life, because death is larger than life. On Día de Muertos our death-dealing is nakedly honest.

Festivalization

For "A Day to Remember" Disney made a creative decision to represent the holiday as a secular cultural festival devoid of any sacred, spiritual, ritual, or religious components. It did this through key omissions and privileging Festival as the holiday's exclusive performance genre. While this may make Día de Muertos more acceptable, familiar, and inviting to primarily non-Latinx audiences, the cost is, once again, a misrepresentation of the holiday's essence.

The secularization of Día de Muertos that happens in this episode comes as little surprise. Disney, after all, has managed to walk a fine nonreligious line in its ninety years of existence. Numerous film historians, cultural scholars, and biographers have noted that there is almost never any overt religious symbolism, religious substance, or even mention of God in Disney productions. According to biographer Bob Thomas, in his books *Walt Disney: An American Original* and *Building a Company: Roy O. Disney and the Creation of an Entertainment Empire*, Walt Disney strongly insisted that his films avoid religion and religious concepts because he didn't want to alienate any portion of his potential audience. This stance carried over from Disney as a production company to Disney as an entertainment empire. Por ejemplo, there are no churches or chapels in Disney's theme parks or anywhere on Disney-owned property, and there are no places of worship on Disney's cruise ships. These decisions were made because Disney didn't want to favor one religion or faith over another. Thus, all religions are excluded. However, as Mark Pinsky notes in his book *The Gospel According to Disney: Faith, Trust, and Pixie Dust*, the company's decisions to eschew religion and religious symbolism weren't grounded in principled humanism, diversity, and inclusivity. They were commercial decisions made to ensure that their products would be profitable and reach a global, multicultural, and multifaith market. In short, secularism sells! Yet, the "A Day to Remember" episode of *Elena of Avalor* seems to be an exception to a long-standing Disney rule. They've chosen to situate a princess story in the context of a religious holiday. However, the episode uses some subtle and not-so-subtle maneuvering to neutralize the religious nature of Día de Muertos.

For starters, not once is it mentioned in the episode that Día de Muertos is a holiday. The word "holiday" is omitted entirely. Instead, the writers rely on a number of other terms. These include "celebration," "special day," "favorite day," "a day to celebrate," "a day we all await," and "festival." While these words signify that Día de Muertos is an important day, they don't indicate that this annual observance is sacred in nature and grounded in religion. The result of this critical omission is that the holiday is reduced to a cultural celebration, albeit a meaningful one. Disney would have the audience believe that Día de Muertos is little more than a tradition, a mere aspect of Latinx cultura, no different from our music or food.

The word that gets used more than any other to characterize the holiday is "festival." This appears most noticeably in the musical number "Festival of Love," where the term is repeated a dozen times. Certainly "holiday" could've been substituted without messing up the lyrical cadence or rhythm of the song. But "festival" is what the creators chose. Even beyond the musical number, "festival" is used to characterize the holiday throughout the rest of the episode, so as to completely immerse the audience in the idea that Día de Muertos is first, foremost, and exclusively a festival performance genre.

In my particular field of performance studies, it is generally recognized that *performance* is a broad term that applies to any and all enactments of human behavior, while also being a large umbrella concept that contains a variety of typologies and genres that are differentiated according to their qualities and characteristics.[4] Festival is but one performance genre among myriad others. A variety of scholars have identified the unique attributes and elements that differentiate Festival from other performance genres.

Anthropologist and folklorist Alessandro Falassi, whose life's work involved examining Festival, provides a general definition, which is that Festival is a specially marked time of celebration that showcases a series of overt values that a community recognizes as essential to its worldview, social identity, and historical continuity (Falassi 2). While that definition might also apply to other performance genres as well, social scientist John MacAloon notes that one of Festival's fundamental and unique characteristics is that it requires and invokes a particular mood and spirit—fun and revelry (MacAloon 246). Indeed, "festival" derives from the Latin term *festum*, meaning public joy, merriment, liveliness, and gaiety. Furthermore, Falassi summarizes that Festival is governed by four cardinal points of behavior: "At festival times, people do something they normally do not; they abstain from something they normally do; they carry to the extreme behaviors that are usually regulated by measure; they invert patterns of daily social life" (Falassi 3). These are the key features of Festival.

Given these defining qualities, Día de Muertos can easily be identified as a Festival performance genre. To be sure, a survey of celebrations across Mexico and the United States would show an abundance of all the qualities outlined above. My argument, however, is not that Festival is the wrong performance genre. Rather, it's my contention that Festival is not the *only* performance genre that describes Día de Muertos. Día de Muertos is expressed as an idiosyncratic performance type that contains multiple, hybridized performance genres operating simultaneously and interdependently. While Día de Muertos contains genres such as Festival, Spectacle, and Game, the beating heart at the core of the holiday is Ritual.

Ritual is generally understood as a genre of performance in which individuals, groups, or communities enact deeply held beliefs through codified and symbolic behavior that takes place in a consecrated or specially designated time and place. Although in our globalized postmodern world there exists an increasing number of secular rituals, Ritual is still primarily associated with religion, spirituality, the divine, and the supernatural. While Ritual and Festival may have a variety of overlapping characteristics, folklorist Roger D. Abrahams saw that many of the formal qualities and symbolic meanings of these two performance genres stand in opposition to each other. For Abrahams, at the most basic level Ritual is "for real" and usually marked as a serious occasion, while Festival is "for fun" and not to be taken seriously. Furthermore, Ritual tends to reinforce social harmony, cultural norms, and authority (religious, political, social), while Festival tends to challenge or disrupt authority, cultural norms, and social harmony. Finally, Abrahams notes that unlike festivals, rituals are usually devised to mark and bring about definitive life transitions and transformations, or they're devised to help people cope with individual, social, and natural changes that occur in life (Abrahams).

All of these characteristics of Ritual apply to Día de Muertos. Despite its festive attributes, it's still a holiday (holy day) anchored to religion, which allows people to manage difficult and complicated feelings concerning death. The connection to the supernatural during Día de Muertos is not "for fun" but "for real," and it's achieved by employing symbolic behavior and sacred technologies like the ofrenda and copal incense to bring the spirits of the dead back to the land of the living. Underneath the colorful revelries there is a reverence for the dead that is absolutely serious. Yet despite this, Ritual aspects of Día de Muertos go completely unacknowledged in the "A Day to Remember" episode of *Elena of Avalor*.

Time and again Disney portrays the holiday exclusively as Festival. Prior to the musical number "Festival of Love," Elena provides a definition and explanation of Día de Muertos. She states, "It's like a party, and everyone we love is invited!" The simile she utilizes, "like a party," places the holiday squarely within the confines of Festival, as per the definition and characteristics outlined above. This signals to audiences that the festive qualities of Día de Muertos are what give the holiday its unique identity. Elena's definition of the holiday gets reinforced throughout the episode by other characters who refer to it either as a "party" or a "celebration." This includes her fox spirit guide, Zuzo. He appears in the episode to explain to Elena how Día de Muertos gets celebrated in the spirit world. Zuzo provides a wealth of exposition in less than a minute of screen time. He tells Elena that "the parties can be pretty epic" down in the spirit world, and that "this is the one day a year ghosts come to party with the living!" His emphasis on Día de Muertos as a "party" is made all the more pronounced for audiences by virtue of the fact that Zuzo is not usually one to party. He's a character defined more by his steadfast devotion to Elena and the sage counsel he provides her. Regular viewers of *Elena*, then, can hardly be blamed for thinking that Día de Muertos must be just a festive and epic party if Zuzo is decked out in a costume and leading conga lines.

Any traces of the holiday's Ritual components and sacred nature are completely omitted in the episode. There are no scenes depicting any of the ceremonial aspects of Día de Muertos. There's no procession through the graveyard. There are no prayers offered to the dead, and no blessings offered to the four cardinal directions, heaven, and earth. Even the deepest ceremony of Día de Muertos, the creation and dressing of the ofrenda, is mostly bypassed. The ofrendas are shown only in their fully completed state.

Perhaps the most egregious omissions in the episode are the missing religious items and imagery one would normally find on a traditional ofrenda. Absent are images of the Virgen de Guadalupe, Jesus, or any of the saints. Gone too are Catholic artifacts altogether—rosary beads, the crucifix, the sacred heart. Gone too are the ritual tools and components related to Indigenous spirituality. There is no copal, the Mesoamerican tree resin that gets burned as a smoky incense to cleanse the air and guide the spirits back to the land of the living. The altars in "A Day to Remember" are even missing some of the four elements fundamental to the ofrenda—water, earth, fire, and wind. While the ofrendas in the episode contain fire (in the form of candles) and earth (in the form of marigold flowers and food), there is no water placed on the altar to quench the thirst of the spirits when they return from the land of the dead, nor is there any *papel picado*, the decorative craft paper traditionally hung over an altar to signify the movement of the wind. It's possible that I'm nitpicky with the details, but none of the sacred objects, elements, and iconography I've catalogued are trivial or peripheral to the holiday. These aspects of Ritual are foundational and fundamental to Día de Muertos celebrations everywhere, from Chihuahua to Chicago. By omitting the religious nature and elements from its version of Día de Muertos, Disney transforms this sacred holiday into a secular cultural festival.

Conclusion

Although it's inexcusable that *Elena of Avalor* has chosen to omit death from Día de Muertos, Disney can hardly be blamed for representing the holiday as a Festival performance genre. In many respects they are merely mirroring a trend that's been happening for much of the twenty-first century in both the United States and Mexico. As a scholar who's spent the last decade conducting field research, I've watched many community and institutional celebrations decenter Ritual in order to center Festival, all while this holy day gets further unfastened from the sacred. In many urban celebrations I've seen individuals create elaborate ofrendas for no one in particular. Instead, the altar becomes a conceptual installation artwork influenced by the aesthetic and intellectual trends of the contemporary "high art" world. Whereas skeleton costumes and calavera face painting were rare idiosyncrasies a couple decades ago, now it's almost expected for holiday participants to be adorned in festive attire. A whole secondary industry has been born, with makeup artists operating booths at event sites to decorate your face calavera style for fifty dollars. Many Día de Muertos celebrations now also feature on-site food and alcohol carts to encourage participants to feast and indulge themselves, often to excess (porta-potties don't lie). And especially in the United States, Day of the Dead celebrations have become music, dance, and arts festivals with a full day of programming on multiple stages, transforming an ancient ceremony to honor the dead into an opportunity to showcase Latinx cultura writ large. In all these ways the festivalization of Día de Muertos is becoming as real as Disney represents it.

What's at stake is the very identity of this holiday. Many of my Latinx/Mexican/Chicanx informants have expressed trepidation over what their holiday is becoming. I too am nervous. There's a legitimate concern that Día de Muertos is becoming a culturally permissive excuse to wear festive costumes, paint one's face like a skull, eat and drink to excess, and party. Day of the Dead is not, of course, "Mexican Halloween." However, the crucial ways that it's not Halloween are getting more and more difficult to discern. Or to put it in terms that hit a little closer to our cultural home, marinate on these wise words from a woman I spoke with last year at a Los Angeles Día de Muertos celebration: "We can't allow this holiday to become another Cinco de Mayo!" Her fear of the festivalization of Día de Muertos is a valid one that resonates deeply with Latinx folks of all generations, ethnicities, races, genders, classes, and backgrounds.

Representation matters. The Día de Muertos that appears on television isn't just a reflection and representation of our real-world tradition. These media representations, especially those aimed at children, actively influence and affect the trajectory of our tradition in the real world. It's already happening. The Día de Muertos that we can expect to see celebrated in the future will carry the indelible imprint of mass media, animation and cartoons specifically, as has been the case with the holiday for more than a century. We may find in the coming years that the character of the holiday is tossed into a deeper identity crisis, with Festival elbowing out Ritual as the preeminent performance genre. Disney's influence, through a TV series like *Elena of Avalor* or feature film like *Coco*, may prove larger than imagined. If that's the case, then it turns out the joke is on us. Disney won't need to have trademarked Día de los Muertos legally, because it will have done so culturally.

Notes

1. The most descriptive sources on the Nahuatl Feasts for the Dead come from ethnographic reports compiled by two Franciscan missionaries—Fray Diego Durán and Bernardino de Sahagún. Although their ethnographies have been rightly criticized for their Eurocentric analysis of Nahuatl beliefs and cultural practices, they nonetheless provide serviceable description of rites and ceremonies. See Diego Durán's *History of the Indies of New Spain* and *Book of the Gods and Rites; and the Ancient Calendar*, and Bernardino de Sahagún's *Florentine Codex: General History of the Things of New Spain*.

2. A variety of sources have explained Día de Muertos's syncretism. These include Elizabeth Carmichael's *The Skeleton at the Feast*, Juanita Garciagodoy's *Digging the Days of the Dead*, and Stanley Brandes's *Skulls to the Living, Bread to the Dead*. Perhaps the most in-depth survey of the syncretic process is Hugo Nutini's *Todo Santos in Rural Tlaxcala*.

3. Perhaps the most popular text to explore Americans' anxiety and avoidance concerning death is Jessica Mitford's *The American Way of Death*. See also Furer and Walker's "Death Anxiety."

4. The "broad spectrum" approach is foundational to the field of performance studies. Although it has been elaborated on by scholars over the past several decades, the theoretical and conceptual basis was first put forward by Richard Schechner. See Schechner's *Performance Studies* (2002) and "Performance Studies" (1988).

Works Cited

Abrahams, Roger D. "An American Vocabulary of Celebrations." *Time Out of Time: Essays on the Festival*, edited by Alessandro Falassi, U of New Mexico P, 1987, pp. 173–83.

Brandes, Stanley. *Skulls to the Living, Bread to the Dead*. Wiley-Blackwell, 2007.

Carmichael, Elizabeth. *The Skeleton at the Feast*. U of Texas P, 1992.

Cox, Meredith, et al. "Death in Disney Films: Implications for Children's Understanding of Death." *Omega*, vol. 50, no. 4, 2004–5, pp. 267–80.

"A Day to Remember." *Elena of Avalor*, created by Craig Gerber, written by Sylvia Cardenas Olivas and Craig Gerber, season 1, episode 9, Disney Channel, 16 Oct. 2016.

Durán, Diego. *Book of the Gods and Rites; and the Ancient Calendar*. Translated by Fernando Horcasitas, U of Oklahoma P, 1971.

Durán, Diego. *History of the Indies of New Spain*. Translated by Doris Heyden, U of Oklahoma P, 2010.

Falassi, Alessandro. "Festival: Definition and Morphology." *Time Out of Time: Essays on the Festival*, edited by Falassi, U of New Mexico P, 1987, pp. 1–10.

Furer, Patricia, and John R. Walker. "Death Anxiety: A Cognitive-Behavioral Approach." *Journal of Cognitive Psychotherapy: An International Quarterly*, vol. 22, no. 2, 2008, pp. 167–82.

Garciagodoy, Juanita. *Digging the Days of the Dead: A Reading of Mexico's Días de Muertos*. U of Colorado P, 2000.

Graham, James A., et al. "Death and Coping Mechanisms in Animated Disney Movies." *Social Sciences*, vol. 7, no. 10, 2018, p. 199.

Macaloon, John J. "Olympic Games and the Theory of Modern Spectacle." *Rite, Drama, Festival, Spectacle: Rehearsals Toward a Theory of Cultural Performance*, edited by MacAloon, Institute for the Study of Human Issues, 1984, pp. 241–80.

McDermott, Maeve. "How Disney Brought *Elena of Avalor*'s Latin Heritage to Life." *USA Today*, 12 July 2016, www.usatoday.com/story/life/entertainthis/2016/07/12/meet-disney-channel-first-latina-princess-elena-of-avalor/86982644/.

McLennan, Cindy. "*Elena of Avalor*: Second Season Renewal for Disney Channel Animated Series." *TV Series Finale*, 11 Aug. 2016, tvseriesfinale.com/tv-show/elena-avalor-second-season-renewal-disney-channel-animated-series/.

Mitford, Jessica. *The American Way of Death*. Simon & Schuster, 1988.

Nutini, Hugo. *Todo Santos in Rural Tlaxcala*. Princeton UP, 2014.

Pinsky, Mark. *The Gospel According to Disney: Faith, Trust, and Pixie Dust*. Westminster John Knox Press, 2004.

Sahagún, Bernardino de. *Florentine Codex: General History of the Things of New Spain*. Translated by Arthur J. O. Anderson, U of Utah P, 2012.

Schechner, Richard. *Performance Studies: An Introduction*. Routledge, 2002.

Schechner, Richard. "Performance Studies: The Broad Spectrum Approach." *TDR*, vol. 32, no. 3, 1988, pp. 4–6.

Thomas, Bob. *Building a Company: Roy O. Disney and the Creation of an Entertainment Empire*. Disney Editions, 1998.

Thomas, Bob. *Walt Disney: An American Original*. Simon & Schuster, 1976.

Umstead, R. Thomas. "Disney's 'Elena of Avalor' Delivers Royal Ratings." *Multichannel News*, 28 July 2016, www.nexttv.com/news/disney-s-elena-avalor-delivers-royal-ratings-406725.

Willis, Clarissa A. "The Grieving Process in Children: Strategies for Understanding, Educating, and Reconciling Children's Perceptions of Death." *Early Childhood Education Journal*, vol. 29, 2002, pp. 221–26.

THESE ARE THEIR HISTORIAS

Latinx Cops and Prosecutors in Police Shows

Mauricio Espinoza

In reviewing the highlights of the 2014 report *The Latino Media Gap*, two findings quickly jump off the page. First, there's the unfortunate but unsurprising fact that at the time the report was made there were fewer Latinx lead actors in the U.S. entertainment industry than there were seven decades before, even though the Hispanic population had significantly grown during that period (Negrón-Muntaner 1).[1] Two, "51.9%, or 14 of the 27 Latino main cast roles in top ten scripted TV shows, have been related to criminal activities, law enforcement, or security" since 1984 (Negrón-Muntaner 16). That Latinx actors continue to be cast predominantly as criminals is also unsurprising, considering the traditional "bandit" stereotype to which Hispanics have been subjected in American law, culture, and media (Ramírez Berg 66). In fact, according to the report, 24.2 percent of Latinx TV characters were linked to crime from 2012 to 2013, compared to only 6 percent in 1994 (Negrón-Muntaner 16). But the finding that most interests me here is that the portrayal of Hispanics as law-enforcement officials has grown: law enforcement constitutes one of the main types of roles given to Latinx actors in film and TV, even as the range of roles and stories in which Latinxs appear has become significantly narrower in both media. For example, of all Latinx-specific roles across the top ten TV shows in 2012–13, 23 percent were law enforcers—just slightly below the 24.2 percent who played lawbreakers (Negrón-Muntaner 16). This trend doesn't appear to have slowed in the years since 2014. Latinx actors, both males and females, have continued to play cops, federal agents, and prosecutors on TV, as evidenced by their casting in shows such as *Brooklyn Nine-Nine*, *Criminal Minds*, *Blue Bloods*, and *Shades of Blue*.

While law enforcer is a common role for Latinxs, this doesn't mean that they are adequately represented in crime shows when compared to other ethnicities. Marilyn Yaquinto concludes that the "omission among screen cops and crimefighters that is the most flagrant, though, is that of Latinos, given the statistical changes to both the nation's population and within law enforcement agencies" (27). As Latinxs now account for 18.5 percent of the total U.S. population, this demographic shift has also led to an important increase in the number of police officers who are Hispanic.[2] According to the latest data available (2013) from the Bureau of Justice Statistics, Hispanics accounted for 60 percent of the increase in minority local police officers between 1987 and 2013. About 12 percent of all local cops were Latinx in 2013, compared to an estimated 5 percent in 1987 ("Percentage of Local Police"). In large cities where police shows are commonly set and Latinx populations are large, the percentage of Hispanic police officers is close to mirroring the cities' Latinx population: in New York City, 26.1 percent of officers are Hispanic (a −2.7 percent difference with respect to population); while the Los Angeles Police Department has 43.4 percent Hispanic officers, for a 5.2 percent underrepresentation ("Diversity on the Force"). In other words, the number of Hispanic cops that appear on television—typically one, two at most in the main ensemble of popular crime shows, still dominated by white male cops even in minority-majority cities—lags behind their growing presence in the country's police forces.

With these statistics as a backdrop, in this essay I examine the presence and portrayal of Latinx cops and prosecutors in U.S. television police shows during the twenty-first century. While I list and briefly discuss representative programs that have featured Latinx law and order characters in main and recurring roles during the past two decades, my analysis will concentrate on two shows that represent the two main genres within fictional crime shows: drama and comedy. They are *Law & Order: Special Victims Unit* (*SVU*) (1999 to present), which has included in its ever-changing cast Det. Nick Amaro (Danny Pino) and Assistant District Attorney Rafael Barba (Raúl Esparza); and *Brooklyn Nine-Nine* (2013 to present), which features detectives Amy Santiago (Melissa Fumero) and Rosa Diaz (Stephanie Beatriz). Here, I'm interested in comparing how drama and comedies approach issues of minority representation and characterization differently, and what that means for Latinx characters. Additionally, I look at how race, ethnicity, gender, sexual orientation, and class intersect within Latinx representation in these series. Finally, I delve into how the shows and their Latinx characters deal with (or ignore) larger societal issues such as racism and police brutality.

TV Crime Shows and the Latinx in Them

Stories dealing with crime solving have been a staple of U.S. film and television since the advent of each medium. As Timothy Lenz states, this may be in great part due to the fact that law appears to be everywhere in modern American society: "Indeed, criminal law has always been an especially popular topic for film and television where crime stories are familiar viewing. Gangster films, cop shows, and lawyer programs are just some of the visual media genres whose continued popularity is based upon the public's fascination with law in general and criminal law in particular" (Lenz 1). In his study of crime television shows over the decades, Douglas Snauffer asserts that "crime dramas, whether they've focused on uniformed police officers or private investigators, have more closely mirrored actual society than any other genre" (1). While this claim is problematic in some regards (as will be discussed later), it is hard to argue with Snauffer when he writes that "as a society and a viewing audience our perceptions of the good guys and the bad guys have changed since the inception of television in the late 1940s, along with our definitions of what constitutes heroes and villains" (1).

Crime media, particularly television, also play an important role in providing a certain level of knowledge of legal procedures and shaping public opinion about the legal system and its actors. For Lenz, a key reason for this is that legal fiction is often related to fact: "Popular films and television strike a chord with the public because they 'ring true,' because they depict both events and human reactions to events and situations in ways that make the work seem to be an accurate reflection of the real world. Crime fiction is not real, but it can be virtually realistic" (8). The plots of these shows are usually based on real events or cases, and although they are not true stories, "they may describe events that an individual or even a whole community have actually experienced or can realistically imagine happening to them" (Lenz 8). Additionally, crime fiction "can tell us something about the way the legal system works because legal writers and script consultants are employed to make sure that the story line and dialogue use accurate terminology" (Lenz 9). Popular crime shows such as the long-running series *Law & Order* and its spinoffs supply important information to the public and even citizens who serve on juries, shaping their perceptions about how the justice system works. "Because most people (fortunately) do not have much direct, personal experience with crime and criminal justice, realistic television programs are one of the influences on thinking about the law" (Lenz 13).

Crime television programming debuted in the late 1940s in the United States and closely resembled the radio dramas that began broadcasting in the 1920s (Snauffer 1). Three main types of crime shows would develop during the twentieth century: dramas, which are the most common; comedies (either sitcoms or a hybrid of the sitcom and the realist crime drama, best represented by *CHiPS*); and true-crime or reality police shows such as *Unsolved Mysteries* and *Cops*, which began appearing in the 1980s. The proliferation, growing quality, and immense popularity of crime and police-related shows is undisputable: by 2001, about 25 percent of all prime-time TV programming was delivered in the form of a crime show (Potter and Kappeler 7). Their popularity has persisted over the past twenty years. As Jonathan Nichols-

Pethick explains, much of the longevity and success of crime shows has to do with the fact that the genre "has proven to be an incredibly flexible form, almost infinitely renewable and malleable across a range of different contexts" (20). Since their appearance more than seventy years ago, crime programs have both reflected and engaged with the changing attitudes, approaches, and technologies of police work and the legal system. Additionally, they have evolved (albeit slowly and still not sufficiently) with shifting U.S. and police department demographics in addressing issues of racial, ethnic, gender, and sexual orientation diversity. The study of Latinx cops on the screen can help us elucidate some of these changes and remaining challenges.

Latinx actors and/or characters have been a part of television shows dealing with the law since their early days. *Dragnet* featured a Mexican American cop, Sgt. Ben Romero (played by Barton Yarborough in the show's radio and TV formats from 1949 to 1951). Another notable pioneer is Disney's *The Nine Lives of Elfego Baca* (1958–60), a western about the real-life New Mexico lawman whose heroics in the late 1800s became legendary; although the leading character is Hispanic, he was played by Italian American actor Robert Loggia. The first Latino cop star, however, was California Highway Patrol officer Frank "Ponch" Poncherello in *CHiPs* (1977–83). The character "Ponch" was originally supposed to be Italian American, but actor Erik Estrada purportedly convinced the producers to make him Hispanic (Rothman). Still, the character's ethnicity was not a central part of his construction and was little explored in the show.[3] While informant "Huggy Bear" in *Starsky & Hutch* (1975–79) is ethnically ambiguous, he was played by Afro-Latinx Antonio Juan Fargas, who is of Puerto Rican and Trinidadian ancestry. In *Barney Miller* (1975–82), which featured a surprisingly diverse cast for its time, Gregory Sierra played Puerto Rican Sgt. Miguel "Chano" Amanguale.

The 1980s and 1990s saw additional Latinx characters in popular crime shows. The ensemble cast of *Hill Street Blues* (1981–87) included Lt. Ray Calletano (played by René Enríquez), who is prominently featured in several episodes, including one in which he receives the Hispanic Officer of the Year award. In *L.A. Law* (1986–94), Jimmy Smits played attorney Victor Sifuentes. The superior officer to protagonists Sonny Crockett and Ricardo Tubbs of *Miami Vice* (1984–90) was also Latinx; the character (Lt. Lou Rodriguez) was originally played by Gregory Sierra, who quit soon after and was replaced by Edward James Olmos, who stepped in as Lt. Martin Castillo (Snauffer 137). *Miami Vice* also included a Latina detective, Gina Navarro Calabrese (played by Saundra Santiago). In *NYPD Blue* (1994–98), Smits (whose parents are from Suriname and Puerto Rico) played Det. Bobby Simone, who is of French and Portuguese descent. Cheech Marin starred as Insp. Joe Dominguez, partner of the title character in *Nash Bridges* (1996–2001), while Jaime Gomez

Figure 9.1 The Latinization of private eyes: Tom Selleck's 1980s *Magnum P.I.* (left) gets an ethnic makeover with Jay Hernandez in the title role of the 2018 reboot.

played another San Francisco Police Department inspector (Evan Cortez). Finally, Benjamin Bratt played Det. Reynaldo Curtis in both *Law & Order* (from 1995 to 1999) and in a few episodes of *Homicide: Life on the Street* (also between 1995 and 1999).

Supporting Frances Negrón-Muntaner's findings about the preponderance of law enforcement roles for Latinx actors in the past few decades, the twenty-first century has seen a steady increase in the appearance of these roles on TV shows. More importantly, the screen Latinx cops, federal agents, and attorneys of the past two decades are more diverse in terms of race, gender, and sexual orientation, and they hold more leading roles and higher police ranks than in the previous century. In addition to the shows analyzed in this chapter, there are a few recent crime programs with Latinx leads or recurring roles that are worth mentioning here to get a better idea of the way representation has evolved in this TV genre over the decades. For instances, Tia Texada played Sgt. Maritza Cruz in *Third Watch* from 2002 to 2005, also guest-starring as a cop in other police procedurals such as *The Unit* (2006–7) and *Criminal Minds* (2008). Meanwhile, *Without a Trace* (2002–9) featured two Latinx FBI agents, Elena Delgado (played by Roselyn Sánchez from 2005 to 2009) and Danny Taylor (also known as Danny Alvarez), who was played by Enrique Murciano during the duration of the show. Murciano has also played the role of law enforcer in other series, including in *CSI* (as Det. Carlos Moreno, 2009), *NCIS* (Agent Ray Cruz, from 2011 to 2012), and in the Netflix original series *Bloodline* (as Det. Marco Diaz) since 2015. In two other series, we see the all-too-common Hollywood phenomenon of actors playing different ethnicities or races. In *NCIS*, Chilean-born actress Cote de Pablo has played Israeli Mossad officer/NCIS agent Ziva David (2005–13 and 2019–20); while in *Criminal Minds*, Italian American actress Lola Glaudini plays FBI Special Agent Elle Greenaway (2005–6), whose mother is Cuban.

Murciano is not the only actor who has made a career out of cop shows. Other notable examples include Danny Pino (who will be discussed later in detail) and Adam Rodriguez. After playing officers in the late 1990s in *NYPD Blue* and *Brooklyn South*, Rodriguez was cast in *CSI: Miami* (2002–12) for his best-known role to date as Det. Eric Delko, who is of Russian and Cuban ancestry. In 2016, Rodriguez joined the cast of *Criminal Minds* as FBI Special Agent Luke Alvez, a role he played until the show's final episode in early 2020. Another *CSI: Miami* Latinx agent is Natalia Boa Vista, played by Eva LaRue (2005–12). In addition to Luke Alvez, notable roles of the 2010s include Det. Antonio Dawson, played by Jon Seda. Dawson was a crossover character in the *Chicago* franchise, first appearing in *Chicago Fire* in 2012, then joining the cast of *Chicago P.D.* in 2014, and finally moving on to *Chicago Justice* in 2017. *Castle* featured two main characters played by Latinx actors: Javier Esposito (Jon Huertas), a homicide sergeant who remained in the series from beginning to end (2009–16); and Captain Roy Montgomery (2009–14), played by Afro-Latinx Ruben Santiago-Hudson. One crime drama, *The Bridge* (2013), featured a Mexican police detective—Marco Ruiz, played by Demián Bichir—who works with an American detective solving transnational murders. Latinas have continued to garner important law enforcer roles in the past decade. They include Maria Baez, a *Blue Bloods* detective played by Marisa Ramirez (2013 to present); and Officer Vanessa Rojas (Lisseth Chavez), who joined the main cast of *Chicago P.D.* in 2019.

Latinxs have also appeared as law enforcers and attorneys in shows other than police procedurals. Examples include DEA agents in the Netflix biographical crime dramas *Narcos* (2015–17), with Pedro Pascal in the role of Javier Peña; and *Narcos: Mexico* (2018 to present), with Michael Peña as Enrique "Kiki" Camarena. Meanwhile, in the dark fantasy series *Penny Dreadful: City of Angels* (2020), Daniel Zovatto plays Tiago Vega, the LAPD's first Mexican American detective. There are also two legal dramas in which Smits plays the lead character, a significant achievement for Latinx representation, although both shows were canceled after the first season. They are *Outlaw* (2010), about Cyrus Garza, a former Supreme Court justice who returns to private practice; and *Bluff City Law* (2019), about civil rights attorney Elijah Strait. Finally, it is important to highlight two police series in which Latinxs play the main roles, which may signal a move in the right direction toward increased and more visible representation in the next decade. In NBC's *Shades of Blue* (2016–18), Jennifer Lopez was executive producer and starred as Harlee Santos—a troubled, single-mother NYPD detective who is forced to work for the FBI's anti-corruption task force. And in the reboot of *Magnum, P.I.* (2018 to present), the investigator originally played by Tom Selleck is now played by Mexican American actor Jay Hernandez. It took almost forty years after *CHiPs*, but Latinx police stars are a thing once again.

"Your Little Spanish Dandy Here": *SVU*'s Latinx Problem

Spanning over two decades and still going strong, NBC's *Law & Order: SVU* is not just the longest-running police procedural in U.S. television but also the longest-running prime-time live-action series, with twenty-one seasons to date (Ausellio). Its longevity and popularity could be explained by Americans' fascination with crime-and-punishment stories and the inner workings of the legal system (as discussed earlier), but what might set it apart from similar series is the combination of crime-fighting and another topic that also fascinates audiences: sex. The show features Manhattan's sexually oriented crimes division, focusing on a small ensemble of elite detectives in the NYPD's Sixteenth Precinct, their captain, and the assistant district attorneys (ADAs) who prosecute their cases, often "ripped from the headlines." From its inception in 1999, the show's main cast has featured a decent amount of gender and racial diversity that has remained fairly stable over the years: an African American, one to two women, and two to three white males (one Jewish and one Catholic) among the detectives; a female captain (former detective Olivia Benson) in the last few seasons; several female ADAs; and, as recurring characters, two Asian males (an FBI forensic psychiatrist and a technical analyst). However, despite the fact that New York City's Latinx population is about 29 percent and more than a quarter of the NYPD's officers are Hispanic, *SVU* did not have a main Latinx character—Det. Nick Amaro—until its thirteenth season, in 2011. Soon after, during season 14, the "law" side of the *Law & Order* equation would also get a Latinx character when ADA Rafael Barba joined the show in a recurring capacity, being promoted to series regular prior to the season 15 premiere. The absence of main Latinx characters for such a long time in *SVU* was certainly an anomaly among major police procedurals, as even the original *Law & Order* had a Latinx cop back in the 1990s. Notwithstanding, once this omission was corrected, the series did something similar prime-time programs hadn't done before: promote a Hispanic lawyer to a permanent ADA position, which helped to diversify the range of roles given to Latinxs in crime shows. It also featured two Latinxs in prominent roles simultaneously, something not unprecedented but still unusual among top crime series.

Before joining *SVU*, Danny Pino (the son of Cuban parents just like his character, Amaro) had plenty of experience with police procedurals, having played Det. Scotty Valens in *Cold Case* (2003–10). Following his departure from *SVU* in 2015, Pino played FBI agent John Bishop in *Gone* (2017–18), before joining the cast of the *Sons of Anarchy* spinoff *Mayans M.C.* in 2018, where he has played drug cartel leader Miguel Galindo to date. While at *SVU*, Pino also played Amaro in *Chicago P.D.* during two crossover episodes in 2014–15. In other words, almost all of Pino's TV career has consisted of roles within crime shows, either as a cop or as criminal, further confirming findings of *The Latino Media Gap* study. Amaro also exemplifies the limitations facing Latinx law enforcers when it comes to character development and cultural representation. Amaro came in to replace Det. Elliot Stabler (Christopher Meloni), who had been the show's costar alongside Benson (Mariska Hargitay) since its inception. In an effort to retain the program's successful formula of personality types and team interactions, the Amaro character had many of Stabler's traits: he's Catholic and heavily influenced by his faith; values family and fatherhood but has a troubled marriage that ends in divorce; plays protector to the women in the squad; and has trouble controlling his emotions and temper, often getting in trouble for using unnecessary violence and taking the law into his own hands. Like Stabler (an Irish American), Amaro is the hypermasculine, impulsive justice-doer so common in U.S. police dramas and action films. In Marilyn Yaquinto's words, he is the "redeemable rogue crimefighter" who migrates from the Old West to the uncivilized urban landscape, carrying with him "a particular performance of masculinity" and a "sense of entitlement and noble purpose with this added frontier-bred taste for regenerative violence" (5–7).

As a result of this preferred characterization of leading male cops in *SVU*, two key issues are at play when it comes to Amaro's depiction in the show. First, the updating of ethnicity in the transition from Meloni to Pino is problematic because, as Yaquinto further elaborates, the rogue crime-fighter prototype also includes "an ever-adaptive nod to white supremacy," with the mythic cowboy reemerging in contemporary times "as the white, male 'everyman' able to prosper in uncharted lands, survive challenges by the Other, and rely on his own discretion to distinguish law from disorder—his gender, race, and denial of class all woven into his foundational construction" (5). While the inclusion of Amaro in the show provides an undeniably Latinx material presence (in the way Pino looks and talks) and specific cultural nuances (the use of Spanish and other markers of Latinidad) that were simply not there with Meloni, the rigid hypermasculine construction of Pino's character and his rogue qualities play into the reproduction and perpetuation of a prototype that carries with it racist overtones and lacks class and ethnic solidarity.

This dynamic is best exemplified in two episodes from season 15. In "Spring Awakening" (episode 23), Amaro brutally beats up a man who's taking pictures of children behind the fence of a school playground. We soon find that the man is a suspected child molester who was recently found not guilty at trial, but whom *SVU* detectives firmly believe to be a disgusting criminal. The transition from cop to vigilante is almost instantaneous, and audiences are cued to believe the "perp" is guilty anyway and deserves his punishment, identifying in the process with the troubled but handsome and noble cop—because, after all, who likes a child molester? This dominant narrative is further supported by Amaro's peers. Retired *SVU* detective John Munch (Richard Belzer) posts Amaro's bail and reassures him: "You fight for the victims, for the survivors. That's who you are." Meanwhile, in "Amaro's One-Eighty" (season 15, episode 10), the detective ends up shooting a fourteen-year-old Black African immigrant boy during a chase, erroneously believing he was armed and was shooting at the Black female officer Amaro was backing up—while in actuality, the boy had no gun and what hit the cop was her own ricocheted bullet. Amaro faces tremendous backlash from the African American community and is accused at grand jury deliberations of being quick to intervene to "rescue" women and of being (along with the rest of the NYPD force) a racist. While he is deeply shaken by the incident, Amaro is acquitted. Status quo, then, remains undisturbed, and the rogue cop can continue to work. In the end, Amaro is in many respects *Stabler in brownface*.

The second issue I want to address is more Latinx-specific but problematic nonetheless. Amaro's construction as a tough but charming cop whose behavior is often erratic and whose emotions get the best of him coincides with another long-standing stereotype of Latinx men in U.S. popular culture: the macho, which borrows characteristics from both the bandit and the Latin lover stereotypes (Ramírez Berg 66). The intersection of these traditional tropes is at work in Amaro's Latinx characterization. During his first appearance in the series ("Personal Fouls," season 13, episode 2), it is revealed that Amaro previously served in the Narcotics Division, working the "MS-13 (Central American transnational gang) case" and infiltrating drug-trafficking rings as a *narcotraficante* known as "Carlos el colombiano." Thus, Amaro enters the show making the transition from "playing" a criminal to rejoining the police as a cop—the two roles more readily available for Latinx men on TV and strong determinants of their screen representation. Soon, we also find out about his abusive father, his troubled marriage, and his anger issues. In "Street Revenge" (season 13, episode 20), Amaro punches a guy he suspects is having an affair with his wife, Maria (Laura Benanti), and angrily confronts her—only to find out she has been seeing a psychiatrist and confiding in friends to deal with trauma from her time deployed in Iraq with the military. Ultimately, Amaro's machoness and his inability to properly deal with emotions and relationships is his undoing. In the finale of season 16 (2015), Amaro decides to retire, haunted by an injury from a recent shootout and his inability to move up police ranks because of the fallout from his multiple anger-related episodes. He moves to California to live closer to Maria and their daughter, Zara, as well as to his son, Gil—the result of a relationship with the sister of a drug lord during his years undercover. However, Amaro's departure also reveals the show's failure to imagine and construct a more nuanced Latinx character who could embrace a healthier masculinity and move away from stale stereotypes.

On the plus side, Barba's characterization is more flexible and complex. He is close to his mother and grandmother (his father had died of diabetes) and has strong community ties, hailing from a working-class background in the Bronx barrio. At the same time, he is an independent bachelor with no children, attended Harvard on a scholarship, is smart and well read, is eloquent and well spoken, and is known as an impeccable dresser, sporting high-fashioned suits and his signature suspenders. As a prosecutor, Barba is ambitious (he sees his transfer from Brooklyn to Manhattan as a positive career move) and has an aggressive, sometimes ruthless style in the court-room. As a police captain describes him, "He has big brass . . . ego" (season 14, episode 3). Despite his lawyer demeanor, Barba is typically composed and has a no-nonsense approach to personal and professional relationships. Pre-cisely what makes his character more interesting and nuanced are his efforts to reconcile the two sides of his identity, which are often odds: his humble origins in a poor neighborhood and his drive to succeed in a cutthroat, pre-dominantly white profession. Barba's internal conflict fully comes to life in "October Surprise" (season 15, episode 6), the most "Latinx" of *SVU* episodes in the sense that all main parties involved (police, prosecutor, and the accused and his relatives and friends) are Cuban Americans and use untranslated Spanish and Cuban expressions throughout. Additionally, Barba finds him-self in a tough situation where doing the right thing by the law also means (in his mind) betraying the community and culture from which he hails.

In the episode, Barba's childhood friend Alex Muñoz (Vincent Laresca) leads the polls just days before the election and is on the cusp of becoming New York City's first Hispanic mayor, running on a progressive platform of fair housing and equality. When another mutual friend and Muñoz's body-guard, Eddie García (Kirk Acevedo), gets in trouble, *SVU* detectives uncover a sex and political favors scandal involving the mayoral front-runner.[4] Deeply conflicted, Barba tries to give Muñoz the benefit of the doubt and warns him about the investigation, risking his job and professional integrity. Amaro— who has an antagonistic relationship with Barba because of his harsh style

Figure 9.2 New York City assistant district attorney Rafael Barba (left) and Det. Nick Amaro during a season 15 episode of *Law & Order: Special Victims Unit.*

and stuck-up personality—catches on and reproaches the ADA for his behavior and lack of objectivity. The tense conversation they have in the precinct elevator is revealing of their personal and cultural conflict:

> BARBA: I'm not cutting Muñoz a break just because he's my friend.
>
> AMARO: I get that. It's not about friendship. It's about you. That you're afraid to go after Muñoz because while he stayed in the 'hood, *en el barrio*, and played man of the people, you went off to Harvard to pretend you were one of the *gringuitos.*
>
> BARBA: I know where I come from.
>
> AMARO: And so does Muñoz, and he's playing you so he makes you feel like a sellout, *un arrepentido.*
>
> BARBA: Thank you very much for the bodega psychoanalysis, detective.... *Compay, no te equivoques conmigo.*[5]

In the final exchange between Barba and Muñoz, his friend also accuses the prosecutor of being a sellout to the white elite he claims is trying to frame him. Then he tells Barba: "She [Muñoz's wife, Yelina, with whom Barba had a relationship in their youth] thinks you've always been jealous of me because you can't stand seeing another *cubano* get ahead. You think there's room for only one of us at the top." At the end of the episode, Barba (displaying a vulnerability not seen in him thus far) admits to Benson he's always been jealous of his friend and that he isn't sure he was only doing his job in this case: "Alex is a winner. When I was little, my mom told me, 'Stick with Alex. He will be mayor of New York City one day.' She never said that about me."

Finally, I would like to talk about the ways *SVU* deals (successfully and unsuccessfully) with issues of representation and racism that reflect larger societal conversations and which are connected with its Latinx characters. The episode I just referred to is a good example of how to get representation right and wrong. On the one hand, the writers did a great job of exploring the difficulty for many successful Latinxs in bridging the gap between one's culture and assimilating into a white man's world and culture without losing touch with their origins. Conversely, the show made the unfortunate decision of introducing a successful Latinx politician (a rarity in prime-time shows) just to quickly dismiss him as a horny criminal. The problem here is not quality (Muñoz clearly did commit several crimes and deserved the consequences), but quantity—that is, Viet Nguyen's concept of *narrative scarcity* ("Viet Than Nguyen"). If series like *SVU* showed many prominent Latinxs of integrity alongside a few "bad apples" like Muñoz (as it does with white men and women), then the bad ones would be dismissed as an anomaly. The problem is, it doesn't: Muñoz is the only one, and he's crooked. Other times, the show has empowered its Latinx protagonists to use their wits and privileged positions to bring racist and sexist cops to justice. In "Forgiving Rollins" (season 16, episode 10), Barba prosecutes an Atlanta police chief who is accused by one of his detectives of rape when they were both in New York City for a conference. Accustomed to getting away with sexual abuse because of his position and connections in the South, the chief refuses to plead guilty and mockingly tells Barba's boss, as he stares at the Cuban American ADA dressed in a pink shirt and tie: "I don't know about your little Spanish dandy here, but I'm straight as an axe. That girl got what she wanted." To which Barba replies, using Spanish as a weapon to counter the doubly prejudicial remark: "That won't work for me. . . . *Nos vemos en los tribunales, amigo*."[6] In the end, Barba gets a conviction and much more than poetic justice. In the end, too, Barba exited the show after the conclusion of season 21 in early 2020 (Esparza decided he was done with the character), leaving *SVU* Latinx-less once again.

"Nine-Nine!": Comedy Gets Serious—and Gets It Right

The sitcom *Brooklyn Nine-Nine*, which follows the hilarious personal and professional lives of a motley crew of cops from Brooklyn's Ninety-Ninth Precinct, has been hailed for its diverse cast and for its ability to tackle sensitive issues such as racism, sexism, sexual orientation, and the role of police in society in a more progressive and open-minded manner than other "serious" shows—including police dramas. *Entertainment Weekly* has even called it "the most inclusive show on TV" (Baldwin). The reviewers are not wrong. The Fox and NBC sitcom has featured from the very beginning a cast that includes a Black, openly gay captain (Raymond Holt, played by Andre Braugher) who is married to a white man; a Black sergeant (Terry Jeffords, played by Terry Crews); a Jewish American detective (Jake Peralta, played by Andy Samberg); and, of course, two Latina detectives—one of whom, Rosa Diaz, is bisexual. The inclusion of two Latinas in main roles in a prime-time show cannot be underestimated. As Argentinean-born immigrant actress Stephanie Beatriz has written in *Latina* magazine, when she found out Melissa Fumero (the daughter of Cuban parents who migrated to the United States) had gotten the role of Amy Santiago, she figured she was "screwed": "There's no way in hell a major network is gonna cast two Latina actresses in such a tight ensemble. . . . Normally, the Latina is a singular element of the ensemble she is working in. She's there to provide contrast, or sexuality, or humor. Or she's there to clean the floors and/or steal your man" (Beatriz).

Brooklyn Nine-Nine marks an important point of departure from police procedurals in the way it addresses Latinx representation as intersecting with issues of gender and sexuality in a changing society and for new generations. For example, *SVU* never had a main female LGBTQ character and had not had a woman of color in a main cop role since season 2, when African American detective Jeffries (Michelle Hurd) left the show. This finally changed in season 21 (2019–20), when Lebanese American detective Kat Azar Tamin (played by Jamie Gray Hyder) joined the squad and came out as bisexual. The show had the perfect opportunity to introduce a gay character of color with Barba, since Esparza is bisexual. In a 2015 interview with *E! Online*, Esparza said he welcomed the idea of drawing from his own personal experience (just as he did with his Cuban-ness) to play a gay Latinx character and for the show "to think about representing anything beyond sort of the standard white guy that's always been at the center of it" (Harnick). What *SVU* never did with Barba and what it just started doing in 2020 with Tamin, *Brooklyn Nine-Nine* was already doing in season 5 (2017), when Diaz told her coworkers she was bisexual. Holt, meanwhile, had been openly gay for decades, constantly facing discrimination and obstacles to move up the ranks of the NYPD.

In addition to their sexual orientation, the Diaz and Santiago characters are different in every way possible. The fact that they are both Latinas and cops are about the only things they have in common, and even in that they have their differences of ancestry: Diaz is Mexican American, while Santiago is Cuban American. Diaz is tough, physical, street-smart, prone to angry outbursts, mysterious, secretive, hates the rules, and doesn't care what other people think of her. She rides a motorcycle, wears all black, has a menacing stance and scowl on her face, and refuses to smile—as she considers smiling or showing any sign of emotion for that matter a weakness. Her coworkers often feel intimated by Diaz and have a hard time reading her, although Terry believes her appearance and behavior are a front to hide the fact that deep down she's a "softy." Additionally, Diaz doesn't have a good relationship with her family, preferring to avoid gatherings and spend the holidays alone or with her coworkers. Meanwhile, Santiago is book-smart, a nerd, dresses conservatively, always follows the rules, often behaves awkwardly in public, and is eager to please her superiors. She is extremely ambitious and puts the advancement of her career (which she achieves by passing her sergeant test and leading her own police unit) above all else, but also feels like a pushover. She comes from a family of cops and is extremely close to her parents. In other words, Santiago is the good girl and good cop to Rosa's bad girl and rogue cop—although, this being a comedy, Rosa doesn't actually beat up anybody. Such opposing characterizations allow for humor to work better, as comedy thrives on contrast and stereotypes—not in the harmful sense but in regard to their narrative function coalescing a set of stable and expected traits that audiences can easily recognize and quickly react to (Aldama and González 40). It also helps to provide varied depictions of Latinas across a wide representational spectrum, avoiding the "THE Latina" stereotype (in its negative connotation) that Beatriz has referred to in interviews about her role (Beatriz).

Brooklyn Nine-Nine pushes back against harmful stereotypes in various other ways. Going back to the characterization of Diaz and Santiago, we can

Figure 9.3 *Brooklyn Nine-Nine*'s two Latina cops (Rosa Diaz, left, and Amy Santiago) show their contrasting personalities during a junior detective class for at-risk youth.

see how the extreme ways in which they are depicted—Rosa as "looking like a villain" and "terrifying" and Amy as "too nice" and "so by the book" she once gave her aunt a jaywalking ticket—actually punctuate their characters' radical departure from trite Latina tropes commonly found in U.S. media. Rosa unabashedly appropriates the "bad boy" look and behavior of Hollywood films, turning it into a weapon to fight expectations of Latinas as submissive or overtly sexualized for the male gaze. Likewise, Amy also resists the Latina spitfire stereotype by dressing and behaving modestly and being a terrible dancer. More importantly, she offers an alternative and aspirational representation that's seriously lacking in the media, especially for young women of color: the intelligent, driven Latina who's not afraid to show her smarts and won't temper her ambitions. A notable accomplishment of this show is the intersectionality of its depictions of people of color. Diaz's and Santiago's identities as Hispanic and as women are intimately woven into the narrative and are presented as inseparable. In season 1, episode 10, Amy is jealous because Rosa has been offered a police captain job, feeling she's much more qualified than her colleague. Amy tries to justify her reaction: "I'm competitive. I have seven brothers and always had to fight for a place at the table." To which Rosa replies: "You're not the only girl at the table anymore. We work at a police force full of dudes. We have to have each other's backs, OK?" Brown female solidarity comes through as the most effective vehicle to dismantle both racism and sexism.

Family relationships are used quite commonly in *Brooklyn Nine-Nine* to explore matters of identity as well as changing social and cultural norms. While Amy is close to her large family, she resents the way her parents (especially her mom) favor her older brother David (played by Lin-Manuel Miranda), who is also a cop, is just as competitive as Amy, and seems to always be a step ahead of his sister in terms of accomplishments. Amy believes her mother's preferential treatment of David has to do not so much with his success but with his gender, and she resents such traditional attitudes in her family. Likewise, Amy speaks up about the patriarchal behavior of her father, who disapproves of Jake—reminding him that it's not the 1950s and men don't own women. Family life on Rosa's side of the equation is far more complicated and conflictive. After not wanting anything to do with her relatives, Rosa begins to get closer to them following her time in prison due to a setup by dirty cops. After coming out as bisexual to the squad (season 5, episode 10), Rosa asks Jake to help her tell her parents—Oscar Diaz, played by Danny Trejo, and Julia Diaz, played by Olga Merediz—about her sexuality at dinner because "they are very traditional" and this might hurt their relationship. However, her parents end up assuming the two of them are dating even as Jake and Amy are engaged. The conversation then gets real:

> JULIA: We understand. Love is complicated.
>
> OSCAR: *M'ija*, when you called this dinner, you were so nervous I was afraid you were gonna tell us you were gay.
>
> ROSA: So you'd rather me being some dude's mistress than being in a loving relationship with a woman? Well, Jake and I aren't dating, but guess what? Your worst fear is real . . . I'm not straight. I'm bisexual. And I don't care what you think about it! Screw this, I'm outta here!

Oscar insists Rosa is just "going through a phase," to which Rosa replies she just wants to be accepted for who she is. Days later, Oscar apologizes to his daughter and tells her he's trying hard to accept her as she is. "Mom," however, "still needs a little more time."

In other instances, the show employs what it does best (humor) to make fun of cultural insensitivities and prejudicial expectations, calling them out in the process. After Santiago and Peralta begin dating, Jake's parents invite Amy's parents to Thanksgiving dinner. As the Santiagos arrive, Jake's mom greets them with "Hola! Feliz Thanksgiving! Jake told us you're Cuban." Embarrassed, Jake retorts: "And now I regret it" (season 5, episode 7). In response to the Peraltas' assumption that because they are Cuban they might not fully understand English, the Santiagos begin condescending to Jake's parents—highlighting how their family is much better because they are supportive and have always been together, while the Peraltas are divorced and Jake has trust issues stemming from his father cheating and leaving him when he was a boy. Speaking of language, unlike in *SVU*, *Brooklyn Nine-Nine*'s Latina characters don't speak Spanish. This may come from restrictions of the comedic genre, as jokes are infamously difficult to translate due to language and cultural differences. Or it may simply reflect the reality that many Latinxs (particularly U.S.-born) don't know or choose not to use the language, which in itself would constitute another effort to challenge assumptions about such a linguistically diverse culture and the personal experiences within it.

Other times, the squad's two white, middle-aged, largely incompetent cops (Scully and Hitchcock) are the ones who bring up sensitive issues. On Cinco de Mayo during season 6, Hitchcock shows up in a colorful poncho followed by a mariachi band, appropriating a celebration that the two Latinas in the precinct don't even talk about. However, in season 7 they redeem themselves and shatter the mostly negative perceptions about them. When asked why they didn't include the name of a key witness in a report, the food-loving cops reveal that the witness was undocumented—proceeding to tell Rosa and Amy that undocumented immigrants don't like to talk to the cops because they are afraid of ICE. The two Latinas respond that of course they knew that, but act surprised that Scully and Hitchcock did—or even cared. Scully resents their assumption. Understanding the significance of their colleagues' actions and the fact they are on the same team on this issue, Rosa later apologizes and tells them: "You did the right thing."

Conclusion

Following the murder of George Floyd by a Minneapolis police officer in May 2020 and the massive Black Lives Matter protests that ensued, cop shows (both reality and fictional) have come under fire more than ever before for glorifying officers as heroes, justifying the use of illegal practices, burnishing the police's image for recruitment, and perpetuating "the idea that people of color are more likely to commit crime" (Blake). In June 2020, the long-running reality show *Cops* was cancelled, while police procedurals and even sitcoms like *Brooklyn Nine-Nine* are struggling with how to properly respond to the backlash. Samberg has said that the writers and actors are "discussing how you make a comedy show about police right now, and if we can find a way of doing that that we all feel morally OK about" (Kiefer). This juncture truly feels like "mission impossible" for police series. On the one hand, "research literature leaves no doubt that media representations of crime, whether for news or entertainment purposes, or both, has exaggerated public fears about crime and generated ever-increasing support for repressive and punitive crime control policies" (Potter and Kappeler 3–4). On the other hand, law-enforcement programs have been providing Latinx actors with a good percentage of their limited appearances on prime-time TV—even if those roles are as criminals or public servants who are increasingly viewed as pariahs of American society. This is what Santiago must have felt when she literally became the "poster girl" of an NYPD public relations campaign (a huge accomplishment for a Latina), only to find out that angry New Yorkers quickly drew devil horns and pig noses on her portraits all over the city because of what her uniform represented to them. "There's no right way to shoot a fourteen-year-old," Amaro says to the grand jury, wondering why doing what you think is right according to your training and respect for the law can have such terrible consequences ("Amaro's One-Eighty"). Is there a right way to do a cop show that avoids complicity in glorifying police violence against Latinxs and other people of color?

Notes

1. Another study, "Inclusion or Invisibility? Comprehensive Annenberg Report on Diversity in Entertainment" (2016), found that only 5.8 percent of speaking or named characters in U.S. film and TV were Latinx (Smith et al.).

2. U.S. Census Bureau, 2019 estimates, www.census.gov/quickfacts/fact/table/US/IPE 120218. The U.S. Hispanic population grew from 35.3 million in 2000 (12.5 percent of total population) to 60.6 million (18.5 percent of total population) in 2019.

3. A film version of *CHiPs* was made in 2017, directed by Dax Shepard and distributed by Warner Bros. Pictures. Michael Peña plays a Miami FBI agent named Castillo, who is given an undercover assignment with the California Highway Patrol under the alias of Frank "Ponch" Poncherello. The film also includes two female officers, Sgt. Gail Hernandez (Maya Rudolph) and Officer Ava Perez (Rosa Salazar).

4. Barba quips that the three friends used to be known as "Los Tres Mosqueteros de Jerome Avenue": he had the brains, Alex the heart, and Eddie the muscles.

5. "Buddy, you're getting me all wrong."

6. "I will see you in court, friend."

Works Cited

Aldama, Frederick, and Christopher González. *Reel Latinxs: Representation in U.S. Film and TV*. U of Arizona P, 2019.

Ausellio, Michael. "*Law & Order: SVU* Renewed for Season 21 at NBC, Will Become Longest-Running Live-Action Series in History." *TV Line*, 29 Mar. 2019, tvline.com/2019/03/29/law-order-svu-renewed-season-21-record-longest-tv-show-history/.

Baldwin, Kristen. "Huzzah for *Brooklyn Nine-Nine*, the Most Inclusive Show on TV." *Entertainment Weekly*, 11 May 2018, ew.com/tv/2018/05/11/brooklyn-nine-nine-b99-canceled-fox-inclusive/.

Beatriz, Stephanie. "On My Radar: Stephanie Beatriz Shares Why Diversity on TV Is Important." *Latina*, 6 Aug. 2014.

Blake, Meredith. "After 32 'Egregious and Cruel' Seasons, 'Cops' Was Canceled." *Los Angeles Times*, 11 June 2020, www.latimes.com/entertainment-arts/tv/story/2020-06-11/running-from-cops-live-pd-canceled-podcast-police.

Brooklyn Nine-Nine. Fox, 2013–18; NBC, 2019–.

"Diversity on the Force: Where Police Don't Mirror Communities." *Governing the States and Localities*, Sept. 2015, media.governing.com/documents/policediversityreport.pdf.

Harnick, Chris. "It's 'Absolutely' Time *Law & Order: SVU* Introduced a New Gay Character—So Where Are They?" *E! Online*, 30 Sept. 2015, www.eonline.com/news/696074/it-s-absolutely-time-law-and-order-svu-introduced-a-new-gay-character-so-where-are-they.

Kiefer, Halle. "Andy Samberg Says *Brooklyn Nine-Nine* 'Rethinking' How to Make a Police Comedy." *Vulture*, 6 July 2020, www.vulture.com/2020/07/andy-samberg-brooklyn-nine-nine-rethinking-police-comedy.html.

Law & Order: Special Victims Unit. NBC, 1999–.

Lenz, Timothy. *Changing Images of Law in Film and Television Crime Stories*. Peter Lang, 2003.

Negrón-Muntaner, Frances. *The Latino Media Gap: A Report on the State of Latinos in U.S. Media*. Columbia University, 2014, ecfsapi.fcc.gov/file/7522909797.pdf.

Nichols-Pethick, Jonathan. *TV Cops: The Contemporary American Television Police Drama*. Routledge, 2012.

"Percentage of Local Police Officers Who Were Racial or Ethnic Minorities Nearly Doubled Between 1987 and 2013." *Bureau of Justice Statistics*, 14 May 2015, www.justice.gov/tribal/pr/percentage-local-police-officers-who-were-racial-or-ethnic-minorities-nearly-doubled.

Potter, Gary, and Matthew Kappeler. "Introduction: Media, Crime, and Hegemony." *The Harms of Crime Media: Essays on the Perpetuation of Racism, Sexism, and Class Stereotypes*, edited by Denise Bissler and Joan Conners, McFarland & Co., 2012, pp. 3–17.

Ramírez Berg, Charles. *Latino Images in Film: Stereotypes, Subversion, and Resistance*. U of Texas P, 2002.

Rothman, Michael. "5 Things You Never Knew about 'CHiPs' and Erik Estrada." *ABC News*, 23 Mar. 2015, abcnews.go.com/Entertainment/things-knew-chips-erik-estrada/story?id=29793423.

Smith, Stacy L., et al. "Inclusion or Invisibility? Comprehensive Annenberg Report on Diversity in Entertainment." University of Southern California, 2016, annenberg.usc.edu/sites/default/files/2017/04/07/MDSCI_CARD_Report_FINAL_Exec_Summary.pdf.

Snauffer, Douglas. *Crime Television*. Praeger, 2006.

"Viet Than Nguyen and Vu Tran: Narrative Plentitude | Talks at Google." *Viet Than Nguyen*, vietnguyen.info/2018/viet-thanh-nguyen-and-vu-tran-narrative-plentitude-talks-at-google.

Yaquinto, Marilyn. *Policing the World on Screen: American Mythologies and Hollywood's Rogue Crimefighters*. Palgrave, 2019.

¿QUIEN MANDA IN *STAR WARS*?

Disidentifying with the Bandido in *The Mandalorian*

Carlos Gabriel Kelly González

The genre of science fiction (SF) has great potential to transport viewers into new worlds, new possibilities, new ways of seeing the world we inhabit, and the transmedial experience of *Star Wars* certainly possesses that promise of possibility. The *Star Wars* franchise has an enormous and far-reaching influence, making its way into books, Legos, cartoons, movies, television, video games, comics, fancy Dutch ovens, and so on. When it comes to TV, *Star Wars* has utilized animation as a way to make its mark with *The Clone Wars* (2008–20) and *Rebels* (2014–18) series, but *The Mandalorian* (2019–) generated unparalleled anticipation as the first live-action TV *Star Wars* project. After my share of binge-watching Westerns during the COVID-19 pandemic (such as *Godless* [2017] and *The Good, the Bad, and the Ugly* [or *GBU*, 1967]), I knew I wanted to revisit Mando's gunslinging ways. The space Western *The Mandalorian* uses grand music akin to composer Ennio Morricone's famous score for *GBU*, gunslinging, and quest-driven character development that, together, drive unique identificatory experiences for audiences.

Many questions inspire this trek into *estar warslandia*, but one central question has dominated my viewing of *Star Wars* films and TV: do Latinx people exist in *Star Wars*? Obviously, we do . . . *pero like, do we*? The Mandalorian gunslinger (portrayed by Pedro Pascal) is almost always referred to as "Mando." If we, as audiences, understand that we can insert our experience into texts to create new meaning, then perhaps Latinxs like myself can query the usage of this naming device.[1] Spanish etymology adds layers to the usage of "Mando," because it comes from the word *mandar*, which brings up the question of *¿quien manda aquí?* Or, who is in charge here? While the *Star Wars* franchise typically utilizes features of SF and action-adventure genres (typical for a space opera), I choose to classify *The Mandalorian* as a space Western because of how Western influence permeates the show. Take, for instance, how Mando, in order to find the Child must learn to tame and ride a Blarg (horselike creature) inside of a corral. There is also the continual use of landscape shots, saloons, wild animals (who are dangerous parts of unknown frontiers), and the tension from duels/standoffs with guns drawn and at the ready. Through these similarities, *The Mandalorian* may conjure images of the *bandido*, but Charles Ramírez Berg and José Esteban Muñoz provide the language to resist and challenge this stereotype. This chapter aims to illustrate the implications of the use of *mandar* as well as argue that Pedro Pascal's performance of Mando challenges the bandido stereotype.

In recent years, there has been an explosion of Latinx actors in speculative and SF TV, making Pascal's Mando one of the newest iterations of Latinx performance to the genres. To more adequately address the promise of the speculative and SF, Frederick Aldama and Chris González detail how "speculative genres potentially allow for more capacious and imaginative re-creation of the building blocks of reality. They offer the possibility for creators to think of ways that Latinxs, for instance, can be reimagined in a future or fantasy world" (*Reel Latinxs* 133). But we know this is not always the case, especially for Latinx characters and performers in *Star Wars*, who always seem to be absent, hidden, or side characters—that is, until *The Mandalorian*.

Though I cannot name every Latinx star who has appeared within the genres of speculative fiction and SF, I do want to highlight a few notable and recent performances by Latinxs in speculative TV. Netflix's series *Umbrella Academy* (2019–) features Diego Hargreeves (played by David Castañeda), a telekinetic, knife-wielding, expert warrior who joins other superheroes fighting to save the world across dimensions of time. Amazon's *Undone* (2019–) features the ever-curious Alma (played by Rosa Salazar), who moves across space and time through the potential powers of her schizophrenia.[2] Additionally, Netflix's *Seis Manos* (2019–) features Mexican orphans who become kung fu fighters (starring Latinx actors Johnny Cruz, Aislinn Derbez, Angélica Vale, and Carlos Luna). Their plan is to save their pueblo and avenge their master by killing the supervillain, El Balde (played by Danny Trejo).

However, if we are interested specifically in a legacy of science-fiction television (which typically features world-building components, an integration of a novum technology, and alien species who exist as extended metaphors for difference), we can look to the presence of Latinx performers. Consider *Star Trek*'s Khan Noonien Singh (played by the adored Ricardo Montalbán, famous for his Latin lover roles in the mid-twentieth century), Raquel Welch (née Jo Raquel Tejada)—who appeared in films like *Fantastic Voyage* (1966), *One Million Years B.C.* (1966), and Westerns like *Bandolero!* (1968)—and Edward James Olmos's Admiral William Adama in the reboot of *Battlestar Galactica* (2004–9). Of Olmos's performance, Aldama writes: "we get our very own zoot-suiter in space with Olmos. . . . Here he's a great rhetor, strategist, leader of the people, and savior of a new generation of existence: the human-cylon era" (72). The roles performed by actors like Montalbán, Welch, and Olmos create lineage for Mando, as he shares history with Latinx actors who have performed in SF, speculative fiction, and Westerns.

More recent representations of Latinx performers in SF and speculative genres include Aubrey Plaza's Lenny Busker in FX's *Legion* (2017–19), Jeanine Mason's role of Liz Ortecho in The CW's *Roswell, New Mexico* (2019–), and Latinxs like Rubén Blades, Colman Domingo, and Danay García in *Fear the Walking Dead* (2015–). Finally, Michael Peña's character (Peter) in the film *Extinction* (2019) exemplifies the leadership and intelligence akin to Admiral Adama. Peña portrays a hyperintelligent hero who—unlike the white father who immediately gets his family killed—is able to save his family and other survivors.

When we shift from SF to the Western, the failures in stereotyping Latinxs prove even more pervasive. William Nericcio speaks to how varying media worked together to solidify and reproduce stereotypes about Mexicans. He writes: "By the time cowboys, and bandits ([we've played] so many Mexican bandits that it appears to be our vocation, our calling), made their way to the boob tube, pulp fiction magazines and cinema had laid the groundwork for the naturalization of the 'Mexican' as pejorative" (Aldama and Nericcio 64). Competing media images of dangerous Latino men in the mid-twentieth century metastasized to create the unending stereotypes we continue seeing today. In *Border Bandits: Hollywood on the Southern Frontier*, Camilla Fojas expands our reading of Westerns, writing: "Westerns are a genre of western expansionism, of a manifest destiny west of the Mississippi River; for this reason, the genre has rarely been identified with the southern frontier, though the relationship of U.S. citizens to Mexico and Mexicans is a dominant trope of the genre" (28). Thus, the genre itself serves as a nation-building device that benefits white, heterosexual, wealthy, Anglo men, and includes Latinxs and Natives only as characters to build up the white protagonist. In other words, these narratives exist without centering people of color and without including the possibility for Latinxs to identify with on-screen characters who look and act like them. To highlight this media mishmash, look no further than the Frito Bandito (voiced by Mel Blanc), a marketing scheme's plea for people to protect their chips from Mexicans. The popularization of the bandido clues us into the historically inescapable nature and acceptance of viewing Latino men as threats.

In *Talking #browntv: Latinas and Latinos on the Screen*, Nericcio and Aldama take readers on a nostalgic superhighway documenting the presence of Latinxs on TV to highlight dominant stereotypes as well as norm-busting representations. Nericcio wrestles with the dialogue of a Mexican bandit appearing in a children's variety hour in the 1950s: "I'm Mexican Pete, zee bad bandit / Zee bad bandit I always 'ave been. . . . Señor Hank he must pay ze fat ransom / Before little Cassy I free" (Aldama and Nericcio 66). Accents are an excuse (a wildly exaggerated and stereotypical trope) to represent Latinxs as incompetent. Consider the infamous accented line, "We don't need no stinkin' badges," by Alfonso Bedoya in the Western film *The Treasure of the Sierra Madre* (1948), or non-Western characters like Bumblebee Man from the *Simpsons*, or Jack Black's horrid Latino face in *Nacho Libre* (2006). Going back a bit, Western actor Gilbert Roland's affinity for costuming reveals how Latinxs can subvert the Western or at least their role from within. Ramírez Berg, through investigating Roland's filmography, concludes Roland used "attire to make himself the center of visual interest . . . even when he was at the [frame's] margins" (100). Roland's actions portray how Latinxs can subvert their positionality in early film. Between the Western and SF (within speculative spaces), the roles are limited, the stereotypes are many, and the promise of possibility is slim. Set against heavy expectations involving the history of Latinx representation within the genres explored above, *The Mandalorian*—like Roland—breathes new life into a genre typically riddled with Latinx stereotypes.

At this point, I want to provide a brief recap of *The Mandalorian* to situate us in the show's narrative progression. In the show's first scene, Mando's character (AKA Dyn Jarren) enters a saloon and stands at the entrance of the doorway, not speaking (which is his general MO). After a roaring display of masculine tension over a spilled drink, other saloon-goers attack Mando. He defends himself by throwing fists, drawing his blaster only when fired on. Mando disarms his assailants and claims his bounty—easy-peasy. As we travel across new worlds with Mando, the screen fills with highly imaginative landscapes echoing a frontier motif generated by landscape shots familiar to the Western genre. Mando's calm demeanor shows in every situation: from a chase scene in space where he outmaneuvers and kills a pilot on his ship's tail to destroying an IG unit hellbent on killing the Yoda-like child in chapter 2. In chapter 4, "Sanctuary," Mando's selflessness shines as he works alongside Cara Dune (played by Gina Carano) to train a small village to fight against invading pirates and their AT-ST.[3] At one point, he answers Dune's fearful remark of "You cannot fight that thing" with "Unless we show them how" (20:20). Mando's absolute combat skills shine in chapter 6, "The Prisoner," where his old crew betrays him, stranding him on a New Republic prisoner ship where wits and patience secure his escape. In chapter 8, "Redemption," Mando saves the day by utilizing his new Z-6 jetpack to attach himself to Moff Gideon's (played by Giancarlo Esposito) TIE fighter. No matter what, Mando is in charge, *el manda*. Perhaps the strongest challenge to his in-charge-ness comes from Mando's reliance on others, which I explore later.

Let us now turn to the Spanish etymology and definitions of *mando/mandar*. The word *mandar* "comes from the Latin *mandare*, made up of *manus* (*mano*/hand) and *dare* (*dar*/give). Originally it refer[red] to a commission. That is, something one gave in the hand of another, so [they] could keep it or give it to a third party. Hence also the words . . . errand, errand boy" ("Mandar," Etimologia de Mandar). Consider Mando's bounties as errands that he takes from his hands and gives to Greef Karga (played by Carl Weathers), the middleman in the bounty transaction underworld. Mando demands different currency than the imperial credits offered by Karga, reflecting his choice in securing pay. Mando's agency in this scene is a precursor to his later actions to save the Child, reflecting his ability to transgress guild protocols and carve out a unique path from others. Thus, although he might "run errands" or be an "errand boy," he chooses his errands, taking control of his destiny—*el manda*. Add to this reading the Spanish colloquial usage of "Yo mando aqui," or "I'm in charge here," which affirms Mando's authority as he picks and chooses who to deal with and what bounties and/or payment he accepts. In Spanish, the word *mando* means: "facultad o capacidad para mandar," or "capacity to take charge."[4] This definition affirms Mando's decision-making power and his ability to take charge or lead as one of the most revered warriors in the *Star Wars* mythos—a Mandalorian.

An interesting moment from the series complicates the reading above, but only slightly as the refrain of this series mostly revolves around Mando, yes, but also the help he receives. Consider how *mandar* may also mean a way "to control (a bull) by aggressive action in bullfighting."[5] The moment where Mando confronts the Mudhorn adds depth and mystery (à la force) to the claim of being in charge.

In figure 10.1, we see Mando standing up after having resigned himself to defeat, barely holding up his knife with two hands while awaiting the Mudhorn's final charge (chapter 1, 20:30). Mando takes on the charging Mudhorn, but like anyone he cannot be in charge all the time. In fact, this encounter highlights his vulnerability and reliance on others for help. Help from Kuill

(UPLIFTING MUSIC PLAYING)

Figure 10.1 After Jawas scrapped his ship, Kuill negotiates for Mando to find a delicacy (the Mudhorn's egg) in a trade for his stuff (*The Mandalorian*, chapter 2). Disney+.

(an expert mechanic and fixer who also helps rebuild Mando's ship) ensures Mando is able to retrieve his gear. Additionally, Mando survives only with the help of the Force (which is a myth neither Mando nor his compatriots truly understand). Mando's powerlessness here reveals that the idea of *quien manda* is more nuanced, that taking charge in this frontier-filled landscape requires the strength of a crew, or even the power of the Force.

Mando's crew grows as the story progresses, challenging warrior narratives that place "lone-wolf" men (especially Latinx men) at the forefront in stereotypical ways. The strength of a crew shines in Westerns like Scott Frank's series *Godless* (2017), where an entire town of women band together to fight against Frank Griffin's vicious gang. Akin to this, Mando forms a crew made up from random encounters with shock trooper Cara Dune, the Child, IG-11, Kuill, the Armorer, and many others who cross his path. Ramírez Berg explains warrior narratives as being "rooted in the Hollywood Western" and that "their common defining feature is a protagonist who possesses and displays his fighting capability" (227). Ramírez Berg continues: "the genre centers on a *lone male protagonist* who possesses *special physical skills*" (228). Indeed, Mando is a highly skilled warrior; our introduction to him in the cantina affirms this idea. However, the fact that he is not alone for most of the series (often being accompanied by the Child, IG-11, Kuill, and/or Cara Dune for the remainder of the chapters) provides new ways of viewing Pascal's Mando as standing apart from the lone hero of typical Westerns.

Mando's experience with IG-11 also works to upend the solo nature of the bandido stereotype while also complicating the warrior narrative. Let me paint another scene from chapter 1: Mando arrives at the bounty location to find IG-11 attempting to take the bounty for himself. The scene quickly devolves into a shoot-out; after IG-11 mistakenly shoots Mando, Mando declares his guild status and convinces IG-11 that they should work together. Mando appeals to IG-11 with, "I have a suggestion. Let's split the reward," to which IG-11 responds, "This is acceptable." The duo squares off in a shoot-out with the gang holding the Child. Viewers experience shifts in perspective from IG-11 to Mando as the characters maneuver together through an exchange of blaster fire, seeking refuge behind corners, barrels, and pillars. IG-11 and Mando's enemies succumb to their blasters, some screaming and falling from rooftops. After Mando commandeers a Gatling-gun-like blaster to kill all remaining enemies (preventing IG-11's third attempt to self-destruct), IG-11 and Mando break into the building.[6] But, before Mando escapes with the bounty, IG-11 proclaims: "The commission was quite specific. The asset was to be terminated." A blaster goes off. Smoke enters into the scene, revealing the now decommissioned IG-11 and Mando as he reaches his finger toward the Child in a moment resembling *The Creation of Adam* by Michelangelo (chapter 1, 31:00). Ultimately, this scene's allusion foreshadows a powerful connection between Mando and the Child. The partnership between Mando and IG-11 also illustrates trust between guild members (although short-lived), as well as Mando's intelligence and strategizing prowess. The situation compels him to work with a droid, even though his aversion to droids was made clear early in chapter 1.

Mando not only finds a partner in IG-11, but he plans and strategizes on the spot to avoid death and losing IG-11's firepower. When IG-11 announces the beginning of its self-destruct mechanism, Mando shouts, "Do not self-destruct, cover me," spurring IG-11 into action instead. This first chapter reveals how Mando's proclivity toward teamwork will be a motif, as he is willing to ally himself with a droid to complete the mission.

The scene above highlights Mando's cool demeanor, and how he approaches IG-11 contradicts the definition of a bandido. Ramírez Berg defines a bandido as "vicious, cruel, treacherous, shifty, and dishonest; psychologically, he is irrational, overly emotional and quick to resort to violence" (68). Tuco (played by Eli Wallach, in a rousing performance of Latino face) in *GBU* comes to mind as a spot-on example of the bandido, especially when deputies—before attempting to hang him—declare the long list of atrocities the smiling Tuco committed. Mando, however, thinks rationally to overcome the situation, and through actions like saving the Child, he becomes a direct challenge to the bandido stereotype seen in Tuco. I want to clarify that just because a Latino actor like Pascal is the central gunslinger in *The Mandalorian* does not mean he is automatically a bandido. But the Western genre does raise questions about the stereotypes most often seen in roles given to Latino men or to those pretending to be Latinxs. Thus, Pascal's Mando—by not being afraid of assistance—gives Latinxs an opportunity to identify with a character who works against stereotypical roles and narratives.

Figure 10.2 Mando saves the Child from IG-11 (*The Mandalorian*, chapter 1). Disney+.

Mando's actions of acquiring a crew signals to viewers how teamwork can lead to disidentifying with the bandido stereotype. According to José Esteban Muñoz, disidentification "works on and against dominant ideology. . . . [It is] a strategy that tries to transform a cultural logic from within, always laboring to enact permanent structural change while at the same time valuing the importance of local and everyday struggles of resistance" (11–12). Latinxs hover between 2 and 3 percent of all media representations; therefore we have no choice but to actively disidentify with stereotypical representations. Mando, however, works against dominant ways of viewing Latinxs in the Western. Muñoz's book *Disidentifications: Queers of Color and the Performance of Politics* works to understand how the dominant culture (one ruled by the hegemony of heterosexuality, patriarchy, and white supremacy) creates the need for LGBTQ and marginalized communities to disidentify with said dominant culture. Thus, "disidentification can be understood as a way of shuffling back and forth between reception and production" (Muñoz 25). Latinxs in SF hardly appear as protagonists, and if we do appear in SF or SF-inspired Westerns, it might be as the literal bandido Hector Escaton in *Westworld* (played by Rodrigo Santoro) or sidekick to the white villain Lawrence (played by Clifton Collins Jr.). Thus, the production and reproduction of the bandido continues, as Ramírez Berg argues, quite literally or in two updated forms as "the Latin American gangster/drug runner . . . [and] the inner-city gang member" (68). Mando's ability to best his enemies comes from his unique skills, but also his characteristically unmacho reliance on teamwork, which sets him apart from the bandido and works to reimagine how Latino men can appear on the screen.

Mando represents a new way for Latino men to exist, and although his mask can complicate viewer identification, there is still opportunity. In chapter 8, "Redemption," Mando and his crew are surrounded by Moff Gideon and his battalion of imperial stormtroopers, but Mando's decision to unmask saves the day. The newly reprogrammed (for care) IG-11 unit reassures Mando they are not human, therefore affirming Mando's claim of "no living thing" seeing him without his helmet.[7] Mando was willing to die in this moment to hold off the enemy to save his friends (pretty stubborn and macho-like), but IG-11 convinces Mando to fight on (an amazing parallel to chapter 1's gun-slinging showdown) by surviving to ensure his friends' escape. Applying a spray to his head trauma, IG-11 saves Mando's life, allowing Mando to continue taking charge, to continue leading. While this moment undoubtedly reveals how Latinidad is rendered invisible (for the majority of the series), it is also an opportunity. The opportunity lies in identifying with the masked Mando—to be in charge, to *mandar*—for so many quests, through so many interactions with varying species of humanoids, nonhumanoids, and droids. Mando's mask allows viewers to experience the possibilities that *Star Wars* can imagine. After his unmasking, audiences (if they were unaware Pedro Pascal is Mando) must reckon with identifying with someone whom they once may have deemed Other.

Thus, Mando's mask presents powerful identificatory experiences for viewers, as we suture ourselves to his perspectives, to the power and intelligence behind the beskar.[8] A Mandalorian's helmet is sacred; once taken off "it can never be worn again," as Dyn Jarren solemnly recounts to Dune after defeating the pirates and AT-ST (chapter 4). Here, let us consider Jessica Benjamin's work on recognition theory and the concept of "the Third" in her book *Beyond Doer and Done To*. In it, Benjamin interrogates the relationship between mother and child and analysand and analyst. However, in this case, Benjamin clarifies the identificatory experiences provided by Mando's mask—a fusion between Mando and viewers similar to how in video games players become player-characters.[9] Benjamin argues toward a liminal space between analyst and analysand she calls "the Third," defined as the position in which

> we implicitly recognize the other as "like subject," a being we can experience as an "other mind." The Third refers to the position constituted through holding the tension of recognition between difference and sameness, taking the other to be a separate but equivalent center of initiative and consciousness with whom nonetheless feelings and intentions can be shared. (4)

In this case, the Western motifs combined with *Star Wars'* settings add to the already present tension of difference and sameness between the Mandalorian and the viewer, but Mando's unmasking in chapter 8, "Redemption," furthers the complexity. Mando's mask positions viewers to read into the emotions hidden behind the mask, connecting viewers into experiencing the Other, the mythological Mandalorian.[10] Thus, viewers may spend the majority of the series in the tension highlighted by Benjamin's liminal Third, where they share Mando's feelings and intentions, becoming closer to the Other that is our masked protagonist. The audience can feel as though they are Mando through the continual use of close-up shots on his mask, and how he constantly strategizes to gain the upper hand. Similarly, Mando's mask, as in *Spider-Man: Into the Spider-Verse*, where Miles Morales confirms that "anyone can wear the mask," creates the possibility of anyone being Mando or a Mandalorian. TV and film provide space for viewers to identify with protagonists or other characters through varying camera angles as well as shifting perspectives. Possible connections to identifying as Mando stem from his always being masked, but also through the power of music to shape emotions.

The Mandalorian's focus on questlike narrative and emotions situates readers in a narrative full of moments with which to identify with Mando. In order to progress forward, Mando (or viewers) needs new gear, but to do that Mando takes on a quest to find the Child (bounty), returning immediately afterward to the Armorer (played by Emily Swallow), who provides him the upgrades to fight on. While on the main mission of protecting the child, Mando gets sidetracked into protecting and training a town from space pirates (another quest or side quest.)[11] Lacking funds and needing repairs, Mando reunites with an old crew to get paid; Mando continues to trek the frontiers of space until he finds his way to the final boss fight against Moff Gideon. Torben Grodal's work on audiovisual realism informs our understanding here, especially through the idea that "a strong feeling of reality demands that vital human or animal concerns are at stake [and that] realism is more often attributed to those representations that portray negative emotions" (267). Mando's trajectory clues viewers into the idea of progression: how one must continue to develop their skills and gear to advance. The negative emotions here revolve around lacking the means to fight on, the dangers associated with avoiding capture by bounty hunters hired by the empire, and with the frontier, where several times wild animals attack Mando and/ or his crew. There are consequences for breaking guild protocols and playing trickster to the Empire, such as becoming the hunted. The looming threat of Mando's unmasking reminds me of watching lucha libre as a kid, where a wrestler's identity hinged on their ability to stay masked and why unmasking a rival *luchador* was the ultimate way to defeat someone. These negative emotions reinforce the suturing of audiences' perspectives to Mando—like the luchador, we want the protection of the mask.

However, Mando always has his mask on (except for one moment in chapter 8), so where do these empathic connections lie? Anthony Breznican's *Vanity Fair* interview with *The Mandalorian*'s composer, Ludwig Göransson, explains his creative decisions for the music. In speaking about the mask, Göransson asserts, "[Mando] wears a helmet, so he doesn't have any facial expressions. *I'm* the facial expression. The *music* is the facial expression, telling how he feels going through this journey" (Breznican).

Music and Mando's mask work on the viewer to shape distinct moments of emotion. Although viewers cannot readily decipher the feelings behind Mando's unflinching mask, the music and accompanying close-ups of his mask help to connect viewers to a slew of possible emotions. Thus, the mask in combination with the questlike narrative and Göransson's epic music as emotional proxy work on viewers to increase identification with Mando. This identificatory experience is yet another reason for viewers to disidentify with the bandido stereotype, as it invites us to be Mando, unlike in Leone's *GBU*,

Figure 10.3 Mando in the cockpit of his ship with the Child during chapter 8's final moments (*The Mandalorian*). Disney+.

where viewers are expected to identify with Clint Eastwood's Blondie over the criminally violent Tuco.

Additionally, viewers can disidentify with stereotypical representations of the bandido through Mando's emotional intelligence and his access to new worlds. The shifting landscapes point to how Pascal's Mando exists without borders. For example, "in many Westerns, the border replaces the western frontier and provides a different line of access to the freedoms that once typified the roaming frontiersman" (Fojas 28). Although Fojas refers to the southern border between Mexico and the United States, the unending frontiers found on the different planets in *The Mandalorian* reframe Pascal's access. Indeed, this new access to perspectives (through the freedom of space travel) materializes in Mando's conversation about Tusken Raiders with wannabe bounty hunter Toro Calacan. In chapter 5, "The Gunslinger," when Toro and Mando ride out to hunt a dangerous bounty (another unexpected side quest and partnership), they come across Tusken Raiders guarding their territory.[12] Toro remarks, "Tusken Raiders . . . I heard the locals talking about this filth," to which Mando responds: "Tuskens think they're the locals. Everyone else is just trespassing" (25:40). This moment alludes to the powers of colonizers to displace and remove Native populations. For *Star Wars*, this is quite a step forward in recognizing the implications of a storyworld based on the premise of empire.

In this instance, we have someone (who is Othered as a Mandalorian) recognizing the marginalized Tusken Raiders. This act reminds me of how Benjamin argues "[an] act of recognition confirm[s] that I am seen, known, my intentions have been understood, I have had an impact on you, and this must also mean that I matter to you" (4). Thus, viewers see like Mando sees, full of nuance and recognition for the atrocities performed by the colonizing forces in *Star Wars*. Mando shows his respect for the Tusken Raiders by communicating with them using his hands to sign an exchange, which gains him and Toro passage through the Tuskens' land—*el manda*. Adilifu Nama's work underscores how important this moment is through his description of how things usually go down in *Star Wars*:

> The robots and nonhuman aliens of *Star Wars* are similar to the type of racial impersonation found in early Hollywood cinema, . . . [where] African Americans, Native Americans, Asians, and Latinos have all had the dubious honor of having white actors use makeup and adopt exaggerated mannerisms to achieve their racial identities. (30)

Nama points to the constant use of alien as Other in famous moments like the cantina scene where Obi-Wan and Luke negotiate for safe passage with Han Solo.[13] As symbolic stand-ins for displaced Natives, Tusken Raiders are given new life and empathetic understanding, which is a drastic change from their most violent representation in Anakin Skywalker's murderous rampage in Episode 2: *Attack of the Clones*. Though Nama's criticism holds true through various iterations of *Star Wars*, *The Mandalorian* ushers in a new perspective on the infamous Tuskens.

Fojas helps to further contextualize Calican's ideas about Tuskens, writing: "Racial difference is associated with some anxiety-provoking occult powers; the racialized other is powerful and alluring at the same time. The Anglo subject, out of fear, neutralizes the racial other's difference to better facilitate domination by interpreting it as a sign of being simply less evolved or primitive" (40). Calican reduces Tusken to "filth" so that he may justify his (and the "locals") trespass onto their land, which fits well within the project of manifest destiny so often replicated in Western films.[14] However, Mando's actions remind me of how Muñoz argues that "the minoritarian subject employs disidentification as a crucial practice of contesting social subordination through the project of worldmaking. . . . Our charge as spectators and actors is to continue disidentifying with this world until we achieve new ones" (200). The charge to disidentify with these images takes shape in Pascal's Mando, where viewers sutured to Mando's perspective begin to see how new worlds can be imagined and populated with Latinxs as protagonists. In addition, the world-making processes (through space-traveling between worlds) generates opportunities for Latinxs to challenge borders, to see themselves as intergalactic.

Part of this new world takes shape via a reimagining of masculinity or machismo to be less reactionary and more strategic. Frederick Aldama and

Chris González identify machismo as "refer[ring] to the patterns of being strong, aggressive, brave—protector of the family, often denigrating the role of women and gay or lesbian members" (*Latinx Studies* 181). Although Mando possesses this mysterious masculinity that carries all the marks of using violence to solve problems, the violence isn't guns blazing kill-all end-all. Rather, Mando is not aggressive unless he needs to be, and his taking off his helmet shows he is willing to be vulnerable. He protects his crew or family without denigrating anyone. In critiquing the multicultural presence in the film *Lone Star*, Rosa Linda Fregoso discusses how reframing the border frontier requires an intersectional approach. She argues that "genuine multiculturalism involves the redefinition of the nation, a rearrangement of center-margin power relations, insisting upon the interplay of multiple and plural identities" (Fregoso 56). Mando may certainly represent phallocentric narratives where the male hero dictates the trajectory of the story. *Pero el Mando manda* without excess violence and through a strong reliance on women throughout the series, forming partnerships in key moments of his travels. Cara Dune saves his life after a bounty hunter finds them hiding in the village they saved from pirates. Mando pleads with Dune to accompany him on his final mission against the Empire, which isn't just about Mando's quest to save the Child but also Dune's contempt for the Empire (as she fought against them in the war). Ultimately, Mando does use violence to subdue enemies, but it isn't akin to bandidos where revenge, pride, or even lust dictate intentions—*esta tranquilo*, he is calm, and he is willing to accept help from the homies.

A few other things challenge the trope of the solo masculine hero. For example, Mando willingly adopts the Child; so that at the end of the series they become "a clan of two," according to the Armorer. He put himself at risk to protect the Child, possibly remembering the demise of his parents as they scurried him into hiding only to be saved by a Mandalorian and to be taken into the creed as a foundling himself. But perhaps the strongest challenge to *mandar*, or being in charge, as being a man's game is the prowess and knowledge of the Armorer. She is the last remaining Mandalorian who can morph beskar and other metals into Mandalorian armor. In chapter 8, "Redemption," stormtroopers enter the secret tunnels looking for Mando (Dyn Jarren) and stumble upon the Armorer, where one asks: "Hey Mando, where are they?" (39:50), referring to Dyn Jarren and his crew. The Armorer defeats the stormtroopers using her forge tools as weapons, signaling that she too possesses unique fighting skills. This is the only time in the *entire series* where the term "Mando" is utilized to describe anyone other than Dyn Jarren, which ensures that *quien manda* is certainly not men alone, simultaneously reinforcing how Mando (as a term) acknowledges all Mandalorians as equals.

Mandalorians have always been one of the most exciting character classes in *Star Wars*, with Boba Fett leading the way with his mysterious mythos, his patented jetpack, and iconic green armor. Now we can add Pascal's rendition as one of the most appealing characters to come out of the *Star Wars* universe. Pascal departs from the bandido and the way stereotypes narrow what is possible for Latinxs in SF; like Peter in *Extinction*, Mando reflects the promise of speculative spaces. Purposefully, I have waited until now to address a couple of questions from the beginning of this essay. *The Mandalorian* does a wonderful job illustrating that *quien manda* can be a collaborative team effort, that all the power doesn't always reside in the macho man. Simultaneously, it challenges what is possible for Latino men in SF and in *Star Wars*. However, for Latinxs, *los que mandan* in *Star Wars* can be boiled down to men: Diego Luna, Jimmy Smits, Pedro Pascal, Benicio Del Toro, Oscar Isaac, Lin-Manuel Miranda, and so on. Latinas have been present but with far less visibility. Consider Lupita Nyong'o as the orange Maz Kanata in the newest trilogy, or Margarita Fernández as an Ewok in *Return of the Jedi*, or Verónica Segura, who played Cordé, the decoy posing as Senator Amidala in Episode 2: *Attack of the Clones*. This is why I believe Latinx people do not really exist in *Star Wars*, because we are more diverse than the majority white-passing men who populate these narratives.

Interrogating the question of *quien manda* brings me to the presence of the Martez sisters, Rafa and Trace (voiced by Latinas Elizabeth Rodriguez and Brigitte Kali Canales, respectively) in episodes 5–8 of the final season of *The Clone Wars*. How can their presence further complicate the question of *quien manda* in *Star Wars* projects? Could the presence of Latinas in the animated show translate to a live-action series dedicated to centering Latinas? Even with their presence, the Martez sisters circle the law in precarious ways via spice running (AKA drug smuggling). Their representation is akin to Oscar Isaac's Poe Dameron's past as a spice runner and Benicio Del Toro as a shifty weapons dealer. Television seems an apt place for *Star Wars* to branch out and to insert more diversity into its projects, but the galaxy far, far away continues to fail Latinxs by replicating stereotypes with an intergalactic spin.

As a fan, I've been asking myself what I want from *Star Wars* in regard to Latinidad. For starters, hiring women and Afro-Latinxs for major roles—enough of the side character treatment. At the time of writing much of this piece, Disney had yet to release season 2 of *The Mandalorian*, which features Afro-Latina Rosario Dawson as Ahsoka Tano, as well as several women in prominent roles, such as Ming-Na Wen's reprisal of the assassin Fennec Shand (from season 1), and Sasha Banks and Kathryn Ann Sackoff as the tag-team duo of Mandalorians, Koska Reeves and Bo-Katan. In season 2, chapter 16: "The Rescue," viewers can see for themselves what a more diverse approach to casting looks like, and honestly, just how much better the stories can be with a more inclusive group of characters. Perhaps Disney finally got the memo about being more inclusive to women and Latinxs beyond the male-dominated storytelling we're used to. Apart from Ahsoka Tano being one of my favorite Star Wars characters, Latinxs can also celebrate that an Afro-Latina is not only making a significant appearance in *The Mandalorian*, but we will soon be able to enjoy Star Wars' world-making possibilities through the first show centering an Afro-Latina as a protagonist in the galaxy far, far away. Saying that I am excited for season 3 of *The Mandalorian* and for Rosario Dawson's Ahsoka Tano series is a severe understatement.

Also, isn't it possible (especially with the grandiose budgets of Disney) to create a *Star Wars* world that is wholly Latinx? I wonder what futuristic influence and design Latinx artists could bring to a world inspired by the fusion of Mesoamerican mythology and contemporary Latinidad? Could a world like this finally bring Latinidad into the *Star Wars* mythos? If that is too difficult, perhaps we can look to language and how it is central to *Star Wars*; how it creates imaginative ways to understand other beings like Chewbacca's speech, famous droids like BB8 and R2D2, humanoids from other planets, iconic characters speaking Jawaese or Huttese. If English exists in this faraway galaxy, then why not Spanish? Perhaps, the new TV series where Diego Luna will reprise his character Cassian Andor will bring Latinxs onto the screen in new ways like *The Mandalorian* does. Whether or not more diverse representations of Latinidad make their way into *Star Wars*, Latinxs must continue to disidentify and cocreate with characters whose Latinidad exists nowhere in *Star Wars* but in the credits.

Notes

1. See Frederick Aldama's theory on cocreation in *Latinx Superheroes in Mainstream Comics*.
2. For scholarship on *Undone*, see Danielle Orozco's chapter in this volume, "Inhala, Exhala: Mental Health and Accessible Shaping Devices in Latinx TV."
3. Two-legged walker droids that are used famously on Endor when Luke Skywalker and company fight with Ewoks to take down the Death Star's shields in the film *Return of the Jedi* (1983).
4. This definition come from the website Spanishdict.com.
5. According to Merriam-Webster.
6. IG-11 is an assassination droid whose manufacturing protocols dictate that he cannot be captured. If he is at risk for capture, he must self-destruct, which he makes clear to Mando several times.

7. IG-11 went from being programmed to kill to being reprogrammed by Kuill. IG-11 had to relearn all motor skills and was the only reason Mando, Dune, and Karga survive in chapter 8.

8. Beskar is the famous material utilized to craft Mandalorian armor.

9. In video game studies, a player-character takes form as a player's concerns morph or fuse with those of the character they play, becoming a way for players to more fully embody character experiences and enhancing empathy through sutured identificatory experiences. In other words, through the journey and through questing, players become the character. See chapter 1 in David Owen's *Player and Avatar: The Affective Potential of Videogames*.

10. With the Mandalorians' home world in shambles, all Mandalorians have been pushed into hiding. Thus, not only are Mandalorians followed by their reputation of being mighty warriors, but they are also Othered in the *Star Wars* universe due to their low surviving numbers.

11. Side quests in video games provide more exposition or further narrative development beyond the main quest line.

12. Tusken Raiders from the planet Tatooine are most notably remembered from Luke Skywalker's encounters in Episode 4: *A New Hope*, and when Anakin Skywalker slays an entire village after his mother's death in Episode 2: *Attack of the Clones*. Season two of *The Mandalorian* kicks off with chapter 9: "The Marshal," which continues to humanize Tuskens in ways we don't see in other *Star Wars* productions.

13. From Episode 4: *A New Hope* (1977).

14. See the discussion in the documentary *Latinos Beyond Reel* (2013) of a scene in *Red River* (1948) where John Wayne feels entitled to land already claimed and owned by Mexican ranchers.

Works Cited

Aldama, Frederick. *Latinx Superheroes in Mainstream Comics*. U of Arizona P, 2017.

Aldama, Frederick, and Christopher González. *Latinx Studies: The Key Concepts*. Taylor & Francis, 2019.

Aldama, Frederick, and Christopher González. *Reel Latinxs: Representation in U.S. Film and TV*. U of Arizona P, 2019.

Aldama, Frederick, and William Nericcio. *Talking #browntv: Latinas and Latinos on the Screen*. Ohio State UP, 2019.

Benjamin, Jessica. *Beyond Doer and Done To*. Routledge, 2018.

Breznican, Anthony. "How Ludwig Göransson's Music Reads the Mind of *The The Mandalorian*." *Vanity Fair*, 9 July 2020.

Fojas, Camila. *Border Bandits: Hollywood and the Southern Frontier*. U of Texas P, 2008.

Fregosa, Rosa Linda. "The Bronze Screen Looking at Us Looking." *Bronze Screen*, U of Minnesota P, 1993.

Godless. Created by Scott Frank, Netflix, 2018.

The Good, the Bad, and the Ugly. Directed by Sergio Leone, United Artists, 1966.

Grodal, Torben. "The Experiences of Audiovisual Representation." *Realism and Reality in Film and Media*, edited by Anne Jerslev, Museum Tuscalanum Press, 2002, 67–92.

The Mandalorian. Created by Jon Favreau, Disney+, 2019.

"Mandar." Etimología de Mandar, *DeChile.net,* etimologias.dechile.net/?mandar. Accessed 1 July 2020.

"Mandar." *Merriam-Webster.com Dictionary,* Merriam-Webster, www.merriam-webster.com/dictionary /mandar. Accessed 1 July 2020.

Muñoz, José Esteban. *Disidentifications: Queers of Color and the Performance of Politics.* U of Minnesota P, 1999.

Nama, Adilifu. *Black Space.* U of Texas P, 2008.

Owen, David. *Player and Avatar: The Affective Potential of Videogames.* McFarland & Co., 2017.

Ramírez Berg, Charles. *Latino Images in Film: Stereotypes, Subversion, Resistance.* U of Texas P, 2002.

"Yo mando aquí." *Spanishdict.com,* www.spanishdict.com/translate/yo%20mando%20aqu%C3%AD. Accessed 1 July 2020.

Carlos Gabriel Kelly González

208

PART IV

#BorderlandLatinxsReclaimed

UNDOCUMEDIA

Documentary Media and the Spectacle of Enforcement

Camilla Fojas

You can watch a documentary and you can say, "well this is too bad." But at the end of the day, it's just something that you're watching on TV, and you can turn that off and you can go about your life.

AWA, *LIVING UNDOCUMENTED*, 2019

The raid on the Postville, Iowa, Agriprocessors plant by Immigration and Customs Enforcement (ICE) as part of Operation Endgame in 2008 was one of the largest immigration raids in U.S. history. On May 12, the plant was surrounded by hundreds of agents on the ground and in the air, creating an atmosphere of terror that resulted in nearly three hundred arrests, children detained in improvised holding areas, family members held for questioning, and general uncertainty about the fate of those in various forms of ICE custody. The raid was designed to be spectacular and to overwhelm the small town in a manner that would capture media attention the world over and broadcast the power of the U.S. immigration enforcement regime. The immensity and scale of the raid and its devastating impact on the local community inspired outrage and a wide-ranging media response. There are a number of documentary films about the aftermath of the Postville ICE operation, including *abUSed: The Postville Raid* (2010), *Postville: Where Cultures Collide* (2016), and *America First: The Legacy of an Immigration Raid* (2018). These documentaries exposed ICE abuses and disregard for the rule of law and due process and laid bare the machinery of deportation to the public. The documentary form of storytelling gave context, historical depth, and meaning to the individual stories of migrants targeted by the raid, marking a key moment in the history and legacy of documentary filmmaking challenges to the U.S. immigration system.

After Postville, ICE excesses became the subject of individual videos and witness accounts captured on phones and cameras and circulated digitally through YouTube, Facebook, MigraCam, and Notifica. YouTube in particular became a venue for the contestation of the immigration and deportation regime by undocumented youth, many DACAmented, who use the platform to launch "coming out" videos that tell their personal narratives about being undocumented. These media helped to amplify the Abolish ICE campaign throughout the world and most notably in the halls of the U.S. Congress. Moreover, the burgeoning of streaming platforms and digital content providers—Netflix, Amazon, and Hulu—has created an aperture for the proliferation of docuseries that combine engaging storylines with socially aware and politically oriented content for wide audiences.

The Netflix docuseries *Living Undocumented* (2019) combines the exposé of ICE with coming-out stories of undocumented individuals and families who face untold risks in this exposure. It interweaves eight stories of undocumented migrants from various parts of the world—including Mexico, Honduras, Israel, Laos, and Colombia—disabusing viewers who believe the undocumented derive only from Mexico and Central America. Many have created a life in the United States over years and sometimes decades. Each faces deportation by ICE, and the series unfolds as they wait in fear, anxiety, and hopelessness while their cases are adjudicated. The series is about the violent impact of ICE on these migrants and their families as the net of apprehension expands in the post-2016 political environment that links migration to national security. The then acting director of ICE in a 2018 report makes this association explicit: "Aliens who illegally enter the United States, or even those who overstay or otherwise violate the terms of their visas, have violated our nation's laws and can pose a threat to national security and public safety" (Homan 3). The series traces the experience of social and political accommodation to everyday terror as families and individuals living undocumented are suddenly deemed a criminal class targeted and ferreted out by agents of Homeland Security.

Living Undocumented is not part of any undocu-movements, nor does it employ undocumented artists and staff in its creative or production ensembles. It does not partake in the genre of youth media activism, from YouTube videos to Instagram media campaigns such as #UndocuMedia and other media that register ICE abuses. However, the subjects of the series are political actors and activists who take their cases to lawyers, politicians, and the media to contest their individual cases and, as a consequence, the entire immigration regime. Its modes of address and support are mainstream and popular, evinced by its production team and media platform, while the codirectors, Aaron Seidman and Anna Chai, have independent filmmaking pedigrees as Emmy award-winning documentarians. Actress and recording artist Selena Gomez, one of the executive producers, promoted the series across mainstream media outlets. She wrote a notable opinion piece for *Time* magazine about her family history of immigration and recounts her identification with the stories of the series within a narrative arc that tends toward the mythos of the American Dream; "It captured the shame, uncertainty, and fear I saw my own family struggle with. But it also captured the hope, optimism, and patriotism so many undocumented immigrants still hold in their hearts despite the hell they go through" (Gomez). Gomez is the show's media ambassador, ensuring its reach and amplifying its message.

Living Undocumented addresses an audience not acculturated to alternative messages about migrants and immigration. It provides a visual space of witness to record the impact of policy on families and the manipulations and violent conduct of ICE agents. In its function as mainstream media, it tells a story that ultimately exploits its subjects through storylines shaped by melodrama guided by simple moralism—good normative people against a bad system—that ultimately supports an immigration system that sorts migrants according to their moral value. Nonetheless, the series succeeds in documenting forms of resistance against ICE in the era of "zero tolerance" policies for a public uninitiated to the human rights and legal abuses of this agency. This show, while it uses mainstream tropes and storylines, might be read in the context of the corpus of anti-ICE narratives and critical immigration media.

Living Undocumented (2019) directly challenges the audience to consider the show as not "just something that you're watching on TV." The series begins with Awa, who, through direct address, demands that we imagine being in the place of those impacted by a repressive immigration regime. Awa's father is from Mauritania, where human rights abuses are so severe that leaving the country is the only means of survival. In the wake of her father's removal by Immigration and Customs Enforcement (ICE), she speaks directly to the camera and, as tears stream down her face, asks us to experience her situation.

> I want you to imagine waking up one morning and your father is just gone. I want you to imagine just going home and trying to tell everybody that everything will be okay when you yourself aren't even sure of that. I want you to imagine trying to sleep every night only to find yourself lying awake for hours because you can't sleep. That worry will end you and it will try to break you. You can watch a documentary and you can say, "well, this is too bad." But at the end of the day, it's just something that you're watching on TV and you can turn that off and you can go about your life.

After this powerful address, it is unlikely the audience will remain unmoved, even if they do not continue watching and follow each of the eight stories that make up the six-part series. The series is characterized by documentary media's critical principles of exposing social realities of injustice for the purpose of moving audiences to transform their ways of thinking and perhaps their social or individual realities. While Awa obliquely refers to the show as something on "television," evoking the documentary genre prevalent on TV, reality TV, the show is more accurately a docuseries on a streaming platform in a manner that distinguishes it from the more televisual genre. It follows a documentary format that explores the conditions of living under the constant threat of ICE removal and provides insight about the state of "living undocumented" under the terror of this agency. The scenes are interspersed with informational screens, initiated by the assertion that, "immediately following his inauguration, President Trump directed Immigration and Customs Enforcement (ICE) to pursue a 'zero tolerance' policy. ICE would no longer solely focus on detaining and deporting criminals. Instead, they would now target every undocumented man, woman or child." Thus, while the title, *Living Undocumented*, points to the conditions of precarity for its subjects, it is actually about the impact of the expansion of the interior enforcement of the U.S. border regime.

Immigration and Customs Enforcement (ICE) is a division of the Department of Homeland Security whose remit is internal enforcement of immigration policy. The intensifying border security regime, particularly through the expansion of Immigration and Naturalization Services' enforcement capacity through ICE, advanced the concepts of "illegality" and the "illegal alien" that forced migrants into the shadows and margins of the social order (Nevins 11). Todd Miller notes the unprecedented "scope and intensity" of ICE operations as a result of a massive influx of funding and support for interior policing as part of the expansion of the detention and deportation machinery of the DHS (214). ICE is part of the militarized approach to immigration and border control in a war on immigration in which migrants are deemed enemies of war—dramatized in a number of border media docuseries, including *Homeland Security: USA* (ABC, 2009), *Bordertown: Laredo* (A&E, 2011), *Border Wars* (National Geographic, 2010–13), *Law on the Border* (Animal Planet, 2012), and *Border Security: America's Frontline* (National Geographic, 2016–). ICE combines its warlike campaign of raids with a national and international network of detention facilities that punish detainees as criminals (Dow 535). Since the early 2000s, the agents of interior enforcement have become infamous, as in the case of the Postville raid, for organized and militarized raids on workplaces and private homes. ICE created the deportation spectacle as a dramatic scenario meant to elicit fear and awe, to dazzle onlookers with a surprise attack that leverages the symbolic power of border and immigration control. Activists and documentarians shift the field of power of the visible; they redeploy the ICE spectacle to expose its violence, manipulation, and deceit.

Documenting the Undocumented

One of the primary objectives of undocumedia is to make politically visible those migrants living in the shadows of their communities in the United States. This media reflects a history of activism for immigrant rights that began to gather force in the 1980s during an era of immigrant phobia and nativism. This activism intensified during the era of the "war on terror," which was stalling early attempts to pass legislation to grant legal status to children of undocumented parents, known as the DREAM Act, and its imperfect compromise policy of Deferred Action for Childhood Arrivals, DACA, which provides relief from deportation and work authorization for undocumented youth (Nicholls 10–12). DACA is under continual threat of being terminated, and while it remains in effect, those who receive it must renew their status every two years. The policy creates uncertainty and insecurity; it forecloses the possibility of building toward a future and places migrants in the abysmal shadow of criminality. In fact, immigration policy after 9/11 became more stringent and shifted definitively to coalesce with security initiatives so that all immigrants are framed as a security threat and undocumented migrants associated with criminality and lax border security.

Living Undocumented follows a typical trope of immigrant narratives and Hollywood film and television storylines of undocumented migrants intent on creating humanizing portraits that reveal the injustices of the immigration system and the social mood of nativism and exclusion. It is a trope inaugurated by the story of Central American migration in *El Norte* (1984), followed by other tales from the Americas, including *Mi Familia/My Family* (1995), *Under the Same Moon* (2007), and *A Better Life* (2011), along with stories of undocumented migrants from Asia, as in *Take Out* (2008) and the documentary by Filipino undocu-activist and journalist Jose Antonio Vargas, *Documented* (2013). In *Living Undocumented* the main characters are portrayed as industrious, moral, and upstanding community members deserving of but excluded from attaining all of the entitlements of citizenship and national belonging. While these depictions are not deleterious in themselves, they coincide with the divisive political sorting of migrants into normative and deserving and undeserving non-normative migrants who are readily marginalized. In this case, these portraits of "good" migrants are strategic interventions that expose ICE excesses and resist the insidious association of undocumented migrants with criminality and crime. Each case is presented against a backdrop of exclusionary policies and the daily experience of living with the unremitting threat of arbitrary removal by the state.

Living Undocumented is unique for its reimagining of undocumented experience beyond source countries in the hemisphere, adding other histories of migration that lead to the state of being undocumented in the United States. The framing of each individual and family as deserving accomplishes a strategic intervention and resistance to the overwhelming ICE directives and decisions on each case. We witness the unfolding of an increasingly restrictive and punitive process that results more often in removal and deportation or deferment than entry or permission to remain. Also, it is increasingly difficult to embody the "good" migrant category, particularly after the 1996 IIRIRA (Illegal Immigration Reform and Immigration Responsibility Act) expanded the categories of offenses deemed grounds for deportation to include fraud, forgery, and controlled substance violations. The series exposes one such instance of this in which an alleged false statement by one of the subjects when he was a child entering the United States makes him ineligible for legal status.

Documentary media exposes hitherto unseen realities with an emphasis on the documentary genre's (often contested) relationship to veracity and authenticity, from exposing a social issue to the intimate self-disclosure of the first-person confessional. The various tributaries of meaning of the documentary, from Latin *documentum*, from *doceo*, "to teach," signify the written expression that constitutes proof or evidence, much like the artifacts of national belonging that authenticate identity. The state of being undocumented means a lack of a documentary connection between a person and the state. It also means evading the web of surveillance and control into which legal documents embed its subject. These documents authenticate identity and provide certainty in a manner that renders social sorting more efficient. A lack of documents does not exclude subjects from surveillance but exposes them to an expanded net of detection since their identity is not certain. Also, these documents sustain the bureaucratic organization to which they refer; refusal or subversion of this system threatens its existence (Rule et al. 226). In their study of documentation, Rule and associates note the ease with which documents might be obtained fraudulently and thus undermine the credence placed in them. The documentaries about the undocumented legitimate migrant stories and justify their right to migrate in a manner that undermines a system based on the hegemony of documentation as verification of legal claims—rather than other processes of establishing identity and other matrices of membership and inclusion. The undocumented migrant is an existential threat to the state and treated with violence and force as an enemy combatant.

Those who appear in the United States without the proper documentation or with false documentation undermine the global border regime premised on identity verification as an alibi to maintain the global inequities of racial capitalism. Writer and activist Harsha Walia describes how the global border regime is an outcome of the intersecting logics of security and racial capitalism through four "overlapping and concurrent structurings":

> First, the mass displacement of impoverished and colonized communities resulting from asymmetrical relations of global power, and the simultaneous securitization of the border against those migrants whom capitalism and empire have displaced; second, the criminalization of migration with severe punishment and discipline of those deemed "alien" or "illegal"; third, the entrenchment of a racialized hierarchy of citizenship by arbitrating who legitimately constitutes the nation-state; and fourth, the state-mediated exploitation of migrant labor, akin to conditions of slavery and servitude, by capitalist interests. (5)

Border imperialism refers to modes of governance in which the bounded nation, defined by its exclusions, operates in conjunction with the dictates of global capitalism to sustain the inequity between the Global North, in this case the United States, and the Global South, including most of the nations represented in each story of undocumented migration in the series. Critical media about migration critiques the larger institutional frame of migration, particularly the U.S. role in creating the conditions that lead to forced mobility and economic exile. This series is critical of aspects of the immigration regime, particularly of ICE, but not of the imperial chauvinism of Washington in relation to the Global South. Nor does it fully disabuse audiences of the allure of the capitalist myth of the "American Dream" that draws each migrant to the United States. The "good" migrant is enterprising, hard-working, and enjoys financial success, while the "bad" migrant must repent and align with the moral values of the good and law-abiding citizen. For instance, Vinny from Laos lost his permanent residency status due to a drug conviction and is slated for deportation, yet he demonstrates—by religious conviction, family values, and community involvement—that he has fully repented, in a juridical and moral sense, and is framed as deserving of our hope that ICE will permit him to remain. Moreover, the portrait of the good industrious migrant seeking fulfillment of the American Dream serves other aims: it offsets the larger threat to the very system of global capital that a lack of documentation represents.

The series reveals the expansion of the surveillance state in which immigration is deemed a security issue to justify foreclosure of any path to legalization. In each case, what had been routine check-ins with ICE have become automatic deportations under an intensified version of "zero tolerance" policy. The drama of each story ensues from the ongoing threat of deportation and from the hope, most often thwarted, that there might be an outcome that allows each petitioner to remain. ICE is framed as a shadowy and omnipotent threat with the power to destroy lives. It stands in for the entire immigration system, not just its enforcement arm. It is experienced through its agents and the complex and ubiquitous network of nondescript ICE facilities—these unassuming buildings add to their menace as sites that could be anywhere and appear from nowhere.

While the series bears few activist credentials linking it to undocumented politics, it furnishes a storyline punctuated with scenes that expose the violence, extra-legal manipulations, duplicity, and social engineering of ICE agents. We are not "just watching" these events on TV; we are witnessing illegal activity and civil rights violations take place.

The series begins by foregrounding the storyline that furnishes the primal scene of the era of extra-legal "zero tolerance" immigration enforcement. The opening monologue in which Awa describes the feeling of being separated from her father is voiced against the image of a man walking hand in hand with a child, which initiates a montage of the various subjects in the series, many in the moment when they face separation from their families. The image of a man and his child is our first introduction to Luis, who arrived undocumented from Honduras and works in the construction industry, having participated in the building of major aspects of U.S. infrastructure, including schools of every kind, parking lots, and even a jail. The montage is followed by an intertitle about the function of ICE and the expansion of its targeting to all undocumented migrants, not just, as was its original remit, those who have committed crimes. Moreover, ICE operates in murky legal territory, partly as a consequence of what the American Civil Liberties Union calls the hundred-mile Constitution-free zone that characterizes the border region, where the Fourth Amendment protections against warrantless searches are lifted and where racial profiling is standard practice and a principle of the Secure Communities program. The latter marks the integration of ICE with the Department of Justice and local law enforcement through information-sharing protocols; this means that a simple traffic stop may result in arrest, detention, and deportation. This is how the story of Luis and his partner Kenia and their son, Noah, begins, with a simple traffic stop. Kenia, though five months pregnant, is held in detention, and Noah, a toddler, remains with Luis as they await a decision on her case. Their story contains the most spectacular and egregious ICE violence and violations, catching the attention of immigration lawyers, activists, and the news media, all of whom appear at the scene of the early morning surrender of Noah, who will be deported with his mother.

The immigration attorneys, Andrea Martínez and Megan Galicia, took Kenia's case as an unprecedented instance of detention of a pregnant woman, a sign of an inhumane change in policy. The scene of reunification of Kenia with her son is fraught with risk; if Luis enters any ICE facility, he could be detained. According to the producers, "ICE agreed that Luis could hand off Noah outside the facility and briefly unite with Kenia." This accords with the admission by agents to the lawyer, Martínez, that they were too understaffed to pursue an arrest. Yet this reassurance is just a ruse. With the news media, the series camera crew, and immigrant rights activists as witnesses, the ICE agents attempt to lure Luis into the lobby of the detention center so "they can personally have their time as a family together." The violence in this scene is initially subtle, apparent in the mingling of the forces of coercion and desire. As the lawyers return to Luis in the parking lot, one of the agents accompanies them and reiterates they he does not "intend" to detain Luis but that he is "not here to negotiate custody." He suddenly takes Luis's arm and firmly directs him into the building, the promise of reunification of Kenia on the horizon. As they remove and detain him, Martínez tries to block them and is beaten back by the agent and suffers a broken foot and lacerations on her leg. The lawyers, as proxies for the audience, are shocked at the false lure, outright duplicity, violent display, and disregard for the welfare of the child and his expectant mother. This scene begins unfolding in the first episode and establishes expectations about how ICE operates, as a deceitful and manipulative agency that functions according to the ever-changing principles of zero tolerance policies. Luis, against ICE testaments to the contrary, is arrested and detained for almost two months.

The second installment of the series, in which Luis's detention unfolds, is appropriately titled "The World Is Watching," a message drawn from one of the activist placards. The episode follows the scene of the ICE deception as it reaches its dark denouement, revealing the violent predations of ICE operations. This episode offers the first instance of the obscene reality of the border regime as it extends deep into the interior of the nation and becomes ever more exclusionary, defaulting to automatic detention and deportation. The filmmakers secure an interview with a former ICE attorney, Patricia M. Corrales, who worked on the front lines of the immigration regime under the administrations of former presidents Bill Clinton, George W. Bush, and Barack Obama. She notes that the current administration is characterized by the intensification of consequence in immigration matters, notable in the removal of the role of "discretion": "I can tell you as a matter of my seventeen years of experience working with the Department of Homeland Security, I was proud of the work I did because there was discretion. There was the ability to decide whether or not we were really going to enforce law against this individual who's paid their taxes for 15 years, who has three U.S. citizen children." Under the new enforcement regime, there is no nuance or humane application of the rule of law; everyone without papers is treated with "zero tolerance," subject to detention and deportation.

The condition of statelessness, deprivation of rights, and the constant threat of removal is evident across all of the cases in the docuseries, while Luis's case strikingly exemplifies ICE manipulations and coercive tactics of expulsion from the United States. The state of "living undocumented" is one of the unknown, a perpetual and anxious present, an inability to plan for a future, and constant threat of upheaval and expulsion. The scene in which ICE compels Luis to enter the detention center with the false promise of family unity captures the violent coercion of the new border regime, the mingling of forces that impel, persuade, and address the desire for cohesion.

While the series does the work of documentary, particularly its critical aim of exposing contemporary issues that demand critical attention, it presents engaging storylines that create tension as each story builds toward the official determination about deportation in each case. Each outcome is predetermined by the political climate and nativist principles animating the rule of law; yet we, the audience and the immigrants and their families, hope against hope that the events will conclude otherwise. This is the crux of the tragedy of each story, that we are witnesses to stories fated to end badly, with deportation or the deferral of a decision that leaves deportation an ever-present threat. Each of the cases ends with either a deferred ICE determination and continued "check-ins," pending decisions on asylum claims, or outright forced or willing deportation.

Each of the cases in the series benefits from media visibility and political attention from lawyers, activists, and politicians. Rebecca Schreiber, in her analysis of documentary accounts of undocumented activists, describes this media framing as counter-visibility, or a strategy that shields activists from the state, from detention and deportation (38). Yet her work, published in 2018, begins to account for but cannot anticipate the unimaginable: the increasing brutality, arbitrary use of power, illegal actions, and inhumanity of ICE, in which the protective shield of media visibility vanishes. All of the cases of the program, on their own and by virtue of the series, are politically visible, and almost all of the petitioners must leave, are deported, or remain under the threat of deportation.

While the Department of Homeland Security deploys ICE in deportation campaigns to publicize its work and create a spectacle of deterrence, *Living Undocumented* and other forms of undocumedia show how the same scenario might be reframed to expose the brutality and inhumanity of the immigration enforcement regime. The series captures the deployment of the "spectacle" against ICE. In response to a lawsuit filed by the ACLU on behalf of Andrea Martinez that charges ICE with the use of excessive force, violation of her Fourth Amendment rights, assault, battery, false arrest, false imprisonment, and infliction of emotional distress, U.S. Attorney Timothy A. Garrison claimed that "in light of circumstances created by more than 30 people who came to a routine law enforcement operation at 3 a.m. for the purpose of making a spectacle, the officer's actions were justified in order to secure and control access to the ICE office entrance from unauthorized persons" (qtd. in Fernandez). Martinez argues that the case is about protecting civil rights and the consequences of ceding the ground of representation to the state: "We really believe that this is a matter of principle and it's a matter of not letting ICE agents get away with hurting people and making sure these individuals are held responsible. My opinion differs from the U.S. attorney. People have a right to peacefully protest in public spaces, and there's no excuse for violence on the part of law enforcement just because they don't know what to do when they're being filmed" (qtd. in Fernandez). In ICE deportation dramas, they maintain control of the visual and political discourse. This is among the reasons that the filmmakers of *Living Undocumented* declined to incorporate representatives from ICE, since, as with all filming of state agencies, the state reserves editorial control over the content and framing of the story.

One of the core objectives of undocumedia is to question the role and function of the current regime of immigration enforcement in order to dismantle and abolish it. The docuseries and less mainstream forms of undocumedia serve as the cultural arm of efforts to unsettle, disrupt, and dismantle the entire border security complex. ICE describes those it targets as "removable" aliens within an ever-wider net of apprehension and ongoing threat of detention. Detention is incarceration, a form of terrorizing punishment as the site of the unknown, of the indefinite stay, and uncertain future in which deportation is the only known variable. The uncertainty of "living undocumented" breeds fear, fear of detection and the abandonment to insecurity rendered more dangerous after the pandemic. Undocumented activists decry the politics of fear and exploitation and resist by refusing to be afraid. Visibility through the exposure of their stories enables this resistance and becomes prolegomena to political power. The stories in *Living Undocumented* end badly with disrupted lives and uncertain futures. Their difficult and painful individual tragedies are documented for mainstream national and global audiences unacculturated to the violent deportation machinations of ICE. Their stories disrupt the nativist politics circulating in the hemisphere and the world and offer some hope that audiences will not turn away from ICE abuses as "just something . . . on TV" and instead help change the political fate of the most vulnerable among us.

Works Cited

Dow, Mark. "Designed to Punish: Immigration Detention and Deportation." *Social Research*, vol. 74, no. 2, 2007, pp. 533–46.

Fernandez, Maria Elena. "Lawyer from Netflix's *Living Undocumented* Files ACLU Lawsuit Against ICE." *Vulture*, 10 Oct 2019, www.vulture.com/2019/10/living-undocumented-lawsuit-ice-andrea -martinez.html.

Gomez, Selena. "I Feel Afraid for My Country." *Time*, 1 Oct. 2019, time.com/5690070/selena-gomez -americas-immigration-crisis/.

Homan, Thomas. "Statement of Thomas D. Homan, Acting Director, U.S. Immigration and Customs Enforcement, Department of Homeland Security, Regarding the Fiscal Year 2018 President's Budget Request," 13 June 2017, p. 3.

Living Undocumented. Directed by Aaron Seidman and Anna Chai. Netflix, 2019.

Miller, Todd. *Border Patrol Nation: Dispatches from the Frontlines of Homeland Security*. City Lights, 2014.

Nevins, Joseph. *Operation Gatekeeper: The Rise of the "Illegal Alien" and the Making of the U.S.-Mexico Boundary*. Routledge, 2002.

Nicholls, Walter J. *The Dreamers: How the Undocumented Youth Movement Transformed the Immigration Rights Debate*. Stanford UP, 2013.

Rule, James B., et al. "Documentary, Identification, and Mass Surveillance in the United States." *Social Problems*, vol. 31, no. 2, 1983, pp. 222–34.

Schreiber, Rebecca. *The Undocumented Everyday: Migrant Lives and the Politics of Visibility*. U of Minnesota P, 2018.

Walia, Harsha. *Undoing Border Imperialism*. AK Press, 2013.

PARTY OF FIVE REBOOT

The Denaturalization of Undocumented Latinx Suffering

Stacey Alex

This chapter analyzes recent developments in the TV representation of undocumented Latinx communities. It offers an overview of changes to immigration policy that make it particularly urgent that undocumented characters be more complex and that they have more substantial roles. Many undocumented characters are limited to one episode and/or included only to highlight the positive attributes of main characters, who are typically white citizens. The 2020 Freeform reboot of *Party of Five* is unique in that its main characters are undocumented and the plot revolves around their legal status. While the original 1994 drama is a white-centered story, I argue that the 2020 version is a standout contribution to undocumented Latinx narratives because it offers complex undocumented characters, accurately portrays immigration policy, and challenges the naturalization of undocumented immigrant suffering and criminalization. In the original series, the Salinger children must come together after their parents are killed in a car accident caused by a drunk driver. In the new series, the Acosta parents are alive but deported to Mexico. The show makes a concerted effort to underscore how the Acosta family's struggles stem from a government-made disaster resulting from a broken immigration system and collective inaction.

Familiar Yet New

Critical observers may have cause for concern in the opening scene of the series, which shows the oldest Acosta child, Emilio Acosta, played by Brandon Larracuente, as a Latin lover stereotype. As the lead singer whose audience awaits him and whose bandmate begs him to start the show, he opts to stall a few more moments to continue kissing a fan backstage whose name he does not know. While this characterization of a Latino character could be read as othering, the show's creators characterized each Acosta child to mirror the original Salinger children. The oldest character in the original series, Charlie Salinger, played by Matthew Fox, was also a womanizer. While this may not completely erase the Latin lover problem, the context at least shows that these qualities are not only attributed to Latinx culture. Moreover, the setup underscores Emilio's transformation. The end of the pilot episode returns to Emilio's guitar, but rather than use it to win over hearts, he sings a lullaby to his baby brother after their parents have been deported: "si me necesitarás, yo vendría por ti, cruzaría el mar para aliviar tu dolor" ("Pilot"). This highlights the shift from his lack of romantic commitment to his newly made promise to help raise his younger siblings.

Amy Lippman, cocreator of both the original show and the reboot with Christopher Keyser, explains that they preserved the character traits that served them well in the original. While the oldest brother struggles with losing his independence, the oldest girl, Lucía Acosta, played by Emily Tosta, is a talented student who rejects traditional maternal responsibilities such as domestic chores. The second eldest brother, Beto Acosta, played by Niko Guardado, struggles in school but feels more comfortable as a caregiver to his younger siblings. The youngest sister, Valentina Acosta, played by Elle Paris Legaspi, is resourceful, and the youngest, Rafael Acosta, is a one-year-old. Overlaying Latinx characters onto the white originals may at first glance appear limiting. However, each Latinx character also has their own characteristics and is differentiated from the original by their unique circumstances and identities. While the series centers on the family's mixed immigration status, the characters are not restricted only to this issue.

The four older Acosta children's characters are developed through complex intersections of gender, sexuality, socioeconomic class, language, and immigration status. Moreover, the show highlights their agency. Tragedy is not just happening to them; they actively navigate multiple oppressions. For example, Valentina insists they take the baby, Rafa, to the emergency room after he shows various signs of sickness. They discover he was exposed to lead poisoning from a secondhand crib at his daycare ("Rafa"). This detail underscores how families of low socioeconomic status and families of color are disproportionately affected by environmental hazards. As they feel helpless for having not realized sooner, they are also portrayed as determined to find the source of the problem. When Valentina takes on the name "Amanda Davis," the girl that her mother nannies in Mexico, her siblings worry about her mental health and brainstorm ways to support her. When Beto suggests there must be doctors who specialize in this kind of identity crisis, Lucía rebuffs the idea: "You think a lot of brown people who can't afford lawyers to help them avoid deportation are working through their emotional issues in therapy?" ("Dos y Dos"). Here, the show marks the lack of mental health resources for undocumented communities while also underscoring the children's support for one another.

In another example highlighting agency and intersectionality, Lucía challenges unfair policies at school in echo of her disillusionment with immigration policy. When she refuses to retake a test because other students cheated, she defies the teacher, "Your rules are full of shit" ("Pilot"). Lucía later joins an immigrant activist organization and helps arrange a fundraiser for immigrant families facing deportation at the Acosta family's restaurant. At the same time, she struggles against heteronormativity and her family's expectations as she begins to fully realize her feelings for a female activist leader. Her friendship with an undocumented transgender man, Matthew, contextualizes Lucía's experiences as potentially part of a LGBTQIA+ community. They also belong to the same church, highlighting her faith-based community. At first, Matthew rejects her friendship because she cannot understand what it means to have no family support. Matthew later helps Lucía understand the complexities of intersectionality since he could have applied for DACA but refused to retake his original female name on his birth certificate.

Secondary characters like Matthew bring multiple privileges into view and invite the audience to consider their own positionalities. While Matthew underscores Lucía's privilege as a cisgender citizen with a supportive family, other minor characters reflect the Acosta family's disadvantages and the taboo they continue to face as a mixed-status family. In one case, Emilio and Beto wait in the pediatrician's office across from a white mother. The woman assumes they are a homosexual couple and asks how they selected or combined their sperm to produce baby Rafa. She seems to congratulate herself for being so liberally open-minded while asking such an invasive question. When Emilio and Beto explain they are Rafa's brothers, she applauds them for being so involved, implying that her own young adult daughter should be so responsible. However, when they clarify that Emilio is now Rafa's guardian because their parents were deported, the woman sinks back in her chair to disengage with them physically and emotionally. Beto smirks and Emilio sighs; they understand that white left-leaning liberals can pick and choose who deserves to be human; supporting LGBTQIA+ rights is trending, but undocumented rights is not.

Another minor character, Beto's physics teacher, refuses Lucía's request to make an exception for Beto when he fails the class because of stress at home. The teacher, who is herself Latina, invokes "law and order" rhetoric to argue that her parents' decisions have consequences and "it makes things worse for the rest of us who have to prove over and over again that we have the right to be here" ("Margin of Error"). This conflict draws attention to the diversity of Latinx identity politics and the widespread resentment toward undocumented communities. This episode's title, "Margin of Error," points to Lucía's realization that there will be no allowances made for them. They are not allowed to make the same kinds of mistakes as privileged children born to citizen parents. Beto feels this mercilessness for himself when he is caught kissing his future love interest, Ella Barnett, the white daughter of a man who hired them to cater a party and perform *mexicanidad* by wearing brightly colored ponchos. Emilio tries to excuse Beto as just having made a mistake, but the man insists that he "drop him off at whatever corner he picked him up" ("Authentic Mexican"). Emilio defends his brother, but the scene reveals how any brown Latinx body can be assumed to be undocumented and undeserving of basic dignities.

It is in the face of these hostilities that the 2020 reboot makes a standout contribution. Cocreator Amy Lippman endeavors to distinguish their motivation for remaking the show from the recent reboot trend by claiming that the central themes of the original, youth trying to remain a family without their parents, has become a daily headline through family separation. She explains: "So our interest in reviving the series didn't come about because we wanted to join this wave of 'How can we take a successful series and repurpose it?' We saw an opportunity in the zeitgeist. The story we told 25 years ago was no longer fictional; it was happening every day around the country. That seemed to be a reason [for a reboot]. And it seemed in some ways a much more urgent story to be told" (Sarner). Of course, this kind of violence was commonplace before the Trump administration's "zero-tolerance" policy. However, this new policy constituted a glaring shift: adult border crossing was prosecuted a hundred percent without exception for those seeking asylum or accompanied by minors, and therefore justified the separation of children from their parents.

Immigration Policy: A Brief History

Long before the Trump administration's family separation policy, deportation separated families. The Clinton administration begin a pilot program for mass deportations during Operation Gatekeeper in California (1994). Patrisia Macías-Rojas reveals how the immigration debate was shaped by the War on Crime's failed mass incarceration policies. In "Immigration and the War on Crime," she argues that the crime politics of both the GOP and Democratic Party under the Reagan and Clinton administrations led to criminal provisions of the 1996 Illegal Immigration Reform and Immigrant Responsibility Act that restructured it and provided resources needed for immigration enforcement to detain and deport a broad range of immigrants beyond those with convictions. Many of these policies to criminalize migrants would then be used nationwide by the Bush administration and the newly formed Department of Homeland Security's post-9/11 War on Terrorism. Immigration and Naturalization Services (INS) became three separate entities, including Immigration and Customs Enforcement (ICE), in 2003. The continued shift of focus from immigrants who had committed violent crimes to immigrant workers meant that massive workplace raids were used to justify a rapid growth of the enforcement budget. Fueled by a fear of terrorist threats, the continued political popularity of nativism, and economic conditions, workers who previously had not been the focus of surveillance, detention, and deportation were criminalized and targeted as committing identity fraud to meet quotas (Camayd-Freixas). The Obama administration, perhaps in part to bolster support for DREAMers and a pathway to citizenship for youth that would never materialize, continued a tough deportation regime promoted by earlier administrations.

The consequences of deportation on families are documented across journalistic and artistic forms. Luis Argueta's documentary *abUSed: The Postville Raid* (2011), for example, exposes the traumatization of children following the Postville, Iowa, ICE raid of 2008, the largest workplace raid of its time, detaining nearly four hundred individuals. Prominent public figures have also catalyzed the issue into popular culture contexts by sharing their own experiences as formerly undocumented or the children of undocumented parents. One example is *Orange Is the New Black* and *Jane the Virgin* actress Diane Guerrero, who writes in her memoir *In the Country We Love: My Family Divided* (2016) that no one from the government ever checked on her well-being as a fourteen-year-old after her parents were deported.

Undocumented communities have been waiting quite some time for any substantial change to immigration policy. The last major shift was the Immigration Reform and Control Act (IRCA) passed by the Reagan administration in 1986. It provided amnesty for nearly 2.7 million immigrants but failed to help those who arrived after 1982 (Plumer). While some scholars, advocates, and artists call for reform, others argue that reform is simply not enough to undo the violence of an unjust and racist system that must be dismantled altogether. Yet, grassroots organizing for immigration reform gained enormous momentum during nationwide protests beginning in 2006. Latinx politics scholar Cristina Beltrán argues in her book *The Trouble with Unity* that this movement constitutes world-building as described by Hannah Arendt and, therefore, points to a new undocumented subjectivity that can be wielded in the public eye but should not be used to insist on pan-Latino uniformity and solidarity.

In tandem with the intensified criminalization of undocumented communities through immigration policy, dehumanizing TV representations of Latinx immigrants are common along with a lack of TV portrayals to counter contemporary anti-immigrant rhetoric. TV news has experienced some pushback. For example, the public pressure of the "Basta Dobbs" campaign organized by political strategist Roberto Lovato appeared to contribute to the retirement of Lou Dobbs. On the CNN show *Lou Dobbs Tonight*, Dobbs thrived on racist rhetoric, such as pathologizing Mexican immigrants as spreading leprosy and inaccurately citing data in 2005. This rhetoric was accompanied by a steady rise in hate crimes against Latinx individuals in the United States that spiked in 2008 (Negrón-Muntaner et al.).

While apparently running counter to demonizing caricatures, narratives that focus on youth to support the right of DREAMers to remain in the United States often run the risk of reinforcing liberal rhetoric that implies parents are to blame. For example, President Obama defended the Deferred Action for Childhood Arrivals (DACA) program by claiming that its recipients were here "at no fault of their own" (Obama). In contrast, *Party of Five* (2020) stages its undocumented parents, Gloria and Javier (played by Fernanda Urrejola and Bruno Bichir), as central characters. The audience is invited to empathize with their decisions and tough adjustment to guiding their children only over videoconferencing. While the mother is conflicted, they originally determined all the children should stay in the United States to avoid depriving the youngest of the privileges of U.S. citizenship and of being with one another. However, they are eventually persuaded by Beto that Valentina and Rafa need to stay with them in Mexico. The parents' decision-making process is portrayed as a complex struggle rather than static or unthinking. While *Party of Five* is to be commended for underlining the agency of undocumented characters, many TV representations fail to move beyond overly simple resolutions to undocumented status, promoting the exceptionalism of undocumented youth, or using their stories to heroize non-Latinx characters.

Problems with Representation: White Saviors and Incredible Escapes

Relatively few TV shows have been centered on undocumented characters or the issue of undocumented immigration status. One exception is the 1987 ABC sitcom *I Married Dora*, about a man who marries his housekeeper to prevent her deportation. Of course, a sham marriage is far from representative of most undocumented experiences in the United States. The show was also cancelled only halfway through its first season. A 2019 Netflix original docuseries directed by Aaron Saidman and Anna Chai, *Living Undocumented*, provides an important contribution by following eight undocumented individuals along with immigration attorneys to expose the growing humanitarian crisis. Two recent examples of positive representations in Latinx-based fictional shows are the dramedy *Jane the Virgin* and sitcom *One Day at a Time*.

In the first season of *Jane the Virgin* (2014–19), it is revealed that Jane's grandmother, Alba Villanueva, is undocumented, as she immigrated from Venezuela without a visa. This is the reason that Jane cannot pursue a lawsuit for being artificially inseminated by mistake. Later in the first season, Alba faces medical repatriation when she falls into a coma and the doctor informs the family that the hospital will be calling ICE to have her deported to Venezuela since she does not have insurance. Jane's first love, Detective Michael Cordero, halts the deportation by telling ICE he needs Alba as a witness for a Miami Police Department case ("Chapter 10"). Even more unbelievably, considering the risk of applying for those already flagged by ICE, Alba attains a green card in season 2 ("Chapter 30"). In season 3, filmed during the first year of the Trump administration, Alba is moved to attend an immigrant rights march after reading about ICE raids and witnessing a white customer tell someone to speak English in the store where she works. She later realizes her romantic interest, Jorge, is undocumented after he refuses to join her at the march ("Chapter 61"). As in *I Married Dora*, the characters resort to a sham marriage to secure Jorge's green card, but ultimately fall in love. While the resolutions to both Alba and Jorge's undocumented status are far-fetched, even for a telenovela, the show does repeatedly return to the issue and create characters struggling against an unjust immigration system. One of the show's narrative devices, displaying texts and hashtags to relay background information and tone, calls audiences to action by announcing "#immigrationreform" in relation to Alba's potential deportation ("Chapter 10") and "#vote #vote #vote" when Alba's lawyer consults on her green card application and tells her that immigration law is constantly changing ("Chapter 27").

Like *Jane the Virgin*, *One Day at a Time* (2017–20) returns to the issue of immigration over several episodes. A remake of the 1974–85 original series, the new sitcom centers on three generations of the Cuban American Alvarez family. High school student Elena Alvarez reveals that her best friend Carmen has been spending more time at their home because her parents were deported. Elena's mother, Penelope (Justina Machado), and grandmother, Lydia (Rita Moreno), are supportive and confirm Elena's belief that their family helps others. Penelope decides Carmen should eventually move to Austin—not for lack of caring, but to respect the parents' wishes that she live with her brother. Although the undocumented parents never make it on screen, Carmen justifies their decision by affirming they did nothing wrong. Her defense relies on her parents both working two jobs and her academic achievements, which may run the risk of reinforcing exceptionalism and justifying the exclusion of less-than-ideal immigrants. However, the show does manage to confront the injustice of deportation. When Elena expresses disbelief that the government sent Carmen's parents "home," Penelope replies,

"They didn't send them home. They sent them away" ("Strays"). Here, the show rejects the premise that undocumented individuals do not belong in U.S. society. Rather than drop the character altogether, which is often the case in other shows, Carmen appears in two more episodes later in the first season to show the continuation of their friendship and the impact on the Alvarez family.

Although its undocumented character is Filipino and not Latinx, America Ferrera's sitcom *Superstore* (2015–21) about workers at a big-box store also merits attention. Crucially, it takes its time developing the intersectionality of its gay, Asian, undocumented character, Mateo. Like many undocumented individuals who arrive as children and do not discover their status until later in life, and in parallel with journalist Jose Antonio Vargas's experience, Mateo does not realize he is undocumented until a coworker suggests his paperwork is fraudulent during the premiere of season 2. The show consulted with Vargas through Define American, a nonprofit dedicated to using media to humanize immigrants. Mateo is detained by ICE during a raid prompted by the store to stop unionization at the end of season 4 and is out on bond during season 5 while he awaits deportation proceedings. Mateo's ankle bracelet is removed in season 6, but he continues to worry that he will be deported if he loses his job. These details confront the violent nature of the immigration system; even if immigrants can avoid deportation, they may face years of uncertainty and fear about the future of their immigration status. *Superstore* is commendable for doing its research and committing multiple episodes to the issue.

While there are exceptions that strive to humanize and debunk myths about migration, one common characteristic of undocumented TV characters and plots revolving around undocumented status is that they are short-lived, appearing for only one episode, or are used to underscore positive aspects of more central, non-Latinx characters. One early precursor to undocumented characters that follows this pattern is played by the dimpled thirteen-year-old Mario Lopez, who plays Dorothy's student in *The Golden Girls* episode "Dorothy's Prized Pupil" in 1987. Dorothy unknowingly outs her student to Immigration and Naturalization Services (INS) by entering his essay in a contest. Dorothy, despite being to blame for her ignorance and naivete about her student's everyday reality, is portrayed as a fearless advocate as she promises Mario's character to look for legal solutions to his problem. He is deported anyway, even after Dorothy assures him that telling the truth is always the right answer.

In a clip for *Today.com*, Mario Lopez reflects on the experience and says that he was the "original Elián González," because his character was deported. González was a Cuban child whose mother died at sea as they attempted to cross the Caribbean Sea to the United States. González was the focus of a months-long media saga about the custody battle between his late mother's family waiting for him in the United States and his father's family back in Cuba. This comparison is apt because it reveals the individualized and sensationalized nature of media portrayals of undocumented suffering. Roberto Suro argues that this kind of TV news coverage erases the systemic and racialized oppression behind immigration policy that affects millions of individuals (5). The end of the episode exposes the real problem: Dorothy's pain at having lost her student becomes the focus, while Mario's character is never mentioned in any future episode.

Meredith Grey (Ellen Pompeo) of *Grey's Anatomy* is also characterized as a heroic defender of vulnerable undocumented Latinx bodies. The fourteenth season of the show features Dr. Sam Bello (Jeanine Mason), who is revealed to be Salvadoran and works at Grey Sloan hospital under the Deferred Action for Childhood Arrivals (DACA) program. Although she appears in several episodes as the romantic interest of Dr. Andrew DeLuca, viewers are not made aware of her status until the character's last episode ("Beautiful Dreamer"). Like *The Golden Girls*, *Grey's Anatomy* banks on liberal rhetoric that focuses on innocence and implicitly blames parents as a defense strategy. When an ICE officer shows up to question Sam, she tells her colleagues that a friend who arrived as a two-year-old was just deported to Mexico and does not even speak Spanish.

While bringing awareness to the very real possibility that ICE can deport despite DACA protections, such as in the case of Juan Manuel Montes in 2017 (Gomez and Agren), this portrayal also raises the question: Do older, Spanish-speaking undocumented individuals deserve to be deported because they do not qualify for DACA? Proponents of DACA also point to the professional qualities of recipients, particularly their contributions to the medical field during the COVID-19 crisis. Undocumented writers such as Karla Cornejo Villavicencio reject this capitalistic assignment of value that treats undocumented individuals as "brown bodies made to labor" (14) and euphemizes them as "undocumented workers," "as if there was something uncouth about being just an undocumented person standing with your hands clasped together or at your sides" (13). Meredith's opening monologue suggests that Sam's fifteen years of training to become a surgeon will be wasted, while Sam lists her academic accomplishments as reasons why she should not have to change her identity. Both run the risk of reinforcing the immigrant-as-economic-asset mindset that justifies the exclusion of "less valuable" immigrants.

Meredith Grey is characterized as righteous when she tells Sam to take the moral and ethical high ground: "You can't run. Listen, I'm all for driving the getaway car, but right now, they are treating you like someone who snuck into this country in the trunk of a car. Don't become what they're trying to make you. If you run, you're a criminal. If you're a criminal, you could never practice medicine again. Do not give them that" ("Beautiful Dreamer"). Although the show consulted with the organization Define American, as did *Superstore*, this monologue misses the mark by buying into criminalizing rhetoric. Like Dorothy, Meredith conforms to the rules of an unjust system. She is heroized for finding Sam a job with Cristina Yang in Switzerland without standing up to oppressive forces that rip Sam from her home. Furthermore, this speech criminalizes the many who *did* cross the border in the trunk of a car without acknowledging the complex history of U.S. imperialism and foreign policy that drives this migration.

While time does not allow for a more extensive list of examples, the final two offered here are CBS courtroom shows that incorporate undocumented immigration to underscore the heroic advocacy of its privileged protagonists. The first, *The Good Fight*, is like *Superstore* in that the undocumented character is not Latinx and does not know he is undocumented until adulthood. The Nigerian-born character Jay discovers his status only when he is pulled over by federal authorities looking to arrest the witness that he is transporting for a case he is working as legal investigator. Although the issue is limited to one episode and does focus on the heroism of non-Latinx women who team up to save Jay from deportation, the show is well crafted to underscore tension between federalism and the asylum policies of individual cities, as well as the unjust nature of immigration policy. Jay is saved by a deus ex machina ending in which his legal team convinces an immigration judge that Jay's comic art merits him an EB-1 "Einstein" visa ("Day 485"). While this is hardly representative of most undocumented experiences, the show challenges the reasons Melania Trump was given such a visa for her modeling career and points to the way that immigration policy has always favored white, privileged groups (Agard).

A second recent CBS courthouse show, *All Rise*, limits its attention to undocumented status to just one episode and uses the love shared between an imprisoned undocumented Nicaraguan activist and his girlfriend to underscore the budding romance between two recurring characters, lawyer Emily Lopez and Deputy Sherriff Luke Watkins. However, it also offers a nuanced look at Black and Latinx relations as Latino ICE officer Sal Soto and Black judge Lola Carmichael compare their complicity within institutions that continue to oppress their own people. Carmichael's character invites audiences to consider how TV representation can shift public perception by revealing her framed photo of Nyota Uhura, the first Black character from the original *Star Trek*, and sharing how that character made her feel she could be anyone ("Long Day's Journey into ICE"). By recognizing the importance of racial and ethnic representation in pop culture, *All Rise* maintains that un-documented characters are crucially needed to shape public attitudes, even if their stories are mediated by those in privileged positions.

Immigration Consultation

Party of Five breaks the molds by focusing on the issue of immigration and undocumented characters throughout the series. A second major achieve-ment was to have writers work with an immigration consultant across ep-isodes to make sure that the plot and dialogue rang true to contemporary experiences within shifting immigration policies. The show hired Edgar Campos to provide this perspective and a realistic portrayal of what would and would not happen in the Boyle Heights neighborhood of L.A. Although he is not an immigration attorney himself, he conferred with attorneys, has various experiences in community leadership positions such as a campaign manager for several local elections, was a policy researcher for the Los Ange-les Unified School District, and worked with My Brother's Keeper and Cali-fornians for Justice. In my conversation with Campos, it was clear that he felt a deep sense of responsibility to get the details right.

One of Campos's primary concerns was that legal proceedings and de-tention in the show would not misrepresent the current climate in Los Ange-les. As L.A. was a sanctuary city, it was important to Campos that the plot did not unduly aggravate everyday uncertainty and the fear that undocumented immigrants walk with daily. For example, he felt that the Netflix original *Gentefied* (2020), which also takes place in Boyle Heights, was problematic in that the father of the family, Casimiro Morales, is arrested by ICE at the end of the season 1 finale. Since Casimiro's only trouble with the law was a mis-demeanor for urinating in public, this could lead undocumented immigrants to believe that the Los Angeles Police Department would cooperate with ICE. Campos made a number of recommendations to make sure legal details were accurate, such as the appearance of an administrative warrant and confirming that a detention center wouldn't have a commissary, leaving Javier without access to a new razor. Campos helped writers navigate immigrant activist Sully's interactions with ICE officials and the workers' mixed reactions at the restaurant raid, since their statuses would most likely be heterogenous. He also warned writers about potential cultural and racial issues, such as the insulting tone of "mock Spanish" and the risk of having too many white allies create a white savior dynamic (Campos). These efforts combined constitute a show striving to do justice to the representation of undocumented expe-riences as well as resist the popular notion that undocumented suffering is unavoidable.

Challenge to Naturalization of Immigrant Suffering

Migrant suffering is often made to seem natural across politics, pop culture, and the media. Even sympathetic portrayals of migrant suffering can reinforce this naturalization. In her essay "Poor Enrique, Poor María," theater scholar Ana Elena Puga argues that migrant melodramas make suffering appear inevitable through what she calls a political economy of suffering, or the active trading of migrant suffering as a commodity in publishing/film and as currency for empathy, sympathy, or solidarity (228). Popular migrant narratives such as Sonia Nazario's *Enrique's Journey* allow readers to be unreflective about their investment in this system and encourage sympathy with youth, only to blame parents' decisions to migrate as irresponsible (241).

Party of Five works against this naturalization in several ways. First, it relies on the audience's familiarity with the original series premise for contrast. While the original parents die at the hands of a drunk driver, the reboot reminds viewers repeatedly that the Acosta family is suffering not because of one person's actions but rather the injustices of government-made immigration policy and our collective acquiescence. The pilot capitalizes on immigration proceedings to raise awareness of changes to immigration policy. In an appeal to halt their deportation, Valentina gives a heartfelt explanation of how she needs her parents, and their lawyer explains that there is precedent to claim the children would face exceptional hardship if Emilio's DACA status were to change and the children were sent to foster care. However, the judge rules that their case does not qualify as exceptional because, "Unfortunately heartbreak is anything but uncommon, especially in these cases. So is the wrenching apart of families" ("Pilot"). While he apologizes to the children, he tells the parents only that his hands are tied because the law is clear. Viewers are invited to consider how the family's fate has become common and expected, and that this is the consequence of changing attitudes and government actions.

Later in the episode, Val makes a GoFundMe web page to raise money for their family. She explains she got the idea from a family who raised $200,000 after their father drowned on vacation. Beto cynically replies, "Just forget it. No one cares. There are tons of families like ours" ("Pilot"). The contrast is striking; a natural disaster would earn the family more sympathy than deportation. Here, the show prompts viewers to consider the unnaturalness of their situation. Unlike the "rogue wave" that washed away the father that Val describes, their situation could be avoided through legislative action. This denaturalization is hinted at from the very beginning of the series when Emilio announces from the stage, "We are the Natural Disasters! Homegrown here in the city of angels, baby" ("Pilot"). The very name of the band, as it is repeated throughout the season, invites viewers to consider the cause of their circumstances. Moreover, the show underlines the brutality of an immigration system that forecloses the compassion that might be felt for the family if not for the polarization of the issue for political gain.

The unnatural denial of basic human dignity is felt again when the children visit their parents in detention and a guard yells at them for holding hands ("Pilot"). Later, during their fundraiser for other immigrant parents, Lucía describes to the crowd how her father is dehumanized in detention. Since her father shaved every day, she mentioned his stubble to him. During the next visit, his face was shaven but showed multiple cuts. He attempted to dismiss it lightheartedly; he could not find a mirror. However, Lucía realizes that the men probably all had to share a disposable razor. She concludes this is not the result of a shortage or problem with a lack of funding, but rather an act of cruelty: withholding anything that makes people feel cared for ("Speak for Yourself"). Again, the show directs audiences to consider how detention is anything but natural, as it works to strip individuals of their sense of identity and agency.

Promotional materials for the show such as *TV Guide* endeavor to draw in viewers by sharing a "heartbreaking clip" so that viewers can "get ready for an emotional journey" and downplaying immigration as simply background: "The new series has an immigration twist" (Vik). While this rhetoric may ease viewers' worries and assure them that the show will not be too emotionally burdensome, I argue that the show's storytelling resists viewers' wish to simply experience catharsis and move on. Part of this is accomplished by making sure the parents' perspectives are well established. As Javier and Emilio say goodbye before deportation, Javier recounts and stands by his decision to carry Emilio across the desert in 106° heat because he can now live the life he wants: "You be what you want to be, OK? I'm so proud of you" ("Pilot"). Viewers may not easily dismiss the parents as irresponsible nor simply feel relieved that they do not share the same fate.

The parents did not migrate on a whim, but for the promise of employment for Javier and a better life for their family. Moreover, episode 9 provides a series of flashbacks in which Gloria and Javier attempt to navigate their new jobs and childless lives in Mexico after deportation. Tension mounts when, after Javier suggests a fresh start and job in another town, Gloria explains that she already uprooted her life once for their move to the United States and does not want to do it again. Gloria wants to remain in her job as a nanny, and Javier expresses his discomfort as she becomes more involved with work. While it is clear he wishes he could continue to support her, the show is careful not to portray him as controlling but sensitive to the pain Gloria feels from their separation, mournful of the lives they had, and worried they are growing apart; he even suggests they have another baby to maintain their sense of family ("Mexico"). These scenes remind viewers that immigrant parents are not unthinking or naïve, but rather must negotiate complex power dynamics that would deny their agency.

Manipulating Windows: Resisting Criminality

Party of Five (2020) lets audiences see undocumented Latinx characters without the all-too-familiar trappings of criminality. They are entrepreneurs, mothers and fathers, and decision makers capable of navigating complex situations. It then attempts to shift viewers' focus and denaturalize that criminality by bringing it to the center of the frame. The final challenge to the naturalization of immigrant suffering considered here is the careful framing of shots to turn viewers' attention on the windows through which the public perceives the issue of immigration. New, alternative framing through the Acostas' experiences asks viewers to consider how their perspective of the immigration system is manipulated by dominant narratives that criminalize immigrants. By bringing the framing of immigration policy into view, audiences may more easily reflect on how their own privileges shape their ability to ignore these injustices and perhaps spur them to action.

One scene that calls for this kind of reflection is featured in the pilot. Gloria and Javier are told they must leave, as visiting hours are over and their deportation is imminent. They move down a chain-link fence opposite their children, sharing last kisses and touches through the wire mesh. A handheld camera quickly alternates between the parents' and children's perspectives to emphasize the fleeting and rushed nature of the moment. As agents pull Gloria away, she pleads with them that she is not ready. The camera then pans out away from the children as a wooden door with a glass window momentarily obstructs them from view. As it is shut behind the parents, the window is squared around the children huddled together. The blurring of the wooden door on both sides of the frame focuses viewers' attention on the children's pained expressions and the barrier separating the family from one another. Hopefully, viewers will also notice that the children are not alone. Many other families facing this same violence and criminalization have been present in the periphery of every shot of this scene (see figure 12.1).

A further example of this framing appears in episode 8 when the youngest sister, Val, runs away to be with her parents. The family receives a call from a U.S. Border Patrol officer that she is waiting in their facility to be picked up. While Val sits in an office by herself, an officer comes in the room to drop off a file. She follows him with her gaze as he leaves, which draws her attention to an older immigrant sitting in the hallway. She smiles and waves at him; maybe he reminds her of a grandfather or elder in her church. Her smile dis-

Figure 12.1 *Party of Five* pilot episode: detention and goodbye.

Figure 12.2 Val waves to an immigrant at the border.

Figure 12.3 Val waves to an immigrant at the border.

Figure 12.4 Val waves to an immigrant at the border.

Figure 12.5 Val waves to an immigrant at the border.

appears when he waves back, and the image of his handcuffed hands come into the frame and her view. Val looks off to the side as if remembering her own parents in the detention center in the pilot episode and the sound of the door locking behind them that replays in her dreams (see figures 12.2–12.5).

The sign beneath the window between Val and the immigrant reads "Do not tamper with the window / *No manipular la ventana*" ("Dos y Dos"). Like the previous image in the detention center, this signage prompts viewers to consider what they can and cannot see. How much of our daily lives is spent considering the violence immigrants face under surveillance, detention, and deportation? The shot seems an attempt to alter the viewers' perspective and interfere with dominant stories meant to keep the public from questioning immigration policy. At the same time, the scene may dare the audience to continue "tampering" with limited and privileged views by engaging with the systemic nature of this violence. The Acostas are not the only family to experience these injustices. Crucially, the following shot also recognizes the potentially ephemeral nature of this engagement. As the other Acosta children arrive and burst through the doors of the office to hug Val, the immigrant is sent back out of focus. This may visually work to imitate U.S. society's tendency to show a sudden wave of compassion, only to fall back into its habitual amnesia as issues such as family separation and human rights violations at the border are erased by other headlines. Will viewers continue to consider the massive number of immigrants affected by zero-tolerance policies, or will the immigrants fade from view at the end of the episode?

Conclusion

As with many other narratives about undocumented immigrants, *Party of Five* (2020) runs the risk of prioritizing idealized immigrants only to reinforce the exclusion of others. Where are the undocumented single parents or undocumented individuals without children? Where are the laborers working multiple jobs who do not have the time or resources to become bilingual? When will they make it on the screen alongside the typical "American" family? Despite these limitations and unlike shows that limit representation to youth, such as *The Golden Girls* and *One Day at a Time*, *Party of Five* resists liberal privileging of DACA recipients and exceptionalism by staging undocumented parents' voices as central to its story. Moreover, it avoids using undocumented Latinx experiences only to showcase the qualities of non-Latinx protagonists, such as in *Grey's Anatomy* and *All Rise*. Through careful consultation, *Party of Five* accomplishes more thorough representation of undocumented identities by developing complex characters, accurately portraying immigration policy, and confronting the naturalization of undocumented immigrant suffering. It visually invites audiences to question criminalization of undocumented Americans and consider their own limited perspectives and engagement with systemic injustices.

Party of Five (2020) offers a unique focus on contemporary undocumented Latinx experiences, and yet it was cancelled by Freeform just a month after the season finale (Andreeva). The creators' concerns that the show would be perceived as just another repackaging of 1990s nostalgia may have been warranted. Nielson Company data reports that *Party of Five* averaged 252,000 same-day viewers, with 442,000 viewers for the pilot and only 143,000 for the finale ("*Party of Five* Season One"). Live +3 viewers also dropped off, starting with 652,000 for the premiere and 350,000–360,000 during the show's final weeks (Andreeva). Other Freeform shows were renewed despite having only slightly higher or even lower total same-day viewership. For example, *Good Trouble* was renewed with 255,000 same-day viewers but only 0.10 for the 18–49 demographic, while *Party of Five* had 0.11. *Everything's Gonna Be Okay* was renewed with less total same-day viewership, 175,000, and a lower 18–49 demographic at 0.6 ("Freeform TV Show Ratings").

The lack of industry support for undocumented Latinx representation, such as that offered by *Party of Five*, is disappointing considering the urgent need to continue shaping national conversations about our increasingly unjust immigration system. Without the kind of public support behind other Latinx-centered shows such as *One Day at a Time*, *Party of Five* was not taken up by another distributor. However, the show is worth further attention as a model for future shows and the potential to continue this kind of critical storytelling.

References

Abused: The Postville Raid. Directed by Luis Argueta, New Day Films, 2011.

Agard, Chancellor. "*The Good Fight* Recap: The Firm Battles ICE and Makes a New Enemy." *Entertainment Weekly*, 20 May 2018, ew.com/recap/the-good-fight-season-2-episode-12/.

Andreeva, Nellie. "'Party of Five' Reboot Canceled by Freeform After One Season." *Deadline.com*, 17 Apr. 2020, deadline.com/2020/04/party-of-five-reboot-canceled-Freeform-one-season-series-1202910922/.

"Authentic Mexican." *Party of Five*, created by Amy Lippman and Christopher Keyser, directed by Jenée LaMarque, written by Amy Lippman, Christopher Keyser, and Gabriel Llanas, season 1, episode 4, Freeform, 22 Jan. 2020.

"Beautiful Dreamer." *Grey's Anatomy*, created by Shonda Rhimes, directed by Jeannot Szwarc, written by Shonda Rhimes and Meg Marinis, season 14, episode 19, ABC, 12 Apr. 2018.

Beltrán, Cristina. *The Trouble with Unity: Latino Politics and the Creation of Identity*. Oxford UP, 2010.

Camayd-Freixas, Erik. *US Immigration Reform and Its Global Impact: Lessons from the Postville Raid*. Palgrave Macmillan, 2013.

Campos, Edgar. Personal interview. 14 Mar. 2020.

"Chapter 10." *Jane the Virgin*, created by Jennie Snyder Urman, directed by Elodie Keene, written by Jennie Snyder Urman, Meredith Averill, and Christopher Oscar Pena, season 1, episode 10, The CW, 19 Jan. 2015.

"Chapter 27." *Jane the Virgin*, created by Jennie Snyder Urman, directed by Jann Turner, written by Jessica O'Toole and Amy Rardin, season 2, episode 5, The CW, 9 Nov. 2015.

"Chapter 30." *Jane the Virgin*, created by Jennie Snyder Urman, directed by Uta Briesewitz, written by Carolina Rivera and Paul Sciarrotta, season 2, episode 8, The CW, 14 Dec. 2015.

"Chapter 61." *Jane the Virgin*, created by Jennie Snyder Urman, directed by Melanie Mayron, written by Paul Sciarrotta, season 3, episode 17, The CW, 1 May 2017.

Cornejo Villavicencio, Karla. *The Undocumented Americans*. Random House, 2020.

"Day 485." *The Good Fight*, created by Robert King, Michelle King, and Phil Alden Robinson, directed by Ron Underwood, written by Jacquelyn Reingold and Marcus Dalzine, season 2, episode 12, CBS All Access, 19 May 2018.

"Dorothy's Prized Pupil." *The Golden Girls*, created by Susan Harris, directed by Terry Hughes, written by Susan Harris and Christopher Lloyd, season 2, episode 21, NBC, 14 Mar. 1987.

"Dos y Dos." *Party of Five*, created by Amy Lippman and Christopher Keyser, directed by James Larkin, written by Amy Lippman, Christopher Keyser, and Gabriel Llanas, season 1, episode 8, Freeform, 19 Feb. 2020.

"Freeform TV Show Ratings." *TV Series Finale*, 17 July 2020, tvseriesfinale.com/tv-show/Freeform -tv-show-ratings-33382/.

Gomez, Alan, and David Agren. "First Protected DREAMer Is Deported Under Trump." *USA Today*, 18 Apr. 2017, www.usatoday.com/story/news/world/2017/04/18/first-protected-dreamer-deported -under-trump/100583274/.

Guerrero, Diane, and Michelle Buford. *In the Country We Love: My Family Divided*. Macmillan, 2016.

"Long Day's Journey into ICE." *All Rise*, developed by Greg Spottiswood, directed by Michael M. Robin, written by Gregory Nelson, season 1, episode 2, CBS, 30 Sept. 2019.

Macías-Rojas, Patrisia. "Immigration and the War on Crime: Law and Order Politics and the Illegal Immigration Reform and Immigrant Responsibility Act of 1996." *Journal on Migration and Human Security*, vol. 6, no. 1, 2018, pp. 1–25.

"Margin of Error." *Party of Five*, created by Amy Lippman and Christopher Keyser, directed by Rodrigo García, written by Amy Lippman and Christopher Keyser, season 1, episode 2, Freeform, 8 Jan. 2020.

"Mario Lopez Remembers Guest-Starring on 'The Golden Girls.'" *Today.com*, 11 Dec. 2019, www .today.com/video/mario-lopez-remembers-guest-starring-on-the-golden-girls-74904133752.

"Mexico." *Party of Five*, created by Amy Lippman and Christopher Keyser, directed by Edward Ornelas, written by Amy Lippman and Christopher Keyser, season 1, episode 9, Freeform, 26 Feb. 2020.

Negrón-Muntaner, Frances, et al. *The Latino Media Gap: A Report on the State of Latinos in U.S. Media*. Columbia U, 2014, asit-prod-web1.cc.columbia.edu/cser/wp-content/uploads/sites/70 /2020/03/Latino-Gap.pdf.

Obama, Barack. "Immigration Can Be a Controversial Topic." *Facebook*, 5 Sept. 2017, www.facebook .com/barackobama/posts/10155227588436749.

"*Party of Five* Season One Ratings." *TV Series Finale*, 18 Apr. 2020, tvseriesfinale.com/tv-show/party -of-five-season-one-ratings/.

"Pilot." *Party of Five*, created by Amy Lippman and Christopher Keyser, directed by Rodrigo García, written by Amy Lippman, Christopher Keyser, and Michal Zebede, season 1, episode 1, Freeform, 8 Jan. 2020.

Plumer, Brad. "Congress Tried to Fix Immigration Back in 1986. Why Did It Fail?" *Washington Post*, 30 Jan. 2013, www.washingtonpost.com/news/wonk/wp/2013/01/30/in-1986-congress-tried-to -solve-immigration-why-didnt-it-work/.

Puga, Ana Elena. "Poor Enrique and Poor María, or, the Political Economy of Suffering in Two Migrant Melodramas." *Performance in the Borderlands*, edited by Ramón H. Rivera-Servera and Harvey Young, Palgrave Macmillan, 2011.

"Rafa." *Party of Five*, created by Amy Lippman and Christopher Keyser, directed by Patricia Cardoso, written by Amy Lippman, Christopher Keyser, and Michael Zebede, season 1, episode 5, Freeform, 29 Jan. 2020.

Sarner, Lauren. "How the 'Party of Five' Reboot Was Ripped from the Headlines." *New York Post*, 31 Dec. 2019, nypost.com/2019/12/31/how-the-party-of-five-reboot-was-ripped-from-the-headlines/.

"Speak for Yourself." *Party of Five*, created by Amy Lippman and Christopher Keyser, directed by Michael Medico, written by Amy Lippman, Christopher Keyser, and Mike Skerrett, season 1, episode 7, Freeform, 12 Feb. 2020.

"Strays." *One Day at a Time*, developed by Gloria Calderón Kellett and Mike Royce, directed by Phill Lewis, written by Peter Murrieta, season 1, episode 5, Netflix, 6 Jan. 2017.

Suro, Roberto. "Introduction." *Writing Immigration: Scholars and Journalists in Dialogue*, edited by Marcelo M. Suárez-Orozco, Vivian S. Louie, and Roberto Suro, U of California P, 2011, pp. 1–18.

Vick, Megan. "Freeform's *Party of Five* Reboot Announces 2020 Premiere Date Along with New Footage." *TVGuide*, 13 Sept. 2019, www.tvguide.com/news/party-of-five-Freeform-premiere-date/.

Stacey Alex

STORIES VALUED, BODIES EXCLUDED

Immigrant Narratives in *Jane the Virgin,*
On My Block, and *Party of Five*

Irma J. Zamora Fuerte

Undocumented immigrant narratives in the post-2016 media focus on either the "bad" (e.g., Trump's "they're rapists" comments) or the "good" and "deserving" (e.g., conversations regarding DREAMers and DACA recipients). Mostly, these representations of "good" undocumented communities fall into the "moral regulation" or "deservingness" narratives, which limit which immigrants are celebrated and deemed successful in their integration into American society (Andrews; Chauvin and Garcés-Mascareñas). In television shows led by Latinx casts and/or directors, the narratives use the concept of "deservingness." The narrative mold of the "deserving immigrant" is one of the archetypes of what Isabel Molina-Guzmán terms "post-racial-era TV" (2007–16) in *Latinas and Latinos on TV: Colorblind Comedy in the Post-Racial Network Era.* This was "an era of increasing inclusion," where television show casts became increasingly diversified, both narratively and visually (Molina-Guzmán 3). Latinx-led television shows certainly push representative narratives by including unDACAmented storylines. (The neologism "unDACAmented" is used by various immigration rights activists to recognize the separate yet intertwined fate of undocumented and DACA-mented communities living in a United States with ever-shifting immigration laws and in fear of deportation.) However, Latinx TV still falls into a pattern that proves "post-racial-era TV comedies are often both progressive and regressive at once" (Molina-Guzmán 9). In this case, shows are often progressive in their nuanced Latinx stories and in including unDACAmented characters/arcs but prove regressive in perpetuating assimilationist ideologies for unDACAmented communities.

Following Molina-Guzmán's critiques of post-racial-era TV and the debate over "deservingness" in unDACAmented communities, this chapter focuses on the representation of immigrant narratives and figures in the Latinx shows *Jane the Virgin* (*JTV*), *On My Block* (*OMB*), and *Party of Five* (*POF*). Specifically, I focus on the arcs of Alba Villanueva in *Jane the Virgin,* Olivia in *On My Block,* and the Acostas in *Party of Five.* I choose to focus on these shows because they all have at least one character who is unDA-CAmented or from a mixed-status family. Two out of the three shows have also proved incredibly successful—running for multiple seasons and winning multiple awards. The fact that they are deemed award-winning shows is worrisome given the shortcomings of their unDACAmented narratives. This chapter observes that these shows successfully tell nuanced stories of Latinx communities and contribute to the cultural citizenship of immigrant Latinxs in the United States. However, they fall short in imagining stories of unDACAmented immigrants. So the shows are not fully inclusive of the general Latinx immigrant experience, furthering ideals that only white-acting, family-oriented, and gendered "good" and "deserving" immigrants are worthy of empathy. The foregrounding and elevating of these narratives in these television series are detrimental to unDACAmented communities since the narratives outline who and what type of immigrants audiences should and should not support, thus determining and declaring who does and does not belong with us.

Immigrant "Deservingness" and "Moral Regulation"

A significant tension in the unDACAmented community and the immigrant activist movement is the question of whether citizenship should be granted based on vulnerability or on merit (Chauvin and Garcés-Mascareñas 426). With this tension comes the rhetoric of the "deserving" immigrant and of "moral regulation" within undocumented and DACA communities (Andrews; Chauvin and Garcés-Mascareñas). The idea of "deservingness," according to sociologists Sebastien Chauvin and Blanca Garcés-Mascareñas, comes down to unDACAmented communities trying to make themselves "less illegal" and "less deportable," which is usually tied to performing civic duties (e.g., paying taxes, not committing petty crimes to avoid police interactions, etc.) and proving "good" conduct via third parties, like NGOs, churches, or other institutions (426). This "good" behavior ties in with "moral regulation" patterns of undocumented communities, including policing other immigrants' actions when they break the "good" behavior framework. According to sociologist Abigail L. Andrews, "moral regulation" within undocumented communities not only involves creating the perception of "productive" members but also policing other immigrants' behavior as "bad" (i.e., if not working, they are lazy) and placing sole responsibility on the individual for behaving as "good" (2491). Policing also involves gendering of "deportability," with men often treated as susceptible to "bad" behavior and women seen as less criminal (Andrews 2492). Furthermore, acting "good" involves "acting white," embodying behaviors that are coded as "white" (speaking English,

Irma J. Zamora Fuerte

being "less noisy," etc.) and refusing attributes or behaviors that are deemed Indigenous (Andrews 2496). With these ideals in mind, it is no coincidence that most of the representations of unDACAmented folks in television today are female and white passing and why two of the characters of focus in this chapter are white-passing (mostly) religious women. The whiteness of these characters seems purposeful in conveying how much an unDACAmented body is allowed to disrupt notions of Americanness. Additionally, the racial ambiguity of these characters along with their gendering ties in with the idea that "the bodies of women, specifically racially ambiguous but ethnically marked U.S.-born and immigrant women, are central to imagining what it means to be 'American' and who belongs in the United States" (Molina-Guzmán 104). In the case of these unDACAmented narratives, the bodies of Latinx women indicate what and who can become "American." Television narratives of unDACAmented characters who represent mostly female, white-passing, and "good" immigrants perpetuate ideas of moral regulation. After all, now audiences are able to see not only what "good" immigrant characteristics are but also who these immigrants look like. If they do not match what is depicted on television, they must be the "bad" immigrants.

These tensions regarding "good" and "deserving" immigrants are exemplified with the debate about Deferred Action for Childhood Arrivals (DACA) and the DREAMers. As they fought for their rights, DREAMers often got portrayed as "deserving" and "exceptional," with "attributes [like] . . . normal Americans, best and brightest, no fault of their own" (Nichols 56). This in turn emphasized the difference between the "deserving" and "undeserving," with DREAMers' parents now grouped in the "undeserving" group and causing a separation of communities in the fight for human recognition. Furthermore, with these stories of "exceptionalism," those who did not fit the "cream of the crop" description were left in the "undeserving" category (Nichols 56). That is to say, immigrants who are "unassimilated, adults, poor and low skilled" are relegated to a status of "less deserving" and incapable of integrating into the United States (Nichols 56). I refer to this debate about DACA as a jumping off point for my discussion of the television shows. This tension of separating the "deserving," "good," "moral," and assimilated immigrants from those "undeserving," unassimilated, and "bad" undocumented immigrants plays out in the unDACAmented stories of *JTV*, *OMB*, and *POF*, particularly in the characters focused on.

Jane the Virgin: Alba's Arc

Jane the Virgin (2014–19) is a soap-opera comedy that originally aired on The CW Network. Set in Miami, Florida, *JTV* tells the story of Jane Villanueva (Gina Rodriguez), a young virgin Catholic Latina, who is accidentally artificially inseminated during a regular checkup. The show also stars Andrea Navedo as Xiomara Villanueva, Mexican telenovela star Jaime Camil as Rogelio de la Vega, and Ivonne Coll as Alba Villanueva. The show has the format of a telenovela, with many coincidences and miracles along with comedic effects shaping the plotline. Focusing on a Latinx family and with an almost entirely Latinx cast, the show gives a nuanced representation of Latinx families, specifically with conversations about Latinas and sexuality. A very direct example of this comes in Chapter 62, where Jane finally has a casual fling after becoming a widow. In these moments, Jane seems to subvert initial stereotypes of Latinas on television—she is portrayed as a thinker, intelligent and logical for the most part. Still, she fits the archetype of a Latina señorita (Molina-Guzmán 15). This is the crux of my critique: although *JTV* pushes the envelope for the possibility and success of Latinxs on television, it remained complacent in other ways, including the representation of its undocumented character. Still, this show proved successful and incredibly popular among mainstream media. The show and cast were nominated for multiple awards: Primetime Emmy Awards (2015, 2016), People's Choice Awards (winner 2015, nominated 2017), and the Golden Globes (2015–17), with Gina Rodriguez winning for "Best Actress" in 2015.

Although the main focus of the show is Jane's life as a newly pregnant (later mom and widow) woman, the show also revolves around the life experiences of the Villanueva women. The matriarch of the family is Alba, the mother of Xiomara and grandmother of Jane. Alba is a Venezuelan undocumented immigrant, a very devout Catholic, and was previously a nurse. Throughout the show, Alba's citizenship status shifts between taking the forefront and a secondary role. For example, in Chapter 8, Jane is in the process of suing Rafael's (Justin Baldoni) sister, Luisa (Yara Martinez), who accidentally inseminated her. However, from intermittent flashbacks and an explicit reveal toward the end of the episode, the audience is told that Alba is undocumented. This drives a major plot point, because Jane decides to drop the lawsuit because she is nervous Alba's status could be brought up in a court of law.

When compared to other shows, *JTV* does an incredible job showing the trials and fears of undocumented and mixed-status families (especially after the 2016 election). Nevertheless, Alba's arc still falls within the rhetoric of the "deserving" and "moral" immigrant. Alba is portrayed as someone who is extremely good: she does not break *any* rules (she even gets anxious and mad about Xiomara's parking ticket in Chapter 8), is *devoutly* Catholic (hence the whole "flower" metaphor at the beginning of the show), and even plays the role of a caretaker (the caring grandmother, a homemaker, and a nurse).

Figure 13.1 Alba and her top priorities are introduced in *Jane the Virgin*.

When the narrator introduces her, Alba's priorities appear with the word "God" underlined and, right below, "Jane."

With this introduction, Alba's devotion to religion and her family (via Jane) are set as her prominent characteristics. As Chauvin and Garcés-Mascareñas point out, all of these characteristics fall within the category of "good" immigrants and immigrants who are integrated into the community—in the case of Alba, her family (426). Furthermore, Alba's gender, along with her religiosity and morality, is tied to pleas for empathy, in particular for women. Since women are often seen as less criminal and "often detained in lower numbers," Alba's gender and characterization definitely play into the concept of the "moral" and "good" immigrant whom outsiders must empathize with and who therefore "deserves" to receive U.S. citizenship (Andrews 2492).

An example of the convergence of these ideals placed on Alba comes in Chapter 10 of season 1, where she is hospitalized after being pushed by Petra's mom at an award party. After the narrative recap, the episode starts with a flashback in which the audience sees Alba teaching a young Jane how to pray using a rosary. Halfway through the episode, the doctor treating Alba (who is in a coma) tells Xiomara that after the storm is over the hospital will have to report her to Immigration and Customs Enforcement (ICE) for deportation because she "is in this country illegally. She has no insurance. And the hospital cannot afford to absorb the cost of her care.... It's called medical repatriation" (18:53–19:20). Although Rogelio very much tries to fix this problem through his connections to "a UN ambassador and Gloria Estefan," the issue is resolved through Michael Cordero (Brett Dier) and his role as a police officer. Although it is Alba's status that propels considerable tension in the episode, she is, ironically, without a voice throughout much of the episode. She speaks for only about fifty seconds throughout the entire episode, and the bulk of her dialogue is her teaching "proper" religion to her granddaughter. Through the foregrounding of her religiousness and her family values, and showing her as a victim who is saved by the white love interest of her daughter (who happens to be in a position of authority), Alba is revealed as someone to empathize with and who deserves to remain in the United States. It is no coincidence that the storyline is resolved on a happy note, where Alba is able to stay with her family, keeping Jane's family intact. As Molina-Guzmán points out about minority characters in TV comedies, "the visual and comedic existence of ethnic and racial minority actors on TV rarely challenges dominant ethnic and racial values and is never portrayed as explicitly threatening to whiteness, white privilege, and the norms of white civility" (10). This extends to unDACAmented narratives, as is seen through Alba's character. Through her familial values and religious devotion, she does not challenge "the norms of white civility" and is therefore framed as worthy of being saved by Michael. In having Alba comply with the norms of white society, *JTV* relies on the rhetoric and narrative-building of the "deserving" immigrant who should be able to stay. She belongs to the "American" way, but only as a guest who is permitted a seat at the table by a white character. Because she is a (great-) grandmother, does not break any rules, is very religious, and plays the role of caretaker, by the end of the show she is portrayed as having deserved her green card and the ability to work lawfully in the United States.

On My Block: Olivia's Arc

On My Block (2018–) is a Netflix teenage dramatic comedy original series that stars mostly young actors of color. A coming-of-age story, *OMB* is set in Los Angeles and focuses on the lives of longtime friends Ruben "Ruby" Martinez (Jason Genao), Monse Finnie (Sierra Capri), Jamal Turner (Brett Gray), and Cesar Diaz (Diego Tinoco) as they navigate high school life and attempt to rescue Cesar from further involvement in gang life. With its mixture of genres and an exclusive focus on young people of color, the show has received rave reviews and has won multiple awards from the Imagen Foundation, which recognizes the industry's "portray[al of] the Latino community in a positive and accurate manner" ("About Imagen"). In 2018, it was deemed the "most binged" Netflix show (Nakamura). It is still going strong in popularity, with a third season released in 2020.

Although the overarching storyline focuses on the inner circle of friends Ruben, Monse, Cesar, and Jamal, the first season spends a majority of its focus on Olivia (Ronni Hawk). Shortly after the show begins, Ruby's parents tell him that his "cousin" (actually the daughter of his mom's friend Rosa) Olivia is staying with them because her parents were deported (Chapter 2). Even though it is deportation that brings Olivia into the storyline, most of her character's arc does not center on the impact of the deportation. Olivia's parents' deportation is brought up or alluded to four times in the whole season (briefly in Chapters 2, 6, 7, and 10), and we never get a full story about them nor get to hear or see them directly. The only background that viewers receive about the parents are the brief mention of Olivia's mom's name, Rosa, and any other details that Olivia shares in other episodes.

Olivia's parents are literally always marginalized whenever we see them. The first instance we see them (or rather an image of them) is in Chapter 2 where we see the framed family photograph that Olivia has kept with her. Next, we see them as life-size picture cutouts for Olivia's quinceañera in Chapter 7 (literally on the edge of the scene). Toward the end of Chapter 10, we finally get to see and hear from them, but only very briefly and only through a phone screen. In all of these instances, Olivia's parents are boxed in, never seen entirely and never heard besides the four lines praising, missing, and loving Olivia on the day of her quinceañera. We never get to know details about their life outside of contacting Olivia; their fate is left to the imagination of the viewer.

By limiting the voices and narratives of Olivia's parents, viewers' empathies depend entirely on Olivia's behavior and whatever details she decides to share about her family. This strategy of focusing on the children parallels strategies employed during the debate about DACA in the United States and other international immigration debates (Nichols 177). The parents and adults are stigmatized and denied a voice in telling their stories and instead are framed as voiceless and harmful in the lives of their children (Nichols 57). In the case of *OMB*, the parents are not villainized, but they are relegated to the outskirts of their own narrative. *OMB*'s depiction of Olivia's voiceless undocumented parents is a parallel narrative strategy to *JTV*'s voiceless Alba, steering audiences to feel empathy for the essentially orphaned Olivia, who is the only visible victim of this deportation.

Even ignoring the fact that the parents never voice their own stories, the way that Olivia's behavior and reflections about her parents are framed still shapes them as "deserving" and respectable immigrants. Two examples of this: the way that Olivia is characterized, and her parents' framing as responsible, caring, nuclear family members. Olivia is characterized as assimilated to U.S. culture: she speaks English well, rarely uses Spanish, and is never involved in the gang-related events that occur in the show, thus showing her as "innocent." These traits parallel those of young DACA adults who attempt to show deservingness through "assimilation into the American value sys-

Figure 13.2 A framed photograph of Olivia's parents is centered in Ruby's room. From *On My Block*.

Figure 13.3 Ruby presents Olivia with life-size cutouts of her parents. From *On My Block*.

tem" (Nichols 56). Furthermore, Olivia is presented as white passing, visually tying her innocence and assimilation to whiteness and being American. By depicting Olivia in this manner, the parents are tied into family and "good" American values.

In Chapter 2, with the framed photograph, we see Olivia and her parents in a family portrait. Through this photograph and knowing that this is a valued possession of Olivia, the parents are presented as loving and caring. Viewers get another sample of this "good parents" and nuclear-family narrative in Chapter 7, where a tearful Olivia shares to the group all the dreams and expectations her parents had for her quinceañera. Having Olivia's parents' narrative rely heavily on the fact that they are loving, caring parents and heads of a nuclear family fits the rhetoric of "a family unit that [is] hardworking, nuclear, and free of all the typical dysfunction of immigrants," a strategy of "deservingness" employed in France in the mid-1990s (Nichols 177). Additionally, through the presentation of an idealized nuclear family, the show connects Olivia's happier times to when her family mostly complied with "whiteness, white privilege, and the norms of white civility" (Molina-Guzmán 10). Through these one-sided depictions of Olivia's parents, they are shown as "good" immigrants whose post-deportation fates viewers are left to imagine. The way the show neglects to substantially include the parents highlights broader critiques of comedy television today, especially for characters from marginalized communities. Just like Alba in *JTV*, Olivia and her parents are unique in that they are a mixed-status family but not in disrupting American expectations of behaviors for good immigrants. While the storyline of a mixed-status family breaks the norm, the family is still presented as compliant with "norms and values of white heterosexual familial domesticity" (Molina-Guzmán 75). The parents' limited appearance on screen allows writers and creators of *OMB* to touch on but not face the consequences of the deportation of unDACAmented brown bodies. Not only does this portrayal limit the possibilities of unDACAmented representation on screen, but it is also heavily reliant on rhetorics of deservingness. In a time when immigration politics center merit-based ideologies, the narrative of *OMB*, like that of *JTV*, complies with these demands. By relying on deservingness as the primary form of representation for unDACAmented narratives, television producers/writers/directors are also perpetuating ideals of who deserves to be represented on the screen. These portrayals seem to indicate that unDACAmented individuals who are closely assimilated, come from a nuclear family, and promote "white civility" are the only ones whose stories are worth seeing on-screen. Everyone else is unworthy.

Olivia is not present in the second season, and, as of the third season, no other prominent unDACAmented character has been included in the *OMB* storyline. We never get to see what happens to her parents, but Olivia's death highlights her innocence (and through her, that of her parents) and serves as a plot device in season 2. Still, why include a mixed-status family in the storyline but not more? Why is there only one prominent character impacted by immigration law in a story set in East Los Angeles and why is that character's storyline limited to the first season? These questions become more urgent when considering that the series' writers and director all claim that Olivia's death was planned from the beginning. Why include the storyline at all? That Olivia's mixed-status narrative is introduced to bring her into Ruby's household problematizes representations of immigration on television. Just like in *JTV* with Alba, the deportation of Olivia's parents is brought up in *OMB* to propel the group's storyline. The priorities in representations of immigration stories in television are revealed when Olivia's story is relegated to narrative propellant. *OMB* is focused on idealizing the victimhood of the nuclear family Olivia belonged to and the damage the forced family separation had on Olivia's short life. Once the audience empathizes with Olivia and her parents, especially after her tragic death, her story is brought up no more.

The Acostas in *Party of Five*

A Latino-fied reboot, *Party of Five* (2020) launched on the streaming platform Freeform in January of 2020. The updated *POF* takes the general premise of the 1994 original of five siblings who struggle to survive without their parents and adds the urgency of deportation—the Acosta parents are forcibly removed from their family via deportation. The show focuses on the impact immigration regulations have on this mixed-status family. The show stars Brandon Larracuente as Emilio Acosta, the oldest brother; Niko Guardado as Beto Acosta, the second oldest brother; Emily Tosta as Lucia Acosta, the oldest sister; and Elle Paris Legaspie as Valentina Acosta, the youngest sister. There is also baby brother Rafael. Although a necessary show for today's times, the show was cancelled after its first season, primarily because of its low viewing ratings (Goldberg).

Through its short run, *POF* showed the darker reality of the American immigration system and dealt with it head-on. As Stacey Alex presents in this anthology, *POF* deserves commendations for doing its due diligence in portraying the stories of mixed-status families (even hiring a consultant) and in centering the stories of the Acosta parents much more than other shows. Building on her assessment, this section questions who and what kind of undocumented immigrant stories *POF* helps expand. Through the voices of the Acosta children, who seem mostly assimilated to American culture, audiences are presented with nuanced representations of Latinxs and of immigration. Both of the parents, Javier (Bruno Bichir) and Gloria Acosta (Fernanda Urrejola), are presented as undocumented. Emilio is presented as a DACA recipient, and Lucia's friend Matthew (Garcia) is presented as a young, undocumented, trans homeless boy. In many ways, *POF* does an impressive job in representing the nuanced stories of unDACAmented folks.

One of the highlights of the show is the penultimate episode, "Mexico," in which there are flashbacks of the Acosta parents' deportation and forced relocation to Tijuana. Unlike *OMB*, where the deported parents remain literally boxed in whenever they appear on screen, *POF* fills in the gaps of post-deportation for the parents. This works narratively to show how much all the Acostas are hiding from each other in the name of family. But through this purposeful narrative unveiling, *POF* also demonstrates the impossible breaks family separation imposes on mixed-status families—with irreparable damages. Interestingly, this episode shows the audience the limitations of "boxed-in" narratives, since we see the children also boxed in on the screens of the Acosta parents' phones when they chat in the flashbacks.

Retrospectively, the audience is presented with the limited view the Acosta parents have of their children and how much they are not seeing outside that frame. Similarly, the audience is then presented with the world beyond the framed Acosta parents—one in which they are struggling economically, their marriage is falling apart, and they are considering separation. Their readjustment to a new life and their struggle to maintain their nuclear family relationship demonstrate the limits to success in Mexico's economic structure. When contrasted with *OMB*, this is a far more progressive depiction of unDACAmented families. Through the depiction of the parents, the undocumented bodies are officially given a voice—even if it is for only one episode.

Although in many ways *POF* provides crucial representation of unDACAmented stories and pushes boundaries in these representations, for the most part it remains tied to promoting "deserving" and assimilationist ideals. Just like characters of color are used in comedies to promote white heteronormative ideals, the trauma and drama of the family separation in the courtroom and detention center of *POF* promote these ideals of assimilation.

Figure 13.4 Beto on video call with his mother, Gloria, in *Party of Five.*

Yes, there are characters who are queer and trans and hence question a bit of the heteronormative aspects. (Lucia is later revealed to be questioning her sexuality as well.) However, their romantic relationships are not the central focus; they are portrayed as exceptions to the rule. Throughout the series, the ideology that "we are a good family" and "our parents came with nothing and created something" pervades the logic of the characters. At the end of the day, the show focuses on three heterosexual relationships: that of the parents, of Emilio and Natalia (Sol Rodriguez), and Beto and Elle (Audrey Gerthoffer). Furthermore, these characters all promote the ideals of a nuclear family—at the end showing that Emilio could not fully take care of Valentina and Rafael, who end up moving in with their parents in Mexico. The trauma of the family separations—the trial and the parents in the detention center—heightens the visual cruelty. It is this trauma porn that makes the audience especially empathetic toward the family. The gut-wrenching scene of a mom handing back her baby to her daughter and a father not able to hug his children longer leads to a larger critique of how and when Brown bodies are allowed to be human and empathized with. This scene, however, does serve to depict the Acosta parents as good parents of a nuclear family. When Gloria gives up Rafael so he can stay with her other children, it is understood to be a necessary sacrifice—elevating this act as a mother's sacrifice. The fact that the Acostas are presented as innocent, hard-working, and moderately economically successful in the United States makes them and their family especially worthy of citizenship in this narrative. Through this storyline, *POF* promotes the ideal that a nuclear family is the only way to prove the worthiness of someone's belonging. As with Alba and Olivia in *JTV* and *OMB*, the ideal family values promoted ensure that audiences feel empathy toward the Acostas and their situation. Javier and Gloria are depicted as having raised at least three adjusted American citizens and contributed to their community—physically, economically, and socially.

But *POF* also includes the necessary lawbreaking/dubious areas that the Acostas (and most immigrants) navigate in order to survive and support their community: they employ other undocumented folks in their restaurant, give most of their restaurant profits to someone else for their liquor license, and Lucia even takes a Social Security number from a deceased man to give to Matthew so he can get a job (episode 5, "Rafa"). These legal gray areas bypass the pure and innocent ideals generally attributed to "good" immigrants. This is a step forward in the representation of immigrant stories, since these stories do not make us question the Acostas' belonging, but rather make the audience question the morality of immigration laws that set up immigrants to break more laws. They further portray the legal mazes that undocumented and mixed-status families must navigate in order to survive in the United

States. Furthermore, these unlawful acts by the Acostas, when compared with the actions of ICE agents who separate the family, emphasize that following the law to the letter does not a moral person make.

Conclusion

Although shows like *JTV*, *OMB*, and *POF* do an amazing job in creating nuanced Latinx storylines, their vision of unDACAmented Latinxs remains one-dimensional. This is not to say that they are not positive portrayals: Alba in *JTV* is not always depicted as a saint (she reveals her regret over suggesting Xiomara get an abortion); Olivia is shown to participate in typical teenage things (i.e., partying); and the Acostas are not depicted as a flawless nuclear family. Nevertheless, these shows still follow the rhetoric of gendered (mostly female) "deserving" immigrants, who are extremely moral and "good," focused on family, and exhibit "American values." Although the unDACAmented and mixed-status storylines are valuable on their own, they play to both the progressive and regressive sides of Latinx television today. In the case of Olivia's parents (and to some extent, Alba), the stories of undocumented immigrants in these shows are marginalized and pushed to the side. Even in *POF*, where the mixed immigration status of the family is at the forefront, the deservingness of the Acostas is always foregrounded. By boxing in the experiences of unDACAmented community members as "deserving," these shows fall short in portraying a nuanced and human side of immigration as it impacts the immigrant Latinx community at large. Furthermore, through this deservingness rhetoric these narratives perpetuate the white heteronormative values as central to becoming and belonging in American culture. By highlighting the narratives of mostly white-passing religious women, Latinx shows are placing value on these bodies and stories over those of Black and Indigenous, non-Christian, non-heterosexual individuals. So, even if their stories are valued, their very bodies are excluded from their own narratives. In this way, these narratives leave much to be desired. It is important to recognize these narratives as problematic because with this marginalization comes an understanding of who and what unDACAmented communities should strive to be. And they also tell audiences which type of unDACAmented immigrant should ultimately be allowed in the United States and whom we should and should not feel empathy toward.

Works Cited

"About Imagen." *Imagen Foundation*, 9 July 2017, www.imagen.org/about/.

Andrews, Abigail L. "Moralizing Regulation: The Implications of Policing 'Good' versus 'Bad' Immigrants." *Ethnic and Racial Studies*, vol. 41, no. 14, 2018, pp. 2485–2503.

Chauvin, Sébastien, and Blanca Garcés-Mascareñas. "Becoming Less Illegal: Deservingness Frames and Undocumented Migrant Incorporation." *Sociology Compass*, vol. 8, no. 4, 2014, pp. 422–32.

Goldberg, Lesley. "'Party of Five' Reboot Canceled at Freeform." *Hollywood Reporter*, 29 July 2020, www.hollywoodreporter.com/live-feed/party-five-reboot-canceled-at-freeform-1290647.

Jane the Virgin. Created by Jennie Snyder Urman, The CW, 2014–19.

Party of Five. Created by Amy Lippman and Christopher Keyser, Freeform, 2020.

Molina-Guzmán, Isabel. *Latinas and Latinos on TV: Colorblind Comedy in the Post-Racial Network Era*. U of Arizona P, 2018.

Nakamura, Reid. "What Is 'On My Block'? Netflix's Most-Binged Show of 2018." *TheWrap*, 11 Dec. 2018, www.thewrap.com/what-is-on-my-block-netflixs-most-binged-show-of-2018/.

Nichols, Walter J. *The DREAMers: How the Undocumented Youth Movement Transformed the Immigrant Rights Debate*. Stanford UP, 2013.

On My Block. Created by Eddie Gonzalez, Netflix, 2018–20.

Irma J. Zamora Fuerte

254

MYTH, FORCE, AND THE BURDEN OF PRESTIGE

Narcos: Mexico as Case Study

Ryan Rashotte

Only once in my life, during a period of restless confusion, did I ever seriously consider becoming tattooed. This was during the final weeks of my undergrad education. My grades had begun to slip. I had no job, or job prospects. I had a girlfriend (who had a tattoo) and a very tenuous hold on her heart.

To solve the latter problem, I suspected, would require a bit more edge in my life. And what easier way to snag some edge than with a little gentle scarification? Nothing too fancy; my intended design was simple, but classic: the ancient Greek word for "glory": *kleos.* Here's how it looks in the original lettering: κλέος.

Please understand, this is not run-of-the-mill glory. Kleos is the glory of immortality. It was the glory that drove Achilles from his sexy life among the princesses of Skyros to face down and smite hundreds of wily Trojans on the battlefield. More importantly, it was the glory that inspired Homer to snap all that smiting into dactyls, which, almost three thousand years on, are still being recited in lecture halls across the world, still stressing their beats to eternity.

Before opening the search for a tattoo artist proficient in classical alphabets, I thought it would be a smart idea to confirm the word's denotations with my old classics professor. At the same time that I received a form email telling me that that excellent adjunct was no longer with the college, the department head himself sent a personal, interventional email warning me that while, yes, *kleos* did refer to the literary glory I coveted, it also meant "rumor," as in, a lifetime of being whispered about and laughed out of symposiums is surely in store for anyone dumb enough to inscribe feats of ill gain on his left bicep.

My takeaway from this experience, other than the knowledge that I am not a tattoo person, was that the ancient Greeks had a prescient understanding of modern celebrity. Glory and rumor, reverence and controversy. Each side weighs in a delicate balance of stardom, the slightest disruption to which can send careers plummeting at speeds and to depths that, in our digital age of celebrity, may be nothing short of epic.

Netflix's *Narcos* (2015–19), a serial drama about Colombian narco-culture in the 1980s, offers a moving lesson in what can happen when the idol is made over into a scapegoat. In the final episodes of season 2, we find Pablo Escobar, drug kingpin, erstwhile Robin Hood, and likely the most globally recognizable Colombian in history, pursued to the edge of fame with a bounty on his head the size of his country's GDP. Holed up in his father's farmhouse, the last of his pesos literally rotting away, Escobar spends his days working as a campesino: laying fences, gutting hogs. In his downtime, he wanders the fields at the magic hour with a roach pasted to his lip, squinting at natural phenomena as though they held the riddle of his demise: how a life of money, power, and women could be so abruptly stunted into a few final hours of poverty, sweat, and shame.

In Colombia, narcoculture is a theology: the cult of Pablo Escobar. Audiences expect this kind of agony as a prelude to his resurrection as national icon. In Mexico, however, narcoculture is a mythology. And when *Narcos* rebooted, in 2018, for a new series about the rise of the Guadalajara Cartel, the producers made the wise decision to spread the kleos across a much wider pantheon. For the price of one Escobar, we get Amado Carrillo Fuentes (José María Yazpik), Lord of the Skies, an airborne smuggler with three-day stubble and *Top Gun* good looks; we get his uncle, Ernesto Fonseca Carrillo (the formidable Joaquín Cosío), an earthy old-schooler who subsists on beer, rocks of cocaine, and glucosic stores of Sinaloan vengeance; we get Joaquín "El Chapo" Guzmán (the adorable Alejandro Edda), a human mole who rules an illicit kingdom of underground tunnels running money and drugs below the border.

In the first part of this chapter, I will probe further into this mythology of *Narcos: Mexico*, examining how the series anneals the history of the Guadalajara Cartel to fit the molds of legend. Second, I'll explore how violence in particular is used to develop and embellish that legend. Finally, after demonstrating how the series accords with the formal conventions of prestige TV, I'll consider both the ethical and neurochemical implications of representing cartel violence as a fine televisual art.

Myth

Of all the narcos whom the series mythologizes, Rafael Caro Quintero (Tenoch Huerta) appears the most classically Grecian: buff physique, dark clots of curly hair. The role he plays is that of a farmer, but not just any farmer: a horticultural expert, a botanical intuit. Rafa displays a paternal care for the sinsemilla plants he is credited here with inventing: cradling them, sniffing the nutrition deep into their stalks, wincing at the slightest deficiency.

But like his vegetation cohorts from other pantheons, the sensitive Rafa has a violent, volatile streak. In episode 1.2, his subplot has him stymied by the impossible task of building a marijuana plantation in the desert of Chihuahua. After fruitless days spent mining the sand for groundwater, Rafa gives into a feverish pique, dumping a box of grenades into the barren sands. Five explosions later, a geyser thick as Rafa's outstretched arms erupts from the dry earth, drenching his chorus of thugs, and, as fate would have it, ensuring the creation of Rancho Búfalo, the largest marijuana plantation in narco history: twelve square kilometers of Rafa's handiwork (Bowden 149).

There are many synchronistic moments like this in season 1 of *Narcos: Mexico*: simple twists and berserks of fate. As the villains run through their plot points, racking up kills and leveraging vendettas, they seem more and more destined to succeed no matter how fantastically their story evolves. It's as though the deep, mysterious power that drives their misdeeds lifts them above the gravity of human agency. (Season 2 takes on the countertask of dismantling these legends, especially that of Félix Gallardo, who—spoiler!—will end the season in jail. My focus in this section is mainly on season 1.)

In theory, this should pose a narrative conundrum. How do you create suspense for characters who appear untouchable, characters whose real-life counterparts (a basic Wikipedia search will confirm) are mostly still alive, many of them out of jail? How do you build tension into a story when, twenty seconds into the pilot episode, the voice-over narrator spills the beans by saying, "[this story] doesn't have a happy ending; in fact, it doesn't have an ending at all"?

One solution is to lean in and make this untouchability an aesthetic principle. In episode 1.1 ("Camelot"), when the narcos transplant themselves from rustic Sinaloa to glitzy Guadalajara, they approach the city's reigning crime lord with a partnership deal. When said crime lord rejects their deal, in a giggle of contempt, he is promptly shot in the face: executed in the middle of the day, in the busy lobby of the city's most glamorous hotel. As hordes of shrieking guests scamper for the exits, the Sinaloans linger at the crime scene. One of them pulls out a map, and they begin to pore over it, the corpse bleeding over the tiled floor posing less concern to them than the question of where to establish their next grow-op.

This scene crosscuts for several minutes, and when we return to the hotel, the Sinaloans appear even more at ease, sitting at a table, enjoying a drink and a cigarette, the corpse splayed beside them completing a pleasant, if ironic, three-shot of afternoon repose.

There is a narrative purpose for this insouciance: the narcos, we'll discover in a moment, are waiting for the police to arrive so they can bribe the captain onto the cartel's payroll. But the narcos' general indifference to their crime, played here for comic effect, sets a tone for the series: it epitomizes the show's mythical conceit that in Mexico the system is so corrupt, the ideal

Figure 14.1 A pleasant three-shot of afternoon repose. From *Narcos: Mexico*.

of justice so warped, that it elevates its criminals into heroes, even gods. The DEA will have no chance against an entire nation that conspires to let its deities rule as ferociously as they please.

Of all these divine criminals, it's Miguel Ángel Félix Gallardo (Diego Luna) who seems destined to rule this mythic land. A graduate of the Don Draper school of brooding protagonists, Félix is typical of the dark alpha males who rule today's prestige TV: he's dapper, pensive, too morally complex to fail. The narrator calls him "the Rockefeller of marijuana," and it's Félix's entrepreneurial instincts that pave the narcos' path to success. By the middle of season 1, the Guadalajara Cartel, under his rule, will be pulling in $30 million a week ($93 million by today's standards—about $3 million more than Netflix's weekly revenues at the time of this writing) (Watson).

One notable, and somewhat odd difference between Félix and the other dark alphas of prestige TV is that Félix's hardscrabble origins are fast-forwarded so the series can get right to its mythmaking. Like with the legendary Nahuatl warrior Popocatépetl, a giant impressionistic portrait of whom hangs opulently in Félix's office, it's the grand struggles that matter most to his national legend. Félix's backstory—the years he spent working as a police officer and PRI bodyguard in Sinaloa—are obscured by the omnipotent spotlight the series is constantly shining on his criminal labors.

This isn't to suggest Félix has it easy. They are plenty of mettle-testing adventures for him in season 1, including kidnappings by both Nicaraguan contras and Colombian narcos (in back-to-back episodes). But only once in the first season does his vulnerability seem legitimately a cause of dramatic tension. This moment comes at the end of episode 1.6 ("La Última Frontera"). The DEA has hatched a plan to lure Félix across the border into the United

States. Once he's on America soil, the good guys can finally nab him, try him in federal court, and lock him away for a few dozen lifetimes.

In order to sneak across the border, Félix has to assume the identity that matches the one in his fake passport. This means trading his designer suit for a casual jacket and baseball cap, his 1980 Mercedes Benz SLC for an '86 Volkswagen Corsair ("Narcos: Mexico: 2018–2020"). It means offsetting the glare of his Rolex with the blankness of his face, the vacant look of a god blinking out from behind mortal drag.

In the episode's climax, as Félix sits alone in his brown VW, crawling closer and closer to Mexican Customs at the speed of bottoms sliding farther to the edge of seats, the DEA agents adjust their haunches, spying him in their binoculars from across the border. "Come to papa!"

The tension of this scene is motivated by Félix's celestial demotion. The Mexican capo, a mythic figure in his homeland, is reduced by the power of the border to an illegal migrant, a persona non grata forced to secure his livelihood in a country whose authorities have already begun plotting his persecution. This is a rare moment in the series when the spectacle of brutal violence (about which, a lot more in a moment) is superseded by the threat of structural violence, that is, the kind of violence that reveals "the unavoidable limitations that societies place on groups of people, which prevent them from achieving the quality of life that would otherwise be possible" (Adlam et al. 31) (i.e., the kind of violence that would be central to the series if David Simon were its showrunner).

Fortunately for Félix, before he can clear Mexican Customs, myth asserts its own authority. The customs officer hands Félix a telephone: it's the Mexican secretary of defense on the line, and he warns Félix that a phalanx of municipal, state, and federal gringos is waiting with guns cocked just a few yards north.

As far as dei ex machina go, this one is completely improbable. Even Félix looks shocked. But as *Narcos* is intent on showing us, in Mexico, improbable does not mean unbelievable. In a land where politics is the stuff of myth, the cipher of human ethics can discern some very bold shapes, but it can never unscramble the will of the gods.

Force

If myth sets a tenor for *Narcos*, its corresponding vehicle is violence: not an uncommon match in classical aesthetics. Simone Weil wrote that "the true hero . . . of the *Iliad*" is not a god or a warrior, but rather the idea of force itself: "Force employed by man, force that enslaves man, force that . . . turns anybody who is subjugated to it into a thing." "Exercised to the limit," she writes, "it turns man into a thing in the most literal sense; it makes a corpse out of him." And corpse-making "is a spectacle the *Iliad* never wearies of showing us" (6–7).

Narcos: Mexico takes similar relish in displaying the destructive, dehumanizing power of its mythic force.

There are two main forms of violence in the series, distinguishable by scale. The more grandiose form is the battle scene. In the eighth episode of both seasons, we get one big *Iliad*-grade slaughterfest. These battles run, respectively, 4:30 and 2:30 (not counting the long culminating standoff that takes place after the raid in the latter scene), and they take advantage of the narrative's cross-border tensions by pitting U.S. federal agents (of various departments) against Mexican narcos.

There is an energetic video-game-like quality to these battle scenes. Once the helicopters deposit the Americans on Mexican turf, we follow the ensuing ground action over the shoulders of avatars racing steadily forward, machine guns pointed ahead and sending stutters of gunfire into the shimmering distance. Abandoned trucks and empty buildings provide momentary shelter for these avatars to recock their weapons before reemerging into the fray. Allies spiral to the ground, dust blooms in the ricochet of bullets, new foes pop from behind new obstacles, fervently stalling the mission's completion. At the end of the sequence, the catharsis of a high body count is counteracted by the thrilling realization that the main characters on both sides have survived the onslaught.

Protracted battle scenes like this are obviously nothing new. If anything, they meet the Hollywood standard for film violence, set in the late 1960s. According to film scholar Marsha Kinder, kinetic orchestrations of slaughter are to the action movie genre what songs are to musicals: "'numbers' [that interrupt] the linear drive of the plot with their sensational audio and visual spectacle [while] simultaneously [serving] as dramatic climaxes that advance the story toward closure" (68).

One notable difference in *Narcos* is that the first-person perspective toggles between gringo and narco. For a few seconds, you play as a DEA agent, dodging bullets and strafing militarized campesinos, before switching over to become Rafa, mashing a *federale's* face with the butt of your machine gun. An idealist might see this as a democratic approach to the masochism. A steadfast structuralist would insist it's just another way to stir the chaos.

The second form of violence we find in *Narcos* (and the one most often perpetrated solely by Mexican characters) takes place on a smaller scale. Typically, it portrays the murder or torture of individuals or small groups of people. Sometimes, and maybe to compensate for the reduced body counts, this kind of violence can be extra brutal.

The ultimate example is the torture and murder of kidnapped DEA agent Enrique "Kiki" Camarena (Michael Peña). (For info on cinematic representations of the Kiki affair, see my monograph *Narco Cinema*, 54–88.) So much of *Narcos'* narrative tension is built around this moment, whether its anticipation (season 1) or its aftermath (season 2). The act itself is stretched out for four minutes, over three scenes and two episodes, during which time we see Kiki, tied to a chair, blasted with a cattle prod, penetrated with an electric drill; we see a doctor inject adrenaline into his heart so that his body may be dragged for several victory laps around the battlefield. The bloodier and more corpselike Kiki appears from scene to scene only underscores that the worst is happening off camera.

This torture sequence is primordial to the series' narrative—the root cause of its violent pathology—but it is hardly singular. There are regular, seemingly random moments of violence scattered throughout *Narcos*, luring the gorehounds out to feast: scenes of bodies separated by airplane propellers, of severed heads delivered in gift boxes. These scenes are designed to shock not through their originality, but rather by evoking a gory verisimilitude to the real-life atrocities of the drug war.

Occasionally in *Narcos*, this mimesis achieves an auteur level of craftmanship, with stylized acts of violence so unsettling that they momentarily overwhelm the plot, forcing us to reflect on their entrancingly grisly mise-en-scènes. The raid on don Neto's beach house (episode 1.10: "Leyenda") is a good example. (Other notable auteur sequences: the bridge scene from episode 2.10 ["Free Trade"], and the Sofia Coppola-esque target practice scene that opens episode 2.5 ["AFO"].) In this scene, we adopt Neto's perspective as he sits on a deck chair on the craggy beachfront of his Puerto Vallarta estate, watching calmly as federal officers barge through his villa, shooting every bodyguard and reveler in sight. Bullets maul through the bodies of topless sunbathers, ranchero bruisers twist to the ground or tumble off balconies in slow-motion sync with the '80s ballad "Mamá ven a sentarte aquí" leaking into the soundtrack from Neto's earphones. Meanwhile, from the vantage of his deck chair, Neto takes in the massacre wistfully, as though scanning a poem about life's impermanence. The blood splatter collecting on his face sends a lone red teardrop down his cheek as he glances at the tide crashing on the shore below him. Scenes like this elevate the show's violence into something aesthetic, something to appreciate. They recall Godard's smart-aleck response to accusations of excessive violence in *Pierrot le fou*: "That's not blood," he said, "that's red" (qtd. in French 2).

Studies of film violence in recent decades have tended to highlight the postmodern, referential quality of that violence, often charting the array of influences that steady the hands of today's auteurs of red (Bruder; Self; Slo-

Figure 14.2 A lone red teardrop.

cum). But the best moments of auteur violence in *Narcos* don't compromise gut-level affect for intertextual reflection (nor do they, I think, in many of the films these studies examine). Rather, they evoke a profound creepiness that is enough to remind us that "uncanny" is not synonymous with "irony." To be fully unorthodox here, I'd even suggest that it's this unsettling feeling that makes these fabricated displays of violence feel "authentic." Eric G. Wilson argues that "most Hollywood violence is too meaningful to be disturbing. . . . Actual brutality often escapes meaning, and this is one reason it unsettles." But under the pretense of being a fact-based historical drama, maybe *Narcos* is able to have it both ways: it can represent the unsettling brutality of "real life" narco violence through depictions whose auteurist flourishes momentarily trouble the show's otherwise largely conventional narrative (and our habit of reading it as such).

Opening up the border between reality and representation obviously raises big ethical questions about the artist's responsibility in depicting real tragedy. If it makes us uncomfortable to think that actual atrocities of the drug war have been mined for script beats and jump scares, it may be genuinely disturbing to realize that the movement from real to mimetic violence has not always been unidirectional in *Narcos*. In September 2017, Carlos Muñoz Portal, a thirty-seven-year-old production scout for the series was gunned down while taking photos in Temascalapa, a town north of Mexico City. Though Portal's murder remains unsolved, given that the location he was scouting has been the scene of multiple drug-related homicides, the attorney general speculates that local traffickers mistook Portal for a police officer gathering intel (Bitette).

I'm probably overthinking this, and I really don't mean to sound disrespectful, but at this point, having watched the series several times, I find it hard not to see Portal's murder as another example (albeit, an extra-extra-diegetic one) of the vacillating seriality of violence on which *Narcos* forges its casual, quippy, gritty, nihilist take on the drug war. My problem with the series, what makes it kind of obscene, is not any particular moment of violence; rather, it's the larger fetishization of Kiki's death, and the constant effort the show undertakes to ensure that his murder monopolizes the viewer's mourning.

In episode 1.7 ("Jefe de Jefes"), when two American tourists wander into the wrong seafood restaurant only to be butchered with an icepick by a coke-addled Rafa, their stories are quickly dropped from the plot, their corpses cast atop the ever-growing stack of bodies whose foreshadow stretches closer and closer toward Kiki. It may be a trope of the action genre that minor characters are fleshed out as minimally as necessary to energize the spectacle of killing them off—brown skin and an intense expression often being all they get—but does this make the practice any less warped?

Narcos is just as susceptible as its heroes to being "modified by its relations with force," as Weil writes, "swept away, blinded by the very force it imagined it could handle . . . deformed by the weight of the force it submits to."

And whether it's the lionization of the lone hero's struggle, or the transposition of real massacres into high art, these deformations of *Narcos*, we'll see, have proven very popular, and highly lucrative, in the age of streaming TV.

The Burden of Prestige

Season 1 of *Narcos: Mexico* opens with a montage of 1980s newsreel footage from the trenches of the drug war: images of body bags hauled away on stretchers, of corpses lining the streets in neat gory rows. As these images cycle, the voice-over narrator informs us that half a million people have died in the drug war. He then proceeds to exercise the first of the series' many uses of dramatic license by telling us, "A lot of people don't want to hear this story. They want to pretend it never happened."

Any rhetorician worth his sneer would identify this claim as a stacked evidence fallacy: while there are certainly a few living people who'd sleep better with this story off the air—maybe, say, a dozen elderly politicians (including Mexico's former minister of defense, a minor character whose name the show coyly, and kind of annoyingly, bleeps whenever spoken aloud)—clearly there are many more people who do want to hear this story. When season 2 debuted, in February 2020, it was the fifth-most streamed show in the United States, garnering 49,651,373 weekly "demand expressions" (an obscure, propriety measurement of online interest that, according to its developer, collates comments on social media, illegal downloads of the show, as well other data points withheld by the company; take that for what you will [Clark]). And if fan reviews are any indication—the series holds a 91 percent average audience score on Rotten Tomatoes ("Narcos: Mexico")—there are a lot of people who do want to pretend that this story happened in just the way Netflix says it did.

Who are these people? What makes a teenager from Japan or Sweden suddenly so invested in the mythic feats of Mexican capos from the 1980s? Now that neurological studies are undermining the classical argument that watching violence on stage or screen inspires a general feeling of catharsis (Gentile 492), how can we understand the kind of pleasure *Narcos'* global audience derives from the show's gruesome spectacles of "Mexican history"?

One catalyst for this pleasure may simply be generic. *Narcos* fits the mold of the "prestige drama," "prestige" being the trendy misnomer for "prestigious" in the rhetoric of the digital age. More specifically, "prestige" denotes a high-quality TV project, often produced by a cable channel or streaming service, and formally earmarked for critical acclaim. Unlike regular TV, prestige is treated as a highbrow art form, equated with literature: seasons are "10-hour novels," episodes "chapters" crafted to elicit close readings from podcasters and online fans (Thurm). And the genre's emergent tropes—dampened color schemes, complexly troubled male protagonists, boobs, and the participation of celebrity actors and directors (VanArendonk) promise viewers a connoisseurial pleasure in tuning in, a virtual congratulations in knowing that the algorithms that monitor their browsing histories have placed them among the cognoscenti of streaming TV.

But how does this pleasure of discernment influence the viewer's reaction to *Narcos'* layers and layers of brutal violence? Violence scholars John Adlam, Tilman Kluttig, and Bandy X. Lee suggest that the attempt to understand violence is driven by an innate human need to find symbolism in something profoundly irrational (37). If we accept this definition, we might suggest that the series' auteur moments satisfy this critical desire, allowing us to interpret violence as a fine art, but also encouraging us to reconcile our understanding of that violence within larger ideological or historical frameworks.

The problem with this theory is that, for many viewers, the "search for meaning" is not primarily a scholastic endeavor. The medium itself—online streaming TV—plays a big role in viewer motivation. It'll come as no surprise to anyone reading this essay in 2022 that another key trope of prestige

TV is its propensity for addictive viewing. In 2015, more than 70 percent of Americans admitted to "binge watching" their favorite shows (Steiner and Xu 1, 3). Encouraged by the cheap, instantaneous access to a seemingly infinite store of movies and series, today's audiences have turned excessive TV consumption into a cultural phenomenon. Netflix admits that 61 percent of its subscribers "regularly watch between 2–6 episodes of a show in one sitting" (Page).

Psychologists who study this phenomenon are less interested in the tropes that make streaming TV so addictive than they are in the mental and physical effects of indulging this addiction. What these psychologists are finding is that, like any pleasurable act (analogies range in the literature from eating chips to having sex to shooting heroin) (Camart et al., "'Potato Chips' Effect"; Page), binge-watching produces heavy doses of dopamine, the hormone responsible for stimulating attention, motivation, and pleasure (Perry). The more we watch, the more dopamine we produce, the more addicted we may become (Page; Riddle et al. 592).

These studies also reveal that habitual binge-watchers exhibit the signs of traditional addicts: they neglect their work and social lives, they have problems sleeping, their diets go to McHell, they regularly feel irritable, anxious, self-loathsome, and they have difficulty controlling the consumption of their chosen vice (Camart et al., "Between Pleasure and Risk" 46; Romo et al. 57, 59; Steiner and Xu 12). Binge-watchers who break the habit commonly describe the experience with terms like "overdose" and "withdrawal" (Steiner and Xu 12).

Like binge-watching, screen violence also shakes and stirs the chemical cocktails of our brain in ways that may encourage our consumption of it. When we watch violent media, adrenaline, cortisol, and testosterone enter our bloodstream in heroic doses, triggering our fight-or-flight response. This "makes us feel alive and excited" in the moment, and then pleasantly exhausted in the aftermath—a pattern that sounds similar to, but is not physiologically congruent with, Aristotelian catharsis: our aggressive feelings are never "purged"; on the contrary, they stay primed between the action scenes, anxious for the next adrenaline blast (Gentile 505–6).

Studies of viewer motivation also find that audiences prefer watching depictions of real over fictional violence on TV, particularly when those depictions are assumed to shed light on larger events or issues, like the drug war (Cano 10–12; Fernández Villanueva et al. 588–91; Fernández Villanueva et al. are talking about documentary violence, so I'm extrapolating here). Psychologist Concepción Fernández Villanueva argues that this kind of violence offers the viewer rare insight into the reality of criminal life. This insight may be sympathetic, affording details into "the emotional impact on the victims . . . [or] the motives of the aggressors," or it may be aesthetic, presenting "nuances of cruelty [and] explicitness" we wouldn't find in other formats (588) (and a big cf.: note that 24 percent of binge-watchers also claim "information/knowledge" as a cause for their compulsive viewing) (Camart et al., "Between Pleasure and Risk" 45–46; Steiner and Xu 9).

Before its recent connotation with "achievement," prestige, we should remember, used to mean "deception." I wonder if *Narcos'* audience—yours truly included—feels a delusive sense of self-improvement when we watch Héctor Palma split Rafael Moreno's face apart with a baseball bat: a specious insight into the course of Mexican history as it transposes itself, crack after bloody crack, into the show's mythology; if the neurochemical recipe that produces these feelings of insight and connoisseurship is crafted to leave us craving more; if it's not violence at all, but addiction that is the true force of the show's epic narrative.

Despite the ambivalent enjoyment I get from the violent spectacles, my favorite moment in *Narcos* isn't any of the big battle scenes, nor is it one of the auteur moments discussed earlier. It's actually a scene that goes out of its way to withhold the violence we expect.

This scene comes in episode 1.8 ("Just Say No"). The Lord of the Skies and the Ojinaga Fox have tracked down two coke smugglers who claim to have lost their shipment when their truck hit a rock and slid off the road just across the U.S. border. The Lord of the Skies isn't buying it: he raises his shotgun to the first smuggler and solicits the Fox to "Kill these fuckers!" You can almost hear billions of dopamine receptors tingling across the Netflix multiverse for their next hit.

But rather than shoot, the Fox decides to give the smugglers the benefit of the doubt. The next night, he and the Lord of the Skies set out to cross the

Ryan Rashotte

Figure 14.3 "Kill these fuckers!"

border and locate the missing truck. The Lord of the Skies worries they're being set up by the Americans, just as Félix was set up two episodes earlier. But the Fox insists they find out. "If they're telling the truth," he explains, "I'd be shooting two innocent men."

In the end, the missing truck turns up, the coke still intact. The smugglers were telling the truth, and their lives are spared.

Not only does this scene delay, and then ultimately confound, the compulsive desire for violence the series routinely rewards, it goes out of its way to make nonviolent behavior something positive, even heroic. This is the god on the battlefield, seeing how easy it is to take a human life, but choosing to act with mercy. "I love people more than money," the Fox tells the Lord. (This action is very much in keeping with Fonseca's persona as the noble bandit. His *aristeia* in season 2's battle sequence demonstrates the best example of kleos in the series.)

There is an obvious moral to this, and my attempt to blow it into some larger lesson about how best to represent the drug war would be a factitious way of wrapping up. After all, my feelings about this scene are just as much the result of neurochemical manipulation as my feelings for the battle scenes. Maybe it just so happens that my noggin is better wired for oxytocin than testosterone that I could do with more scenes like this one.

But as *Narcos* goes forward into new territory, delving into new decades, new deeds and new massacres, I hope that, like the cartels it mythologizes, Netflix understands that a diverse pharmacopeia can be very good for business.

Vengeance and fury make for fine poetry, but love and sympathy are worth binging forever.

Works Cited

Adlam, John, et al. *Structural Violence and Creative Structures*. Jessica Kingsley Publishers, 2018. Vol. 1 of *Violent States and Creative States*.

Bitette, Nicole. "'Narcos' Locations Manager Shot Dead While Scouting in Mexico." *New York Daily News*, 17 Sept. 2017, www.nydailynews.com/entertainment/tv/narcos-locations-manager-killed -scouting-mexico-article-1.3500168.

Bowden, Charles. *Down by the River: Drugs, Money, Murder, and Family*. Simon & Schuster, 2002.

Bruder, Margaret Ervin. *Aestheticizing Violence, Or How to Do Things with Style*. 2003. Indiana U., PhD dissertation.

Camart, Nathali, et al. "Between Pleasure and Risk: The Psychology of TV Series Watching." *Combining Aesthetic and Psychological Approaches to TV Series Addiction*, Cambridge Scholars, 2018, pp. 36–54.

Camart, Nathali, et al. "The 'Potato Chips' Effect: TV Series' Addictive Additives." *Combining Aesthetic and Psychological Approaches to TV Series Addiction*, Cambridge Scholars, 2018, pp. viii–xiv.

Cano, Maria Alejandra. "The War on Drugs: An Audience Study of the Netflix Original Series *Narcos*." *Digital Commons @ Trinity University*, 2015, digitalcommons.trinity.edu/cgi/viewcontent.cgi ?article=1023&context=infolit_usra.

Clark, Travis. "The Top 9 Shows on Netflix and Other Streaming Services This Week." *Business Insider*, 23 Feb. 2020, www.businessinsider.com/top-netflix-streaming-shows-this-week-narcos-mexico-clone-wars-2020-2.

Fernández Villanueva, Concepcíon, et al. "Violence on Television: Unpleasant, Interesting, or Morbid?" *Revista Latina de Comunicación Social*, vol. 16, no. 68, 2018, pp. 582–98.

French, Karl. Introduction. *Screen Violence*, edited by Karl French, Bloomsbury, 1996, pp. 1–11.

Gentile, Douglas A. "Catharsis and Media Violence: A Conceptual Analysis." *Societies*, vol. 3, no. 4, 2013, pp. 491–510.

Kinder, Marsha. "Violence American Style: The Narrative Orchestration of Violent Attractions." *Violence and American Cinema*, edited by J. David Slocum, Routledge, 2001, pp. 63–102.

Narcos. Created by Chris Brancato, Carlo Bernard, and Doug Miro, Gaumont International Television, 2015–17.

Narcos: Mexico. Created by Chris Brancato, Carlo Bernard, and Doug Miro, Gaumont International Television, 2018–20.

"Narcos: Mexico." *Rotten Tomatoes*, www.rottentomatoes.com/tv/narcos_mexico.

"Narcos: Mexico, 2018–2020." *Internet Movie Car Database*, www.imcdb.org/movie_8714904-Narcos--Mexico.html.

Page, Danielle. "What Happens to Your Brain When You Binge-Watch a TV Series." *NBC News*, 5 Nov. 2017, www.nbcnews.com/better/health/what-happens-your-brain-when-you-binge-watch-tv-series-ncna816991.

Perry, Susan. "Dopamine and Movement." *Brain Facts*, 22 Oct. 2015, www.brainfacts.org/thinking-sensing-and-behaving/movement/2015/dopamine-and-movement.

Rashotte, Ryan. *Narco Cinema: Sex, Drugs, and Banda Music in Mexico's B-Filmography*. Palgrave Macmillan, 2015.

Riddle, Karen, et al. "The Addictive Potential of Television Binge Watching: Comparing Intentional and Unintentional Binges." *Psychology of Popular Media Culture*, vol. 7, no. 4, 2018, pp. 589–604.

Romo, Lucia, et al. "Serials / Passion or Addiction?" *Combining Aesthetic and Psychological Approaches to TV Series Addiction*, Cambridge Scholars, 2018, pp. 55–77.

Self, Will. "The American Vice." *Screen Violence*, edited by Karl French, Bloomsbury, 1996, pp. 71–81.

Slocum, J. David. Introduction. *Violence and American Cinema*, edited by J. David Slocum, Routledge, 2001, pp. 1–36.

Steiner, Emil, and Kun Xu. "Binge-Watching Motivates Change: Uses and Gratifications of Streaming Video Viewers Challenge Traditional TV Research." *Convergence*, Jan. 2018, pp. 1–20.

Thurm, Eric. "It's Not Prestige, It's Just TV." *Esquire*, 27 Apr. 2017, www.esquire.com/entertainment/tv/a54762/the-flaws-of-prestige-tv.

VanArendonk, Kathryn. "13 Signs You're Watching a 'Prestige' TV Show." *Vulture*, 28 Mar. 2017, https://www.vulture.com/2017/03/prestige-tv-signs-youre-watching.html.

Watson, Amy. "Revenue Generated by Netflix from 1st Quarter 2011 to 1st Quarter 2020." *Statista*, 22 Apr. 2020, www.statista.com/statistics/273883/netflixs-quarterly-revenue.

Weil, Simone. "The Iliad, or the Poem of Force." *Chicago Review*, vol. 18, no. 2, 1965, pp. 5–30.

Wilson, Eric G. "The Problem with Aesthetic Violence." *FSG Work in Progress*, fsgworkinprogress.com/2013/01/31/trainwreck.

FROM BORDER "REALITY" TO NARRATIVE POSSIBILITIES IN LATINX TV AND FX'S *THE BRIDGE*

J. V. Miranda

Dangerous. Lawless. Frightening. These are some of the words I have heard students use to describe the border between Mexico and the United States. Such responses may not be surprising, but what is striking is how few of these students have visited a border city, much less crossed the border at a physical checkpoint. This is not to say the students are misinformed; indeed, many of them demonstrate awareness of the current debates and concerns associated with the border. What intrigues me about these descriptions is how they reflect perceptions that are formulated absent any firsthand knowledge of the region or people of borderlands. So how do the students arrive at these descriptions?

The short answer to this question can be gleaned from the assortment of sources that students often cite when explaining their responses, such as movies, television, books, and the news (among others). For example, a student will launch into a documentary on drug trafficking before suddenly turning to the TV series *Narcos: Mexico*; or, another will carefully detail a scene from the movie *Sicario*, which leads them to reference a news article on the dangers of crossing the border. As these examples suggest, the borderlands is a mediated setting culled from fiction and nonfiction representations to create a narrative framework that shapes how the "reality" of the borderlands is perceived. Representations, in other words, not only hold up a mirror to the "real" world but reveal the underlying structures that make it possible to perceive this world absent any firsthand knowledge. These *representational frameworks* offer a more complicated answer to my question, including how perceptions of the Mexico-U.S. border are formed by crossing and blurring the lines between fiction and nonfiction narratives.[1] Such narratives grapple with a material reality that exists at a distance while also projecting a symbolic reality that is made close by its mediation and consumption. The "reality" of the border is perceived as dangerous and frightening because these stories traffic in representations that trouble an imaginary that envisions the U.S. territory as safe, stable, and secure.

I open with these descriptions because much of what follows can be read as a distillation and extension of my conversations with students while teaching texts, films, and other mediations of the Mexico-U.S. border. One of the topics we discuss is the outsized role that televised borders play in structuring perceptions of the borderlands and Latinx communities.[2] Depictions of the border on television (and in popular culture more generally) reinforce the perception that this region is a lawless zone, thus stoking fear and implying a need for a militarized response to (im)migration and drug trafficking. That the presence and representation of Latinx people is tied to these depictions, which are projected into the domestic space, further implies the encroachment of a Latinx people consisting of criminalized, deplorable, and abject border crossers who pose an urgent threat to national security and an existential threat to "American" culture. But whereas depictions of the border capitalize on the spectacle and fear of a Latinx threat, other examples of Latinx television—most often those set within the United States—challenge these perceptions by showing an amenable Latinx community that is committed to U.S. middle-class and working-class values. I am less interested in interrogating the accuracy of this representational spectrum than in examining how these unresolved mediations of Latinx identity are often mapped onto the Mexico-U.S border.[3] Therefore, and as I do with students in my class, this chapter invites us to consider how representations help us understand the mediating function of border narratives on television.

The role Latinx narratives play in mediating the formation of local, national, and transnational communities has been a recurring theme within Latinx scholarship. Scholars such as Monica Muñoz Martinez have called attention to the way these narratives challenge U.S. nationalist mythmaking and recuperate the theorizations, struggles, and activism of local communities. As such, narratives provide a means for extending the collective memory of communities and can be read as archival sites that require researchers to embrace alternative forms of knowledge production. This affirmative role of local narratives—as both a collective act of community formation and as an archival site—according to Muñoz Martinez, demands "a public reckoning with the legacies of racialized and sexualized forms of terror" and violence (664). Yet, this emphasis on the impact of local narratives becomes less clear when considering the broader history and transnational scope of Latinx storytelling. On one level, this transnational history involves reading Latinx narratives, following Juan Bruce-Novoa, as a "topological space" (146) where particular plots, tropes, and genres create the sense of a connection across Latinx communities through shared symbolic relations. In other words, when taken together, Latinx narratives produce a topology that offers a sense of solidarity and unification across racial, gender, and national differences. On another level, a focus on narrative recalls Ramón Saldivar's "dialectics of difference," which includes making distinctions about form and content based on efforts at "demystifying the relations" between minorities and the dominant culture (5). Latinx narratives, from this perspective, are the product of historical differences and articulate these differences by separating themselves from dominant cultural forms. As these approaches suggest, the mediating function of narrative not only provides insight into the formation of Latinx communities but the tensions that arise when considering how these representations may function differently based on their relationship to local, national, and transnational audiences.

These representational tensions raise important questions when moving toward a narrative theory of Latinx television. For example, how do we read Latinx stories—in particular those set in the borderlands—whose popular status and wider circulation (and accessibility) call into question the distinction between local and national narratives? Then there are Latinx stories that adopt dominant cultural forms such as genre television. Do these narratives inevitably reinforce a U.S nationalist imaginary? Or can these televised narratives provide a framework for better understanding historical differences? And finally, what role do popular Latinx narratives on television play in extending collective memory and recuperating histories that have been silenced?

It is within the context of these questions that I turn to the FX series *The Bridge*, which adopts the genre of the neo-noir crime procedural while also centering the gendered, racialized, and national violence taking place on the Mexico-U.S. border. The first section of this chapter will situate *The Bridge* in the context of recent television shows premised on the "reality" of the border. The second part will focus on the adoption of the neo-noir crime genre, which structurally limits Latinx representation while also reorienting the perceptions of U.S. viewers by moving them across the border. Finally, the chapter will place *The Bridge* in the context of the historical use of bridges as a trope within Latinx cultures (which opposes borders) to examine how narratives frame our perceptions about what connections are possible and desired and what connections are impossible and potentially harmful. These final two sections—which consider tropes and genres, respectively—can be read analogously as a move from local to transnational narratives, thus positing *The Bridge* as a useful entry point for examining the role of culturally specific tropes within generic cultural forms and the limits and possibilities of mediation between different audiences and contexts. In this sense, I posit the series as suited for a study in the contradictions and tensions that are evident in Latinx TV representations, while also demonstrating how these narratives take up tropes and genres to challenge the dominant representational framework that envisions the border, and by extension Latinx people, as dangerous, lawless, and frightening.

Televised Borders: An (A)bridged "Reality"

No end in sight. This vague adage serves as the title for the first episode in the National Geographic television series *Border Wars*, which, on its airing in January 2010, claimed to take viewers into the "battleground" that has developed at the U.S. southern border. The series, as the title suggests, pits immigration and customs agents against undocumented migrants and drug traffickers in a purported endless game of "cat and mouse," thus glorifying the devoted soldier-agents who preserve U.S. national security from the criminal-enemy border crossers. Privileging U.S. citizens, and to a lesser degree documented immigrants, *Border Wars* filters this "us versus them" formula through a pseudo-documentary style, thus blurring the line between a police reality TV show premised on giving viewers an unvarnished peek into law enforcement and a cinematic documentary aimed at educating and informing its audience. These generic qualities provide a format for exploiting the spectacle and rhetoric surrounding the border and U.S. (im)migration. And, as Noam Dorr, Emine Fidan Elcioglu, and Lindsey Gaydos argue, *Border Wars* mediates this proposed conflict in a manner that reaffirms "border militarization as the solution rather than the source of insecurity" (59), thus suggesting the necessity of border enforcement.[4] The plots of the series adhere to this narrative, creating scenarios where the border patrol officers act as the first (and last) line of defense against those who threaten the security of U.S. citizens.

This narrative structure can be traced to what Camilla Fojas refers to as a "border genre" that depicts a violent setting where illicit activities proliferate, and Mexican border crossers are represented as a threat to U.S. morality and governance (36). In this sense, Mexicans are both feared and fetishized in these narratives since their portrayal as characters lacking traditional U.S. morals and the moral dilemmas they provoke in their white counterparts are central to driving the plot. Historically, Mexicans provided this genre with a racialized "Other" whose presence and border crossing meant they must be tamed, conquered, or vanquished if the U.S. territory is to be redeemed and made safe for white settlement. Such narratives reflect both the paternal structure that guided U.S. relations with Mexico, often represented by white saviors protecting meek and submissive Mexicans, and the gendered depictions of Mexican antagonists. For example, if a Mexican man stood in the way of the "American" protagonist, they were often brought to heel or eliminated, whereas the women were subdued by sexual conquest or the promise of matrimony. Modern-day narratives perpetuate this mythos, which, in the case of visual media, often takes the form of shifting between images of a landscape caught between a pastoral past and militarized present. Here border agents

272

serve as stand-ins for the rugged "American" cowboys while "Indians" and "Mexican bandits" are replaced by lowly migrants and ruthless drug traffickers. But unlike this history of the border genre, television shows such as *Border Wars* claim to offer viewers direct access to the "reality" of the border while continuing to distort and exploit this region in order to justify the force necessary to hold back those who are framed as threatening the United States with the deviance they bring to an otherwise morally upstanding U.S. citizenry.

This shift to "reality" produces a more complex and a less stable racialized geography, which Camilla Fojas attributes to narratives that involve both Latinx border agents and the Latinx border crossers they pursue, thus disrupting the discursive use of racial difference (41). Race, as noted above, frames representations by posing the decency and moral rectitude of white authority figures against the dishonesty and immorality of a racialized (often Mexican or "Indian") criminal. As Fojas points out, what emerges from this focus on "reality" is a "typology of citizen and alien" (41) that does not easily break down along racial lines. The distinction between "good" and "bad," in other words, cleaves along documented and undocumented, citizen and alien, lines as opposed to clear-cut distinctions of race. Yet, and despite racial ambiguity, these narratives continue to superimpose a moral and racial geography onto the Mexico-U.S. border. It is in this sense, and perhaps unwittingly, that *Border Wars*' opening episode, "No End in Sight," can be read as an admission that there is no foreseeable resolution to this racialized geography and that this ambiguous racial composition threatens a U.S. imaginary underwritten by racial difference. In other words, the mere presence of Latinxs on border "reality" television troubles the U.S. imaginary by depicting a "reality" that must be abridged, or edited, to maintain and secure a racial geography that is representative of the United States.

The Bridge also appeals more directly to the "reality" of the border by drawing on news sources and contemporary issues to shape the narrative. Adapted from the Nordic series *Bron/Broen*, the series premiered on FX in July 2013, several months after *Border Wars* aired its final episode, and is set in the El Paso–Juárez corridor, where it follows a joint investigation into a murder by police officers and journalists from opposite sides of the border. The U.S. detective is a woman, Sonya Cross, who is an effective and dedicated investigator but has difficulty reading and following basic social cues, suggesting she struggles with interpersonal relationships. The Mexican detective is a man, Marco Ruiz, who is torn by his duty to uphold the law amid the systemic corruption of the Mexican police force, and whose troubled masculinity becomes central to the storyline in the first season. Journalists Adriana Mendez and Daniel Frye are also from opposite sides of the border, although both work at the *El Paso Times*, where Frye is a cynical, alcoholic U.S. veteran and Mendez a new reporter who challenges the cynicism of her senior colleague. In centering these cross-border, racially different relationships, the series examines the gender politics, cultural tensions, and social inequalities that mark the relationship between the United States and Mexico. *The Bridge*, therefore, offers a more complicated representation of the televised border "reality" by narrativizing the national tensions that manifest from the depictions of border enforcement and the desire to maintain this perverse racial framework that cannot reconcile the presence of Latinx bodies within the United States.

This violent effort to police a racialized geography is especially evident in episode 7, entitled "Destino," when Cross and Ruiz believe they have located the man responsible for the murder. The detectives arrive at his trailer, and when he does not answer they enter to find military-grade weapons, maps of the border, and a monograph titled "The Dialectics of Paso Del Norte by Jack Childress." It is made clear that Childress is not a border agent when Ruiz discovers a bathtub filled with medications, leading the detective to assume the man is insane. Ruiz's assessment that Childress suffers from psychosis is further confirmed when he skims a chapter title from the monograph that reads "On the Extraterrestrial Origins of the Mexican People." Soon after this discovery, Childress returns home and chooses to take up a sniper position as opposed to going on the run. He is eventually apprehended but not before telling Cross that he wants "the truth to come out" that "there is a war happening here at the border." When asked by Cross at the station why he did not run when he saw the police, he says the "job" was not done since his intention was to "kill the Mexican." This violence is further contextualized in the next episode when he asserts that "dialectics" is the reason he had built up a cache of weapons and that "equilibrium" explains why he wanted to kill Ruiz. For Childress, the dialectic he ascribes to demands he draw hard lines between the United States and Mexico based on race and culture, but it also leads him to admit that El Paso del Norte, which was the name given to El Paso and Ciudad Juárez by the Spanish prior to the separation of the two cities, was "falsely split."

We can read Childress as a representation of the vigilantes and militias that operate along the border and who take it upon themselves to "defend" U.S. territory against the threat of foreign entities. He voices the ideology of these extrajudicial agents with his appeal to dialectics, while his failure to resolve these divisions suggests he is driving himself "insane." For example, he expresses the understanding that these divisions are "falsely" imposed, yet he seeks to violently police them despite this knowledge. Taken metaphorically, Childress's insanity represents the impossibility to reconcile and make sense of Latinx presence in the United States, which manifests in the arbitrary, yet seemingly necessary, violent policing of the border. His mad dialectic separates and connects these two nations who are, as was noted in *Border Wars*, caught in an endless battle between the forces of "good" and "bad." The specter of mental illness also disassociates Childress from both the legal framework through which the Border Patrol operates and the espoused patriotism, and oftentimes white supremacist ideology, that drives many of the vigilante groups. As such, the series isolates the ideological premise that the United States is engaged in an unending war and misses an opportunity to further explore the systemic forces that promote and tolerate cooperation between border agents and these border vigilantes. So while *The Bridge* challenges viewers to reconsider the televised "reality" of the border, it too draws on the notion that there is no end in sight to the *border wars*, thus reinforcing the perceived need for committed, honest, and competent law enforcement that can simultaneously police this racially ambiguous geography and the senseless violence it supposedly engenders.

Bridging Genres and Nations in Latinx Narratives

Shut the border. This phrase concludes the opening sequence of *The Bridge*, whose end emphasizes the U.S. military-grade surveillance equipment and tactics used by the Border Patrol at the international Bridge of the Americas. Agents are shown tracking a black sedan as it enters the bridge. But when the power suddenly goes out, the control panels, monitors, and bridge lights go momentarily dark—as does the viewer's screen—and the Border Patrol agents are thrown into confusion amid this technological failure. With their screens rendered useless, the agents lose sight of the international bridge in what has become a wall of static televisions. Then, just as suddenly, the power is restored, and an agent zooms in to reveal the body of a woman who has been carefully placed on the international line separating Mexico and United States. The startled border agent utters into his headset, "Shut the border."

In using this phrase, *The Bridge* draws on the resurgence of U.S. nativism and racial fears that are exploited by border "reality" television. This imagined closure of the southern border can be heard in demands for a border wall that will stop the illicit "flow" of people, drugs, and crime that are claimed to be crossing into U.S. territory. These sentiments are not new, but, as the opening sequence shows, this rhetoric can be linked to the militarization of the border, comprising a technologically enhanced police force, surveillance, and inspective apparatus. Alejandro Lugo argues that these technical strategies and advanced technological tools not only enforce territorial boundaries but also facilitate the management, discipline, and regulation of "other" populations. Such technologies, in other words, shape the actions and perceptions of those crossing the border. It is possible, from this perspective, to argue that pseudo-documentaries of the border, like those described above, be included as soft technologies aimed at managing perceptions of this border "war zone."

But if the opening sequence of *The Bridge* situates the narrative within this framework by drawing attention to the constant surveillance and technological warfare deployed at the border, then it also suggests the failure of border enforcement, as gaps in surveillance reveal the inability to see everything and everywhere at once. Moreover, the disposal of a dead body on the international borderline brings with it a specter of the violence often associated with the Mexico-U.S. border. This violence crosses national boundaries, causing juridical ambiguity and rupturing the illusion that increased surveillance will result in a border that is enforced, much less secured. The series, in this sense, recontextualizes U.S. nativist rhetoric by suggesting the futility and paradox of calling for a closed border when people, goods, and stories are routinely crossing national boundaries. Here the genre of *The Bridge*, as a neo-noir crime procedural, offers a contrasting narrative to "reality" border television that guides the viewer in what will be a meticulous, even procedural, deconstruction of the notion that the border can be closed. Not only does this deconstruction move the viewer from a national to transnational perspective, but it also suggests that this transgressive act stages the possibility for meaningful connections between the United States and Mexico.

The series was one of the first U.S. television shows to explore U.S. and Latin American relations in a global context, attempting to grasp the national, cultural, and racial tensions that are heightened by the cross-border interactions it sets up. Narrative is central to this effort since the viewer must be introduced to both a decentered national perspective and the complexities of the global world. R. A. Saunders refers to this when he writes that *The Bridge* (both the Nordic series and the U.S. version) is an example of the growing trend in "geopolitical television," aimed at constructing "affective imaginary worlds" that offer viewers a glimpse into global issues (997). In the case of *The Bridge*, the crime procedural provides the generic conventions for deconstructing nationalist narratives, which includes unsettling its U.S. audience by routinely crossing jurisdictional lines as the characters and stories cross into Mexico and take into account the corruption of the Mexican police force. But the narrative also works to disrupt the stereotyping of Mexicans in the character of Marco Ruiz, who refuses to take cartel money despite the risk to both him and his family.[5] This deconstruction is also constrained by the generic conventions of crime procedurals, since Ruiz and Cross represent the possibility of international justice that must work against corruption on both sides of the border.

Over the course of the first season, the possibility of justice becomes less likely and what emerges is a narrative of transgression that is associated with porous borders. This would prove influential, as neo-noir narco dramas would take up the narco-inspired storylines evident in *The Bridge*. These transgressions, according to Viorella Manolache, provide viewers a glimpse into the complicated cultural landscape of the borderlands, which she describes as a heterotopic space where different systems come into contact to create a "place of tension" that exists at the "edge of transgression" (84). The neo-noir genre and aesthetics lend themselves to this transgression, which provides viewers a more complicated framework for considering the systemic corruption that affects already vulnerable populations and leaves crimes perpetrated against these populations unpunished. But it also limits Latinx representations, especially those of migrants and drug traffickers; the former become plot devices, while the latter play an expanded role, sometimes given their own storylines as ruthless and uncaring killers. It is in this sense that the first season vacillates between a traditional neo-noir crime procedural and a prototype for the neo-noir narco dramas that have recently become popular on television.

The role of these generic conventions in shaping the representational framework created by *The Bridge* comes into relief when considering the contrast between the depiction of narcos, whose storylines emphasize their agency and power, and the women (outside the main characters) whose lives are directly impacted by violence. Jillian Sandall, for example, argues that the series brings attention to the femicide in the region, which involves the unsolved murder of thousands of women, but "neglects" to mention how women organizations turned El Paso and Juárez into a "significant site of political and cultural protest," by offering support to women, conducting investigations, and taking direct action to make the violence visible (317). For Sandall, the failure to account for this important activist work reduces the women to victims, with the exception of the main female characters who are directly involved in the criminal justice system or investigative journalism. These narrative differences demonstrate how generic conventions can serve as bridges for moving audiences from one cultural context to another while also limiting the perceptions of viewers based on how stories are told. How we read these Latinx narratives in relation to genre, therefore, reveals these complexities and requires not only an account of the accuracy of representations for bridging cultures but a shift in the representative frameworks we use to interpret narratives on television.

The representation of narcos on *The Bridge* foregrounds these concerns since the series serves as an early indication of the potential popularity of these figures in the U.S. imaginary. One of the popular figures to emerge from narco dramas is the cartel leader Miguel Ángel Félix Gallardo, who is portrayed by Diego Luna in the series *Narcos: Mexico*. As Luna explains, Gallardo's story places a spotlight on the system that "creates these characters" and "leads to corruption on both sides of the border" (Luna). He further clarifies that he is merely playing a character and that the actions of the actual Gallardo are unjustifiable; yet, when these actions are contextualized, they dispel the predominant moral imaginary of "good" versus "bad" that prevents audiences from confronting the complexity of narcoviolence. For Luna, this blurring of real and imagined lines leaves the audience to reflect on the connections between the fictionalized reality they are watching unfold on *Narcos: Mexico* and the reality many of them are watching unfold in their communities and on the news. So instead of identifying with the character—which he emphasizes is not real—he suggests that the aim is to immerse the audience in the system that produces narco-traffickers and directs their actions. The story, therefore, is not solely a biographical representation of Gallardo's rise as "El Padrino," or "the Godfather" of the Guadalajara Cartel, but instead offers a representation of a system whose global, national, and local structures create and perpetuate the ongoing corruption and violence wrought by the drug trade and its reactionary counterpart, the U.S. "war on drugs."

Luna's comments can be read as a challenge to the audience of *Narcos: Mexico* to reconsider their representational frameworks—specifically he suggests they shift from the individual storyline to the systemic narrative framework that produces such individuals—in order to recognize how the violence of drug trafficking, border politics, and the disintegration of ethical governance affects not only those in Mexico but everyone. But as *The Bridge* demonstrates, this representational framework cannot be separated from genre conventions that, in the case of neo-noir, fetishize the thin line between criminality and law enforcement and, ultimately, limit the potential of Latinx narratives to mediate the complex experiences and imaginative worlds of Latinx communities.

Becoming Bridges: A Trope

There is also a bridge. Or to be more precise, there are many bridges that cross the Mexico-U.S. border. For this reason, the bridge—a structure premised on crossing, but which also serves as a militarized immigration checkpoint—plays a recurring role in Latinx cultural production, often used as a symbolic and material opposition to the border. This contrapuntal relationship between bridges and borders is perhaps best captured by Gina Valdés, in *Puentes y fronteras/Bridges and Borders*, who writes, "Hay tantismas fronteras /

que dividen a la gente / pero por cada frontera / existe tambien un Puente" (There are so many borders / that separate people / but for every border / there is also a bridge) (2). These lines would be formative for Gloria Anzaldúa, who quotes them in her multigenre, multilingual classic *Borderlands/ La Frontera* in a section entitled "Somos una gente" (We are a people), where she specifically refers to herself as a mediator for potential allies, promoting solidarity across social differences (107–8). This role of mediator takes place on a "thin edge of barbwire" she calls *home*, but instead of submitting to the sharpened divisions imposed by this boundary, she symbolically transforms herself into a bridge: "Yo soy un puente" (I am a bridge) (25). In this transformation, Anzaldúa offers her audience a passageway across the violent divisions authorized by the enforcement of borders that separate Mexico and the United States.

Her appeal to the bridge is paradigmatic of the relationship she has to the borderlands, which involves accounting for how the border doubles space and time to produce oppositions marked by difference (such as here/there, past/present, and us/them) without losing sight of the bridges that span the border and connect these spaces, temporalities, and communities. Her imagery of bridges and borders, in these senses, refracts the material structure of a Mexico-U.S. borderlands that has lines, fences, and walls as well as multiple international bridges designed to facilitate the movement of goods, people, and culture across these national boundaries. Anzaldúa negotiates this contested geography by drawing on the contrasting material and symbolic functions of the bridge, which she embodies as a subject of these divisions; and despite the pain, she struggles to preserve the connections that precede, emerge (from), and transcend these divisions. So while her home may be violently divided by the border, Anzaldúa reminds her readers that it is possible to envision oneself as a bridge that spans the border and the oppositions the border seeks to police and enforce.

Anzaldúa's layered contrast between bridges and borders would emerge within the context of Chicanx feminist interventions that sought, according to Mary Pat Brady, to politically critique "border mechanics" to "show how violence, conflict, and pleasure coalesce" to obscure the complexity and contradictions of living in the borderlands (173). Here the metaphor of the bridge proves an evocative challenge to the polarizing political schema generated and reinforced by the notion of impermeable borders. Moreover, the bridges provide a material repository for channeling the desire to bring disparate worlds together in order to unmask, redirect, and transcend the conflicts— between potential allies—perpetuated and intensified by the rhetorical deployment of borders. In this sense, Chicanx feminist writers (and scholars), alongside their allies, created what we might refer to as a *bridge trope* that is particular but not exclusive to Chicanx cultural production, the U.S.-Mexico border(lands), and the embodied politics of solidarity advanced by Chicanx feminists. A central provocation of the bridge trope involves negotiating the violent mechanistic forces of the national border as well as the struggle to preserve the connections that arise from these cultural, national, gender, and racial differences.

When we consider *The Bridge* in relation to this trope, it becomes clear that the narrative attempts to create meaningful connections across the border through its depictions of law enforcement and the media, where the dovetailing stories of detectives Cross and Ruiz and journalists Mendez and Frye drive the plot. But these relationships and their shared goals of pursuing truth and justice are fraught with divisions that the border enacts, calling into question the potential of sustaining these connections. Not unlike the consideration of genre above, a closer examination of the bridge trope offers an alternative to the impasse presented by the divisive logic of the border by opening up the potential of Latinx representations that defy a U.S. imaginary desperately clinging to a rigid and hierarchical racial geography. I say "impasse" because the notion of bridges as structural connections must be considered alongside the way bridges are used as checkpoints for inspecting and excluding those who seek to cross over.

In fact, as I write this, the international bridges along the Mexico-U.S. border have become the primary site for the enactment of U.S. policies that refuse the rights of migrants seeking asylum, and have produced refugee camps underneath these bridges. The stories emerging from this use of the bridge as a site for exclusion and inhumane treatment of migrants are reminders, following Alexandra Minna Stern, of how structural barriers translate "the boundary line into a construct" that acts on the body itself (68). Borderland bridges, in other words, may facilitate passage and connection, but these bridges have also historically been used to obstruct, discipline, and exclude people from crossing. In this sense, *The Bridge* also serves as a representational reminder of these structural limitations that are evident in its effort to examine this desire for connection, unification, and the possibility of solidarity, but which must contend with a cultural history marked by the criminalization, punishment, and exclusion of people based on national differences.

That *The Bridge* attempts but ultimately falls short in its effort to narrativize a culturally and socially responsive depiction of the border is evident in its failure to fully grasp the symbolic potential of this Chicanx feminist trope. Moreover, the historical impact of this trope on Latinx culture illuminates the mediating function of the series since it underscores how representations—that blur the lines between fiction and nonfiction—operate differently based on the geographical and cultural context of their audiences. A narrative theory of Latinx TV must take into the account the formation of perceptions produced by such representational frameworks if we are to understand the contradictions and connections—the borders and bridges—that span cultural, racial, gender, and national differences. It is these questions that I examine with students, challenging them to consider the way their own perceptions are edited and framed by border media while not losing sight of the way Latinx television reimagines the potential of genre conventions and acts as an archival site for cultural tropes.

The Bridge, from this perspective, provides an instructive and problematic case study for Latinx TV narratives since it resists the dialectic and synthetic operations associated with a fixed national imaginary and racial geography. I have also tried to show how the series certainly fails to fully immerse us in the liminality of the Chicanx feminist *bridge trope*—which emerges from a transnational, multiracial, feminist, queer, and migratory imaginary—but how its insistence on making connections through genre speaks to the potential of Latinx narratives. These contradictory qualities of the series reflect the contradictions we experience when confronted by mediated settings we have little to no firsthand knowledge of, thus recalling the words of Anzaldúa that "we are responsible for what is happening down the street, south of the border or across the sea" (xxviii). When considering this responsibility in Latinx TV, it may be the *bridge inside us* we need to foster if we want to create the connections that will make it possible to tell different border stories.

Notes

1. I am using the concept of "representational frameworks" to describe the dynamics of mediation at play when we discuss the relationship between fictionalized realities and the underlying structures designed to facilitate, direct, and limit how we perceive reality. In this sense, I am drawing a tacit connection with perception theory more generally but am not interested in developing a psychological analysis of border media. My interest in considering these frameworks involves their role in moving toward a formalist approach to Latinx media.

2. In my general use of the term "Latinx," I am appealing to both the inclusive and ambiguous signification of the *x*, which opens up conversations about the cultural mediation and unresolved tensions of fixed identity categories.

3. For a closer look at Latinx representations that do center on the border, see Isabel Molina-Guzmán's *Latinas and Latinos on TV: Colorblind Comedy in the Post-racial Network Era*.

4. As critiques of U.S. policing have become mainstream, how police reality shows endorse policing has come under scrutiny.

5. Ruiz's morality is put into question in the first episode when an ambulance is stopped on the bridge by Cross as they investigate the murder. The ambulance carries a wealthy man suffering from a heart attack, and the wife desperately offers police officers money to allow the ambulance to enter the United States. Ruiz allows the ambulance to drive through the crime scene, suggesting he took the money, but later we learn that he did not, leading the wife to say, "I thought all Mexican cops took bribes."

Works Cited

Anzaldúa, Gloria. *Borderlands/La Frontera: The New Mestiza*. 4th ed., Aunt Lute books, 2012.

Border Wars. Created by Neil Laird. National Geographic, 2010–13.

Brady, Mary Pat. "The Fungibility of Borders." *Neplanta: Views from the South*, vol. 1, no. 1, 2000, pp. 171–90.

The Bridge. Created by Elwood Reid, Björn Stein, and Meredith Stiehm. FX, 2013–14.

Bruce-Novoa, Juan. *Retrospace: Collected Essays on Chicano Literature Theory and History*. Arte Publico, 1990.

Dorr, Noam, et al. "'Welcome to the Border': National Geographic's *Border Wars* and the Naturalization of the Border Militarization." *WorkingUSA: The Journal of Labor and Society*, vol. 17, 2014, pp. 45–60.

Fojas, Camilla. "Border Media and New Spaces of Latinidad." *Latinos and Narrative Media: Participation and Portrayal*, edited by Frederick Luis Aldama, Palgrave Macmillan, 2013, pp. 35–47.

Lugo, Alejandro. "Theorizing Border Inspections." *Cultural Dynamics*, vol. 12, no. 3, 2000, pp. 353–73.

Luna, Diego. "Diego Luna on the 'Big Picture' Message Behind His Final *Narcos: Mexico* Scene." Interview by Jackie Strause. *Hollywood Reporter*, 18 Feb. 2020, https://www.hollywoodreporter.com/live-feed/narcos-mexico-season-2-diego-luna-interview-final-scene-1279684.

Manolache, Viorella. "Text/Image Border Nodes: *The Bridge* as a Splitting Place." *Journal of Humanistic and Social Sciences*, vol. 7, no. 2, 2016, pp. 77–86.

Muñoz Martinez, Monica. "Recuperating Histories of Violence in the Americas: Vernacular History-Making on the US-Mexico Border." *American Quarterly*, vol. 66, no. 3, 2014, pp. 661–89.

Narcos: Mexico. Created by Carlo Bernard, Chris Brancato, and Doug Miro. Netflix, 2018–.

Sandell, Jillian. "What Can Television Do? Cultural Representations of Border Violence in FX's *The Bridge*." *Feminist Media Studies*, vol. 16, no. 2, 2016, pp. 308–24.

Saldívar, Ramón. *Chicano Narrative: The Dialectics of Difference*. U of Wisconsin P, 1990.

Saunders, Robert A. "Geopolitical Television at the (B)order: Liminality, Global Politics, and World-Building in *The Bridge*." *Social and Cultural Geography*, vol. 20, no. 7, 2019, pp. 981–1003.

Stern, Alexandra Minna. "Buildings, Boundaries, and Blood: Medicalization and Nation-Building on the U.S.-Mexico Border, 1910–1930." *Hispanic American Historical Review*, vol. 79, no. 1, 1999, pp. 41–81.

Valdés, Gina. *Puentes y fronteras/Bridges and Borders*. Translated by Katherine King and Gina Valdés, Bilingual Review Press, 1996. (Spanish edition published by Castle Graphics in 1982.)

PART V

"QUIERO QUE VENGAS"

Coming From, Out, and Into the Lesbian Latin(a) Lover

Peyton Del Toro

The trope of the Latin lover in cinema has been widely discussed in popular media as well as in academia, often focusing on effeminate, nationless Latinos played by non-Latino actors who perform exaggerated tongue rolls in butchered Spanish. Scholars have also analyzed the Hollywood Latina archetype, centered on her hypersexuality, with the flares of exaggerated accents and luscious brown locks. (See Frederick Aldama's introduction to this volume for the many Latinx scholars who have deeply enriched our understanding of the Latin lover stereotype.)

This said, there is limited scholarship on the lesbiana lover of Hollywood, likely because very few of them exist. It has been argued that heterosexual, cis-male Latin lovers are inherently queer simply because they cannot commit to one woman, are well groomed and therefore feminine, and can position themselves as the object of desire through dance.[1] However, I beg to shift the queer Latin lover discourse to engage with identities within the LGBTQ community that face the daily repercussions of disrupting patriarchal/machisto heteronormativity. Lesbian Latin(a) lovers promiscuously exist within the contradictions of the exotic hypersexuality assigned to Hollywood and mainstream televisually constructed Latinas as well as the dangerous sexual depravity attributed to male Latin lovers. The Latin lover conversation must shift to interrogate the ways in which Hollywood and mainstream TV construct lesbian Latin(a) lovers as ambiguous culminations of the United States' intensely gendered stereotypes of Latinidad. In this chapter I will focus on Showtime's *The L Word* (2004–9) and how it constructs the lesbian Latin(a) lover type as at once exotic *and* assimilated, safe in her sexual appeal to liberal, white audiences. Finally, however, I argue that the Latin(a) lover type constructed in *The L Word* needs to be reframed within a resistant, hemisexual, and new mestiza ontology.

Showtime's *The L Word* broke new representational ground by being the first show in U.S. TV history to feature a majority of lesbian and other queer characters. It also, however, constructed and fixed in the televisual imaginary the lesbian Latin(a) lover type. One of the only two Latinx lesbian characters to appear in the entirety of the show and the only Latinx character in the

Figure 16.1 Janina Gavankar as Eva "Papi" Torres in *The L Word*.

fourth season, Eva "Papi" Torres, is played by ancestrally Dutch/Indian actor Janina Gavankar; the actor's racial ambiguity allows her to play the Brown character expected of Latin lovers. Papi, along with a few other lesbian of color characters who enter and exit the many seasons, exists within a primarily white and white-passing lesbian narrative space, reinforcing a dangerous exotification that promotes rather than undermines hegemonic notions of race, gender, and sexuality.

Perhaps there's more to *The L Word* narrative's characterization of Papi. Indeed, Paloma Martinez-Cruz and John Cruz identify two constructed types of Latin lovers: "Hollywood's Latin lovers that rehabilitate the logic of White supremacy, and hemisexual Latin lovers that harness the potential of performance to advocate for new possibilities for Latino masculinities" (Martinez-Cruz and Cruz 207). Hollywood Latin lovers, often played by non-Latinx actors, are nationless and dangerous, exempt from the possibility of marriage but guaranteed to be the sexual corruptor of [white] women. On the other hand, hemisexual Latin lovers offer a solidarity toward "a range of sexual orientations and expressions" while accounting for "the political, cultural, and material consequences of settler colonialism, [and] neoliberal capitalism" (207). In other words, the hemisexual Latin lover suggests we cross the "borders" of heteronormative institutions, so that the Americas can create new masculinities outside of patriarchal and colonial ideologies. So, if we consider Papi as a Hollywood Latin lover in the same way that the notorious "Latin" lover Rudolph Valentino was, we can see that they cater to the desires of white women in similar ways. While Papi embodies the hemisexual Latin lover who introduces new masculinities, she is still very clearly marked Latina, emphasis on the *a*.

Priscilla Peña Ovalle has analyzed the myth of the Hollywood Latina's racialized and sexualized image in her chapter "Mobilizing the Latina Myth." Although the Hollywood Latina's presence "appears to diversify the media landscape, the traditions of her representation as a dancing and temporary love interest of white men in fact reinforce and reify the status quo of Hollywood representation and cultural citizenship within the United States" (Ovalle 4). Papi is a temporary solution to the show's clear lack of diversity while also being a new element to "spice up" the plot due to the seemingly endless possible women she can romance. That being said, Papi seems to function within the intersections of the Latin lover and the Hollywood Latina. Her construction depends entirely on the spectacle of her incomparable sexual impulses, and though Spanish is scattered throughout her script and she proudly claims her Latinidad (while the actress that plays her is not Latina), her country of origin remains unnamed. For her characterization to revolve around the fact that she is foreign, the lack of specificity about where she actually is from exemplifies a "more than innocent confusion of one so-called Latin nation for another; instead, these errors highlight the imperial power of the United States" (Ovalle 4). She is just enough "Othered" to be sexually appealing to white U.S. audiences: she lacks an overt tie to a specific foreign country as much as she lacks a relationship with a single woman, therefore allowing her to remain a temporary presence in the women's (and the audience's) lives.

As I mentioned earlier, queerness within the construction of the Latin lover is not a new interrogation. In "(Re)Examining the Latin Lover: Screening Chicano/Latino Sexualities," Daniel Enrique Pérez argues that "the Latin lover does not adhere to heteronormative gender or sexual codes. Although his identity is constructed around his erotic relationship with women, it is equally constructed around his inability to maintain a relationship with one woman" (Pérez 442). While Pérez acknowledges that he is using the word "queer" in a way that includes "a vast range of gendered positions, sexualized subjects, and erotic permutations" (438), I argue that labeling cisgender and heterosexual people (even in their hypersexual state) as "queer" continues to center voices and experiences that benefit from the privilege they receive because of heteronormativity. If we replace the pronouns with "she/her," this does, in fact, become a relevant and perhaps progressive analysis of Papi. However, placing Papi within the existing structural understanding of Latinx heterosexuality does not abolish the binary associated with racialized gender and sexuality, and instead only reifies heteronormativity, just with new actors playing the part.

While at times Papi seems to simply be cut and pasted into existing heteronormative conceptions of the Latin lover, in other ways she does embody the third space, "an interstitial space of intersection and overlap, ambiguity and contradiction" (Licona 11). She is simultaneously the Hollywood Latina *and* the hemisexual Latin(o) lover. But this third-space consciousness must incorporate a process of decolonization in which the lesbian Latina can represent herself: "such consciousness refuses fixed dichotomous structures and their reductive implications for matters of self-representation" (Licona 16). Lesbian Latin(a) lovers, especially those played by actresses with no relation to Latinx communities, should not be mistaken as radical movements toward progress and representation. Instead, this lesbian Latin(a) lover is constructed to embody the men absent from the lives of the queer women she loves through a sort of paternalism. Papi simply performs a mix of the same tropes constructed through caricatures of machista heteronormativity, a highly regressive understanding of expressions of racialized queerness.

So, what can Papi offer to the conceptualization of the Latin lover? Papi as a hemisexual lover *is* attempting to create new possibilities, not only for masculinities but also for femininities of Latinidad. She, as a singular Latina subject, performs the many characteristics typically expected of *either* Latinos *or* Latinas. If the Hollywood Latina depends on the presence of a male protagonist, and the male Latin lover requires an intense female love interest to fully develop his being, does the lesbian Latin(a) lover construct herself? Simply put, of course not. Instead, her existence pushes us to interrogate how Hollywood continues a colonial construction of lesbian Latin(a) lovers through the intersecting confines of gender, ethnicity, ability, and sexuality, relying on the reification of violent binaries to do so. To analyze the regressive nature of the "progress" the lesbian Latin(a) lover seems to promise, I will now examine the scenes central to Papi's characterization in *The L Word*.

We first see Papi in the second episode of the fourth season, which is titled "Livin' la Vida Loca," first aired in 2007. Alice Pieszecki, a character from the show who has her own radio station based on a website she created called "Our Chart," is the one to "discover" Papi on the maplike tool online. "Our Chart" is a fictional website that tracks lesbian hookups, linking women to those they've had sexual encounters with. The site also assigns each woman a number based on how many sexual connections with other women they have had. One of the main characters, Shane McCutcheon, who has been described as a "skinny little white girl," notoriously holds the record "body count."[2] That is, until Papi comes around.

In the episode before Papi's debut, Alice finds Papi on Our Chart with a record high number of hookups and is skeptical that this mystery woman could be real. She makes an announcement on her radio station asking for "Papi" to meet her at a local nightclub; the episode concludes with that meeting. The opening scene of "Livin' la Vida Loca" begins with a close-up of a bright flower pinned into blonde luscious locks, neatly tucked into a bun—a staple look of the Hollywood Latina, but this time on a white girl. Just next to the flower, big gold hoop earrings glimmer as they catch the red lights flashing in the background. The bass of "La Carretilla" by Jenny thumps loudly through the speakers of the nightclub as the camera pans from the flower to the face of a wide-eyed Alice Pieszecki, a journalist and creator of Our Chart, who is known for always performing a classic white femininity. The nightclub is *The L Word*'s pinnacle sight of signifying Latinidad, "rely[ing] on the production of familiar ethnic characteristics that communicate national origin through the use of language, dress, or music, such as the use of Spanish or salsa music to signal Latinidad" (Molina-Guzmán 4). She looks scared, playing into the trope of the overwhelmed white woman about to be corrupted by the Latin lover. The camera finally shifts its focus from lost and confused Alice to a series of long shots that show us the club's demographic. Amid many drag kings and queens of color and people dancing in sombreros, Alice slowly walks around in search of Papi. Various racially ambiguous men and women in drag, as well as some effeminate cis-men, approach Alice and claim to be the Papi she is looking for, attempting to woo her affection with hand kisses and compliments. That is, until someone explains to Alice that "Papi" means "Daddy," so she'd likely find a lot of "Papis" in the club. This feeling of deceit entices Alice and the viewer into the mystery: Who is the *real* Papi? Perhaps this scene represents the show's attempts to interrogate past tropes of the Latin lover, and how "Papi" is a figure many can identify with. The drag queens and kings, sombreros, and fruit hats that are all constructions of the term "Papi" in relation to the Latin lover trope hold significance in relaying what this term signifies to the general U.S. public; however, the search for the authentic, one "true" Papi must continue.

With no luck finding Papi in the dimly lit sea of dancing bodies, the scene ends with the mystery unsolved. Nonetheless, Alice continues on her quest to find Papi in a new scene. Under a charming yellow umbrella that stands out against the background of the dark alley she walks through, Alice approaches the entrance of a place called Jorge's, the sign reading, "Jorges Shoe Shine & Billiards, Anojitos, Chicharron, Tacos, Flautas." This site is a compilation of the service, entertainment, and consumption that the United States is comfortable accepting from Latinx communities. She walks inside to find that the interior of the building is as dimly lit as the dark alleyway. With clear apprehension, she asks the man working behind the counter if he knows anyone by the name of Papi. The camera pans to another Latino—the wrong Papi once again. Frustrated and uncomfortable in the space, Alice hurries out the door. The show is attempting to undermine past models of the Latin lover, displayed through Alice's disappointment seeing a macho, male Latino. As she is leaving, she gets a call from an unknown number, and tells the caller, "Look, I don't know who this is, but I'm really sick of these games, and I'm not going to—." She pauses, listening to the person on the other end of the line. "Where?" The camera pans to show a white limousine. As Alice walks to the car, she is harassed by three Latinos standing by a lowrider in the alley, another reference to the stereotype of Latinos unable to control their sexual impulses. Despite the struggle it has been to discover the mysterious Papi, Alice persists, and finally gets into the car. "What's the plan?" she asks the driver, clearly annoyed. A dark-tinted window lowers to reveal a set of deep brown eyes peering back in the rearview mirror and a dark silhouette. In slow motion, the eyes blink and eyelashes flutter. Alice asks, "Are you taking me to Papi?" The silhouette turns to show a Brown girl in big hoops, lip gloss gleaming around a bright smile in the darkness of the night, who responds, "I ain't got no plan, baby. It's you who wanted to see me." Papi is simultaneously exactly who we expect her to be but also a surprise; with her dark eyes and a piercing gaze that easily penetrates the viewer, she finally disrupts the repetitive trail of Latino men that Alice encountered before her.

The next scene that features Papi and Alice begins with a close-up shot of Brown hands setting down two unidentifiable but colorful plates of food while the buzzing chaos of a restaurant is mimicked by the camera's shaky movements. We hear people yell over each other in unintelligible Spanish in the background. Papi confidently leads Alice through the kitchen, greeting the cooks personally as they celebrate her arrival. She takes a small piece of food off a plate and, while repeating "Try this, try this," she shoves the bite into Alice's mouth as Alice attempts to take in all the frenzy. The line of consent is blurred when Papi forces Alice to consume the food. They walk through the kitchen to the public area of the restaurant, where Papi continues to be greeted by niños and abuelas. Papi escorts "Alicia," her new Spanish nickname for Alice, to sit at a table for the radio interview, and a plate of food immediately follows for the two to share. "Papi, huh?" Alice sighs, and then asks "What are you? Like, the Pope of East L.A.?" Playing up the stereotype of the hyper-Catholic Latinx community and positioning Papi as a leader of the group emphasizes her ethnic identity. Popes, according to church doctrine, cannot be women, so this statement also brings Papi's masculinity to the forefront of her presentation. Furthermore, East L.A. is well known for its predominantly Latinx population, whereas Alice lives in West Hollywood, where the rest of the show is set, marking Papi as foreign even within the state of California. Papi corrects Alice's pronunciation of "Papi," telling her, "It's okay, it's just a little more Latina than your tongue is used to, chica. Here, let me help you say my name right, you might need it later." The emphasis on the foreignness of the Latin lover's way of speech is a classic construction of their exotic being. Tying her linguistic otherness to her sexual availability, Papi is solidified as a sexual interest for her white [inter]viewer. Flustered, Alice begins her interview, informing Papi that she had crashed her website "Our Chart" due to her outrageous number of sexual connections. She continues to interrogate Papi about why so many women are attracted to her. Papi tells her they come to her because "they know I love them." Looking skeptical, Alice says, "Really, Papi? All of them?" Papi slowly lists all the reasons she loves women in a low and sensual voice, maintaining intense eye contact as Alice begins to squirm. Papi finishes her serenading answer by telling Alice, "I can make a woman come just by kissing her," as Alice sits in a romantic daze. In the next scene Papi's assumption that Alice would be saying her name comes true, and the two are shown having sex in the limousine. With Papi whispering to Alice, "Quiero que vengas," translated as "I want you to come," the scene comes to an end.

The colonial undertones of how the audience comes to know Papi are obvious: Papi, an exotic woman discovered by Alice, is constructed as alluringly mysterious and hard to find. It is only because of the advanced technology, bravery, and persistence of the white colonizer, Alice, who comes in contact with multiple dangerous Brown bodies along the way, that we discover who Papi is. Since Papi was discovered on Alice's chart, Alice feels entitled, like a sort of manifest destiny, to meet Papi and claim her findings on her radio show. When they do meet, Alice is happily welcomed into the Latinx space accompanied by Papi. Papi is shown to be a well-known and loved member of her Latinx community as she introduces Alice to the exotic food of her people. Papi then preys on the sexual naivete of Alice, who can't resist the temptation, and importantly, it is Alice who gets fucked by Papi, not the opposite. In other words, Alice is the innocent white woman preyed on by Papi's sexual depravity rather than the actor who sought Papi out to begin with. Papi further represents the Latina body being subject to colonial conquest and desire, only to be exploited until depleted and left behind.

Alice's Chart is a strategy and technology of social surveillance. Out of the thousands of lesbians tracked by Our Chart, Papi stands out because of what she disrupts: she is existing as a Latina in the word "lesbian," disrupting the whiteness, just as much as she is existing as a lesbian in the word "Latina," disrupting machisto heterosexuality. Papi is not quite butch, but she is as

Figure 16.2 Eva "Papi" Torres in *The L Word*.

masculine as the show was willing to go. Similarly, Papi "is not quite white but never black" (Molina-Guzmán 13–14). Papi's Brownness paired with her palatable queerness creates a threat to white heteropatriarchy; she is granted access to white and Black women's bodies for nonprocreative purposes. In her critical essay "Having It All Ways: The Tourist, the Traveler, and the Local in *The L Word*," Candace Moore discusses how *The L Word*'s narrative techniques work to acculturate straight audiences, "allowing them to feel as if they are 'discovering' authentic knowledge of the exotic lesbian 'other'" (5). Alice's curiosity, manifested as her attentiveness to Our Chart, is thus representative of the audience's desire to know more about lesbian culture from the "inside," but from a safe distance. That being said, constructing access to a stereotyped Latinidad only enhances the techniques already employed by *The L Word*. Papi's Latin lesbianism is just one stop for the traveler-viewers on their exploration of lesbianism.

Papi remains on the outside of the "in" group within *The L Word*, emphasized by her East L.A. background but also by how she interacts with the regular characters in the show. In the episode following Papi's debut, Papi tells Alice that the best place to meet women is the local lesbian pickup basketball game. Papi invites Alice to go, and Alice in turn challenges Papi to a game. Realizing that Alice would bring a team of her privileged, white friends, Papi jokingly calls Alice's team the Bougie Asses, and in episode 10 of season 5, it is revealed that Papi's team's name is the Coco Girls. While recruiting her friends to play, Alice tells Shane, "West Hollywood is our territory. We can't just let them have it without putting up a fight." Here, the rivalry marked between Papi and Shane shifts from sex/body count to territory, where Papi does not belong. Papi, with cornrows in her hair to symbolize her racialized masculinity, stands at the court with her team of unnamed Brown and Black bodies in baggy basketball shorts and tank tops. The Coco Girls are shown effortlessly and gracefully dribbling the ball when the Bougie Asses arrive to the court. The game starts and Papi moves through the court with ease, clearly knowing what she's doing. Meanwhile, Alice and Jenny, two white lesbians from the Bougie Asses, run around the court screaming as they are dramatically pushed and shoved by members of Papi's team.

A classic scene of the Latin lover is one where the brown body is seen dancing. As many scholars have argued, this is often the central site of seduction, as the Latin(o) lover displays a racialized femininity, regardless of the gender presentation of the character. Priscilla Ovalle, in *Dance and the Hollywood Latina*, explains:

> Hollywood's alignment of dance with specific interpretations of race, gender, sexuality, and class illustrates the symbolic formation of the U.S. national imagery and its ideological visualization.

In musicals and in other Hollywood films, nonwhite and marginalized white women danced instinctively or compulsively, while sexually naive or innocent white women were taught to dance by male suitors as expressions of their sexual awakening and impending matrimony. (6)

The lesbian Latin(a) lover must be Othered from her heterosexual counterparts; however, she must still be given the opportunity to display her racialized sexuality and amoral behavior through a sort of kinetic knowledge. This is a new site for showing how the Latin(a) lover's body can move, yet she is still restricted by regressive, stereotypical conceptualization of racialized masculinity. For Papi, this "dance" is basketball. Papi sways with a smooth swagger as she prepares for the toss of the ball. She jumps nearly a foot higher than Shane as she swats the ball toward her team, and shuffles gracefully across the court as she scores time and time again. When she shoots the ball, the camera focuses on her furrowed brow and puckered lips, showing the intense exertion as she scores a three-pointer. The subtle masculinity incorporated into Papi's movement and talent is juxtaposed with the white femininity displayed by Jenny and Alice, who scream as they run away from the ball, flailing their limbs in an attempt to protect their bodies.

Ovalle analyzes dance as a site of agency that challenges traditional female passivity for Latina characters, but she also pays attention to the ways in which they are locked into the movements expected of them: the Hollywood Latina's "titillating image compounds, carries, and disseminates a long narrative of colonization enacted through her brown female body" (22). Basketball, for Papi, functions in a similar fashion even though she is subverting the gendered elements of the hyperfeminine, dancing Latina. The erotic danger suggested by her movement remains, not in the way her hips move to a rhythm, but instead in how she caresses the ball as it moves between her hands, head tilted back just the slightest, smirking while dragging her tongue across her teeth. She thrusts the ball in and out as she dribbles it through her

Figure 16.3 Katherine Sian Moenning as Shane McCutcheon with Eva "Papi" Torres in *The L Word*.

open legs, tracing her eyes down the body of her opponent just to look back up and meet their gaze with an irresistible smolder. Dance scenes typically show the Hollywood Latina silently moving her body to the sounds of music featuring someone else's voice; in stark contrast is basketball's on-court communication. Papi's vocality suggests a step toward the lesbian Latin(a) lover reclaiming her subjectivity.

However, with Hollywood it is always one step forward, two steps back. The game becomes more hostile when it pits the only two lesbians of color against each other. With the Coco Girls winning, Papi turns to Bette, a mixed-race Black lesbian who often passes as white, and laughingly says, "Don't be mad, Brown Barbie!" Bette forcefully passes the ball to Shane and responds, "Who the fuck you calling Brown Barbie, you fucking Carmelita Tropicana?" using an intonation that would imply that Papi should be offended by such an accusation. Papi is visibly jarred by the aggressive response and does not attempt to block the pass to Shane, telling Bette in a soft voice, "I'm just playing."

Noticing that the two regular lesbian of color characters are pitted against each other is a crucial first step to unpacking this scene. Papi playing pickup basketball with her team of primarily women of color was an explicit decision the show made to further racialize her:

> As a major public area, sport is a key site of white ambivalence, fear and fantasy. The spectacle of black bodies triumphant in rituals of masculine competition reinforces the fixed idea that black men are all "brawn and not brains," and yet because the white man is beaten at his own game—football, boxing, cricket, athletics—the Other is idolized to the point of envy. (Mercer)

Bette is the only lesbian on her team who knows the game, and uncoincidentally, all of her lesbian teammates are white. The different demographics of Papi's and Bette's teams show where these characters fit in and, quite literally, who they play for. If Barbie is the pinnacle site of girls in the United States, formulating an understanding of womanhood through an ultra-feminine, white doll, Papi teasing Bette about being the Brown version of the doll is a nudge at Bette for supposedly assimilating into white culture. Bette is an Ivy League-educated, affluent, white-passing, mixed-race Black lesbian who presents herself with poise and a high level of assertiveness. Papi's accusation is rooted in a calling-out of Bette being a race traitor, being hyper-legible to and profitable for the white U.S. culture.

In contrast, Carmelita Tropicana is the alter ego of the Cuban American lesbian performance artist Alina Troyano. In many ways, Carmelita exaggerates her Cuban and lesbian identities by embodying an elaborate culmination of stereotypes of both, employing styles of cultural critique that are typically male practices within her performances (Muñoz 39). Carmelita Tropicana often utilizes female-to-male drag in her performances, which Muñoz attributes to functioning as a "dyketactics" of disidentification that decenters male dominance, especially the patriarchal depiction of Cuban American identity (Muñoz 41). Papi is never explicitly identified as Cuban, nor to have origins in any other Latin American country, so Bette's comeback is rooted in an ignorant understanding of Latinidad. Furthermore, Carmelita Tropicana is most consumable for Cuban Americans, especially those who identify as LGBTQ. According to Bette's statement, to be deemed worthy only by one's marginalized community is an insult. She makes this assertion while passing the ball to Shane, Papi's white "rival," showing where her loyalty lies. Claire Carter argues that the scene of the basketball game exhibits lesbian camp. She writes:

> Papi is also Latin American and though, arguably her character is not sufficiently developed and is fairly stereotypical, she nonetheless is a welcome contribution to the diversity of the community. . . . [When Papi invites them to the basketball game,] the main characters' team invest in all of the wrong avenues, such as buying flashy jerseys with their names on the back, instead of practicing or learning the rules of the game. This performance of sporting deficiency stands in direct contradiction to a very common stereotype about lesbians. (Carter)

Unlike Carter, I argue that Papi is not necessarily a "welcome contribution to the diversity" of the friend group, as she remains outside the friend group and is shortly after written off the show. Papi plays on a separate team from the friend group and is antagonized with racially loaded disses throughout the game. At most, Papi contributes to how the show treats diversity; her character is another opportunity to exploit stereotypes and add new exotic romance to the show without actually engaging with the racial identities of the Brown and Black bodies written on-screen. Carter misses the nuance that Bette, the only lesbian of color on her team of regular characters, *does* know how to play and plays hard. So while the scene showing the white characters screaming and complaining about the game might be playing into a sort of lesbian camp, or a humor based on the context of stereotypical lesbians, the scene is also severely racialized in a way that perpetuates non-white bodies as Other. If it is a lesbian camp, it is white lesbian camp.

Papi's series debut follows the exit of the only other Latina character in the entirety of the show, Carmen de la Pica Morales, who was written off when Shane leaves her at the altar. Even Carmen was played by a non-Latinx actress: Sarah Shahi, who is Iranian American. Though neither of the Latinx characters is actually played by a Latinx actress, they fit the physical attributes associated with Latin lovers: "good looks, masculine features/behavior, and ethnic markings (whatever may be construed as 'Latin'—dark hair, olive skin, a foreign accent)" (Pérez 439). But these lesbian Latin(a) lovers are as fleeting as the seasons, quite literally. Carmen was on the show for only two seasons, the duration of her two relationships with white women. The producers featured Papi as a character for only one full season.

The transience of the lesbian Latin(a) lover is the temporal extent to which Hollywood can tolerate the contradictions she embodies. Similar to Gloria Anzaldúa's "new mestiza," the lesbian Latin(a) lover "copes by developing a tolerance for contradictions, a tolerance for ambiguity. She learns . . . to be Mexican from an Anglo point of view" (Anzaldúa 101). While Papi's culture remains unspecified, meaning she may or may not be Mexican just as much as she may or may not be tied to any other Latin American country, she does embody a performance of white Hollywood's construction of Latinidad. Papi's impermanence is solidified by the fact that she has no job or home that the audience knows of, frequently sleeping in the limousine that hosts her sexual encounters. The lesbian Latin(a) lover's constant mobility rejects a static depiction of her queer and ethnic being. Papi's mobility can also be equated to her fluidity of gender, specifically the gender roles she chooses to fulfill.

Throughout the show's six seasons, there is not a single supportive and reliable cisgender man the lesbian or queer characters can depend on. Instead, these characters are consistently betrayed and exploited by men. Cherrie Moraga, in *Loving in the War Years*, explains that oftentimes her students "are hungry to know if it's possible to have both—your own life and the life of the familia" (iv). Papi's function is to be the grand female paternal figure for her lesbian community, who embodies the familial compassion desired by these women. She fills this void of choosing sexuality or family; and yet, she leaves. While the show hints at the similarities of Shane and Papi, the two most masculine woman-identified lesbian characters, their rejection of commitment is entirely different. Papi serves as a culmination of the maternal and paternal figures missing from the lives of the countless lesbians she loves. Shane's fear of commitment stems from her fear of becoming her father, selfishly unable to resist impulse. Papi's relation to embodying masculinity resonates with the juxtaposition Cherrie Moraga poses between herself and her brother: "for unlike him, I could never *become* the white man, only the white man's *woman*" (Moraga 92). Shane's proximity to white masculinity is much closer than Papi's, which is why the show could not continue to position Papi as more powerful than Shane. Her exit from the show can only be attributed to the Othered nature of her being: She cannot escape the trope of the Latin lover, who in the United States is never representative of someone who permanently belongs anywhere.

Conclusion

Though this chapter focuses on Papi, a character developed in 2007, the concept of the masculine lesbian Latin(a) lover being linguistically tied to a sort of paternal Latinx figure has not gone away. While there is no backstory to Papi's nickname, the implication is simple: She takes care of women, sexually and otherwise, embodying the men absent from her lesbian community. Dominga "Daddy" Duarte from seasons 6 and 7 of *Orange Is the New Black* (2018–19) is similarly characterized as a masculine embodiment of the contradictions between male Latin lovers and Latina bombshells. The difference, though, is that *OITNB*'s Daddy is not femme-presenting even in the slightest. Daddy responds to both she/her and he/him pronouns, and since *OITNB* does not explain why Dominga goes by Daddy, Vicci Martinez, the actress who plays Daddy, explained in an interview that she thinks her character received her nickname because "Daddy's taking care of her girls. She definitely has that machismo, just kind of the badass" (Hatchett). Yet, Daddy's backstory for how she ended up in jail shows her running an escort service. In other words, Daddy was a pimp, and once one of "her girls" died on the job, Daddy went to jail. What does it mean for the only butch and/or genderqueer Latinx in mainstream media to equate caring for women to exploiting them? While this is not the question explored in this particular piece, it does resonate with the overarching question of this book: How much can TV representation do to solve real-world problems faced by Latinxs, especially when the representation itself is harmful and half-assed?

Of the contradictions inherent in the lesbian Latin(a) lover's existence, the most important seems to be the implications she brings to lesbian Latinas' lived experience. I am not arguing that Papi was entirely misrepresentative or harmful to real lesbian Latinas, nor that we should overlook the show's mistakes to reclaim her character as liberatory. Rather, in order to effectively consume and critique representations of lesbian Latinas in popular culture, we must not think in such a dichotomy. The lesbian Latin(a) lover's brief sprinkles of Spanish in her otherwise *unaccented* English (I use "unaccented" ironically here) gives her just the right amount of exoticism and assimilation for the comfort and sexual appeal of her white audience. The whispered "quiero que vengas" that leaves her lips reminds her white lover (positioned as the white audience) where she comes from, but also for whom she comes. The liberal, white U.S. audience happily consumes the traces of colonial conquest marked on her. Furthermore, they are under the impression that the insertion of this queer Brown body into the manufactured (Hollywood/TV) whiteness is what the end of racism, sexism, and homophobia in the United States looks like. With Papi's presence being as temporary as those caged and deported by the U.S. government, white America is reminded that the lesbian Latin(a) lover exists only during the times they decide they will allow her to be seen/in scenes.

While the problematics of her construction cannot be ignored, the ways the lesbian Latin(a) lover resonates with Anzaldúa's conceptualization of the new mestiza must also be acknowledged. Similar to the ways Martinez-Cruz and Cruz understand the hemisexual Latin lover as one who creates and allows for an imaginative expression of gendered Latinidad, the lesbian Latin(a) lover can serve as an entry point to exploring non-heteronormative sexualities and romances as well as the creation of unique kinships within queer communities. Anzaldúa emphasizes the ways that "the mestizo and the queer exist at this time and point on the evolutionary continuum for a purpose. We are a blending that proves that all blood is intricately woven together, and that we are spawned out of similar souls" (Anzaldúa 85). Papi is the countryless mestiza, satisfying not only her woman lover's sexual needs, but filling the void of the absent kinship as a result of her lesbian sexuality. Between the pushes and pulls of wanting to be seen and wanting to re-present ourselves, we living lesbianas continue to reach for *the right to passion expressed in our own cultural tongue*" (Moraga 136). Hollywood is not our cultural tongue. We must not rely on institutions that reify the power dynamics and stereotypes that continue our oppressions. We must look to lesbian Latina narratives *produced by lesbian Latinas* in order to achieve this right. With this, I leave us with a call to action: "People, listen to what your *jotería* is saying" (Anzaldúa 107).

Notes

1. In "(Re)Examining the Latin Lover: Screening Chicano/Latino Sexualities," Daniel Enrique Pérez argues that all heterosexual, cis-male Latin lovers are queer. The queerness he defines is not reliant on a presence of homosexuality or gender variance; rather, Pérez's queerness includes hypermasculine, heterosexual men who pursue multiple women at once.

2. When Papi first meets Shane, who is supposed to be her main "competition," Papi scoffs that Shane is just "a skinny little white girl."

Works Cited

Anzaldúa, Gloria. "La conciencia de la mestiza/Towards a New Consciousness." *Borderlands/La Frontera: The New Mestiza*, 4th ed., Aunt Lute Books, 2012, pp. 99–120.

Carter, Claire. "Lesbian Chic, Femme-ininity, and Feminist Dialogue: Reflecting on *The L Word*." *Queer Studies in Media and Pop Culture*, vol. 3, no. 1, 2018, pp. 67+.

Hatchett, Keisha. "*Orange Is the New Black*'s Vicci Martinez Responds to All the Daddy Love: TV Guide." *TVGuide.com*, 4 Aug. 2018, www.tvguide.com/news/orange-is-the-new-black-season-6 -vicci-martinez-daddy-love/.

Licona, Adela C. *Zines in Third Space: Radical Cooperation and Borderlands Rhetoric*. SUNY Press, 2013.

"Livin' la Vida Loca." *The L Word*, created by Ilene Chaiken, directed by Marlene Gorris, written by Alexandra Kondracke, season 4, episode 2, Showtime, 14 Jan. 2007.

Martinez-Cruz, Paloma, and John Cruz. "Hemisexualizing the Latin Lover: Film and Live Art Interpretations and Provocations." *The Routledge Companion to Gender, Sex, and Latin American Culture*, edited by Frederick Luis Aldama, Routledge, 2018, 206–21.

Mercer, K. *Welcome to the Jungle: New Positions in Black Cultural Studies*. Routledge, 1994.

Molina-Guzmán, Isabel. *Dangerous Curves: Latina Bodies in the Media*. New York UP, 2010.

Moore, Candace. "Having It All Ways: The Tourist, the Traveler, and the Local in 'The L Word.'" *Cinema Journal*, vol. 46, no. 4, 2007, pp. 3–23.

Moraga, Cherríe. *Loving in the War Years: Lo que nunca pasó por sus labios*. South End Press, 1983.

Muñoz, José Esteban. *Disidentifications: Queers of Color and the Performance of Politics*. U of Minnesota P, 1999.

Ovalle, Priscilla Peña. *Dance and the Hollywood Latina: Race, Sex, and Stardom*. Rutgers UP, 2011.

Pérez, Daniel Enrique. "(Re)Examining the Latin Lover: Screening Chicano/Latino Sexualities." *Rethinking Chicana/o and Latina/o Popular Culture: The Future of Minority Studies*, Palgrave Macmillan, 2009.

COGNITIVE RICHNESS AND SERIAL INGREDIENTS IN *VIDA*

Héctor J. Pérez

From one episode to the next, Tanya Saracho's *Vida* (2018–20) examines the dynamics of gentrification, the racial and cultural identity of the Latinx community, and Latinx LGBTQ+ identities and practices. One way or another, the show touches on all the issues central to postcolonial and Latinx cultural studies (Aldama 2013). These themes are developed through the main plot of the series—two sisters inherit a property that includes a bar, and they change their lives to take over the business and get it out of trouble—as well as through its subplots that emerge out of the construction of new family life along with the dual protagonists' romantic relationships. As the series unfolds, *Vida* integrates these thematic elements in its narrative progression and inter-episodic arcs in ways that create a rich cognitive experience for viewers. In this chapter, I will explore how the show constructs a narrative that uniquely serves to organize the spectator's comprehension of its thematic diversity.

In approaching the study of *Vida*, I draw on the research on narrative comprehension in television seriality, the concept of mental models (J. E. Saerys-Foy and J. P. Magliano), and scientific advances in understanding the complex cognitive process involved in audiovisual narrative comprehension: eye tracking of events and characters and meaning-making integration, for instance. The psychology of discourse has identified three varieties of narrative comprehension: surface form, textbase, and situation model (4–5). To define more precisely the interaction between cognitive levels and varieties, Jeffrey Saerys-Foy and Joseph Magliano speak of an integrative model that offers front-end processes, which govern the viewer's attention and extraction of information, and back-end processes, which set the viewer's memory in motion so that, through inferences about content with a certain degree of abstraction, they lead us from comprehension of the scenes, even the most complex ones, to enrichment of the mental model. Fundamental activities of this phase of back-end processing include event segmentation, inference generation, and updating. This processing refers to a moment of integration that, for example, leads to an account of the evolutionary processes of characters and events throughout the narrative (6–8).

I use this theoretical framework to examine how two key serial ingredients contribute to the cognitive richness transmitted by *Vida*'s narrative. By cognitive richness, I refer to the interaction of two variables: the diversity of aspects that a series offers to feed the viewer's knowledge; and the continuity with which these aspects are offered, so that the viewer can build a mental model based on the evolution of a narrative process. I develop a cognitive richness model to improve understanding of the multiplot architecture, temporal structure, and character evolution in *Vida*.

Multiplot Architecture, Thematic Diversity, and Cognitive Models

As is common in much fiction capable of enriching the viewer's understanding of reality (Plantinga 2018), the main plotlines in *Vida* serve as vehicles for conveying knowledge through narration. Although the main objective of the two protagonists is to manage the inheritance received from their mother, Vidalia, in the best possible way, viewers following this main plotline will often be able to identify a continuity of central themes. These defining ingredients of the cognitive structure of the plot can lead viewers to redefine their mental models of issues in their own reality.

For example, the main threat to the protagonists' management of the inheritance is the dynamics of gentrification: large companies monopolizing land by engaging in unethical practices, such as predatory lending. This plotline challenges our understanding of gentrification by showing a confrontation with it, an opposing set of values embodied in the people who drive that plotline. Similarly, the vicissitudes that mark the plotline of a secondary character like Mari can further contribute to the spectator's mental model of gentrification, in this case from the perspective of activism. But in both cases, the evolution of the plotlines feeds the mental model that each spectator has in relation to gentrification. In this way, the concept of gentrification is explored in two plotlines, continually, throughout the six episodes of the first season. This is not an isolated circumstance in the narrative but systematic. Indeed, other thematic areas explored in different plotlines can also be identified, such as sexual identity and practices, conflict in family life, romantic relationships, and the identity of the Latinx community in the United States.

The theme of sexual identity and orientation is developed mainly through very open reference to bisexuality in a specific plotline featuring Emma, although Lyn's openness with respect to sexuality also allows her to participate in this theme. Conflict in family life is a theme that by its nature requires the interaction of several characters and their individual plotlines; for example, the burden of Emma's past leads her to a direct confrontation with Eddy. In the case of romantic relationships, each sister features in parallel plotlines that enrich the theme, with different orientations due to the conflict in Lyn's emotional life and Emma's skeptical and individualistic attitude. Finally, the central theme of the identity of the second- or third-generation Latin American immigrant appears in the character plots of Emma, Lyn, and Mari, with very different degrees of significance.

The main section of this chapter explores the way the theme of gentrification is dealt with in the evolution of plotlines in the first season of *Vida*. Although gentrification has been an important subject of research among urban geographers for more than four decades (Bernt and Holm 108), the term came into popular use outside academic circles only a couple of decades ago, coinciding with the acceleration and multiplication of gentrification processes throughout the world. Indeed, there are probably hundreds of thousands of "gentrification stories" in cities around the world, such as Kyoto, New York, Berlin, Sydney, Warsaw, Shanghai, Istanbul, Lagos, or Barcelona. Despite this, the phenomenon is probably still not very clearly understood by the general public, as it has numerous complexities, as revealed by studies of urban geography (Eckerd et al.) and sociological debates (Valle). Moreover, there is not much serial fiction that deals with the subject, which may be what makes its inclusion in *Vida* as a key theme a particular attraction of the series. But to what extent can a series really inform us about such a complex and evolving concept, researched and debated by academic experts around the world? Obviously, it cannot pretend to offer a theoretical perspective on the subject or aspire to the depth of studies like Neil Smith's landmark book (1996).

Nevertheless, *Vida* offers a solid formula for representing a gentrification story because it contextualizes the phenomenon with other ingredients,

Figure 17.1 Emma (from behind), Doña Tita, Eddy, and Lyn at the bar they inherited. *Vida*, season 1.

such as cultural and sexual identity, in a way that is corroborated by contemporary urban sociology. For example, the story it tells about Emma and Lyn, third-generation Mexican immigrants, has parallels with the contradictions of middle-class families in Harlem studied by Monique Taylor, as in both cases their economic status informs a class identity that clearly influences their expectations of urban development. Thus, the two sisters in *Vida* will propose a business that, on the one hand, aims to escape the voracious dynamics of the developer, but that at the same time does not seem to fit the kind of social activism that is not concerned with nuanced positions, being dedicated instead to the preservation of what exists at any price.

The first question to answer is whether gentrification is a plotline in *Vida*. The answer is no, for several reasons. It is present in various plots, being essential for the advancement of each one. Moreover, it is such a big issue that a synthetic treatment of the subject would not cover its many dimensions. As will be shown below, the representation of this subject, and the point of interest for this study, is how this theme unfolds in different moments of different plotlines. This structure is what could be described as the narrative deployment of a thematic cognitive model.

The process of thematic enrichment developed continually over episodes in the diversity of plotlines and their interactions will be explored here using the concept of mental models. This exploration will involve the combination of a descriptive approach, which will allow the reader to understand the narrative properties of the series without even having watched it, with an analytical and selective approach in order to relate the plot developments to the key cognitive processes in the establishment of a mental model.

Episode 1: A Foundation for a Mental Model

Gentrification as a theme is represented and developed in two plotlines. The first starts with the first scene of the series, featuring Mari, a young, second-generation Mexican immigrant with no education and limited financial resources, who lives in the family home taking care of her widowed father and a brother who works in a mechanic's workshop. The scene shows the young woman filming an anti-gentrification manifesto on video to be uploaded to the Web. Before she concludes her impassioned monologue, her father asks her to come down and make him an egg, and the young woman meekly interrupts her protest message. This detail, showing the father exercising absolute control over the activist daughter, is the first contrast inviting the viewer to make an inference about Mari, as a character struggling to reconcile accepting a traditionally patriarchal model of life with the adoption of a more progressive, contemporary stance. The former is associated with the first generation of immigrants, predominantly working class and with minimal education, while the latter is characteristic of the second generation, and is reflected in styles of dress (Mari paints her lips black and dresses like an emo-urbanite) and behavior (such as social activism). Thus, from the very beginning, the series combines the question of the immigrant's contradictory identity with the issue of gentrification by activating the various types of knowledge identified by Saerys-Foy and Magliano: surface knowledge (in this case, the way Mari dresses), and textbase (the content of the monologue Mari is recording), which will lead to the spectator's first activity of retrieval to identify connections between the series content and his or her knowledge of the world. All this serves to build a schematic representation of the first mental model related to gentrification: a model that immediately reflects the socioeconomic identity of the activist.

The second plotline related to gentrification, and the most important because it is linked to the main plot, featuring Emma, contrasts curiously with the first, as it is introduced in an elliptical way, when Emma arrives from Chicago to attend her mother's funeral. This scene lingers on images of the neighborhood, which Emma contemplates while on her way to her family home in the taxi. The various frames we see associated with Emma's gaze are the first spatial illustration of gentrification, the first visualization of the thematic element that will be a central focus of the series. This reflects a cognitive approach based on surface knowledge. As the objective is to establish a mental model in which the spatial condition will have crucial relevance, spectators are offered their first access to it in spatial terms. But this visual technique has another dimension as well: the landscape of gentrification is the product of Emma's gaze, shown for the first time from her perspective. This association is not accidental; it will be maintained throughout the narrative. Emma's perspective on this issue will define the main cognitive contribution to our mental model of it.

After this preparatory step, the main plotline related to gentrification is foregrounded more fully when Nelson (scene 8, 16:51), a real estate broker, seeks to negotiate with Emma to buy the newly inherited property, before Vidalia's funeral has even ended. This introduces the expectation that the sisters' management of the inheritance will become the main plotline of the series.

The first episode not only introduces both plotlines in a very short time but also offers the first and main connection between them. This connection is introduced with the scene in which Mari verbally attacks some white tourists who are taking pictures of themselves in front of a Mexican bar. Mari then rebukes Emma and Lyn as they leave the restaurant (scene 12, 23:43), claiming that she is defending the neighborhood, while Emma responds that what the neighborhood needs is to get more customers into the bar rather than drive them away.

From this moment where the two plotlines first converge, defining the mental model will depend on these newly associated elements, with the "gentrifiers" positioned in opposition to the activists and Emma in the middle, trying to determine what to do about the property she has inherited with her sister. The evolving complexity of the model will result from this multiplot interaction (Pérez and Ortiz).

The first episode concludes by introducing further information to affect the viewer's understanding of the inheritance, with an additional conflict that involves not only the two sisters but also Vidalia's widow, Eddy, who knows the neighborhood well and has her own ideas about the management of the inheritance (believing herself to be one of the heirs). In a scene near the end of the episode (25:26), Eddy warns Emma that Nelson is a loan shark who lends money to people who can't pay it back and that dealing with him will mean trouble, and that his developers buy everything only to destroy it and build something in its place that no one can afford. Emma replies to this that someone can in fact afford it. The key element that this scene adds to the model is a moral assessment of the agent who represents gentrification. At this point near the end of the episode, the spectator can construct an initial hypothesis about the possible course of the narrative, based on a predictive inference about the conflicting elements (Magliano et al.): will Emma face an antagonist like Nelson?

Episode 2: Remembering and Updating

One of the unique qualities of seriality is that its prolonged temporal processes, which are more extensive than in other narrative forms, facilitate the cognitive consolidation of previously acquired models. For example, the appearance of new events associated with a character's objective allows us to form a more fully developed understanding of the character, her attitudes, and her predispositions. Episode 2 begins by consolidating our understanding of Mari as an anti-gentrification activist, as the episode opens with her vandalizing a recently opened hipster shop; shortly afterward, in scene 4 (5:38), she reports on her blog about some new neighbors who are settling into a house supposedly as a result of the gentrification process. The spectator associates these events with a mental model by making characteristic inferences from back-end processes, which lead to their inclusion in a plotline associated with the character's activist objective. To do this, the spectator has had to infer a relationship between this action and the previous one, based on the fact that the character has the same objective in both cases. As

Saerys-Foy and Magliano point out, these processes are based on retrieval cues in the form of surface features, such as consistency in a character's appearance (e.g., clothes or hairstyle). The association of events in the category of "anti-gentrification actions" is of a semantic nature, and possibly activates worldly knowledge possessed by the viewer that supports the construction of the model.

As we have observed, at the end of the previous episode, Emma's position, in principle favorable to Nelson's offer, and contrary to the opposition against gentrification expressed by both Mari and Eddy, seems to be completely oriented to the sale of the property, although she herself has not yet expressed a precise position.

Scene 7 (13:26) introduces a new personal plotline for Emma, when she meets Cruz, a girl from the Argentinean neighborhood who had attended her mother's funeral. They meet in a hipster café, a place similar to the one that Mari was vandalizing shortly before. The conversation quickly turns to the subject of gentrification: Cruz tells Emma that nothing is the same there anymore: the pastries, the coffee, the whole menu has changed. Emma responds to these criticisms with the attitude she has displayed before by remarking that there is good wifi. Once again, the spectator can infer from this moment to help construct the thematic mental model, deducing that these negative qualities of the food are consequences of the gentrification process that Emma has previously suggested she does not support. But this new inference suggests that Emma is not against gentrification; in fact, the main function of this scene seems to be to consolidate the idea that Emma has an indifferent (or even favorable) attitude toward gentrification. This moment is important because Emma's position on gentrification will be what decides the future of her mother's inheritance, thus determining the direction of the main plotline.

Interestingly, the negative consequences of gentrification that seem beyond dispute (the loss of a neighborhood's unique local flavor) appear just after the use of film techniques to intensify the spectator's relationship of empathy and/or sympathy with Emma (Tobón), namely a series of close-up shots that seem to serve to encourage access to her subjectivity. Although it may seem contradictory, it effectively functions to heighten the suspense, because in the second part of this episode there is a change in Emma's position.

This change can be traced to two events that occur during Emma's visit to Nelson's company to explore the offer he made her at the funeral. The first is in scene 11 (19:49), when Emma is in the waiting room and is recognized there by an older woman, the mother of a former schoolmate, who remarks to her: "You always won the spelling, siempre le ganabas a mi hija Chela. Eras bien aplicada . . . But now, you are here just like me. About to lose everything.

Pero don't feel bad, mi hija. Son víboras. These people, they are sucking the blood out of the neighborhood." These words seem to have an impact on Emma, who is shown in several close-up shots with a serious expression as the old lady speaks. The scene prepares us for the important event that comes next, when Emma rejects Nelson's offer. The old woman's opinion reminds the viewer of Eddy's similar criticism of Nelson. However, this is not merely a repetition of Eddy's warning, as it adds new information, given that this lady has a very different profile from Vidalia's partner. There is no reason to associate her with the anti-gentrification movement. She is a second-generation migrant who tells of her expulsion from the neighborhood and the loss of everything she once had; she is simply a victim. All this information can be integrated into the thematic mental model of gentrification as textbase knowledge, leading to a new inference that guides the spectator's process of updating: "If someone else with a very different profile says it, it is possible that what Eddy said is true."

Narratively, this new expression reinforces Eddy's warning, insofar as we see its impact on Emma, with whom we already have a sympathetic connection through a process of alignment, reinforcing our suspicion of the unethical behavior of the "gentrifiers." It may also lead us to establish a hypothesis based on the unwritten rules of storytelling: when an element is activated with intensity, the spectator suspects that this element is going to play a relevant role. And it won't be long before this suspicion is proven correct.

Nelson and Emma meet again in scene 13 (22:50). Nelson reveals that Vidalia's house has two mortgages. Vidalia was rushed from one loan to another, Nelson taking advantage of her illness to grant a loan over the value of the house. Emma immediately acknowledges the situation and blames Nelson for the abusive behavior. He shows her that she is cornered: he makes inappropriate sexual advances and offers to settle the mortgages with a sale. In response, she throws coffee on him and tells him that she will never sell him the bar.

At this point, the mental model of gentrification confirms the previously activated and reinforced moral dimension as a central element, by confirming the predictive inference made earlier. Nelson abuses his position of power not only economically but also sexually. The viewer has all the elements necessary to support Emma's act of conscience. Now, understanding the moral repugnance to the two facts about Nelson raises a new question: will all this change Emma's attitude about gentrification?

The first and second episodes constitute a first phase in the evolution of the cognitive model. The second phase begins when gentrification becomes the key factor that convinces Emma to stay in order to resolve the difficult situation of her inheritance. Thus, early on in episode 3, in scene 5 (5:45),

Emma explains to Lyn that she has already had to pay the interest on that month's mortgage with her own money and that now they have to work out a way to keep the bar and pay the bills until they can sell it. Emma adds that to avoid the inheritance becoming a nightmare, she is going to stay and find a way to make the property profitable.

Emma: Character Model in Evolution

During the second part of the season other plotlines acquire importance, adding elements for even more productive thematic interactions. This process takes place as the viewer delves into Emma's "person schema," defined by Murray Smith as a set of knowledge about the character based on knowledge of "real people." With Emma, the spectator will construct a central character model in cognitive terms based on the evolution of her dispositions and motivations in relation to a new central theme: her identity, both sexual and social.

Emma is initially presented as close to the cliché of young third-generation immigrants who are resistant to and disconnected from their Mexican cultural heritage, as reflected by her distance in the first episode from the various cultural elements present in her neighborhood, and highlighted by the contrast with her sister Lyn, who is much more open and receptive to her heritage. The narrative reveals an evolution of the character model that breaks this cliché little by little, in subtle ways. The main experience that stimulates the model's evolution appears when Emma reveals that her mother sent her to live with her great-aunt after Emma engaged in homosexual activity. This memory is vested with new value when she discovers her mother's real reason for sending her away: her own sexual orientation, which she hid from her daughter all her life. Discovering that her mother was bisexual and being able to be bisexual herself in her former home is the key to a reconciliation with the neighborhood from which she was expelled. The viewer will understand that Emma's position on her heritage, and her decision to stay in her old neighborhood in order to fight the gentrification process and preserve her mother's property, will be nourished by this other source of motivation, reconciliation with a world that excluded her and that can now be inclusive.

Although a detailed account of this process is not possible here, I will highlight one crucial element to underscore the cognitive richness of the series: thanks to the mental model of a character in evolution, the spectator is offered the possibility of connecting one thematic area like the question of sexual identity to another thematic area like gentrification. The result, if the series has succeeded in providing sympathetic access to the character, is to put the viewer in the situation of imagining how certain important experiences in life can redirect our appreciation of a problem.

Emma's rapprochement with the world that rejected her is therefore the key to explaining how the theme of gentrification resurfaces in a last moment of evolution of a mental model that has already been quite clearly defined, toward the end of the season. Viewers will use their prior knowledge of Emma when processing certain information on another event. This event is the conflict between Mari and Emma, which reappears after several episodes in which it has remained latent. It begins in scene 5 of episode 4 (7:35) when Mari criticizes the change of the name of the bar from La Chinita to Vida, but Eddy calms her down. In that same episode two scenes show the succession of events very quickly: in scene 9 (13:38), Mari agrees to protest against the bar; and in scene 14 (23:27) Mari does some graffiti on the outside wall of the bar. But the climax of this conflict, which the viewer will process in terms of event segmentation as a macro event, is not the bar, but when, in scene 15 of episode 5 (16:00), Emma leaves after visiting a house for rent. Mari rebukes her as Emma is leaving the house, in another example of her anti-gentrification activism. The two argue so aggressively that they end up in jail. There the confrontation continues (scene 16, 17:10), as Mari calls Emma a "gringo," while Emma tells Mari that her activism is just a front. However, at the end of the scene they reconcile, and Emma even pays the fine to get Mari out.

Emma's reaction elicits textbase knowledge from the spectator in relation to a previous scene where Emma's attitude is similar. This operation opens the way for another possible inference: Emma has not changed her previous and more neutral position about gentrification, but the gesture of forgiveness and reconciliation with Mari has a moral dimension—perhaps based on the same ethical principles that guided Emma in her encounter with Nelson.

With the conflict between Emma and Mari apparently resolved, episode 6 returns the viewer to the confrontation with Nelson, who tries again to get Emma, Lyn, and Eddy to sell their property. This time, in scene 6 (11:10), Nelson tells Emma that he and she are the same because their parents denied them the good things America has to offer. Nelson's attempt to connect a pro-gentrification attitude with a prejudice against one's own cultural heritage does nothing to change Emma's attitude. She has already moved away from absolute rejection of her neighborhood and has entered a new process of life within it: a life that will by no means be simple, but will have none of the dualism that Nelson suggests the two of them share. Her strong moral compass supported by a capacity for reflection places her above stereotypes and gives her character a nonsimplistic perspective on gentrification. In contrast to Mari's naivete and Nelson's cruelty is Emma's effort to adapt, to fight alone against a complex process, without the weapons of a hero, with no other resource than her conscience, navigating between her reduced Mexicanness and her acquired skills as a self-made woman. She has not renounced her cultural heritage; she lives it and suffers from tensions that cannot be resolved, that are not negotiable in simple terms.

Conclusion

With the help of the theory of mental models, I have begun to explore how a series like *Vida*, with all the narrative structures specific to the medium, presents problems of identity, sexual identity, and gentrification as three interrelated scenarios that define the different stages of the narrative and involve all its elements, which in turn activates all the varieties of knowledge proposed by studies of narrative comprehension. These types of representations and thematic associations configure the plotlines through continuous and flexible interaction between them. The richness of the themes also requires strategies that give the scenes a density of meanings, inviting the spectator to construct diverse levels of knowledge, often of an inter-episodic scope. The spectator, according to the suggestive simile proposed by Ellen Spolsky of "knowledge as nourishment," will be able to use mental models in part or totally, through their reactivation in other life scenarios. Possibly it was the intention of the creators of the series that their public should have a special receptivity toward these models in order to promote critical thinking.

Works Cited

Aldama, Fredrick, editor. *Latinos and Narrative Media: Participation and Portrayal*. Springer, 2013.

Eckerd, Adam, et al. "Gentrification and Displacement: Modeling a Complex Urban Process." *Housing Policy Debate*, vol. 29, no. 2, 2019, pp. 273–95.

Magliano, Joseph P., et al. "Generating Predictive Inferences While Viewing a Movie." *Discourse Processes*, vol. 22, no. 3, 1996, pp. 199–224.

Pérez, Héctor J., and M. Jesús Ortiz. "Multi-Plot Structure in Television Serials." *Contemporary Serial Television: Cognition, Emotion, and Aesthetics*, edited by Ted Nannicelli and Héctor J. Pérez, Routledge, 2022, pp. 47–67.

Plantinga, Carl. *Screen Stories: Emotion and the Ethics of Engagement*. Oxford UP, 2018.

Saerys-Foy, Jeffrey E., and Joseph P. Magliano. "From Shots to Storyworlds: The Cognitive Processes Supporting the Comprehension of Serialized Television." *Contemporary Serial Television: Cognition, Emotion, and Aesthetics*, edited by Ted Nannicelli and Héctor J. Pérez, Routledge, 2022, pp. 97–116.

Smith, Murray. *Engaging Characters: Fiction, Emotion, and the Cinema*. Clarendon Press, 1995.

Smith, Neil. *The New Urban Frontier: Gentrification and the Revanchist City*. Psychology Press, 1996.

Spolsky, Ellen. "Narrative as Nourishment." *Toward a Cognitive Theory of Narrative Acts*, edited by Frederick Luis Aldama, U of Texas P, 2010.

Taylor, Monique M. *Harlem: Between Heaven and Hell*. U of Minnesota P, 2002.

Tobón, Daniel Jerónimo. "Empathy and Sympathy: Two Contemporary Models of Character Engagement." *The Palgrave Handbook of the Philosophy of Film and Motion Pictures*, edited by Noël Carroll, Laura T. Di Summa, and Shawn Loht, Palgrave Macmillan, 2019, pp. 865–91.

Valle, Melissa M. "Globalizing the Sociology of Gentrification." *City & Community*, vol. 20, no. 1, 2020.

Héctor J. Pérez

TRANSLOCA(L) POETICS

Que(e)ring *Mucho, Mucho Amor: The Legend of Walter Mercado*

Lawrence La Fountain-Stokes

The Puerto Rican astrologer and psychic Walter Mercado's enormous success on Latinx and Latin American television was always tied to his baroque excess and gender nonconformity, to the way he mixed popular religiosity, New Age esoteric beliefs, and over-the-top theatrical camp aesthetics to share an uplifting message centered on love and self-affirmation.[1] He is a Puerto Rican *transloca* performer par excellence, that is to say, a bilingual and bicultural, queer (effeminate and androgynous) artist whose translocal life experiences and work reflected particular sensibilities and cultural styles; a gender-nonconforming pioneer who never publicly self-identified as gay, but who negotiated the space of the "open secret" as a strategy to keep homophobia at bay.[2] His self-presentation and media persona included the distinctive use of clothing, particularly of capes and showy outfits, makeup, jewelry, way of speaking, catchphrases—most notably, "mucho, mucho amor"—movements, aesthetic choices, and décor, employed consistently as his audience expanded from the archipelago to Miami and eventually to Europe, Latin America, and all across the United States, from 1969 (when he first spoke about astrology on Puerto Rican television, building on almost twenty years of theatrical experience) until his death in 2019, always maintaining a Caribbean, or what Rosamond S. King would call "Caribglobal," touch. His televisual queerness complemented other queer representations in the 1970s, 1980s, and 1990s Puerto Rican and U.S. Spanish-language mediascapes, which frequently veered toward homophobic depictions (Jiménez 246–65) but also included programs by leading drag queens such as Antonio Pantojas, who clearly advocated for gay rights (Laureano). In many ways, Mercado anticipated the mainstreaming of Latinx queerness and gender nonconformity that is now more visible in programs such as *RuPaul's Drag Race* and *Pose* (La Fountain-Stokes, *Translocas*). However, Walter continues to pose a challenge, as "sexism, homophobia, and racism can still be found in Spanish-language television" (Castañeda 14).

Mercado's insistence on his rootedness in Puerto Rico was accompanied by a vast transnational displacement, by explicit Orientalizing and African religious references to Buddhism, Hinduism, Islam, and Sufism (Mercado,

El mundo secreto 125–49), as much as to Christianity, Judaism, and Santería/Regla de Ocha, and by commercial success in multiple languages, particularly in Spanish and English. At the heart of the artist's televisual appeal was the ability to translate *loca* (queer, or *cuir*) sensibilities for mass audiences, his wide-ranging knowledge of many topics, his uncanny ability to make each spectator feel as if he were speaking to them individually, and his masterful understanding of television as a space that negotiated audience interaction and desire. His success also had to do with the way he promoted an ecumenical, sui generis religious amalgam that combined references to multiple faiths along with astrology, numerology, magic, kabbalah, and the tarot, which he synthesized under the moniker "WALTERISM," identified as a "Universal Movement" (Mercado, *El mundo secreto* 298–301), a synthesis that the scholar Efraín Barradas sees as "eclectic but not syncretic," as "it cannot be said that his ideas form a coherent whole" (747). As a successful mass media spectacle and popular icon, Mercado is a crucial referent for queer Latinx culture in Latin America and the United States, and a key figure in the history of Puerto Rican and Latinx television.

The artist's complex life story is richly portrayed in the Netflix documentary *Mucho, Mucho Amor: The Legend of Walter Mercado*, directed by Cristina Costantini and Kareem Tabsch.[3] The well-received feature-length production was launched in the midst of the COVID-19 pandemic on July 8, 2020, and highlights many pertinent issues. It also sugarcoats or simply omits some of the more troubling aspects of the television personality's life and thought, while also pandering to mainstream audiences, particularly by emphasizing the testimony of heterosexual cisgender masculine Latinx men such as Lin-Manuel Miranda and the frankly homophobic Eugenio Derbez. In this context, it is valid to ask if the mostly nostalgic celebration of Walter Mercado that the documentary proposes, particularly the embrace of his complex gender nonconformity, his profoundly queer persona, his iconic Latinx stature, and his message of love leads viewers to ignore his economic, racial, and political contradictions, in a context in which "the *formal* devices of TV prime-time programs encourage viewers to experience themselves as anti-political, privately accumulating individuals," where "forms express social conflict, containing and diverting the images of contrary social possibilities" (Gitlin 253).

Is Walter Mercado a subversive figure and a victim of his circumstances, as *Mucho, Mucho Amor* suggests? Does everyone agree with Lin-Manuel Miranda's assertion that "we love him without questioning anything and he has great moral authority"? Does Walter's importance as a pioneering symbol of queer Latinidad, his fervent defense of women's equality, and his advocacy of self-care and religious tolerance trump his occasional racial bias and his politically conservative, assimilationist views, for example, regarding the status of

Figure 18.1 Promotion for Netflix documentary *Mucho, Mucho Amor: The Legend of Walter Mercado* (dir. Cristina Costantini and Kareem Tabsch, 2020).

Puerto Rico? And, as the scholar Diana Taylor proposes, given "his privileged status of wealthy, white male" (124), does "Walter's biculturality still [pose] a challenge to normativity" (124) as "he forges a sense of a liberated, bilingual, flamboyant Latino community that is capable of making the rules" (130)?

Building on the skills that he acquired from working in theater, dance, radio, and television (particularly in soap operas) in the 1950s and 1960s, on his academic knowledge of pharmacy, psychology, and ethnobotany, on his passion for world religions and esoteric thought systems, and on mostly successful commercial partnerships with media business experts developed from 1969 onward, Walter Mercado turned himself (or was transformed) into a global celebrity, an iconic television star who demonstrated great empathy for his fans and who was adored by many. Walter's mass popularization within and outside of Puerto Rico occurred through the negotiation of contradictions, entailing strategic silences about his sexuality and the toleration of ridicule of his campy, feminine gender expression, but also through the downplaying of his polemical stances regarding politics articulated in his publications and in interviews that positioned the entertainer as a reactionary anti-communist who openly criticized leftist governments in Latin America,

I just want to enjoy
each moment of my life.

Figure 18.2 Walter Mercado dancing as young man. Photo exhibited at the HistoryMiami Museum, 2019. Screen capture, *Mucho, Mucho Amor: The Legend of Walter Mercado*, Netflix, 2020.

advocated for Puerto Rican statehood (entailing the risk of assimilation to U.S. society), and did not denounce extrajudicial political killings in Puerto Rico.[4] Mercado's queer political conservatism and his "contradicciones ideológicas," or ideological contradictions (Barradas 744), align with those of other queer Latin American gender-nonconforming figures such as the Chilean poet and stateswoman Gabriela Mistral, who led a remarkable life as a masculine, closeted lesbian while simultaneously espousing conservative stances regarding motherhood and holding anti-Black racist views, as Licia Fiol-Matta has documented in *A Queer Mother for the Nation: The State and Gabriela Mistral*. Mercado and Mistral help us to understand how being queer or gender nonconforming does not automatically translate into being a politically radical or progressive figure committed to all forms of social transformation.

The major point of contention in Walter Mercado's contemporary reception continues to be his queerness: the artist's reticence to discuss his personal life, a posture that is perceived by some as anachronistic and apolitical, as the Puerto Rican journalist Ana Teresa Toro suggests, in a context in which homophobic or transphobic individuals continue to express discomfort about his effeminacy and flamboyance.[5] Mixed reception also has to do with Mercado's racial, class, and political views and with his links to extreme right-wing figures in Puerto Rico responsible for political assassinations, most notably his friendship with and praise for the exiled Cuban businessman Julito Labatut, "a florist who was actually the mastermind and financier of right-wing political terrorism" (Quiroga 824), who was directly tied to but never prosecuted for the murder of the pro-democracy, pro-dialogue Cuban activist Carlos Muñiz Varela in Puerto Rico in 1979, as José Quiroga has carefully documented. Chillingly, at the time of Labatut's death, in spite of multiple public sources regarding his activities, Mercado "remarked on his human 'qualities' and called him a 'brother,' mentioning that Labatut 'sent flowers to AIDS patients that had been forgotten by their relatives.' And, he added, 'embelleció a Puerto Rico con sus flores. Lo llevaré siempre conmigo en mi corazón' (He made Puerto Rico beautiful with his flowers. I will always have him close to my heart)" (Quiroga 824).[6] As Ana Teresa Toro, Mari Mari Narváez, and Rafael Acevedo have noted, this relationship, and Mercado's friendship with Angelita Trujillo, the youngest daughter and apologist of the Dominican dictator Rafael Leónidas Trujillo, pass completely unremarked in *Mucho, Mucho Amor*, but are well known in Puerto Rico by those who were affected by this violence.[7]

Mercado's legacy can be celebrated for the artist's gender transgression and expansive mystical/religious worldview, which served to create community among Latinxs and fostered individual well-being, but also criticized in relation to his white privilege (his ability to effect cultural syncretism based on unchallenged appropriation), his focus on individual as opposed to collective social transformation (standard in popular American astrological discourse, as Theodor W. Adorno first noted in 1957), and in relation to economic exploitation and neoliberal commercialism (the tension between Walter as victim of fiscal abuse by his former manager Bill Bakula, which is well explored in the documentary, vis-à-vis Walter as perpetrator of fraud and abuse via his collaboration with the Psychic Friends Network, a telephone psychic service that charged exorbitant fees to dispense questionable advice).[8] The Netflix documentary addresses some but not all of these issues. Walter's televisual (broadcast and Internet) legacy is better grasped by placing *Mucho, Mucho Amor* in dialogue and tension with other cultural productions, including YouTube videos such as "Walter Mercado Vintage Era," his books *Beyond the Horizon: Visions of the New Millennium* (1997) and *El mundo secreto de Walter Mercado* (2010), Noelia Quintero Herencia's made-for-television documentary *Walter Mercado: Más allá de la astrología* (2002), Fausto Fernós's drag cabaret ("The Fire Eating Drag Princess," now available on YouTube), Alexis Mateo's drag parody on season 5 of *RuPaul's Drag Race All Stars* (2020), and the performances of Macha Colón (Gisela Rosario Ramos).

Pinkwashing Walter: *Mucho, Mucho Amor*

Cristina Costantini and Kareem Tabsch's documentary, produced with Alex Fumero, carefully traces Walter's biography, starting with his childhood in

Ponce in the 1930s, including perceptions that he had special magical powers and could heal animals and persons, a messianic strand that will become a constant (for example, in his books); his early training and commercial success in dance, theater, radio, and later on television as a soap opera star (a period that is explored more in depth by Quintero Herencia); and his launch into superstardom thanks to his collaborations, first with the Puerto Rican actor and television producer Elín Ortiz, and later with the Miami-based manager Guillermo "Bill" Bakula, who went on to exploit the artist with an abusive contract signed in 1995 that led to a protracted series of lawsuits from 2006 to 2011, greatly affecting the finances and health of the Puerto Rican star.[9] In the Netflix documentary's narrative arc, the revelation of these lawsuits is presented as the answer to the "mystery" of Mercado's sudden disappearance from television in 2010, which led to great speculation and false rumors.

Structured as a series of segments indicated with tarot card-like intertitles and enlivened with colorful animations, Costantini and Tabsch's bilingual, bicultural, and translocal documentary portrays Walter as an aging figure, who depends on attentive support staff, including his personal assistant Willie Acosta (a major interlocutor in the film), with whom Mercado had a long-standing close relationship and who is described as being "part of the family," as well as his secretary, Wilma Torres. We also have privileged access to Walter's family (his six nieces, including Ivonne Benet Mercado and Betty Benet Mercado), who also assist him and share insightful testimonials about their uncle, and get to see his environs, particularly his lushly decorated home in Puerto Rico, which is marked by worldly, over-the-top, perhaps camp baroque aesthetics (a profusion of adornments, photographs of himself, and religious icons) and that includes a variety of queer signifiers, such as a copy of Eric Chaline's *Gay Planet: All Things for All (Gay) Men*, a painting of Saint Sebastian, a reproduction of Hippolyte Flandrin's *Young Male Nude Seated Beside the Sea*, Anderson Cooper and Gloria Vanderbilt's book *The Rainbow Comes and Goes: A Mother and Son on Life, Love, and Loss*, and an image of Oscar Wilde. The documentary also features interviews with multiple colleagues in the television, radio, and media fields such as Raúl De Molina, Tony Hernandez, Mauricio Zeilic, and Maria Lopez Alvarez, who discuss Walter's standing in the Spanish-language industry (for example, Alvarez discusses his appearances on Univision's *Primer Impacto*), as well as interviews with numerous fans, as I expand on later, who are able to talk of what it means to follow or adore Walter.

Mucho, Mucho Amor is exemplary in portraying Walter's humanity, his foibles and frailty, his daily routines, his negotiations of homophobia, and the process through which he becomes a televisual "spectacle," including hairstyl-

Figure 18.3 Willie Acosta applying makeup on Walter Mercado at home. Screen capture, *Mucho, Mucho Amor: The Legend of Walter Mercado*, Netflix, 2020.

ing, makeup, and costume. Witnessing Walter becoming "Walter," that is to say, seeing an effeminate, elderly (eighty-seven-year-old) transloca becoming their public persona, is a remarkable and aesthetically valuable experience, and confirms an intrinsic femininity that parallels but is not exactly equal to the process of a drag queen coming into character. Given Mercado's extensive training in the dramatic arts and his solid finances, his performative social location is closer to what Esther Newton describes in *Mother Camp: Female Impersonators in America* as a "stage queen" (a professional, middle-class entertainer) but also shares in the feminine continuity that marks "street queens," who do not disavow femininity as part of their daily, lived experience.

The major "drama" of the documentary, besides Walter's negotiation of femmephobia or homophobia (synthesized in Eugenio Derbez's and others' crude parodies, but also indicated in Willie Acosta's testimony), is the evil doings of Bill Bakula and the adverse impact this had on Walter's finances and health. Remarkably, the film includes a lengthy, detail-rich interview with Mercado's former manager, who does not admit any type of guilt but does share valuable information about the commercial dimensions of Walter's internationalization and U.S. crossover success. The documentary culminates with Walter's consecration at the opening of a HistoryMiami Museum exhibit dedicated to his legacy (*Mucho, Mucho Amor: 50 Years of Walter Mercado*, held from August 2 to August 25, 2019), which Mercado attended with his family and friends, as the journalist Connie Ogle noted, preceded by a preparatory fashion shoot with the young Puerto Rican photographer Giován Cordero at Veo Estudio in San Juan, and through encounters with contem-

Figure 18.4 Walter Mercado, Lin-Manuel Miranda, and his father Luis Miranda in 2019. Screen capture, *Mucho, Mucho Amor: The Legend of Walter Mercado*, Netflix, 2020.

porary celebrities such as the diasporic Puerto Rican composer, lyricist, and actor Lin-Manuel Miranda and the renowned Mexican television journalist Jorge Ramos.[10]

One way to read the documentary is as the story of Walter's platonic relationships or "seductions," most clearly with Bakula, but also with Miranda and Ramos. *Mucho, Mucho Amor* highlights platonic romances and terrible deception: how Bakula seduced Mercado with roses and lavish attention, as Walter's nieces Betty and Ivonne Benet Mercado and the television producer Maria Lopez Alvarez point out, only to then break his heart (and pocketbook); how Walter gets to shower handsome men such as Miranda and Ramos (and others, as shown in the archival footage) with his undivided, piquant attention, and gets to glow in their adoration, even if only for the brief duration of a video interview. Latin American *locas* have always felt profound attraction for masculine, heterosexual, cisgender men, whether *bugarrones* or celebrities, as Manuel Puig's *Kiss of the Spider Woman* amply shows, and here Bakula, Miranda, and Ramos play the role of sex object to a T. In this sense, it is irrelevant if Walter verbally acknowledges being gay; we see him being his fabulous, queer self, even openly flirting, as when he states "¡Me desmayo! ¡El hombre que más admiro!" ("I am going to faint! The man I most admire!") on seeing Jorge Ramos (at least in the "Real America with Jorge Ramos: Walter Mercado Is Back" footage on Facebook), and listen to him telling the story of amorous betrayal. Walter's sexuality is an "open secret," clearly visible and audible to all, as Ivonne Benet Mercado indicates in the film.

The Good, the Bad, and the Ugly of
"Walter Mercado Vintage Era"

One of the limitations of *Mucho, Mucho Amor* is its lack of attention to matters of race, specifically of white privilege, in a televisual context that strongly favors white Latinx entertainers such as Walter Mercado and others such as the Cuban American talk show host Cristina Saralegui, where U.S. Spanish-language networks "continually reinforce both Latin American and U.S. racial and ethnic hierarchies, most specifically by prioritizing whiteness" (Dávila, *Latinos, Inc.* 168). The filmmakers and interviewees do not remark on the fraught status of Black representation in Puerto Rican and Latinx television, a topic that the scholar Yeidy M. Rivero has explored at length in her landmark book *Tuning Out Blackness: Race and Nation in the History of Puerto Rican Television* as well as in her scholarship on the performer Javier Cardona, where she "[calls] attention to the pressing need to explore commercial television's racial, ethnic, cultural, and gendered representations across the Latin American and Spanish Caribbean region" (Rivero, "Channeling Blackness" 337). Walter Mercado's success is directly tied to his white privilege, to what the scholar Tace Hedrick refers to as "Mercado's performance of *charismatic* whiteness" (18), in a system that marginalizes Black performers and that aspires to project Latinidad as the visual equivalent of whiteness, as the scholar Arlene Dávila has shown in *Latinos, Inc.* and *Latino Spin*. It also has to do, as media scholar Eliseo Colón-Zayas points out, with the fact that "Mercado resignified the cultural practice of astrology and, subsequently, that of Afro-Caribbean Santería, as a cultural product for the new differentiated consumption market practices of neoliberalism and globalized markets" (10–11, my translation).

The question of Mercado's engagement with and syncretic appropriation of the knowledge and traditions of Santería/Regla de Ocha, Espiritismo, and "Afro-Indigenous creolized spirituality" (@afrolatinoed), and its lack of discussion in *Mucho, Mucho Amor* (in fact, the near absolute absence of Black interviewees in the entire film), generated lengthy Twitter threads originated in July 2020 by two Puerto Rican scholars, William Garcia-Medina (@afrolatinoed) and Jorge J. Rodríguez V (@JJRodV); as Rodríguez wrote, "historically, white, upper class folks were allowed to be 'spiritual' while Black and lower class folks were decried as 'demonic'/'cults.'" Mercado's apparently "benign" practice of racial erasure created a white-only environment reminiscent of Andy Warhol's avocation for whiteness, as when Warhol affirmed, "I want it simple and plastic and white" (qtd. in Crimp 67). This mythification of whiteness appears in *Mucho, Mucho Amor* when Mercado describes waking up at the Cleveland Clinic in Ohio in 2012 after suffering a heart attack and

Figure 18.5 Screen capture, "Walter Mercado Vintage Era," YouTube.

perceiving the blond, blue-eyed nurses and doctors as angels in heaven, a misunderstanding that the filmmakers illustrate with a humorous animated sequence and do not critique.

A short video titled "Walter Mercado Vintage Era," shared on YouTube in 2008, serves to illustrate Mercado's racial shortcomings, particularly the overshadowing effect of whiteness in a context where Black cultural referents are invoked while Black bodies are made invisible, where Walter is selling whiteness along with his other products. Uploaded by a user identified as Emi Zip, possibly from Mexico, the four-minute-long clip begins with blaring trumpets, as we see a title sequence with a gyrating planet Earth, highlighting the American hemisphere in green, with a sepia background that includes several photographic images of Walter. The globe shrinks as the words "La Gran Familia de Walter Mercado" ("Walter Mercado's Great Family") appear around the globe and in the middle of the screen. We then see Walter, who is wearing a highly tailored, pale lime green Mao suit, with several rings on his fingers with large green gems and sporting bouffant blond hair. Walter begins by stating, "Para que sepan ustedes que estamos abarcando al mundo entero. Directamente desde Checoslovaquia, de padres rusos, he traído a una amiga, a una modelo exquisita. Su nombre significa oro, pasión y amor. ¡Zlata!" (This is to let you know that we are embracing the entire world. Directly from Czechoslovakia, of Russian parents, I have brought a friend, an exquisite model. Her name means gold, passion, and love. Zlata!) The camera tilts up, and we then see a smiling white, blond model in a purple bathing suit standing next to a white bathtub filled with rose petals. Zlata proceeds to enter the tub as Walter prepares a ritual bath. At the end of the sequence, Walter switches from Spanish to English to thank the model, asking her how to say "I love you" (presumably in Czech), and proceeds to repeat "Miluji tě," which he first pronounces as "mi lucha" ("my struggle" in Spanish). During this entire segment, the international phone number 01 900 849 8118 appears at the bottom of the screen, with the message "El costo es de $45.00 por minuto" (The cost is $45.00 per minute [in Mexican pesos]), and a note indicating a maximum of thirty minutes for this "servicio de entretenimiento para mayores de 18 años" (entertainment service for persons eighteen and older).

There are many layers to this television clip: it is an infomercial that seeks to promote calls to a telephone service and the sale of Walter-related merchandise but that now has archival value, that serves as document of neoliberal commodification but also partakes in the realm of what performance studies scholar Diana Taylor refers to as "the repertoire," referring to the embodied, sensual, and sensory associations we maintain for the figure of Walter Mercado, particularly of his performance. On the one hand, there is the matter of visual representation, absolutely dominated by a blinding racial whiteness (that of Mercado himself and of his invited guest, Zlata), which is counterpoised by a tropical ritual bath incorporating profoundly Caribbean ingredients (*melao de caña*, or cane syrup; cinnamon essence; honey; Agua Florida, a type of cologne) along with some that are clearly not (champagne, "if you have it," "according to your finances," "or if not sparkling apple cider . . . or beer," as well as drops of red wine) that point to complex histories: the *melao de caña*, to the legacy of slavery and sugar plantations; honey, to the Yoruba deity Oshun, whom Walter invokes stating, "¡Ochún! ¡Ochún Yeyeo!"; Agua Florida, to popular Hispanic customs; champagne (or an equivalent sparkling beverage), to perceptions of French sophistication; red wine, to Spain. The belief in the magical or spiritual powers of a bath with natural substances, spices, perfumes, and alcoholic beverages corresponds directly to the practices of the Afro-diasporic religion of Santería; as the scholar Ysamur Flores-Peña notes, "Ochún, Yalode, Iyalode, Yeyeo, and Orí Yeyeo are common praise names that devotees use to address the most desirable of the divine females in the Yoruba/*Lucumí* heaven. Ochún is the manifestation of beauty both physical and otherworldly" (113).

Walter's invocation of Yoruba/Lucumí practices can be seen as a domestication or taming (a destigmatization) of this spiritual tradition. At the same time, it is undeniable that Walter is encouraging his viewers to partake in a cleansing sensory ritual that is beneficial to the individual, inasmuch as it promotes relaxation, engagement with the self, and a celebration of physical (somatic) experiences, which involve sight and smell as much as taste and touch. This encouragement to partake of a ritual bath might or might not bring about the desired goal (success in love), but nevertheless is a pleasant activity that grounds the body and interrupts daily routines. It is an invitation to focus on the self. Mercado's linguistic usage is also very notable, as he favors inclusive language, using feminine and masculine gender markers when referring to his audience, even while describing a ritual love bath that is strongly coded as feminine.

In this video, Mercado is functioning as the character of doña Geno in Dolores Prida's play *Botánica*, which is to say, as a person who dispenses recipes for personal improvement that combine religious belief with community psychology and self-help, except that the model who is posing for the ritual bath (Zlata) actually does not understand most of what he is saying. And while Walter is inviting potential customers to spend money, he is giving the advice out for free: anyone who understands Spanish can benefit from this ritual bath without sending Walter a payment. While the name "La Gran Familia de Walter Mercado" invokes paternalist tones in a Puerto Rican/Latinx context, Walter can be seen as queering this family, similar to how gay writers such as Manuel Ramos Otero did (Gelpí 137–54). What Walter does not do is radically destabilize white supremacy; in other words, he resists the scholar Arlene Torres's call to recognize that "La Gran Familia Puertorriqueña 'Ej prieta de beldá' (The Great Puerto Rican Family Is Really Black)." In his willful neglect, Mercado creates a clashing environment in which Blackness is physically erased as it is spiritually invoked.

Mercado as Author

Throughout his career, Mercado penned a number of books, including *Enciclopedia de Walter Mercado, Tomo I* (1983), *Enciclopedia de Walter Mercado, Tomo II* (1985), *Beyond the Horizon: Visions of the New Millennium* (1997, ghostwritten by Carlos Harrison and published by Warner Books), and *El mundo secreto de Walter Mercado* (2010, published by Harper Rayo), which brings together sections of his out-of-print 1983 and 1985 volumes. The Puerto Rican scholar Efraín Barradas has pointed to inconsistencies in the books and their political conservatism (namely the anti-communist discourse in *Beyond the Horizon*), but also to how they reflect a worldview that promotes social tolerance and the advancement of women. The final volume, *El mundo secreto de Walter Mercado*, is marred by occasional condescending, paternalist racial attitudes, particularly in the autobiographical passages, but can also be read as a proposal for an expansive religious cosmology based on mutual understanding and appreciation, as a type of interfaith or ecumenical gesture that celebrates multiple global traditions. Most notably, Mercado celebrates organized religion (Buddhism, Hinduism, Christianity), polytheistic religious systems (Santería/Regla de Ocha), as well as esoteric belief (astrology, numerology, palmistry), which he combines in his philosophy of love.

Many passages in these books are troubling. One racially insensitive anecdote appears in the introduction to *El mundo secreto de Walter Mer-*

cado, where Mercado reminisces about a challenging experience he faced when his car broke down in the middle of the night in a deserted location. As he describes, he feared for his life, and started to pray to the Black Catholic saint San Martín de Porres. Suddenly, Walter heard a knock on the car window: "miré y vi a una mano negra. Me asusté tremendamente y salté hacia el otro lado del asiento. Cuando miré bien, vi a un señor muy simpático, negrito, delgado, de rostro muy bello. . . . Algo me llegó al corazón que me inspiró fe en aquel hombre" (I looked and saw a black hand. I grew extremely afraid and jumped to the other side of the seat. When I looked well, I saw a very friendly man, *negrito*, thin, with a very beautiful face. . . . Something touched my heart that inspired trust in that man) (15–16). In this anecdote, Blackness signals religiosity but also inspires fear. The actual hero who aids Mercado, a Black man perceived as a potential manifestation of the divine, is infantilized with the diminutive "negrito," a term of endearment used to minimize the stigma of identifying a person as Black; he becomes a "magical Negro," that is to say, a Black person whose function is to help a white man. The introduction also includes extensive references to Santa Bárbara, who stands for the Yoruba orisha Changó in the syncretized practice of Santería. This type of contradiction (Blackness as divine intervention; Blackness as the source of fear) is recurrent in the autobiographical narrations in the book.

Puerto Rican Documentary Views

How do we step back from these highly charged representations that veer toward nostalgia (*Mucho, Mucho Amor*), commercialism ("Walter Mercado Vintage Era"), and sensationalism (*Beyond the Horizon* and *El mundo secreto de Walter Mercado*)? The Puerto Rican director Noelia Quintero Herencia's made-for-television documentary, *Walter Mercado: Más allá de la astrología* (2002), an episode of the Puerto Rican public television series *Prohibido Olvidar* broadcast on WIPR Channel 6 and 3 (TUTV), is an extremely valuable production that provides a different approach, geared for Spanish-speaking audiences and presented in a national (Puerto Rican) context. Filmed almost twenty years before *Mucho, Mucho Amor*, this limited-budget twenty-five-minute documentary features a much younger and somewhat more masculine and assertive Walter who is able to speak articulately and passionately in Spanish about his career, beliefs, and work. It features interviews with many of the same family members (his nieces Ivonne Benet Mercado and Carmen Mercado) and with professional colleagues such as the actor and legislator Velda González, who speaks at length about Walter's early career. In his testimony, Walter Mercado explains in much more detail his first two decades as an artist and how his 1969 major television breakthrough occurred due

Figure 18.6 *Walter Mercado: Más allá de la astrología* (dir. Noelia Quintero Herencia, 2002), Prohibido Olvidar, WIPR Channel 6 and 3, TUTV, Puerto Rico. Screen capture.

to his chance encounter with the entertainer and producer Elín Ortiz at the studios of WKAQ-TV (Telemundo), when the scheduled main guest failed to appear for Cheíto Bugalú's (Ortiz's) segment on *El Show de las 12*, and Ortiz had Mercado improvise on astrology for fifteen minutes while dressed as a Hindu prince.

Más allá de la astrología also includes the insightful testimony of Luis Felipe Díaz, a (now retired) professor from the University of Puerto Rico, Río Piedras, who is also known as the transgender cabaret and drag performer Lizza Fernanda. Díaz's complex, lucid analysis focuses on how astrology functions as a type of social psychology, even while lacking the same scientific rigor. Díaz highlights contemporary individuals' craving for spirituality and the social function that Mercado played. As Díaz states (in Spanish), "We are still arcane, mysterious beings. We have spiritual needs. And they are precisely the need that the Church cannot fulfill, and that with all of its dogma and restrictions, *la escuela* (the educational system) cannot fill. Nor can the doctor. And Walter Mercado precisely fills that need, of a teacher who transcends pedagogy, of a teacher that transcends traditional medicine, of that teacher that transcends jurisprudence and the modern world" (my translation). Díaz is also able to clearly articulate the nature of Mercado's disruption as an effeminate, gender-nonconforming, highly educated, and highly trained entertainer who has knowledge of psychology and pharmaceutical arts, as well as training in theater and dance. In this sense, Díaz argues that Mercado is unique and without equivalent.

Queer/Latinx Recuperations and Celebration

Some of the most enjoyable and politically salient parts of Netflix's *Mucho, Mucho Amor* focus on Walter's queer Latinx legacy, whether it is the heartfelt and insightful *testimonio* of interviewees such as the New York-based Puerto Rican makeup artist and LGBTQ activist Karlo Karlo, the Los Angeles-based Puerto Rican witch Mireya Lucio, or the Salvadoran American actor and influencer Curly Velasquez, who appears with his grandmother María Gladys García. This queerness is intensified by the presence of fabulous Latina drag queens such as Queef Latina (Antonio Méndez), Lolita Cabrón (Fredo Rivera), Mala Matías (Janh Jemel Matías), and Cherub Borne (Jacob Marrero), who attended the party at the HistoryMiami Museum along with the gay Mexican American deejay Hugo Zazuetta, and through the Instagram fan art or memes that appear in the film, such as those by the Chicana journalist Melanie González (@melanie_gee), the Guatemalan-Dominican spiritual healer and teacher Michelle Melo (@rememberlove), and the queer Salvadoran American street artist Johanna Toruño (@theunapologeticstreetseries), who has a photo of Walter all dressed in blue superimposed over a blue floral bouquet, crowned with the words "Pero sobre todo mucho amor."[11] These homages can be seen as effecting reparative work that transforms Walter Mercado's legacy for contemporary queer/Latinx audiences. They show why Walter continues to be relevant, in spite of his contradictions, and why the documentary is an important intervention. Their views and artwork com-

Figure 18.7 Karlo Karlo. Screen capture, *Mucho, Mucho Amor: The Legend of Walter Mercado*, Netflix, 2020.

Transloca(l) Poetics

325

plement and expand the insights that people such as Willie Acosta (perhaps the queerest presence in Walter's life, who served as a surrogate if not actual partner) and Ivonne Benet Mercado offer on the topic of Walter's gender expression and sexuality.

Karlo Karlo's interview stands out, as he is an openly gay, diasporic, bilingual Puerto Rican activist and media/fashion industry insider who feels that Mercado played a crucial role in his youth.[12] As he states, "Growing up as a queer boy and watching Walter Mercado gave me hope. I saw Walter and I was like, OK, I'm not that different. Here you have a man on television breaking all of these rules." For Karlo Karlo, Mercado's aesthetics are part of the appeal: "He just broke the mold, entirely. And people are mesmerized by the beauty of Walter, by the glamour of Walter." The activist provides a complex critique of the American imperative to "come out of the closet" as the only valid strategy for political progress, indicating that "if Walter Mercado would have come out in the sixties, seventies, eighties, I think it would have hurt his career. Puerto Ricans say often *que lo que se ve no se pregunta.* And I know visibility is very important but not coming out stopped perhaps the homophobia from running wild." Karlo Karlo concludes his testimony affirming the high esteem he has for Mercado: "There [are] so many societal laws that he broke. It goes beyond coming out. You use a cape because you're a superhero. And I see Walter as a superhero."

For the interdisciplinary artist, writer, performer, educator, and witch Mireya Lucio, "Walter was very beloved and very much an integrated part of the culture. But he would also get folded into gay jokes. He was embraced and othered at the same time."[13] As she states, "Somehow, inside a misogynistic super Catholic culture, Walter could thrive. We needed Walter in that landscape." Meanwhile, in his interview, Curly Velasquez, "a Los Angeles-based artist who celebrates all things brown and beautiful" and "lead creator for BuzzFeed's Latinx division Pero Like, a diverse team of Latino content creators from different Hispanic backgrounds and lifestyles" (Rodriguez), points to the currency of Mercado's persona: "Imagine there was a twenty-year-old right now who was like 'I'm going to read you your horoscope. I'm non-binary. I'm asexual.' Are you kidding me? They'd be the biggest on Instagram!" Velasquez also highlights Mercado's referentiality: "He's so nostalgic. He represents moments where we're hanging out with our *abuelitas.* You can put him on a coin, on a T-shirt, and we would all be, 'Oh, I know that!'"

The queer recuperation of Walter Mercado is long-standing and antedates the Netflix documentary. Three quick examples are the Puerto Rican performance artist Fausto Fernós's drag cabaret "The Fire Eating Drag Princess" (2000), now available on YouTube; the Puerto Rican drag queen Alexis Mateo's drag parody of Mercado on *RuPaul's Drag Race All Stars* (2020); and

CURLY VELASQUEZ
Actor & Influencer

MARÍA GLADYS GARCÍA
Curly's Abuela

Figure 18.8 Curly Velasquez and his grandmother, María Gladys García. Screen capture, *Mucho, Mucho Amor: The Legend of Walter Mercado*, Netflix, 2020.

the queer Puerto Rican performance artist/rock singer Macha Colón (Gisela Rosario Ramos), who has adopted Mercado's signature blessing "mucho, mucho amor" as part of her performative persona.

In his "The Fire-Eating Drag Princess" performance at the HotHouse in Chicago, held on April 1, 2000, Fernós appears with Radical Faeries-inspired, exorbitantly colorful makeup and costume, which includes black ink swirls and rhinestones, color patches, polka dots, blue and red wigs, and antennas, combining cabaret skills such as storytelling and singing with circus skills such as fire eating.[14] As part of his performance, Fernós welcomes the audience, has them collectively recite an oath of affirmation, eats fire, and goes on to tell an origins story of Taína warrior Amazons in the rain forest before singing "La Era Acuario" ("Aquarius" from the musical *Hair*) in Spanish. Fernós interrupts his musical rendition to offer horoscope predictions, or rather, "premiere Puerto Rican psychological psychic readings," as an elaboration of a vernacular Puerto Rican transloca queerness. The engagement with Mercado here has to do with the embrace of the Age of Aquarius (the "New Age" Mercado touted) as much as with using astrology as a tool for audience interaction, and with a general desire to uplift people's spirits and create a sense of cohesion grounded in queer camp humor. More recently, Fernós and his husband Marc Felion have dedicated two episodes of their podcast *Feast of Fun* to exploring Mercado's legacy (Felion, "FOF #2801" and "FOF # 2880").

Alexis Mateo's impersonation of Walter Mercado in episode 5 of season 5 of the television reality competition *RuPaul's Drag Race All Stars* ("Snatch Game of Love"), first transmitted on VH1 on July 3, 2020, is somewhat dif-

Alexis Mateo ✓
@AlexisMateo79

The drama can not over shadow this amazing moment in my life. #waltermercado was a Icon in my Latin community. A symbol of hope and faith for many of us. Very proud of my performance on @rupaulsdragrace #allstars5 "mucha paz, pero sobre todo mucho Amor" from me to you!

6:06 PM · Jul 4, 2020 · Twitter for iPhone

1.3K Retweets and comments   **20.4K** Likes

Figure 18.9   Alexis Mateo (@AlexisMateo79), "The drama can not over shadow this amazing moment in my life. #waltermercado was a Icon in my Latin community. A symbol of hope and faith for many of us. Very proud of my performance on @rupaulsdragrace #allstars5 'mucha paz, pero sobre todo mucho Amor' from me to you!" Screen capture, Twitter, 2020.

ferent. Unlike the offensive and demeaning parodies highlighted in *Mucho, Mucho Amor*, Mateo's "archival drag" (to use a term employed by David Román) is a type of tribute performed by a self-identified queer, gender-nonconforming, bilingual, diasporic Puerto Rican performer who is negotiating American mass media, and who puts great effort into translating Walter's persona to an audience unfamiliar with his legacy. While Alexis Mateo did not win the "Snatch Game" challenge, she was praised for her performance.[15] Unfortunately, she was also soon eliminated from the show (@AlexisMateo79). The close proximity of the date of transmission of this episode (July 3) to the release of Costantini and Tabsch's documentary on July 8 served to make Mateo's performance a corporate media event, linking two major media companies (VH1, owned by ViacomCBS, and Netflix), portrayed as a "cosmic coincidence" (Rudolph). As such, Mateo's recuperation is quite faithful to Mercado's explicitly commercial orientation.

Finally, Macha Colón's performance stands out, as her decidedly eclectic, countercultural, noncommercial, punk-inspired, folkloric rock perfor-

Figure 18.10 Macha Colón, "Jayá—Macha Colón y los Okapi." Screen capture, YouTube, 2012.

mance borrows multiple camp elements from Mercado (costume, focus on the audience, self-help), always stressing Puerto Rican referents that create a sense of communal identity for her loyal fans, who are a heterogeneous group of Caribbean-based and diasporic queer and feminist misfits (Cintrón Arbaseti; NALAC). As a large-bodied, Afro-Puerto Rican, queer and transloca Latinx performer and film and video director, Colón's recuperation signals irony but also embraces the radical potential of a philosophy of love in a collapsing Caribglobal society marked by a profound economic crisis, natural disasters, and great despair. Her philosophy of "jayaera" and of "estar jayá" (being *jayá*), espoused in her song "Jayá," which she performs with her woman-led band Los Okapi, echoes Mercado's message of self-affirmation, but this time using a vernacular Puerto Rican Spanish-language term (a variation of the standard Spanish *hallarse*) that signals self-discovery and plenitude, and emphasizing a collective ethos. As Macha states, "Estar jayao es estar en orden con el universo" (To be actualized is to be in order with the universe). The video for this song, directed by Ramos Rosario, envisions a large collective celebration culminating in multiple heterogeneous couples, singles, thruples, and children with pets affirming their vows in a mock marriage celebration in which Colón wishes all much happiness and peace, "pero sobre todo, como dice mi tío Walter, mucho, pero que mucho, amorrrrrr" (but above all else, as my uncle Walter says, much, much looooooove). Macha Colón truly captures the essence of Walter Mercado's jouissance and queers it for the new century.

Conclusion

In a context of profound violence, persecution, and animosity against Latinxs in the United States, and of continuing homophobia and transphobia, Diana Taylor affirms that "Walter's performance . . . makes visible both the Law and its transgression: that which demands compliance and, at the same time, that which can be deciphered only by those in the know" (131), stating that "Walter's performance of a psychic space . . . is complicated, contradictory, yet overall affirming. He is the symptom of the commodification of identities and the hypertrophy of artifice" (131). As Taylor indicates, "Walter makes visible the Latino as Star—on condition that he be white, blonde, male, rich, and entrepreneurial" (131). *Mucho, Mucho Amor: The Legend of Walter Mercado* perfectly exemplifies these contradictions and potentialities, which are transformed and reconceptualized thanks to the critique of committed journalists, scholars, activists, and artists who seek to better understand, challenge, and redirect the legacy of Walter Mercado for a *cuir*, Caribglobal, transloca future.

Notes

1. On Walter Mercado, see Barradas, García, Hedrick, Santiago, Taylor. Colón-Zayas analyzes Mercado's 1960s theatrical and television camp aesthetics and his transition to queer performance in 1969: "a polemical, countercultural performance that located him outside of the representational limits of normative masculinity, placing him in a dissident sexual gender, neither masculine nor feminine," precisely at a historical moment of global shifts regarding social conventions, including countercultural movements that espoused an "androgynous vision of sexuality" (10, my translation).

2. For a longer elaboration on translocas, see La Fountain-Stokes, "Translocas" (2011) and *Translocas* (2021).

3. On *Mucho, Mucho Amor*, see Acevedo, Aguilar, Felion ("FOF #2880"), Luna, Miranda, Rudolph, Schulman, Sierra Arzuffi, Toro.

4. See Acevedo, Barradas, Quiroga, Toro. As Barradas writes, "despite a supposedly apolitical attitude, the Boricua psychic has openly declared himself in favor of the assimilation of Puerto Rico to the United States, although he also defends a cultural nationalism, a not-unusual position among those who defend this option for the island. Walter has also been closely associated with Right-wing Cuban individuals and groups, both in Miami and in San Juan" (744, my translation).

5. For example, the Mexican artist Eugenio Derbez is portrayed in *Mucho, Mucho Amor* making waffling statements about Walter's self-presentation. As the Mexican journalist Ana Sierra Arzuffi correctly points out, "Eugenio Derbez Did Not 'Honor' Walter Mercado, He Made Fun of Him."

6. Quiroga appears to be quoting testimony from *El Nuevo Día* ("Muere en Miami el luchador anticastrista Julito Labatut"), but the source is uncredited. Flattering testimony of Labatut by Mercado also appears in an article by Hernández Cabiya. In "Justicia continúa" and "El caso Muñiz Varela," Delgado indicates that the investigation into the 1979 murder of Muñiz Varela is ongoing, forty years after the crime.

7. Acevedo indicates that Walter Mercado was the special guest of Angelita Trujillo when she presented her book *Trujillo, mi padre* (*Trujillo, My Father*), a defense of the dictator, at an event held at Casa de España in San Juan in 2010. Toro's identification of Julito Labatut as "un comerciante cubano radicado en Puerto Rico que tuvo un historial cuestionable" in her *New York Times* column generated an angry debate on Facebook on July 25, 2020, with the journalist Mari Mari Narváez, who felt that the phrase "historial cuestionable" (questionable past) was an unacceptable euphemism for complicity with political violence. Mari Narváez's brother Santiago Mari Pesquera was murdered on March 24, 1976, "as an apparent spin-off of the planned political assassination and unrelenting harassment of Juan Mari Bras (1927–2010)—founder of the Puerto Rican Socialist Party" (Repeating Islands).

8. Analyzing diverse American astrology columns, Adorno writes: "The striking feature which the personal predictions in the two kinds of publications have in common is their 'practicability' and the almost complete absence of any reference to the major and mostly solemn speculations about the fate of mankind at large. It is as though the sphere of the individual were completely severed from that of the 'world' or the cosmos. The slogan 'business as usual' is accepted as a kind of metaphysical maxim" (26).

9. See U.S. Court of Appeals, First Circuit.

10. On Cordero, see Del Valle.

11. See Cárdenas on Toruño's radical street arts practice.

12. On his website, Karlo Karlo is described as "a celebrity makeup artiste, philanthropist, producer and human rights activist" who "began his career in the 90s as a make-up artist for Christian Dior" and who has also worked with Chanel Beauté and Givenchy. See www.karlokarlo.com/biography.

13. Mireya Lucio's biography is available on her website, mireyalucio.com/About.

14. On Fernós, see La Fountain-Stokes (*Translocas*) and Obejas.

15. On the challenges faced by Puerto Rican contestants on *RuPaul's Drag Race*, see La Fountain-Stokes (*Translocas*).

Works Cited

@afrolatinoed. "I love Walter Mercado but does anyone know of any literature on Walter Mercado's whiteness and afro-indigenous creolized spirituality and astrology?" *Twitter*, 11 July 2020, 2:25 p.m., twitter.com/afrolatinoed/status/1282018172162408448.

@AlexisMateo79. "The drama can not over shadow this amazing moment in my life. #waltermercado was a Icon in my Latin community. A symbol of hope and faith for many of us. Very proud of my performance on @rupaulsdragrace #allstars5 'mucha paz, pero sobre todo mucho Amor' from me to you!" *Twitter*, 4 July 2020, 6:06 p.m., twitter.com/AlexisMateo79/status/1279537089885827074.

@JJRodV. "Important in this convo is how race and class informed the reception of Espiritismo in Puerto Rico versus Santeria: in short, historically, white, upper class folks were allowed to be 'spiritual' while Black and lower class folks were decried as 'demonic'/'cults.'" *Twitter*, 12 July 2020, 10:22 a.m., twitter.com/JJRodV/status/1282319377933664256.

@theunapologeticstreetseries. "I am really excited to watch the Walter Mercado docu that releases today on Netflix—this isn't an ad—I just have a lot of childhood memories in El Salvador watching Walter tell the stories of the stars in between all the coverage of the war at the time and it brought me a sense of peace & joy. I'll be watching it later!" *Instagram*, 8 July 2020, www.instagram.com/p/CCZBXBBpD3c/.

Acevedo, Rafael. "Walter, las estrellas y el terror." *Claridad* [Puerto Rico], 16–22 July 2020, www.claridadpuertorico.com/walter-las-estrellas-y-el-terror/.

Adorno, Theodor W. "The Stars Down to Earth: The *Los Angeles Times* Astrology Column." *Telos*, vol. 1974, no. 13, 1974, pp. 13–90.

Aguilar, Carlos. "Love in the Stars: 'Mucho Amor' Filmmakers on Gender Trailblazing Astrologer Walter Mercado." *Los Angeles Times*, 10 July 2020, www.latimes.com/entertainment-arts/story /2020-07-10/netflix-mucho-mucho-amor-legend-walter-mercado-astrology-gender.

Barradas, Efraín. "El Evangelio según San Walter o de las contradicciones de la Era de Acuario." *Revista Iberoamericana*, vol. 82, no. 257, 2016, pp. 743–55.

Cárdenas, Cat. "Artist Johanna Toruño Is Making the Voices of Queer Latinx People Heard with Her Unapologetic Street Series." *Teen Vogue*, 8 Oct. 2019, www.teenvogue.com/story/artist-johanna -toruno-unapologetic-street-series.

Castañeda, Mari. "Television and Its Impact on Latinx Communities." *The Oxford Handbook of Latino Studies*, edited by Ilan Stavans, Oxford UP, 2018.

Cintrón Arbasetti, Joel. "Estrategias para jayarse: Entrevista con Macha Colón." *80grados*, 18 Jan. 2013, www.80grados.net/estrategias-para-jayarse-entrevista-con-macha-colon/.

Colón-Zayas, Eliseo. "Amanecer en la Era de Acuario Walter Mercado, estrella del performance camp y queer." *DeSignis*, no. 19, 2012, pp. 67–78.

Crimp, Douglas. "Mario Montez, for Shame." *Regarding Sedgwick: Essays on Queer Culture and Critical Theory*, edited by Stephen M. Barber and David L. Clark, Routledge, 2002, pp. 57–70.

Dávila, Arlene. *Latino Spin: Public Image and the Whitewashing of Race*. New York UP, 2008.

Dávila, Arlene. *Latinos, Inc.: The Marketing and Making of a People*. U of California P, 2001.

Delgado, José A. "El caso Muñiz Varela continúa bajo investigación." *El Nuevo Día*, 6 Oct. 2019, www.elnuevodia.com/noticias/locales/notas/el-caso-muniz-varela-continua-bajo-investigacion/.

Delgado, José A. "Justicia continúa la pesquisa por el asesinato de Muñiz Varela." *El Nuevo Día*, 29 Apr. 2018, www.elnuevodia.com/noticias/seguridad/notas/justicia-continua-la-pesquisa-por-el -asesinato-de-muniz-varela/.

Del Valle, Liz Yanira. "Giovan Cordero y su mucho amor a la fotografía." *inSagrado*, 28 July 2020, insagrado.sagrado.edu/giovan-cordero-y-su-mucho-mucho-amor-a-la-fotografia/.

El Nuevo Día. "Muere en Miami el luchador anticastrista Julito Labatut." *El Nuevo Herald*, 18 Aug. 2007, www.latinamericanstudies.org/exile/labatut.htm.

Felion, Marc. "FOF #2801—The Magical Life of Walter Mercado." *Feast of Fun*, 11 Nov. 2019, feast offun.com/podcast/2019/11/11/fof-2801-the-magical-life-of-walter-mercado/.

Felion, Marc. "FOF #2880—Mucho Amor and the Voyage of Walter Mercado." *Feast of Fun*, 13 July 2020, feastoffun.com/podcast/2020/07/13/fof-2880-mucho-mucho-amor-the-voyage-of-walter -mercado/.

Fiol-Matta, Licia. *A Queer Mother for the Nation: The State and Gabriela Mistral*. U of Minnesota P, 2002.

Flores-Peña, Ysamur. "Overflowing with Beauty: The Ochún Altar in Lucumí Aesthetic Tradition." *Osun Across the Waters: A Yoruba Goddess in Africa and the Americas*, edited by Joseph M. Murphy and Mei-Mei Sanford, Indiana UP, 2001, pp. 113–27.

García, Sandra E. "Walter Mercado, Celebrity Astrologer for Millions of Latinos, Dies." *New York Times*, 3 Nov. 2019, www.nytimes.com/2019/11/03/world/americas/walter-mercado-dead.html.

Gelpí, Juan G. *Literatura y paternalismo en Puerto Rico*. Editorial de la Universidad de Puerto Rico, 1994.

Gitlin, Todd. "Prime Time Ideology: The Hegemonic Process in Television Entertainment." *Social Problems*, vol. 26, no. 3, 1979, pp. 251–66.

Hedrick, Tace. "Neoliberalism and Orientalism in Puerto Rico: Walter Mercado's Queer Spiritual Capital." *CENTRO Journal*, vol. 25, no. 1, spring 2013, pp. 2–30.

Hernández Cabiya, Yanira. "Lamentan la muerte de Julito Labatut." *El Nuevo Día*, 18 Aug. 2007.

HistoryMiami Museum. *Mucho, Mucho Amor: 50 Years of Walter Mercado*, 2–25 Aug. 2019, www.historymiami.org/exhibition/walter-mercado/.

Jiménez, Félix. *Las prácticas de la carne: Construcción y representación de las masculinidades puertorriqueñas*. Ediciones Vértigo, 2004.

King, Rosamond S. *Island Bodies: Transgressive Sexualities in the Caribbean Imagination*. UP of Florida, 2014.

La Fountain-Stokes, Lawrence. "Translocas: Migration, Homosexuality, and Transvestism in Recent Puerto Rican Performance." *emisférica*, vol. 8, no. 1, summer 2011, hemisphericinstitute.org/en/emisferica-81/8-1-essays/translocas.html.

La Fountain-Stokes, Lawrence. *Translocas: The Politics of Puerto Rican Drag and Trans Performance*, U of Michigan P, 2021.

Laureano, Javier E. "Antonio Pantojas se abre el traje para que escuchemos el mar: Una historia de vida transformista." *CENTRO Journal*, vol. 19, no. 1, 2007, pp. 330–49.

Luna, Luis. "With 'Mucho Mucho Amor,' Walter Mercado Solidifies His LGBTQ Icon Status." *Latino Rebels*, 22 July 2020, www.latinorebels.com/2020/07/22/waltermercadomuchomuchoamor/.

Mercado, Walter. *Beyond the Horizon: Visions of the New Millennium*. Warner Books, 1997.

Mercado, Walter. *El mundo secreto de Walter Mercado*. HarperRayo, 2010.

Miranda, Carolina A. "Review: 'Mucho Amor' Shows Intimate Moments with Bedazzled Astrologer Walter Mercado." *Los Angeles Times*, 8 July 2020, www.latimes.com/entertainment-arts/story/2020-07-08/review-mucho-mucho-amor-shows-intimate-moments-with-bedazzled-astrologer-walter-mercado.

NALAC. "Macha Colón (Gisela Rosario Ramos)." www.nalac.org/es/members/2708-gisela-rosario-ramos/.

Newton, Esther. *Mother Camp: Female Impersonators in America*. 1972. U of Chicago P, 1979.

Obejas, Achy. "'Feast of Fools'—A Celebration of Diversity. Colorful Fausto Fernós—An Appropriate Host for Radical Faeries." *Chicago Tribune*, 31 Mar. 2000, p. 28.

Ogle, Connie. "Walter Mercado's Entrance at the Opening of His Exhibit Was the Most Miami Moment Ever." *Miami Herald*, 2 Aug. 2019, www.miamiherald.com/miami-com/things-to-do/article233432802.html.

Prida, Dolores. *Botánica. Beautiful Señoritas and Other Plays*. Arte Público Press, 1991, pp. 141–80.

Puig, Manuel. *Kiss of the Spider Woman*. Translated by Thomas Colchie, Knopf, 1979.

Quiroga, José. "The Cuban Exile Wars: 1976–1981." *Las Américas Quarterly*, special issue of *American Quarterly*, vol. 66, no. 3, September 2014, pp. 819–33.

Repeating Islands. "Santiago Mari Pesquera Case at the United Nations," 30 Mar. 2016, repeatingislands.com/2016/03/30/santiago-mari-pesquera-case-at-the-united-nations/.

Rivero, Yeidy M. "Channeling Blackness, Challenging Racism: A Theatrical Response." *Global Media and Communication*, vol. 2, no. 3, 2006, pp. 335–54.

Rivero, Yeidy M. *Tuning Out Blackness: Race and Nation in the History of Puerto Rican Television*. Duke UP, 2005.

Rodriguez, Alexander. "What's the Buzz? Alexander Sits Down with BuzzFeed's Curly Velasquez." *Bear World Magazine*, 25 May 2018.

Román, David. "Archival Drag: or, the Afterlife of Performance." *Performance in America: Contemporary U.S. Culture and the Performing Arts*. Duke UP, 2005, pp. 137–78.

Rudolph, Christopher. "The Cosmic Coincidence of Alexis Mateo's Walter Mercado Impression." *NewNowNext*, 17 July 2020, www.newnownext.com/walter-mercado-alexis-mateo-mucho-mucho-amor-drag-race/07/2020/.

Santiago, Javier. "Walter Mercado." *Fundación Nacional para la Cultura Popular*, 4 Nov. 2019, prpop.org/biografias/walter-mercado/.

Translocaʼ(l) Poetics

Schulman, Michael. "The Improbable Charisma of Walter Mercado." *New Yorker*, 24 July 2020, www
.newyorker.com/culture/culture-desk/the-improbable-charisma-of-walter-mercado.

Sierra Arzuffi, Ana. "Eugenio Derbez no 'honraba' a Walter Mercado, se burlaba de él." *Homosensual*,
13 July 2020, www.homosensual.com/entretenimiento/celebridades/eugenio-derbez-no-honraba
-a-walter-mercado-se-burlaba-de-el/.

Taylor, Diana. "La Raza Cosmética: Walter Mercado Performs Latino Psychic Space." *The Archive
and the Repertoire: Performing Cultural Memory in the Americas*, Duke UP, 2003, pp. 110–32.

Toro, Ana Teresa. "Walter Mercado después del amor." *New York Times*, 24 July 2020, www.nytimes
.com/es/2020/07/24/espanol/opinion/walter-mercado-amor-netflix.html.

Torres, Arlene. "La Gran Familia Puertorriqueña 'Ej prieta de beldá' (The Great Puerto Rican Family
Is Really Really Black)." *Blackness in Latin America and the Caribbean: Social Dynamics and
Cultural Transformations*, vol. 2, edited by Arlene Torres and Norman E. Whitten Jr., Indiana
UP, 1998, pp. 285–306.

U.S. Court of Appeals, First Circuit. *Walter Mercado Salinas Astromundo Inc. v. Bart Enterprises International Ltd*. No. 10–2359, 2011. *FindLaw*, caselaw.findlaw.com/us-1st-circuit/1589009.html.

Filmography

"The Fire Eating Drag Princess—Fausto Fernós—April 1, 2000." *YouTube*, uploaded by Feast of Fun,
6 June 2009, www.youtube.com/watch?v=J2xe7JgkiGg.

"Jayá—Macha Colón y los Okapi." *YouTube*, uploaded by Macha Colón, 22 Nov. 2012, www.youtube
.com/watch?v=i2K__dfInfY.

Mucho, Mucho Amor: The Legend of Walter Mercado. Directed by Cristina Costantini and Kareem
Tabsch, Netflix, 2020, www.netflix.com/watch/81200204.

"Real America with Jorge Ramos: Walter Mercado Is Back." *Facebook*, uploaded by Jorge Ramos,
5 Sept. 2019, www.facebook.com/jorgeramosnews/videos/2324697764414717/.

"Snatch Game of Love." *RuPaul's Drag Race All Stars*, season 5, episode 5, VH1, 3 July 2020.

Walter Mercado: Más allá de la astrología. Directed by Noelia Quintero Herencia. Prohibido Olvidar,
WIPR Canal 6 y 3 TUTV, 2002.

"Walter Mercado Vintage Era." *YouTube*, uploaded by Emi Zip, 25 Aug. 2008, www.youtube.com
/watch?v=kMW9BnjILpU.

PART VI

#StreamingBrown

BEYOND NARCOS AND NOVELAS

The Diverse World of Streaming in Latin America

David Schmidt

In this chapter, I take a systematic look at original series created and filmed in the Latin Americas by the streaming platform and production company Netflix. I consider two questions: (1) To what extent do these series reproduce U.S. expectations about the region, skewed toward the stereotypical genres of the telenovela and the crime drama? (2) To what extent do they reflect the tendencies of Latin American television itself? After briefly considering the history of Netflix and the growth of its original content production, I turn to those Netflix series that are created in Latin America. I first consider the prolific catalogue of shows that reproduce the conventional "narcos and novelas" tropes, and then turn to the unique Latin American series that both promote broader demographic inclusion and open up fascinating new genres: fantasy and supernatural drama, documentary, and science fiction. Finally, I consider Latin American productions created for other streaming services, focusing on one uniquely "pan-Latin American" series. (All text in quotations is my translation of the Spanish original.) Before this formal approach and analysis, I begin with a conversation.

As I rode with my friend on the Metrobús in Mexico City one day, we noticed an ad for a new Netflix series. The floral-themed poster—displayed prominently on the Metrobús platform, in the middle of Avenida Insurgentes—announced *La casa de las flores*, the latest telenovela filmed in Mexico for the streaming company.

"Great," my friend sighed. "Another novela. Don't they think we're able to produce anything other than soaps and narco-dramas?"

I had to agree. The English-language series that Netflix was promoting at the time covered much more diverse genres: the fantasy of *The Witcher*, the horror of *Haunting of Hill House*, the dystopian sci-fi of *Black Mirror*.

"Where's the Mexican *Black Mirror*?" my friend asked. "Where is the Latin American *Stranger Things*?"

Where, indeed?

Her question sparked my curiosity. For too long, Latin American television, and U.S. cinematic depictions of the region, had been skewed toward narcos and novelas. Two sides of the same narrative coin: the former focused on the gritty underworld of the drug trade, the latter on personal dramas among the affluent classes.

But what of Netflix and the other streaming series? What sort of Latin American productions were they creating, and to what extent did these original series follow the old tropes? I set out to examine original streaming content—exhaustively examining all the Netflix series created in Latin America—in search of answers.

While I found much content that was "business as usual," I also found new and exciting exceptions, series that expanded into different genres, with greater representation of social classes, cultures, ethnicities. More and more series are being made for a primarily Latin American audience—rather than focusing on English-speaking U.S. viewers—and are gaining worldwide acceptance.

The Prolific World of Netflix

Founded in Scotts Valley, California, in 1997, Netflix, Inc., began exclusively as a video delivery service, not streaming online content until 2007. In 2012, when they had amassed over twenty million subscribers, Netflix began streaming their first original series, the Norwegian-American crime drama *Lilyhammer*. The series received mixed reviews, currently showing a 60 percent approval rating on Rotten Tomatoes, but paved the way for a new age of original online content. The successful *House of Cards* debuted the following year, and by 2017 the company had invested six billion dollars in one thousand hours of its own original content (Shiff).

Part of the motivation for expanding into original content has to do with increasing licensing fees from studios. As Netflix grew, studios began to demand greater fees. Netflix paid Starz thirty million dollars for licensing rights in 2008; by 2011, the studio was asking Netflix for ten times that amount (Schuker and Wingfield).

Another factor is the rapid speed with which the company approves new productions. Netflix gives each creative executive buying power, rather than following the traditional pilot-episode screening process of network television production (expertly parodied in the self-aware fourth season of *Seinfeld*). As Co-Chief Executive Officer and Chief Content Officer Ted Sarandos told *Variety* in 2017, each creative executive "can greenlight a big-budget show in the room without me" (Sims).

Netflix has seen an explosion in its original content over the past five years. The company spent $6.3 billion on content in 2017, of which 85 percent went to original programming; in 2018, they released 88 percent more than during the previous year (Morris).

Netflix's prolific content—from any genre imaginable—has become a trope for contemporary comedy writers. *South Park* depicts the company's executives answering the phone by saying, "Netflix, you're greenlit! Who am I speaking with?" In a *Saturday Night Live* sketch, a woman pitches a show with one sentence—"So it's about a girl named Jenny . . ."—and the executive throws wads of cash at her. The sketch comedy program *Alternatino* suggests that most of Netflix's show titles are actually placeholders, and they start filming as soon as someone clicks on the title.

To be sure, with this much content, not all shows are bound to be winners. And yet, many of the original series and films still bring in massive viewership. *Extraction*, *Bird Box*, *Spencer Confidential*, *Murder Mystery*, and *6 Underground* have all been watched more than eighty million times each (Soen). After the third season of *Stranger Things* was released in July 2019, forty million views occurred during the first four days (Alexander). *Tiger King* became a cultural icon during the early days of the COVID-19 pandemic, as millions of quarantined viewers engaged in heated discussions about whether or not Carol Baskin really killed her husband.

Not only is Netflix's viewership massive, it is a truly global audience—and Latin America represents one of the largest markets. According to Digital TV Research, five U.S.-based streaming platforms will account for 88 percent of Latin America's streaming market by 2025. The five platforms—Netflix, Amazon Prime Video, Disney+, Apple TV+, and HBO—are expected to reach eighty-five million subscriptions in the region (LABS).

Not content to service Latin American viewers with exclusively foreign content, Netflix and its competitors have created increasingly more original content from and for this region. What is the nature of this content? If we systematically look at the Latin American series created, what does their collective profile look like?

To repeat my friend's question in Mexico City: to what extent does Netflix's catalogue of Latin American series reflect "business as usual," a conventional menu of soapy series and crime dramas?

An Overview of Netflix's Latin American Content

Not long ago, I spoke with a Russian shopkeeper on the streets of Mexico City. He had been trying to market eastern European-style pierogi to local *capitalinos*. "It's tough. The clientele are finicky," he said. "People are afraid to try new things. How do you sell them a dish they've never tried before?"

This dynamic has long informed the decision-making process of television and movie production. It is easier to get money behind a guaranteed blockbuster—a reboot, a sequel, a superhero franchise installment—than a new concept. In the world of television, many U.S.-based networks, like the massive conglomerate Telemundo, have produced content that is tried and tested—namely, narcos and novelas. The argument has often been, "Why would we produce something new if people won't watch it? Let's stick with the sure thing."

And yet, Netflix subscribers in Latin America increasingly *are* watching more diverse genres. Series like *Stranger Things* and *Black Mirror* have become veritable cultural phenomena in the region. Given this fact, are Latin American series being created for these genres of sci-fi, dystopian, supernatural thriller, horror, and mystery? Or are Netflix producers sticking with the conventional world of narcos and novelas?

To answer this question, we will need to examine their catalogue in its entirety.

For the purposes of this essay, I have focused exclusively on those series created in Latin America: screenwriters and actors from the region's twenty countries, filmed primarily in Spanish and Portuguese, and aimed primarily—though not exclusively—at Latin American viewers. While I will consider other streaming services later in this essay, I will be focusing on the pioneer par excellence in the world of streaming: Netflix.

Netflix's original Latin American series come primarily from four countries: Mexico, Colombia, Brazil, and Argentina. This is not surprising, given the economic scale of these nations, with GDPs of USD $1.22 trillion, $331 billion, $1.87 trillion, and $519.9 billion, respectively, according to the World Bank.

But what sort of genres are represented by these shows? How many of them fit the narco and novela mold?

Telenovelas, Netflix Style

The number of Netflix series that could be classified under the telenovela genre is substantial: over twenty, as of this publication. It would be unfair to paint all these series with the same brush, however, as they come in a diverse array of styles and subgenres.

Club de Cuervos, a comedy-drama focused on the soccer club Cuervos FC, was the first Spanish-language production of Netflix, debuting in 2015. *Monarca* is a thriller-drama of scandal and violence, while *Edha* and *Hechas en México* focus on the world of high fashion. Many of the South American productions follow the formula of a woman reinventing herself: *Coisa mais linda, Amar y vivir, Samantha,* and others. *El bandido honrado* is a light-hearted, silly comedy about an ex-con trying to turn his life around.

Many of these series span the genres of narco and novela, such as Mexico's *Ingobernable. El club* follows middle-class Mexican youth who decide to enter the business of selling MDMA. *Sintonia* and *Amar y vivir*, from Brazil and Colombia, respectively, both deal with a young person's search for stardom amid crime and violence.

As is the case with most of Netflix's original content, these series have a significantly high production value. Their slick look is more reminiscent of Colombia's high-budget *Sin tetas no hay paraíso* than of the campy 1990s *María la del barrio*. And yet, their storylines are faithful to the novela genre: interpersonal drama, intrigue, lies and corruption, usually among society's most elite classes. This can be best illustrated by the recent Mexican production *La casa de las flores*.

The story follows multiple generations of the De la Mora family, a wealthy dynasty that has made their fortune with a lucrative florist business. Following a scandal involving the patriarch, Ernesto, the family must pick up the pieces and preserve their apparent opulence.

As with many novelas across the last hundred years, representations of race and class are terribly skewed. The protagonists are a wealthy, upper-class family, with European physiognomy, accustomed to opulent living. If not "the 1 percent," they are certainly within the most privileged 5 percent of the nation.

Their status is clear from the opening scenes of the series. The De la Mora family lives in a sprawling mansion in some unnamed neighborhood, though one can guess it to be in the vicinity of the affluent Lomas de Chapultepec. The sister Paulina speaks with the languid, loose-mouthed affectation of the typical *fresa*, Mexico's upper-crust elites. The family's maid Delia, meanwhile, offers some working-class comic relief to lighten the heavy "high drama."

As I watched *Casa de las flores* and other Netflix novelas, I thought back to my years spent in Russia. Russians did not believe that poverty existed in Mexico, because they had seen too many Mexican soaps. "No, David, there can't be any poor people in Mexico," they would say. "I've seen how Mexicans live. All of them have three cars and live in massive mansions."

This sort of skewed class representation is hardly limited to Latin America. In the United States as well, television series have historically focused primarily on middle- and upper-class protagonists, as covered in the brilliantly titled 2005 documentary *Class Dismissed*.

There is also a racial dimension to the class tension of *Casa de las flores*. In the first episode, Elena (played by Aislinn Derbez, daughter of famed co-median Eugenio Derbez) brings her boyfriend to visit from the United States. Her boyfriend, Dominique, is a Black American. Elena's sister, Paulina, admonishes her father when he refers to Dominique as "el negrito."

"That's not the right word to use," Paulina says.

"What do I call him, then, dear?" Mr. De la Mora asks.

"African-American. But there is no need to talk about his skin or the color of his skin."

"Tell that to your *mother*, then."[1]

Of course, had Dominique been a white American, Elena's parents would likely have behaved quite differently. The upper echelons of Mexican society, as in much of Latin America, display the ethnic heritage of Spanish colonialism. This trend is reflected in much of the region's entertainment industry. Films and TV series have historically overrepresented people with lighter skin, while many countries' media severely exclude the majority of their own population, be they mestizo, Indigenous, or Black.

Despite the widespread African heritage in the Dominican Republic and other parts of the Caribbean, Black citizens are underrepresented in television and film. Dominican author Carlos Andújar describes, in his book *Identidad cultural y religiosidad popular*, the systemic denial of the country's African cultural roots, amid an "effort, by the Hispanophile intellectuals, to convince the population of their own Hispanic—and, therefore, white—origins" (Andújar 117).

This is the primary shortcoming of so much of the telenovela genre: its protagonists are wealthy and white, while the majority of the population appears only as maids and underlings.

Narco Drama

Where would the U.S. entertainment industry be without the infamous narco?

Those pesky scofflaws, ever tunneling under our marvelous border walls, discovering new ways to supply our hungry consumers with the drugs they crave, to the tune of $150 billion dollars a year. How we love to hate them, to plaster their faces on our "Bad Hombre Wanted" posters and present them as the poster children of Mexico, forever shamed, forever on display to demonstrate the "barbarism" of our neighbors. We show our children the severed head of Joaquín Murrieta and assure them that *ours* is the culture of civilization and progress.

The nations of Latin America serve as the perennial backdrop for this savage drama. A yellow camera filter is obligatory—we must show how gritty and dusty "those countries" are. God forbid anyone film a modern, bustling center of commerce and culture in Mexico City, Buenos Aires, or Bogotá.

On television stations across Latin America, as well, the crime drama has long rivaled soapy novelas for supremacy. On Mexican networks like Televisa, one can freely toggle back and forth between the extremes of society: the affluent rich of the novela and the gritty underworld of the narco.

As of this writing, Netflix has at least fifteen original narco and crime series from Latin America. These include police dramas in the style of *NCIS*: *La ley secreta*, *Historia de un crimen*, and *Distrito salvaje*. The Mexican series *Tijuana* covers crime and corruption from the point of view of an intrepid journalist; other series, such as *Las muñecas de la mafia* and *Yanqui*, are focused on the criminal underworld itself. Of course, who could neglect one of this century's most powerful drug lords, the eponymous subject of the three-season series *El Chapo*, a coproduction between Netflix and Univision.

There are documentaries on the world of the drug trade. In *Cuando conocí al Chapo*, famed Mexican actress Kate del Castillo obtains an exclusive meeting with the powerful kingpin. All this, in addition to the numerous other narco series available on the platform that are not Netflix originals: *La Reina del sur*, *El dragón*, and many others.

While the platform's catalogue of crime dramas is extensive, one of the most exemplary series is the one with the most minimalist name: *Narcos*.

Based on the real-life stories of Latin American drug lords, the first three seasons focus on Colombian kingpin Pablo Escobar in the late 1970s. The second two seasons—branded under their own title *Narcos: Mexico*—are set in 1980s Mexico and concern the rise and fall of capo Miguel Ángel Félix Gallardo (played by Diego Luna).

The meticulous attention given to historical detail and cultural accuracy is clear. Although the first seasons received some criticism for using Mexican actors to play Colombian characters—imagine Keanu Reeves attempting a British accent in *Bram Stoker's Dracula*—the dialogue flows smoothly in both English and Spanish. If any elements of the screenplay were translated from English, it doesn't show. The seasons set in Mexico were, indeed, filmed in Mexico City (a fact I can attest to, as I was contracted as an extra for a couple of episodes).

The characters are complex humans, much more reminiscent of the protagonists of *The Godfather* or *The Sopranos* than any sort of Manichean "bad hombre" caricatures. Without excusing their acts of torture and violence, the series examines Félix Gallardo and his cohorts as real humans. Indeed, the main critique I have heard from friends in Mexico City is that "they humanized the narcos too much."

If cultural bias is to be found anywhere in the series, it would be in the depiction of the DEA agents. These are the only characters who come out smelling like roses (throughout the first season, at least). Rampant corruption is depicted among all of Mexico's law enforcement agencies, but the DEA is somehow entirely immune to temptation.

All things considered, *Narcos* is a well-made series about the sordid world of drug trafficking, with a human eye for complex character drama.

Even at its best, though, narco drama is a limited genre. Is this all that Netflix is producing—narcos and novelas? As my friend asked, do the company's executives believe this is "all Latin America has to offer"?

Fantasy and Indigenous, Black, and Working-Class Protagonists

Some of the most exciting new Netflix series lie in a very different genre: fantasy and supernatural drama. Not only do they enrich the company's catalogue, but many of them strive to represent broader social realities, including the ethnic and class makeup of their characters. I would like to consider three supernatural series at length: *Frontera verde, Siempre bruja*, and *Diablero*.

Frontera verde (*The Green Frontier*), released in August 2019, is one of the first original Netflix series created in Colombia. Filmed in the jungle surrounding Leticia, Amazonas, it is set on the border between Brazil and Colombia. Helena, a young detective from the city, is sent to the remote region to investigate the murder of several women from a local all-female sect living in the jungle. She works with local police officer Reynaldo, an Indigenous man whose connection to his own roots is strained at best.

Big names were involved in this Colombian series. The producer, Oscar-nominee Ciro Guerra, earned notoriety for the breathtaking film *Embrace of the Serpent*, based on the lives of real-life ethnobotanists in the Amazon. Cocreator and head writer Carlos Contreras is the brother of the famed Mexican director Ernesto Contreras.

Despite the central role of Helena, the series does not view the Amazon region exclusively from an outsider's point of view. Much of the story is told from the perspective of Yua, an Indigenous man. The first episode begins with a narration in the Ticuna language, and a significant amount of dialogue takes place in Ticuna and Witoto.

The primacy of native traditions in the Amazon region is emphasized throughout. In one scene, Helena comes across a group of Indigenous people preparing the ritual immolation of a body that is part of her investigation. "Are they going to burn her?" she asks. "They can't do that."

"Yes they can," a local elder replies. "This woman is from their tribe."

"I can't stop a police investigation just because of your local superstitions."

The elder responds in no uncertain terms: "They aren't superstitions, young lady. You are on Nai territory here, and you have no say in these matters."

Another Colombian series, *Siempre bruja* (*Always a Witch*), tells an intricate tale of magic, love, and time travel. The series follows protagonist Carmen, a former slave from colonial Colombia who was burned at the stake as a witch. She uses magic to escape death, finding herself in modern-day

Cartagena on the coast of the Caribbean. Her task is to seek out the means to return to her beloved Cristóbal, the son of a wealthy white family.

The setting for this story, based on the novel *Yo, bruja* by Isidora Chacón, is uniquely Colombian. Those familiar with the work of Gabriel García Márquez will immediately recognize the Caribbean context, as the town of Cartagena is the emblematic city of the coastal region where *Love in the Time of Cholera* takes place.

The significance of the Caribbean coastal city of Cartagena, for this series, lies in its strong African heritage. While over 10 percent of Colombia's population claims African ancestry, this community has been historically marginalized in much of Colombia. Maricel Sandoval, an Afro-Colombian human rights activist, recently told the newspaper *El Heraldo*, "For there to be justice, there must be truth . . . a truth that brings together different truths, and one of those truths is that of the Afro [Colombian] and Indigenous peoples" (Agencia EFE).

Afro-Colombian identity and traditions play a central role in the series. In the first scene, the protagonist escapes her execution by reciting incantations in the Anagó (Yoruba) language, one tied to the rituals of Cuban Santería to this day. White clothing is used for rituals in the film, as it is in many real-life rites of Santería and Haitian Vodoun.

Several episodes into the series, a key plot development takes place during the Festival de la Candelaria—a syncretistic celebration honoring one of Latin America's "Black Madonnas," an Afrocentric image of the Mother of Christ. For many Catholics in the region, this imagery teaches that Providence identifies with the oppressed of the world; in other traditions, the Black Madonna is a perfect example of religious syncretism, a melding of African goddesses with European imagery, as with the Haitian deity Ezilí Dantor.

To be sure, *Siempre bruja* is not lacking in detractors. Some Afro-Colombian critics have said that it reinforces stereotypes, and that Black actors are lacking from most of the show's cast. Others call attention to the fact that none of the show's creators are Black. However, even critical articles, such as one written by Anyi Castillo and Alexandra López Asprilla for *Revista Vive Afro*, recognize the woeful absence of Afro-Latina protagonists from much of the mainstream media. "Without a doubt," the authors write, "[an Afro-Colombian protagonist] opens the doors to a discussion about more diverse representations" (Castillo and López Asprilla).

The Mexican supernatural thriller *Diablero* is based on the book *El diablo me obliga* by noir novelist F. G. Haghenbeck. It takes place in contemporary Mexico City, a metropolis beset by demons and unseen forces. Elvis Infante is the eponymous demon-hunter, traversing the back alleys of the capital city with his sister, Queta, as they solve otherworldly mysteries and fight demonic forces.

While the aesthetic of the series is that of authentic, gritty, working-class Mexico City, its creators eschew the leering, sensational gaze so common in Hollywood. If anything, the cinematography defies the quintessential "yellow filter" of gringo cameras, often opting for a soft blue pastiche. (Interestingly, these are the colors that represent the peaceful United States in the 2000 film *Traffic*.) Overall, the setting of *Diablero* is neither the idyllic affluence of novelas nor the grimy poverty-porn of Hollywood. It is simply a real-world metropolis, with all its thorns and blossoms.

The visual representations of witchcraft and magic, likewise, are solidly rooted in the contemporary reality of Mexican traditions. These are not the "Mexican curios" of the gringo imagination, the sombreros and cacti referenced in Oliver Stone's film *Savages*. Rather, the altars and talismans are familiar sights for any urban Mexican viewer, reflecting the living traditions of the *santeros* and *curanderos*. They are exactly the sort of occult items that one would find in a working-class indoor market of Mexico City, most notably El Mercado de Sonora.

The actors' ethnic features are more representative of the general population than in many television series. The protagonist is played by Veracruz-born actor Horacio García Rojas, who has portrayed Indigenous characters in previous Mexican productions.

"This was an opportunity to show a lot of things, to feel proud of them," says José Manuel Cravioto, *Diablero*'s showrunner. "Including the characters. With Horacio García Rojas, the type of casting we used was for him to play a Mexican protagonist, with a Mexican physiognomy. Along with his sister, Queta, who is played by Fátima [Molina]. But we also have light-skinned actors like Christopher Uckermann, and Giselle [Kuri]. We are Mexican too, and we are light-skinned. . . . In other words, there is this mix. This is Mexico, and this was a great chance to show that" (Olivares).

The script also makes a point to incorporate Nahuatl, the native language of the Mexica (Aztec) civilization. Some conversations occur in the language, and the incantations used are in Latin and Nahuatl. As the liturgical languages of the two empires that became the Mexican nation, they are ideal for a fictional representation of ritual life.

"I proposed," Cravioto continued, "that we should have certain parts where people speak entirely in Nahuatl, so that people in other parts of the world would see it and say, 'What language is that?' Well, in Mexico there is a language that existed before the conquistadores came here, and it is called Nahuatl" (Olivares).

By no means perfect, these three fantasy series provide fascinating examples of ethnic, cultural, and class inclusion in the world of television.

Tacos and the Insider's View

Viewers in the English-speaking world have long watched documentaries about other cultures' cuisine. Some are respectful and accurate, others exoticizing and problematic; and yet, even with the best of them, there is a fundamental difference between a series written for outsiders and one made for insiders. Ideally, a good show would be accessible to both groups—and this is the case with a recent Netflix documentary.

Las crónicas del taco (*The Taco Chronicles*) covers the diverse culinary traditions of Mexico, examining several different types of tacos. Many of my gringo friends—from as far away as Nevada, Georgia, and Hawaii—have watched the series and loved it. And yet, they are not the primary target audience.

The series is filmed entirely in Spanish (with the exception of a few chefs' interviews in the United States). While the narration provides sufficient background information on each dish, it does not waste an inordinate amount of time answering basic questions like, "What is *barbacoa*?" It does not feel like a Food Network production, with Guy Fieri patiently explaining: "In Mexico, *chile* means a hot pepper . . ."

There is just enough explanation to include outsiders, but not enough to bore insiders. There are, furthermore, enough insider touches to show who the primary audience is.

Each episode is narrated by the taco in question. The thought of a speaking taco is entertaining enough for any viewer, but Spanish speakers—and Mexican audiences, in particular—will appreciate the subtleties of each taco's regional accent. The *taco de pastor* speaks with a very urban Chilango (Mexico City) accent, while the northern *taco de carne asada* speaks with the unequivocal cowboy twang of a ranching state like Sonora. The diverse collection of *tacos de guisado* speaks like a group of *comadres* chatting over coffee. These details will likely be lost on non-Spanish speakers.

As a food documentary by and for Latin Americans, *Las crónicas del taco* represents a shift of voices and audiences for Netflix. Other series, as well, are geared toward their local audiences, and do not easily fit into the narcos-and-novelas box.

The historical drama *Bolívar* depicts the life of the iconic South American liberator. While *La niña* takes place in the world of crime and violence in Colombia, it is more complex than any typical crime drama, as a story of redemption and reconciliation that examines the longest lasting civil war in the region (ongoing since 1964), as well as the tentative peace process begun in 2016.

Even some series that include the tag "soapy" on Netflix's algorithm are much more complex than most of the genre. *Los Briceño* depicts Colombian *muleros*, semitruck drivers; the protagonist is a single mother seeking to make it in the world of male-dominated truck races. The Mexican series *Desenfrenadas* is a "girl power" road story that involves racial and class prejudice, between middle-class suburbanites and a working-class young lady from Oaxaca.

One series deserves special attention, however, as a pioneer in the world of contemporary science fiction from Latin America.

Brazilian Dystopia

The Brazilian series *3%* is more than an exciting Latin American contribution to the science-fiction genre. I would dare to affirm that it is one of the most intriguing representations of a dystopian future, period—from any country or time period.

The series depicts a near-future world of grinding poverty and environmental degradation. Even the location suggests recent devastation: the province is identified as Amazônia Oriental (Eastern Amazonia), a former jungle now turned into a treeless dust bowl. (This prediction has become even more timely, given President Bolsonaro's policies toward the rain forest.) In this world of hunger and despair, one hope shimmers on the horizon: the possibility of leaving.

Once people turn twenty, they are eligible for The Process. Based on a rigorous selection procedure of interviews, tests, and competitions, 3 percent of them will be chosen to leave "The Continent" and go live in "The Offshore," a prosperous utopia free of hunger and violence. The series follows one batch of candidates as they fight for this chance.

The measure of truly excellent sci-fi and fantasy is whether its story has stand-alone value in and of itself. Are the drama and character development solid and engaging enough to keep one's attention, even if all the otherworldly elements were stripped away? In the case of *3%*, the answer is a resounding "yes."

One of the major critiques of some Netflix productions has been the accusation of "padded run-time"—that some series tread water to fill up their allotted number of episodes, whether or not they have sufficient story to do so. This was my impression of the unfortunately languid reboot of *Unsolved Mysteries*. The opposite is true with *3%*.

One gets the sense that the characters and world-building were developed far beyond the audience's field of vision, as with the rich dystopia of 2015's *Mad Max: Fury Road*. The plot is full of twists, turns, and surprises, with all characters well fleshed out.

The series also avoids a typical pitfall of the genre: the exposition dump. Here, the imagery of this futuristic world is exceedingly rich—glowing earpieces, screens, headsets, strange garments—but many elements are never fully explained. Other aesthetics are only explained later in the series. The Offshore citizens who work at the processing facility wear clothing that exposes a bare patch of their upper arm through a star-shaped hole; it is later revealed that this is to display their vaccine scars, the status symbol of the privileged.

While the series' Brazilian roots are clear, the story has universal appeal. There are no clear ethnic majorities in either The Continent or The Offshore; an even mix of Black and white actors play people from both sides. While some might scoff at the idea of no racial inequality in a dystopian future, the point here is to symbolize the world's inequality on a much broader scale, the dynamics of exclusion in every sense: race, class, nation, gender, sexuality, and so forth. In the process, the series has hired a diverse cast of Brazilian actors that reflects the country's present demographics.

And therein lies the genius of this series: like all the best sci-fi stories, it works on so many levels. The Offshore and The Process are not simplistic, one-to-one metaphors, but rather represent a broad array of present realities.

The scenes of the initial screening process, in the first episode, will bring back unpleasant memories to anyone who has sat through a job interview. They will be equally relatable for anyone who has visited a relative in prison, where a pane of glass may as well mean the difference between two different dimensions. Perhaps one of the closest metaphors, though, is for the gauntlet of any draconian immigration system.

It is telling that a common phrase used in the series for the utopia is "o outro lado." On the southern side of the U.S.-Mexico border, migrants often say this phrase in Spanish—"el otro lado"—when referring to the United States.

I shuddered as I watched these interview scenes, thinking back on the anecdotes of countless friends who had applied for a U.S. visa. Even if you meet all the requirements, only a small number of your fellow applicants will be approved. The interviewer is actively trying to confound you. You are nervous, simultaneously begging and trying to avoid looking desperate. Your entire destiny lies in that interviewer's hands, entirely subject to their mood, their discretion. You are supplicating; they are indifferent. One false move—one nervous tic or sideways glance—and you are eliminated, casually rejected.

You could not be more expendable. They have thousands of other applicants to get through.

The metaphor works for so many other dimensions of the immigration process: the visa lottery, admission at the border, requesting refugee status, deportation proceedings in immigration court. As one friend overheard a government attorney tell an immigration lawyer in court, "Tough luck, you know. But we can't just let *all* of them in."

On a broader level, the language of "the lucky three percent" is applicable to our world in its entirety. It is fitting that this story should come from Latin America, a place historically subjected to colonial and neocolonial economic policies, a region that Uruguayan author Eduardo Galeano described as having "open veins." The capitalism that enriches very few sectors of our world's population is a lottery of its own. Large amounts of exclusion are worked into it by design. It is a grading system that does not allow us all to win, no matter how hard we work, how well qualified we are. Failure is not just the result of laziness but is required by the system. The system needs exclusion to function.

Black Mirror, eat your heart out. *3%* represents dystopian sci-fi at its finest.

Other Streaming Services

While Netflix is the current leader in original online content, the market is becoming increasingly competitive, with other platforms launching their own series as well.

Most recently, Amazon Prime has released several new Latin American programs, including an unnamed horror original from Mexico. The comedy-drama *El juego de las llaves* depicts a group of couples in modern-day Mexico City entering the world of swinging. The same country's true crime drama *El Presidente* will cover the FIFA corruption scandal of 2015. The comedy *Cómo sobrevivir soltero* stars Mexican actor Sebastián Zurita, examining the world of online hookups after his fiancée cheats on him.

One exciting series, *Hernán*, presents a detailed depiction of Mexico during the early years of the Spanish invasion. Javier Bardem stars as the title conquistador, with Tenoch Huerta playing the Aztec emperor Moctezuma II. Gael García Bernal and Diego Luna produced the miniseries, making great efforts toward historical authenticity. The creators contracted linguists, historians, and professors to provide faithful translations of the dialogue into the classical Nahuatl spoken during the sixteenth century.

Unfortunately, I found no Latin American productions among Hulu's original content, which may be because the service is not yet available outside of the United States. And yet, good news is on the horizon: Hulu has announced plans to adapt Isabel Allende's acclaimed Chilean novel *La casa de los espíritus* (*The House of the Spirits*) into an original Spanish-language series, a welcome replacement for the Anglo-heavy 1993 film (Lopez).

Of all these streaming services, though, HBO offers one of the most interesting and original series. The show's fanciful, surrealist world exists at the intersection of the nations of Latin America and the Latino and Latina population of the United States, one not based in any individual country, and yet somehow rooted in the entire region.

A Pan–Latin American World

The series *Los Espookys* follows a group of friends who run a business related to all things horror and paranormal. The group uses their technical and special effects know-how to stage supernatural phenomena for their clients. Meanwhile, paranormal mysteries and interpersonal drama surround them on all sides, in this aesthetically rich world of magical realism and absurdist humor. This is the telenovela-meets-Scooby-Doo, with some of the Dadaist humor of Eugenio Derbez or *Deep Thoughts* author Jack Handey.

While the production is U.S. based—the executive producers are Fred Armisen and Lorne Michaels—I include it in this essay for several reasons. First, it is filmed almost entirely in Spanish, with a diverse group of actors from across Latin America and the U.S. Latino and Latina community. It is filmed primarily in Chile. The imaginary location of the series, however, is more than the sum of its parts. With a quintessentially pan-Latin American setting, the series reflects the richly diverse roots of its creators and actors.

One of the protagonists, Renaldo, speaks with a clearly Mexican accent, peppering his speech with phrases like "güey," "en buena onda," and "neta." The other Mexican actress on the team, Cassandra Ciangherotti, plays Úrsula, the brains of the operation; her Mexican accent is apparent as well. Meanwhile, the character of Andrés (Julio Torres), the heir to a chocolate fortune, has a Salvadoran accent with U.S. undertones.

Ana Fabrega, the showrunner and screenwriter, plays the ingenuous Tati, whose speech patterns are especially peculiar. Her strange mix of English affectations and vaguely Central American tone reflect Fabrega's own diverse heritage: born in Arizona to Panamanian parents. (This is explained, in-series, as the result of an ill-starred trip to the States, where Tati failed to learn English but developed a strange accent in Spanish.)

All these accents coexist in the same universe, along with the native speech patterns of other actors—Venezuelan, Chilean, Caribbean, and so forth. This is the world of *Los Espookys*, everywhere and nowhere all at once.

It is also one of the show's most interesting characteristics—it takes place in a perfectly pan-Latin American world. *Vanity Fair* describes the setting as an "unnamed, fictionalized Latin American nation" (Liebman).

The location of "Anywhere, Latin America" is clearly fictional, with a peculiar-looking flag that has a vaguely Bolivian color scheme. And yet, curiously, this imaginary country still feels more authentic than the "Mexico" of many Hollywood productions.

Cultural references and callbacks are everywhere. The entire aesthetic of the show reflects the style of a 1990s telenovela, with deliberately cheap production value. Characters become melodramatic caricatures; villains are dripping malevolence, heroes exude nobility, and sensuality is around every corner. The U.S. ambassador, Melanie Gibbons, is an extremely ditzy version of the stereotypical gringa—she speaks in fractured, heavily accented Spanish, wears all pink, and her office is adorned with a hot pink Statue of Liberty. Meanwhile, one Chicana character leans heavily into the Spanglish, frequently mixing English curses into her speech.

The show is rich in Easter eggs and nods to cultural insiders. One character's dog is named "Frutsi," the cheapest brand of fruit punch in Mexico. Many shots, angles, and effects hearken back to the early 1990s Mexican horror series *La hora marcada.* In one episode, characters watch a fictional film, *The Woman Without an Eye.* The campy style of the film is reminiscent of the work of Jairo Pinilla, director of *Funeral siniestro* and prolific "father of Colombian horror cinema."

In one scene, characters' faces are all hidden from the camera. This may be an original stylistic choice; likely, though, it is a callback to the Mexican director Carlos Enrique Taboada's *Veneno para las hadas,* a horror film told from a child's perspective, where most adults are shown from the neck down.

One regular feature of *Los Espookys* is its show-within-a-show, a news program dedicated to paranormal phenomena (whose hostess may or may not be human). This is a nod to well-known programs across Latin America, including Jaime Maussan's *Tercer milenio,* Carlos Trejo's *Cazafantasmas,* and the paranormal reporting of Chile's Juan Andrés Salfate.

The resulting cultural setting is pan-Latin American, a unified continent that transcends national boundaries. From the corporate HBO headquarters in New York City, new life has been breathed into Simón Bolívar's dream of a united Latin America. It is a unique, culturally transcendent creation of the digital age.

I recently spoke with Arturo Ramos, retired professor of sociology of the National Autonomous University of Mexico (UNAM), about the globalized trends in society and culture. Ramos commented:

The diverse global channels of communication, thanks to new forms of technology, allow for the integration of identities and struggles for true justice and inclusion, as a projection of the essential human nature which makes us a global community, capable of overcoming the secondary differences that so often divide us.

This is the hope of the new series and voices being produced today.

Wish List

What does the future hold for online streaming in Latin America? If this medium has allowed for a broader spectrum of voices, genres, and national origins, could it be expanded even further? What follows is one possible "wish list" for increasing inclusion, as pertains to new original content in Latin America.

Central America: the forgotten region of Latin America. The Northern Triangle, in particular—Honduras, Guatemala, and El Salvador—is the source of millions of modern migrants fleeing violence and instability. During much of the twentieth century, the region suffered a disproportionate amount of U.S. imperial violence, under Republican and Democratic administrations alike, under the pretext of "fighting Communism." The Caribbean, likewise, has been the frequent target of gunboat diplomacy, stifling the social and economic development of its many island nations.

Given these facts, it is no great surprise that the region has not yet become a major source of television and film productions. And yet, if producers continue to take chances and explore new horizons, that may change in the near future.

Haiti: The cards of geopolitics have long been stacked against Haiti, the poorest country in the hemisphere, with a gross domestic product (GDP) per capita of $756 for 2019. Out of 189 ranked in that year, Haiti's Human Development Index was 169th ("Overview").

However, Haiti also has one of the most remarkable histories in the region. It was the first Black republic, had the first successful slave rebellion, the first modern example of enslaved people breaking their own chains. Given this inspiring history, the fact that Haiti is not a major source of film and television series is nothing short of tragic.

The country's rich Creole roots combine Taino indigenous cultures, diverse traditions from Europe, and—most significantly—those of West Africa. It is high time to reverse the long-standing convention of sensationalizing Haitian spirituality, as in Wes Craven's *Serpent and the Rainbow*. (Itself an echo of earlier anti-Vodoun propaganda, including the 1932 Bela Lugosi film, *White Zombie*.) The spiritual and cultural traditions of Vodoun, in the hands of Haitian screenwriters and directors, could serve as rich sources of inspiration.

Indigenous languages have been historically excluded from much of Latin America's media. This tendency has only just begun to change, with Bolivian president Evo Morales leading the way in 2009, declaring Bolivia a "plurinational state." (That was before Morales's government was overthrown by a U.S.-backed coup of Bolivian white supremacists.)

If streaming can open venues for other genres, why not the native languages and cultures of this continent? If a series like *Frontera verde* can give a central place to the languages of the Amazon, why can't an entire series take place in an Indigenous language?

Indigenous cultures have slowly gained a greater presence in Latin American film over the years. Some recent Mexican films have been shot almost entirely in native languages, including *Eréndira ikikunari* and *La otra conquista*. Imagine a series from Peru or Ecuador, written, acted, and filmed entirely in Quechua. Imagine Argentina winning awards with a Guaraní series. A Mexican series could be filmed in Mixtec, Nahuatl, Mayan, or any of the other sixty-five languages spoken in that nation alone. It is a long overdue opportunity.

To be sure, LGBTQ+ relationships are not absent from the streaming series mentioned. An entire storyline in *La casa de las flores* involves Julián de la Mora and his clandestine relationship with the family's male accountant. And yet, I did not come across any series focused specifically on this community. As LGBTQ+ voices become more present across the globe, they will hopefully occupy central roles in new Latin American series as well.

Conclusion

Despite the ample causes for despair in the years 2020–21—a worldwide pandemic, global unrest, economic crises—there is cause for hope. In the world of literature, film, and television, the winds of change are blowing.

The publishing world itself went through major upheavals in just the first half of 2020. Back in January, the industry was throwing its weight behind the hottest new "migrant story": Jeanine Cummins's *American Dirt*, a highly problematic novel that grossly misrepresented Mexico and its subjects.

Initially, complaints to the publishing world landed on deaf ears: the author was paid a seven-figure advance, Oprah announced it for her book club, and Clint Eastwood's studio slated it for the big screen. Following the novel's release, however, there was a wave of outrage from the Latino community and others across the United States, bringing about a long-needed conversation about diversity of voices in literature.

Since then, publishing houses have committed to greater diversity in their staff and in the authors they publish—including Macmillan, the owner of Flatiron Books. HarperVia, an imprint of HarperCollins devoted to translations of international titles, has released several books from Latin American authors this year.

The same could be said for television and film. Online streaming platforms are offering an exciting array of opportunities to new voices, expanding the medium far beyond the stereotypical formats of the novela and the narco-drama.

To be sure, the future of Latin American productions remains uncertain. As long as the centers of production and finance remain in the United States, issues of creative control are bound to emerge. Even new streaming services focused on providing Spanish-language content to the region are primarily based in the United States. Pluto TV, now providing twelve thousand hours of content to seventeen Latin American nations, is owned by ViacomCBS.

How far can Latin American voices advance and represent the region, when they have to answer to companies based in the United States? As long as this is the case, representation and diversity will depend, largely, on the largesse of these U.S. companies. These questions may find permanent answers only when the nations of Latin America develop their own autonomous streaming services, with their own production studios.

Much work remains to be done, and the road forward can be paved only by those who walk down it. To quote the song "Cantares" by Joan Manuel Serrat:

> *Caminante, no hay camino*
> *Se hace el camino al andar.*

We make the road by walking. Let us continue walking toward a future of diverse new voices in television.

Note

1. The author's translation; does not reflect Netflix subtitles. All translations from Spanish are the author's.

Works Cited

Agencia EFE. "En Video: Activista Afrocolombiana: 'Pusimos los muertos en la guerra . . . y en la paz.'" *El Heraldo*, 7 May 2019, www.elheraldo.co/colombia/en-video-activista-afrocolombiana -pusimos-los-muertos-en-la-guerray-en-la-paz-628966.

Alexander, Julia. "Netflix Needs to Grow, but It's Sacrificing Great Original Series to Do So." *The Verge*, 12 Aug. 2019, www.theverge.com/2019/8/12/20791602/netflix-canceled-shows-originals -tuca-bertie-oa-streaming-wars-disney.

Andújar, Carlos. *Identidad cultural y religiosidad popular*. Editorial Letra Gráfica, 2007.

Castillo, Anyi, and Alexandra López Asprilla. "*Siempre bruja*, la serie que refuerza estereotipos." *Revista Vive Afro*, 3 Sept. 2019, www.revistaviveafro.com/ediciones/siempre-bruja-la-serie-que -refuerza-estereotipos.

LABS. "Five Services Will Account for 88% of the Latin American Video Streaming Market." *LABS English*, 17 Mar. 2020, labs.ebanx.com/en/news/business/five-services-will-account-for-88-of -the-latin-american-video-streaming-market/.

Liebman, Lisa. "*Los Espookys* Breakout Ana Fabrega Isn't Afraid to Let Things Get Weird." *Vanity Fair*, 2019, www.vanityfair.com/hollywood/2019/06/ana-fabrega-los-espookys-hbo-interview.

Lopez, Kristen. "Hulu Is Turning Isabel Allende's 'The House of the Spirits' into a Series." *Remezcla*, 24 May 2018, remezcla.com/film/hulu-isabel-allende-house-spirits-series/.

Morris, David Z. "Netflix Original Content Has Grown by 88% This Year." *Fortune*, 12 Aug. 2018, fortune.com/2018/08/12/netflix-original-content-has-grown-by-88-this-year-but-old-tv-still -rules-the-remote/.

Olivares, Edgar. "*Diablero*, una serie que habla de otro México: Entrevista con J. M. Cravioto." *Código Espagueti*, 22 Dec. 2018, codigoespagueti.com/noticias/cultura/diablero-entrevista-con-j-m -cravioto/.

"Overview." *World Bank*, www.worldbank.org/en/country/haiti/overview.

Schuker, Lauren A. E., and Nick Wingfield. "Starz to Split from Netflix." *Wall Street Journal*, 2 Sept. 2011, www.wsj.com/articles/SB10001424053111904583204576545051871923760.

Shiff, Benjamin. "Is Netflix Making Too Many Shows?" *Geeks*, 2017, vocal.media/geeks/is-netflix -making-too-many-shows.

Sims, David. "Why Netflix Is Releasing So Many New Shows in 2018." *The Atlantic*, 29 Aug. 2017, www .theatlantic.com/entertainment/archive/2017/08/now-dawns-the-age-of-peak-netflix/538263/.

Soen, Hayley. "Ranked: These Are Officially the Most Watched Titles on Netflix Ever." *UK*, 17 July 2020, thetab.com/uk/2020/07/17/most-watched-netflix-shows-ever-167036.

David Schmidt

THE UNSTABLE INTERSECTION OF WITCHCRAFT, SLAVERY, AND REPRESENTATION IN *SIEMPRE BRUJA*

Nicole Pizarro

As a young girl growing up in Puerto Rico in the 1990s, I was lucky to experience a mix of media. As a U.S. territory, Puerto Rico had access to American channels such as the Disney Channel, Nickelodeon, ABC, and others. We also had Telemundo and Univision, not to mention Puerto Rican channels such as WAPA and Tele Oro. I could start my day out watching *Looney Tunes*, then learn to draw with Remi the clown, and end my day with *Ghostwriter*, *Kim Possible*, and *Vigías del sur*. This eclectic mix of television shows informed how I viewed the rest of the world. However, I never really saw myself in these shows, especially not the ones from Latinx channels. The actors from these shows had straight, beautiful hair and gorgeous golden-brown skin. They weren't pudgy with darker skin. They didn't have wide noses or kinky hair. I had to create my own fantasy worlds. I existed in the gray area between U.S. American television shows with African-American characters and Latin American television shows that explored my language, my culture, my values. I learned to cope, and found solace in the recesses of my imagination, where this divide didn't exist. Imagine my surprise when twenty years later, Netflix announced a fantasy television series featuring an Afro-Latina protagonist. The show was everything I hoped for as a kid. Or, so I thought.

On January 22, 2019, the Motion Picture Association of America (MPAA) announced that Netflix had become their newest member. MPAA chairman and CEO Charles Rivkin said that the inclusion of Netflix as a member would "allow us to even more effectively advocate for the global community of creative storytellers." Netflix arguably *has* advocated for the global community by facilitating access to diverse stories, although perhaps not in the most effective ways, as David Schmidt informs in his chapter in this volume. Earlier that same month, Netflix released *Siempre bruja* (*Always a Witch*), a Colombian series about Carmen Eguiluz, an Afro-Latinx witch in the 1600s who upon being sentenced to death at the stake, time travels to present-day Cartagena. In the present, she finds herself relying on her powers to survive as she tries to carry out a mission to save her one true love from death.

Siempre bruja's merits as a representation of Afro-Colombian and Afro-Latinx women by a major studio are overshadowed by the series' problematic plot elements. As a slave woman in a new reality, Carmen becomes an "alien" who is stuck in a place she's unfamiliar with. Therefore, throughout the show Carmen ends up in situations where she's constantly at the mercy of white people. As in her past life as a slave, in the present she's still used as a commodity for the benefit of the white people around her; she is treated as a means to an end. Perhaps what puts the final nail in the coffin in the first season of the show is that Carmen is constantly trying to return to her life as a slave, because she's in love with her slave owner's son. Although Carmen is by all means one of the most powerful witches in the *Siempre bruja* storyworld, she has no agency in her own story. Her naivete makes her an easy target for the villains of the show to take advantage. This choice in storytelling is even more damning considering the show premiered during Black History Month. This unstable intersection of the show's story and the value of Carmen's position ultimately raises the question of whether this problematic take on slavery is a product of the colorism that plagues Latinx communities to this day, or if this choice points to larger issues of representations of Afro-Latinx women in mainstream media.

Carmen, a slave woman in Cartagena in 1646, falls in love with her slave-owner's son, Cristóbal de Aranoa. They write letters to each other and meet in secret from Cristóbal's family. When their tryst is discovered by Cristóbal's mother, Isabel, Carmen is imprisoned under suspicion of witchcraft. At Carmen's trial, Cristóbal tries to intervene on Carmen's behalf, explaining that he taught her how to read and write and renouncing Catholicism in the name of love. Cristóbal's father shouts that he'd rather see his son dead than in cahoots with the devil and shoots Cristóbal. Carmen is taken away to await her execution. In the cell she meets a fellow wizard, Aldemar, who gives her a spell to turn back time in order to save Cristóbal from death. However, Carmen must first deliver a stone to someone in the future. Carmen accepts and chants her spell as she's burning at the stake and is transported to present-day Cartagena. The first season of *Siempre bruja* mainly follows Carmen trying to finish her mission and go back to rescue Cristóbal. Eventually, Carmen figures out that Aldemar is using her for her powers and wants to destroy her, as she is from a strong lineage of witches.

Mediated Representations of Race

Stories where love or lust break the barriers of class are not new. More specifically, stories that showcase love plots between enslaved people and their slave owners are not new. I'm hesitant to use the word "love" here, as the reality is that the power dynamics between slaves and slaveowners render things like love relatively meaningless. In famously problematic films such as

Mandingo (1975) and *Passion Plantation* (1976), slave owners were portrayed as lusting after their slaves, to the point of sexually assaulting them. Both of these films are examples from the blaxploitation era of filmmaking, which was marked by films "starring Black actors—but produced by Whites and mostly directed by Whites—[which] deliberately targeted Black audiences" (Hayward 41). The problem is that "although blaxploitation films provided African Americans with more opportunities to work in the film industry than ever before, many critics and activists problematized the films for their apparent overreliance on violence, sexual content, and drug culture" (Lawrence and Butters 745). These two specific films deal mainly with sexual themes, positioning slaves as objects of desire (and abuse) by their white owners. Although this move leads to a larger conversation about power dynamics and sexual violence in the pre–civil rights era United States, I'm mainly interested in highlighting the fact that whereas *Mandingo* and *Passion Plantation* both (for the most part) recognize the violence that is inherent in slave-slaveowner relationships, *Siempre bruja* exists in a revisionist vacuum. The show insists on ignoring the dangerous implications of Carmen's decisions, instead presenting a story about love, slavery, and fantasy with rose-colored glasses.

In a 2018 appearance at TMZ Live, rapper Kanye West said, "When you hear about slavery for 400 years . . . For 400 years?! That sounds like a choice" ("Kanye West"). This caused a lot of controversy as it was another instance of "decades' worth of revisionist Civil War history with the 'bootstrap' narrative of personal responsibility embedded in American culture" (Burton). When it comes to *Siempre bruja*, which is a show aimed at young audiences, these revisionist histories can be harmful. "Very often, when you appear on the page or on the screen, you are a slave, a servant, or a prostitute—your body is not your own. If you have words, your speech serves only to support the narrative, never to subvert it" (Thomas 24). It is unclear if Carmen could have escaped her imprisonment before being condemned to death. Her relationship with Cristóbal is initially "discovered" when they meet in a secluded area at night. Cristóbal's mother appears with guards and dogs. Before Carmen is taken away, she is staring angrily at the dogs, who seem to be growling at her captors. Cristóbal asks Carmen to stop bewitching the dogs. After he is unsuccessful in defending her, she is taken away and imprisoned. It is implied that she could have escaped, but because she trusted Cristóbal, she allowed herself to be taken away by the guards and imprisoned. At her trial, Cristóbal tries to intervene in her favor. His feelings for her seem to be sincere enough, as he risks being disowned for renouncing his Catholicism. When he is shot by his father, Carmen is distraught. In the prison, Aldemar offers Carmen anything she desires in exchange for help. Instead of requesting freedom, she asks Aldemar for the opportunity to save Cristóbal. Carmen *chooses* to be imprisoned and, had Aldemar not given her the spell to travel to the future, she would have *chosen* to die.

With a rating of TV-14, the way relationships are represented in *Siempre bruja* is more reminiscent of softer, revisionist, watered-down films about interracial and "border-crossing" love, such as Disney's *Pocahontas* (1995). The fact that the show glosses over the larger implications of slavery and Carmen's love for her oppressor are oddly reminiscent of Pocahontas's own choice to be with John Smith. That John Smith and Cristóbal are both parted from their loves because of a gunshot wound to the side is eerily similar. A show with a main character who is a woman from a minority group should be cause for celebration, seeing as representation of minorities in popular media is scarce. However, as Ebony Elizabeth Thomas argues in her exploration of fandom and race in children's media:

> The problem of the diversity gap [in all genres of young adult literature, media, and culture] extends far beyond the mere lack of representation of characters of color in children's publishing and media. Many diverse characters that actually *do* show up on the page, on a tablet, on a television or movie screen, or on the computer are often problematic, as recurring controversies about picture books featuring smiling slaves demonstrate. Stereotyping, caricature, and marginalization of people of color, poor and working-class children and families, gender and sexual minorities, immigrants, and other minoritized groups have been persistent problems in children's literature. (5)

The inherent problem with *Siempre bruja* is not simply that Carmen's character is in love with her slave owner's son and is an overall weak character. The choice to only slightly focus on the horrors of slavery and have an Afro-Colombian slave risk everything for her oppressor—akin to Pocahontas risking her life for John Smith (an account whose veracity has been questioned by scholars)—is a highly problematic move. What's worse is that unlike historical slaves, Carmen has magical powers that could give her freedom. At the very least, they should give her agency. Instead, throughout the show Carmen's agency vacillates, and her characterization is unstable. By virtue of being both Black and Latina, Carmen fulfills multiple stereotypes of people of color on the screen. What's more, an in-depth exploration of these stereotypes demonstrates that this intersection ultimately fails due to the show's lack of emphasis on or gravity regarding Carmen's own agency and story.

Carmen displays a layered existence as a result of the structure of the show. In order to understand the intersections Carmen represents and explain why said intersections simply do not work, we must turn to theories about the construction of gendered and racialized identities. In *The Souls of Black Folk*, W. E. B. Du Bois explains the conflict in the experience "of the darker to lighter races of men in Asia and Africa, in America and the islands of the sea" (8). He calls this conflict a double-consciousness, a "twoness,—An American, a Negro; two souls, two thoughts, two unreconciled strivings; two warring ideals in one dark body" (8). Throughout the years, academics have used this concept to further study the oppression of minorities. In his study regarding Afro-Latinos on the color line, Juan Flores contends that because "in the reigning classificatory schemas 'Hispanic' takes on the status of a 'race,'" there is a "disconnect between Hispanic and blackness [that lends] continuity to the baggage of racial denial in Latin American and Caribbean home countries" (92). Because of this disconnect, Flores argues that Afro-Latinos in the United States are in a "racial fault line," and they experience "a pull in two directions—that of the nationality of Latino pan-ethnicity, and that of blackness and the realities of U.S. American life" (82). Flores goes on to suggest this experience might be a "triple consciousness." Notably, Flores's concept of triple consciousness doesn't account for Afro-Latinos living in Latin American countries where their Blackness is less affirmed due to fact that "the national identities of most Latin American countries are invested in *mestizaje* and predicated on claims of having transcended race" (Hordge-Freeman and Veras 148). To complicate matters further, Nahum Welang argues that Black American women exist "between racial and gendered identities [that are] underscored by the role white patriarchy and black hypermasculinity play in the marginalization of black female voices" (296). Thus,

> Black women, due to the physical and psychological anguish they have historically endured on both fronts of race and gender, are fated to view themselves through three lenses and not two: *America* (represented by the hegemony of white patriarchy), *blackness* (a racial space that prioritises the interests of black men), and *womanhood* (a hierarchical gendered identity with white women at the top and black women at the bottom). (Welang 299)

As both Black and Latina, Carmen exists in a racialized liminal space, which allows her to "move beyond an 'either/or' to a 'both/neither' path of identification" (Romo 404). This liminal space is complicated by the time travel aspect of the show, which positions Carmen in a path of identification where she exists both as an enslaved/colonized subject *and* a free person. Furthermore, as a woman, Carmen's existence is marked by oppression as a result of both colonialism *and* machismo.

Ultimately, throughout the show, Carmen develops a sort of *liminal consciousness* that is mediated through her ability to travel through time. By the end of the first season, Carmen's identity is witnessed through the following lenses:

Womanhood

| Slavery/coloniality | Latinidad/coloniality |
| Blackness | *Mestizaje* |

The time-traveling nature of the show results in Carmen's vacillation between being an enslaved subject, a Black woman, a Latinx woman, and a "racially denied" Latinx subject. In the 1600s she is a slave who is sold to Cristóbal's family. She is at the mercy of her white owners, even though she has powers. She is placed in a caretaker role, even as a child. In a flashback to her childhood, we see her using her powers to heal a slave whose back had recently received many lashes. When she is sold to Cristóbal's family, she is shown cooking and cleaning in her owner's villa. Futhermore, as a slave woman, she would historically be subject to sexual abuse and potentially be subjected to breeding by her owners. On the other hand, in the future, she is a Latina woman. Yes, she's Black, but she's also subjected to the color blindness that exists when it comes to conversations about race in Latin America. Furthermore, she adopts the beliefs of twenty-first-century Latin America. In other words, she sees the injustice of a life of servitude and violence and the possibility of a life where she doesn't have to suffer and be subjected to the horrors of slavery. Carmen's liminality further extends to the fact that she is one of the few major media representations of Afro-Latinx people on the screen. In order to understand the shortcomings of the show, we must analyze Carmen *through* the lens of her liminal existence and turn to critical texts that examine gendered and racialized bodies in media.

The Stereotypes in *Siempre bruja*

Stereotypes of minority populations can be traced across media. There stereotypes have the power to shape the attitudes of the general populace toward these groups. Because Afro-Latinos have been historically underrepresented in Latinx media, it's necessary to turn to alternative means to analyze these stereotypes. Elizabeth Hordge-Freeman and Edlin Veras contend that

> perpetual invisibility and dislocation are recurrent themes that have marked the experiences of Afro-Latinxs in the United States.... They are often racially categorized as Black and ethnically as Latinxs, and so their identities defy the mutually exclusive relationship often associated with Blackness and *Latinidad*. (146)

I argue that this mutually exclusive relationship can be applied to the representation of Afro-Latinx people in media. In his *Interpretive History of Blacks in American Films*, Donald Bogle breaks down some of the major trends in the representation of African American people in film, as these historical stereotypes served the same role: "to entertain by stressing Negro inferiority" (4). I would argue that Carmen Eguiluz is a cross between softer versions of the "Mammy" and the "Magical Negro." Bogle defines a mammy as the female servant who is "fiercely independent" and "headstrong" (8). In terms of African American representation, mammies were usually portrayed as subservient and loyal to the white families they served. "Created to justify the economic exploitation of house slaves and sustained to explain Black women's long-standing restriction to domestic service, the mammy image ... symbolizes the dominant group's perceptions of the ideal Black female relationship to elite White male power" (Collins 72). Typically, mammies were not represented as sexual beings; their job was to take care of their white owners/employers. Carmen's powers give her an edge when she "talks back" to her owners. Throughout the show, Carmen goes back and forth in time. When she travels to the past to be with Cristóbal, she is not afraid to threaten her slave owners, who are afraid of her after witnessing her escape death at her execution. The shadow of her mammy figure follows her to the future, where she usually gets herself involved in situations where she wants/needs to protect her group of (white) friends in modern-day Cartagena. She uses her powers to protect others, constantly. The one time in the first season that Carmen is in a position to actually help people of color, most notably her fellow slaves, the plot of the show conveniently has her lose her powers. Ultimately, these powers are the ones that grant her the ability to somewhat tip the power scales in the show and turn her into a Magical Negro.

Magical Negroes are characters who "focus their abilities toward assisting their White lead counterparts" (Glenn and Cunningham 135). Typically, "instead of having life histories or love interests, Black characters possess magical powers" (Glenn and Cunningham 137). These characters are limited; their existence is ligated to the white characters they aid or assist. In *Siempre bruja*, Carmen's powers mainly serve to solve her and her friends' problems. Because her friends have only limited knowledge of what Carmen can do—at least in the first season—Carmen usually finds herself using her powers to protect her *muggle* friends. Of course, this may be a conscious decision, as the show has a children's telenovela feel. *Telenovelas infantiles* are a subcategory of telenovelas, most popular in Mexican television, that are aimed toward and about children or teenagers. Regardless of whether Carmen's powers are a gimmick by the show meant to appeal to younger audiences, she does "not have depth or [an interior life]" (Glenn and Cunningham 138). Carmen's main defining characteristic in the show is that she is constantly used by the male characters in the show for her powers. Like a true Magical Negro, she's *always* used as a commodity.

The first episode of the series begins with an inquisitor saying, "We fear women because they tempt, they seduce, and they think. We fear women who do not obey, who rise up, who question." As we hear these words, we follow Carmen as she's being escorted to the stake where she will be set on fire for the crimes of reading, writing, and witchcraft. These words are reminiscent of Gloria Anzaldúa's claim that dominant paradigms—such as gender roles—are transmitted through culture. Anzaldúa contends that "woman is the stranger, the other. She is man's recognized nightmarish pieces, his Shadow-Beast" (39). These are courageous and inspiring words to introduce the show, and they build Carmen up to be a larger-than-life figure with insurmountable power. The truth, however, is that at every step of the way, she is used. Early in the show, Aldemar manipulates her to travel to the future. His ultimate goal is to become history's most powerful wizard, and he needs Carmen's powers to do so. He tasks Carmen with bringing a stone to one of his acolytes in the future, in exchange for a spell that will enable her to travel back in time to the exact moment Cristóbal was shot and hopefully turn his fate around. The move to start the show having the main character already be dependent on men, even though she's the one who literally and figuratively *has* the power, is not rare or unique in Latinx culture. "In my culture, selfishness is condemned, especially in women; humility and selflessness, the absence of selfishness, is considered a virtue" (Anzaldúa 40). Even when faced with freedom and liberty . . . with *life*, Carmen's sense of both duty and love comes before her own welfare.

The narrative choices in the show so far set a dangerous precedent for its possible future directions. In her keynote address "The Evolution of Multiculturalism," Lillian Comas-Díaz contends that "people of color's oppression is a form of colonization because as highly visible others, people of color bear the mark of historical subjugation. That is, we have been conquered enemies, slaves, political possessions, servants, et cetera."

Both Black and Latinx people bear the physical mark of being the Other. This Otherness extends to their mediated representations. In *Reel Racism*, Vincent F. Rocchio argues that "the contemporary status of race in mainstream American culture is intimately bound to the process of representation within and through the mass media" (4). What happens, then, when the few Afro-Latinx representations we do get blur or completely ignore the very real implications of slavery in Latin America? This is a major question that we *must* ask in the age of digital media and digital access. Technological advances make stories from people of color accessible now more than ever before, from independent Web series like *Brujos* to *Siempre bruja*. Possibilities are endless. Quite often, "characters of color are limited to the townships of occasional historical books that concern themselves with the legacies of civil rights and slavery but are never given a pass card to traverse the lands of adventure, curiosity, imagination or personal growth" (Myers). *Siempre bruja* excels in its *intention* to break with "traditional" representations of people of color, which focus on the traumatic and historical violence that is often tied to them. However, this intention ultimately does not bear fruit. All possibilities that Carmen could have represented for people of color and representation are lost in the construction of her characterization as a leading character.

Conclusion

In yet another controversial move in 2018, Kanye West doubled down on his remarks about slavery being a choice, saying that if he had been alive during slavery, he would have been more like Harriet Tubman or Nat Turner, both of whom historically rebelled against slavery. In a now-deleted tweet, West misattributed a quotation to Harriet Tubman that reads, "I freed a thousand slaves. I could have freed a thousand more if only they knew they were slaves" (West). What's concerning about this move is that "he corrupted African-Americans' painful legacy in America" (Blades) in order to support Donald Trump. West's rhetorical move is outright dangerous, as "the brutality suffered by these enslaved men and women wasn't only the physical cruelty that ravaged their bodies, but also the mental and emotional trauma that they passed down generationally" (Blades). Likewise, *Siempre bruja* dangerously provides a rose-colored lens about slavery and servitude. In a scene where Cristóbal is trying to convince his parents to allow him to marry Carmen, his father objects to the union because she's a slave, Black, and a witch. Cristóbal replies that those are the three reasons he loves her. Comas-Díaz reminds us that "traumatic oppression is concentrated and inhumane, robbing people of their voices, agency, and identity." Multiple times during the first and second season of the show, Carmen expresses to Cristóbal that they should live their lives in the future. Cristóbal understands Carmen's desire to live a life where she has choices and freedom, but he's hesitant to go. He is never comfortable with the future, or in a reality where Carmen could potentially have the same (or more) power than he does—a future where he doesn't benefit from slavery. In the second season of the show, Cristóbal ultimately makes the decision to return to the past and help free slaves. Carmen's decision to remain in the future is the only time in the show where she acts out of selfishness. However, in the second season Carmen is not necessarily driving the plot forward.

The narrative choices in *Siempre bruja* inspire certain questions about expectations when it comes to representation. Throughout this piece, I have heavily criticized the way that Carmen's character is constructed. Her character blurs or outright smudges history. Is Carmen being used as a scapegoat to tell stories of white people? Let's consider the show's second season, which premiered in early 2020. Although there's a storyline dedicated to Carmen traveling back in time and directing her enslaved friends to San Basilio de Palenque, the first "free town" in the Americas, this is just one of many storylines in the show, and it ultimately doesn't shine through. In fact, Carmen and her story almost take a step back, and the show focuses slightly more on the other characters. This is highlighted by the fact that a Netflix search of the show will show one of the other (white) characters of the show, Alicia, in the show's thumbnail, instead of Carmen herself. Anzaldúa contends that

> alienated from her mother culture, "alien" in the dominant culture, the woman of color does not feel safe within the inner life of her Self. Petrified, she can't respond, her face caught between *los intersticios*, the spaces between the different worlds she inhabits. (Anzaldúa 42)

Carmen is a character relegated to the *intersticios* of her own show. She is almost used as a plot device to tell other people's stories. In the first season, we closely followed Carmen's adventures adjusting to a new world. In the second season, Carmen's story is one of many, and quite often more interesting, stories. In his introduction to *The Routledge Companion to Latina/o Popular Culture*, Frederick Aldama contends that Latinx pop culture creators demonstrate different degrees of willfulness in how they construct their stories: "Put simply, some are driven by corporate profits and others by the desire to innovate, and make new our perception, thought, and feeling about Latina/os in the US" (4). Is it possible that Netflix's decision to fund/acquire *Siempre bruja* was done out of corporate greed, since "the Latina/o demographic represents a one-trillion dollar buying potential" (Aldama 4)? Is Netflix really invested in advocating for the stories of the global community?

What originally made Carmen such an interesting character was that even though she represents a subjugated character, she had the potential to rewrite history. *Siempre bruja* is similar to Octavia Butler's *Kindred*, where the protagonist is a Black woman who travels back in time to slavery times and must come to terms with the fact that she is the product of a slave owner raping her ancestor. Not only that, but she often finds herself in situations where she must save her abusive ancestor. *Siempre bruja*, on the other hand, had the potential of possibility. It offered a historically Othered character the literal power and, more importantly, the *choice* to thrive even in the direst of situations. However, the show is reluctant to highlight these possibilities, opting to focus on a naive Carmen trying to survive in a future world where she has options in order to carry out a mission and return to a life of servitude. Of course, Carmen ultimately decides to stay in the future, with a group of friends who are willing to give up their dreams to save her. However, as with every other representation of people of color on both big and small screens, we must once again ask: Is this *enough*? 'Cause . . . that sounds like a choice.

Works Cited

Aldama, Frederick Luis. *The Routledge Companion to Latina/o Popular Culture*. Routledge, 2016.

Anzaldúa, Gloria. *Borderlands/La Frontera: The New Mestiza*. Aunt Lute Books, 1999.

Blades, Lincoln Anthony. "The Myth of the 'Happy Slave,' Explained." *Teen Vogue*, 2 June 2018, www .teenvogue.com/story/the-myth-of-the-happy-slave-explained.

Bogle, Donald. *Toms, Coons, Mulattoes, Mammies, and Bucks: An Interpretive History of Blacks in American Films*. Continuum, 1989.

Burton, Tara Isabella. "The Insidious Cultural History of Kanye West's Slavery Comments." *Vox*, 2 May 2018, www.vox.com/2018/5/2/17311148/kanye-west-slavery-choice-harriet-tubman-quote -comments-trump.

Collins, Patricia Hill. *Black Feminist Thought: Knowledge, Consciousness, and the Politics of Empowerment*. Routledge, 2009.

Comas-Díaz, Lillian. "The Evolution of Multiculturalism: Past, Present, and Future." Microtraining Associates, 2009, video.alexanderstreet.com/watch/the-evolution-of-multiculturalism-past -present-future.

DuBois, W. E. B. *The Souls of Black Folk*. 1903. Routledge, 2015.

Flores, Juan. "Triple Consciousness? Afro-Latinos on the Color Line." *Wadabagei: A Journal of the Caribbean and Its Diaspora*, vol. 8, no. 1, 2005, pp. 80–85.

Glenn, Cerise L., and Landra J. Cunningham. "The Power of Black Magic." *Journal of Black Studies*, vol. 40, no. 2, 2007, pp. 135–52.

Hayward, Susan. "Black Cinema/Blaxploitation Movies." *Key Concepts in Cinema Studies*, Routledge, 1996, pp. 34–49.

Hordge-Freeman, Elizabeth, and Edlin Veras. "Out of the Shadows, into the Dark: Ethnoracial Dissonance and Identity Formation Among Afro-Latinxs." *Sociology of Race and Ethnicity*, vol. 6, no. 2, 2019, pp. 146–60.

"Kanye West Stirs Up TMZ Newsroom Over Trump, Slavery, Free Thought." *TMZ*, 14 May 2019, www.tmz.com/2018/05/01/kanye-west-tmz-live-slavery-trump/.

Lawrence, Novotny, and Gerald R. Butters Jr. "Introduction: Blaxploitation Cinema." *Journal of Popular Culture*, vol. 52, no. 4, 2019, pp. 745–51.

"MPAA Welcomes Netflix as New Member." *Motion Picture Association*, 22 Jan. 2019, www.motion pictures.org/press/mpaa-welcomes-netflix-as-new-member/.

Myers, Christopher. "The Apartheid of Children's Literature." *New York Times*, 15 Mar. 2014, www.ny times.com/2014/03/16/opinion/sunday/the-apartheid-of-childrens-literature.html?_r=2.

Rocchio, Vincent F. *Reel Racism: Confronting Hollywood's Construction of Afro-American Culture.* Westview Press, 2000.

Romo, Rebecca. "Between Black and Brown: Blaxican (Black-Mexican) Multiracial Identity in California." *Journal of Black Studies*, vol. 42, no. 3, 2011, pp. 402–26.

Thomas, Ebony Elizabeth. *The Dark Fantastic: Race and the Imagination from Harry Potter to the Hunger Games.* New York UP, 2019.

Welang, Nahum. "Triple Consciousness: The Reimagination of Black Female Identities in Contemporary American Culture." *Open Cultural Studies*, vol. 2, no. 1, 2018, pp. 296–306.

West, Kanye. "I Freed a Thousand Slaves I Could Have Freed a Thousand More If Only They Knew They Were Slaves.—Harriet Tubman." *Twitter*, 1 May 2018, 8:38 p.m.

PETER MURRIETA TALKS

A Life of Shaping Twenty-First-Century Latinx TVLandia

Peter Murrieta is one of the most significant of Latinx creators, writers, and producers actively shaping a Brown-ocular twenty-first-century TVLandia. His scroll-long resume includes countless accolades, accomplishments, and awards, including multiple Emmys for *Wizards of Waverly Place* and an Imagen Award for *Mr. Iglesias.* He is also the creator of the comic book *Rafael Garcia: Henchman.* He is a Latinx pop cultural creative without measure. Peter shares his remarkable journey here.

FREDERICK LUIS ALDAMA: Let's start at the very, very beginning. The Murrieta pre-history. Those stories that inform you and your story.

PETER MURRIETA: My great great great great great, five greats, grandfather was named Joaquín Murrieta. He was a gold miner from Sonora. He moved north to California during the Gold Rush; he suffered greatly, as a lot of *mejicanos* did in California. His claim was taken away from him. His cousin was killed. His wife was raped and killed. His reaction: to take up arms. He was not a gunman, not a bandido, but he took up arms. He gathered together a small band and then an army, marauding through gold country. Some say he was a freedom fighter, others that he was a vengeance seeker. No matter! He became a legend, a very, very important legend to Mexican Americans, and especially Californio Mexican Americans.

FLA: He was the inspiration for Zorro. And then, of course, Zorro was the inspiration for Batman. That's some serious Murrieta superhero legacy.

PM: I remember when I was a little kid seeing some of the Clint Eastwood Westerns, featuring a wrongly accused person who sought vengeance. My dad and my mama told me that this was the Joaquín story. Recently, I was watching the film *Blood In Blood Out.* There's a moment when they hold up their shot glasses and do toasts to Joaquín Murrieta. It's a name that means a lot to my family—my dad and my son are both named for Joaquín Murrieta. It's a name that resonates in powerful ways among the Latino community.

FLA: Like me, you're mixed with Irish and Mexican ancestry.

PM: My mom is Irish American. She's from Long Island. She moved to Tucson because her father was a fireman. He developed asthma on the job. Way back in the forties, the cure for asthma was to move to a dry climate like Colorado or Arizona. The story goes, he was in mass and stood up and asked if anyone was going to Colorado or Arizona. Somebody said that their kid was going to college in Arizona, so he got a ride there.

There's a joke in our family that we continue immigrating to this country, no matter what. The original Joaquín *and* my dad moved to the U.S. He came here in the fifties. He met my mom in high school. It's a very Riverdale, Archie and Betty story. My dad spoke English as a second language. My mom asked him to the Sadie Hawkins dance. Where the girls ask the boys to dance. Typically, in the fifties, of course, only the men asked women out. What a time that was! I guess she did it as a joke, a sarcastic joke. He didn't pick up on the joke, got her phone number, and called her house to ask what time to pick her up. I guess she felt bad, and so she went with him. And that was that.

FLA: You grew up in Tucson.

PM: I was born and grew up there. My younger sister was born in California. We moved around a little bit, but I ended up doing high school in Tucson, and I really consider that, because it was where I was born and where I did a lot of growing up, to be my home.

FLA: Can you share a little of your journey as a young adult?

PM: We didn't have a lot of money, so I went to the local college a couple of miles down the road. This was the University of Arizona. I went there with the intention of studying creative writing with the idea that I'd become a high school English teacher and a baseball coach. The big goal: coaching high school ball and teaching some Mark Twain and Charles Dickens. While I was there, I got a paper back that I'd written on existentialism from Professor Donna Swaim in a Humanities class. She wrote: "See me in my office." There was no grade. I remember the chill that went through my heart. I went to her office. She told me how this was the funniest thing she'd ever read. After asking about my grade, she told me to forget about the grade and asked me what I wanted to do. We had this talk that I don't think anybody'd ever had with me before.

From our conversation, I decided to join this comedy group on campus, Comedy Corner. I think they're still going. They do an hour live show every week from campus with improvisation and sketches. I wrote the sketches. I eventually realized I wanted to do something like that for a living. Second City from Chicago came out, toured, and did a show. That's when it hit me. I thought, that's where I need to go. Even though I didn't have my degree in hand and I didn't know what Chicago was like (maybe I'd seen like *Hill Street Blues*), I started making plans almost immediately on leaving.

FLA: How did you move from Second City to writing and producing for TV?

PM: So I go to Chicago because I want to do sketch comedy. I want to be a comedy writer. I auditioned, and I got in. I was in the national touring company acting on stage in front of an audience and coincidentally we had a show at Notre Dame and my mom and dad had traveled to Indiana for his job. They decided to come to a show. As the story goes, they were driving to the venue, and they got nervous. They were afraid nobody would show up. As they pulled around into the parking lot, they saw a local Indiana TV truck with a satellite up, and they saw a crowd waiting to go in. At that moment, they thought that maybe this could work out for me. They didn't have a lot of hope until that moment.

While I was with Second City—theater that's so steeped in *Saturday Night Live* and situation comedies on television—I started to think that maybe I, too, could write for TV. So, I just decided to give it a go.

FLA: How did you get from the I-want-to-do-this moment to writing and producing your first show, *Greetings from Tucson*, in 2002?

PM: I got that bug, and I had a couple of great supporters. David Miner was a college intern, who was at Second City, and he and I became friends. He had announced that he was going to become an agent and that he was going to represent me. Now, mind you, at the time he was still a college intern who was just doing things like answering phones. And I was somebody who was in a van, touring around the Midwest doing shows for two or three hundred people.

With David's guidance, I moved out to L.A. and got started. At first I was doing set construction and doing jobs in show business based on my own set of skills that I had from growing up. But I was writing scripts. I had already learned that process and was getting ready for an opportunity. I got an opportunity with ABC around '95–'96. A student who was taking an improv class from me told me about a writing fellowship for diverse writers. She worked at Disney—that owns ABC. Even though the deadline had passed the day before, because I had a Seinfeld sample ready, she got it in for me. A couple of weeks later, I got a call to come interview. In the waiting room at ABC to interview, this guy with cutoff shorts and wearing flip-flops introduced himself to me as the creator of *Married with Children*. I overheard him say: "Don't let them tell you how to dress, and don't let them tell you that they're right, 'cause they never are." And then he left, like a ghost. I never saw him again.

That fellowship got me started. I got a few TV credits and worked my way up through the ranks. I went on an interview for another show, and in that interview for that other show I was telling stories of growing up with my dad and uncle. It wasn't a formal pitch, but afterwards my agent said they wanted to buy the show I pitched. I said I hadn't pitched a show and that I'd just shared stories about growing up with my dad. He told me to get a formal pitch together based on these stories. David Miner had been managing me, but he had never done this yet either. We figured it out together, and we pitched the show and they bought it.

The rub: I couldn't tell my dad about the show; it was a lot about him and me, and there was a lot about our very, very difficult relationship. I made this promise to myself: I'll tell him about it if they shoot the pilot. So I turn in the script, and they called and they said, "We're gonna shoot the pilot." I still wasn't sure if I really want to tell him about this, so I told myself I'd tell him after they shoot the pilot *and* they pick up the show to series. They did. I remember sending him the script. In it my uncle is the hero, my dad is the villain, and I'm the fourteen-year-old protagonist. He read it and called me, and in his style, he asked if I'd shown it to my uncle. I said no. He then said, "He doesn't come off so good in this. I'm pretty great."

FLA: *Greetings from Tucson* was an extraordinary show for Latinx representation. You carved all sorts of new paths here. Yet, it came and went. I was only able to sleuth out a few episodes on YouTube.

PM: There're some business and creative reasons why it's not out there to be consumed or be seen today. It's so weird.

I'll talk about the business reasons first. It was a production from a company called Big Ticket Television, which was a subsidiary of Paramount. This was headed up by a guy named Larry Little, who used to be president of Warner Brothers Television many years ago. His big show was *Judge Judy*; he had other scripted shows, but *Judge Judy* was the show that made him lots of money. The WB was the network that bought the show.

On the creative side, I can say that we did some especially cool things in this show that ended up being some of the reasons why you can't view it. There was an episode at Christmas (one of my favorites) that involved a lot of pathos about the family. I really wanted to play John Lennon's "Beautiful Boy" over the last sequence. So, I wrote a letter to Yoko Ono and the publishing company, asking her for the rights. She made us send script pages. I sent these along with explanation about the show and how it would work. She gave us the rights. So we had that song in the show. We also had a pretty important song to me, Rolling Stones' "Salt of the Earth," represented by ABKCO—Al Klein's label, and he and the Stones did not get along. I worked out a rights deal where on the premiere night we could use that song. And then I worked out a subsidiary deal with Keith Richards' company, so that we dropped in a Keith Richards solo song in subsequent reruns. We also hired Los Lobos to do all the music; in two episodes of the shows, they also played a bunch of guys that have a garage band living down the road.

I think the music rights issues probably are part of why episodes aren't available today. I also think in the consolidation of all the studios—it's a Paramount-owned thing, but it aired on WB—it just feels like nobody's got the idea to put it back on.

I had Lupe Ontiveros playing the role of my grandma. I had Teri Garr and Martin Mull playing my Irish grandparents. I had Carmen Electra on it, and Vince Neil in a weird, crazy WB crossover thing. I had my pal Jeff Garlin. I met Jacob Vargas, who I've worked with twice since—and will always work with. He's so amazing. Aimee Garcia got her start in *Greetings from Tucson*. It was a thrilling time. We got 22 episodes—a full season. It was a big deal to get a full season.

FLA: You created the first Latinx show that didn't have us as an afterthought or as just a bit of spice. You breathed complexity into multiple generations of Latinos and Latinas. You were way ahead of the game.

PM: I remember getting a call from someone in WB casting. She told me how she was calling all the shows to remind them to be diverse when they cast. I told her how I had six series regulars that are Latin, and one white lady. So I asked her if I should put more white people in the show. She laughed.

FLA: The *George Lopez* show also appeared during this period. You guys launched us into a new era of Latinx TV.

PM: This was a really special time. We came on right at the same time as *George Lopez*. That year, I remember getting a Producer of the Year award at the ALMA Awards. I remember that award ceremony well. It was the day that George Lopez had just got his back-nine order of the first season. I remember some talk that there would be competition between the shows. To me it wasn't a competition; they were on ABC and we were on little WB. When I got up to give my thank you speech at the ALMA Awards, the first thing I did was give a special acknowledgment to George. He was at the table, and people said he got a little tense, thinking that I would go after him or something. I remember saying, "George got his back nine. And when one of us wins, we all win. That's what we've got to keep doing."

This was a special time for me.

FLA: You have a gift for using the sitcom storytelling form to take viewers places that are thoughtful, culturally rich and nuanced, and complex. *Greetings* included the first interracial couple since *The Jeffersons* (1975–85) and a smart, independent young Latina.

PM: Just like in my family, right? She had to go to school. She got to go off to college. But she had to move in with her grandmother because [*laughing*] nobody wanted her anymore.

FLA: You went on to be executive producer for and write the hugely successful TV show *Wizards of Waverly Place*. But of course, there's a lot more to this story than just jumping from success to success. As a writer and creator of TV shows that put front and center Latinx lives, you've chosen a very difficult path. Are there days when you say to yourself, I can't do this anymore?

PM: Every day, man. Every day. Can I get a show? Can I get a job this year? Can I get a pilot sold this month? Can I get a pilot shot next year? I think it's the long, lonely race of the marathoner. You can't think, I have to run twenty-six miles. You have to think about getting to the next street corner, then the next lamppost.

Wizards always has a special place in my heart. That was my show. I've had incredible experiences working for other shows. I got to work on a show called *Lopez* that was really special. It wasn't my show. I was the only Latin writer in the room. Which is a thing that continues to this day. But George was happy that I was there. I did the first season, and then I left that to go do *One Day at a Time*. It wasn't my show, but I was able to be a part of the first season. It was really incredible to be in a room with more Latin people than on the previous show. It was nice to not have to be the only expert. I feel really proud of the work that I did there. I wrote an episode that was about a Mexican American friend who was staying the night over and over again at the house, until people realized he didn't have anywhere to go. And we found out that her parents had disappeared, and that they were undocumented. Then I cowrote an episode with my friends Dan and Benji that focused on the return of the father. It was great to be a part of that.

FLA: You worked on *Cristela* (2014–15). How is it that such a great show got canceled?

PM: New shows are hard, and first seasons are hard. You need support from the studio, and from the network. You need them invested in your success. Now, you would say every network is invested in the success of all their shows. But in the network model of releasing seven new shows every fall, some of those children are better cared for than others. Hypothetically, if you have a show with Kevin Bacon starring in it, and you have a show with Cristela Alonzo, there's one show that people are going to bet on internally more.

 Cristela was always the maverick underdog show. Before I was involved, because the network passed on the script, the studio shot the pilot on their own for a limited amount of money. They gave it back to the network, and the network liked it. But already you know that the show's going get bus ads, not billboards—promos, and not commercials.

FLA: In a magical way, everything came together for you with *Wizards* (2007–12).

PM: *Wizards* was something that I backed into. I had worked on a show in New York and had returned home after the first season. But I came back too late to join another show. So I went and met at Disney Channel. They had this pilot script that needed a rewrite and they needed a showrunner. They were already fans of the realness of the characters and the sibling rivalry in *Greetings from Tucson*. So I brought in shades of *Greetings from Tucson*, including the interracial blended family.

 I remembered a videotape someone gave me of a young Selena Gomez in a single camera pilot that didn't go. I asked if I could bring her in for *Wizards*. They had already promised her to another show. I kind of bullied/convinced them to let me cast her in *Wizards*. With their model of only creating one series out of two pilots, I asked for her to lead *Wizards* so they could have the choice to pick up the series they liked best, and not the series with the actor they liked more. They agreed. So we shot two pilots. I shot mine, and Danny Kallis shot his pilot for *Arwin!* Disney dropped *Arwin!* and picked up *Wizards*.

The journey with *Wizards* was incredible. Watching those kids grow up was incredible. We also had Jeff Garlin, Fred Willard (my son Joaquin's godfather), and David DeLuise; David and I played softball together and I'd worked with David before on *Jesse* (1998–2000) with Christina Applegate. With *Wizards*, we made something really special. We won a couple of Emmys. We made a great movie—that's still, I believe, the second highest rated movie Disney Channel's ever done.

FLA: To pay bills and put food on the table, you have to take work. It seems, however, that you are very careful about the choices you make and where you finally end up putting your creative energies.

PM: I was a low-level writer on a show called *Three Sisters* (2001–2). I learned a lot about how to run a show from my bosses, DeAnn Heline and Eileen Heisler, who later went on to create *The Middle* (2009–18). I love them so much, I forgive them for never hiring me on *The Middle*. But you're right about the careful choices.

With *Aim High* (2011–13), Heath Corson (a pal of mine from Chicago) had written a series and was stalled out. He couldn't get a green light. I was friendly with one of the executives at the studio, and they asked me if I would do a production rewrite to get the green light. It had a YA component, and I was just coming off *Wizards*. I had a little bit of buzz around me for that. So I did that rewrite for them. I stepped away once they got the green light so that when they needed a writer on set, they could bring Heath on as the creator of the show. I do feel a loyalty to writers. When you get hired to rewrite, it never feels good. And so one of the things with that one that I treasure is that I immediately called Heath and asked if he was cool with me doing the rewrite.

Superior Donuts (2017–18) was a blast to work on. Working with Judd Hirsch and Jermaine Fowler was a blessing. The chemistry between the two of them is incredible. To get two seasons out of that at CBS is a huge deal. There was an article about Jermaine Fowler when he was a lead on that show. It said he was the first Black lead of a sitcom at CBS for something like thirty or forty years. Shame on CBS. That said, I'm very happy that we got Diane Guerrero into the second season of the show. We had this polyglot donut shop that had an Arab character, a young Black man, an older Jewish fellow, a woman cop, and an unemployed Boomer. We didn't have a Latina. In season 2, we got Diane Guerrero to come in and fill that void. Incredible!

FLA: You also worked on the show *Level Up* (2012–13).

PM: Working with Latina actor Aimee Carrero who played Angie on that show was amazing. She is so talented. She's also the lead voice role for Princess Elena in *Elena of Avalor* (2016–20) and the lead voice for Adora/She Ra in *She Ra* (2018–20). I can't wait to work with her again.

FLA: You've worked on films like *Holidaze* (2006) and *Dealing with Idiots* (2013).

PM: So the first one was purely a paycheck. Sometimes you have to eat. But it was fun. That was a movie that was brought to me by a producer that I had worked for, and they were trying to do something with Walmart. They were making original movies that were going to be sold at Walmart. Walmart was going to buy airtime on CBS on the nights of their classic Christmas stuff. I got checks the first couple years. It was fun, but it was definitely a grind.

Dealing with Idiots was pure fun. I mean that was Jeff Garlin and I deciding we wanted to write a movie from a 30–40-page outline, with everything else improvised. We cast all of our friends. Jeff shot it and directed it on a shoestring. It's a fun movie that has a short beginning, a very long middle, and almost no ending.

FLA: Peter, when you sit down to write for a movie or for a TV show, is there a difference for you?

PM: Huge difference. TV is like writing a novel. You're going to be with the characters for a long time. In the present, you're writing these character pieces that will allow the characters to move forward incrementally in time. The goal: for lots to happen that will allow them to grow over time. With a movie, you're taking a protagonist through one specific story, where they're going to be changed forever, and then it's over. I've had movie work. I'm happy about it and excited for it. But it's different. It's a different animal.

FLA: You create stories that at once entertain and simultaneously smuggle complexity of emotion and nuance and range of characterization along with hitting on issues that enrich our experience of the story. You entertain and complicate our understanding of where Latinx TVLandia can go.

PM: I would add, I'm more interested in the underdog than I am a successful person. This is the case even in my comic *Rafael Garcia: Henchman*. I like the idea of looking at things from a different slice of class, race, even of geography. Instead of New York, let's set the story in Tucson, Arizona.

I like stories with emotion, and I'm not afraid of it. I don't mean yelling and apology. It means diving into the messy, complicated things that we all go through. There are people we love and we hate, and we still have to see them every day. My stories want to see how this messiness works.

FLA: Can you share a little about the life writing, pitching, and the hustle?

PM: There's a point in the writing process when it clicks. It's this dangerous moment where you are in love with a project. And then the rug gets pulled out, and they tell you it's done. I can't *not* fall in love with a project because that's part of being an artist. You just have to be willing to take that hurt again. For instance, I wrote a pilot called *Henchman* that I had Horatio Sanz from *Saturday Night*

Live attached to. It was born out of my love of comic books—and my disgust with Marvel and DC's movies not including any Latinos anywhere. I was like somebody's got to be mowing those lawns and loading those trucks. Probably Mexicans. Let's write a show about those guys. It fell apart. Nobody wanted to do it. The project went into a drawer. Until I pulled it out to create the comic book *Rafael Garcia: Henchman*, with the publisher Starburns Industries. So, that project came back to life.

The one I created about parenting that had Danny Trejo attached to it was really a tough loss. That one was about pain. It was about what happens if the monster comes back to your life, and they're not a monster anymore. They've changed. But you don't want them to change. It's too easy. You want them to continue to be the monster, the villain that you cast them as when you were younger. It was a show about Danny and his adult daughter, Michelle—not his real-life adult daughter. He doesn't have a daughter named Michelle. It was an amalgamation: the relationship with my father, my relationship with my children, Danny's time in prison and his relationship with his children. It came together in this really special script that ABC decided they didn't want to make.

It gets us back to those ratios. We're 18 percent plus of the U.S. population and only 5.8 percent represented. It's hard, but you got to keep going.

FLA: You entertain, and smuggle into the televisual viewer's imaginary complexity of thought in and around Latinx identities and experiences.

PM: Entertainment can smuggle into households' political-social thought. I'm not saying that you should watch my shows to take your medicine. I know those shows. They are not my favorite shows. But we should have the space to make those shows where, for instance, Mr. Iglesias has a monologue that deals with the concept "Latinx" that's a page and a half, and with a whole bunch of jokes in it. Let us play—and let us grieve inside your world. And we will make it better, I promise.

FLA: The Televisual Industrial Complex and its gatekeeping. The Emmys 2020 is a case in point.

PM: They don't want complexity. They're very interested still in our immigrant stories. In our trauma. They're not interested in who we are.

My first reaction is, screw the Emmys. It's how I feel about network TV right now. If you don't want us, then we're going stop making you important to us. We're just going to go over here where they'll let us do these things: *Mr. Iglesias* on Netflix, *One Day at a Time* on Pop, and *Vida* on Starz.

FLA: Industry awards do seem to matter, especially for creators, actors, showrunners, producers otherwise locked out or swept to the side by the Televisual Industrial Complex.

PM: They do matter. They give notoriety and they give a platform to a broader audience. In a world where a lot of networks don't know how to market to us, this is an easy 101 thing. You won an Emmy. Here's a promo for your show. I think that that's important. I think us celebrating ourselves with things like the ALMAs is important. I think that when we're asked to be on a panel, it's important.

FLA: How many twenty-something white dude shows do we need?

PM: I'm good with those, I've got those. I want to see something different. And that different doesn't have to be me. That different can be anybody. I'm excited when I see *Atlanta*. I'm excited when I see *Insecure*. I'm excited when I see *Crazy Rich Asians*. I want us to have our versions of all three of those shows. I don't think we have them.

FLA: We need more Afro-Latinx representation in our televisual storyworlds—and not just for non-Latinx televisual viewers. Many of our families have internalized legacies of colonial colorism, where the white phenotype is king. #BlackLivesMatter is a call to action, too, to recognize our own internalized racism within our own *familias*. The more representation of Afro-Latinxs, the better for all of us.

PM: #BlackLivesMatter—absolutely. This is the group that needs support right now. This is the group that is in danger, literally, physically in danger.

When it comes to television, if I'm being honest and open, I'm conflicted. I read recently that Netflix bought a library of Black comedies: *Living Single, Girlfriends* . . . They bought a library of Black sitcoms to put on Netflix as part of their move to support #BlackLivesMatter. This makes me go inside my heart and wonder where the Latinx sitcom library is. There's a library waiting for Netflix, if they want it.

FLA: It's the divide and conquer approach to Latinx and Black demographics and televisual representation. It's a question of all of us still not being seen. But you are changing this, as writer and producer behind the camera—and as a professor at ASU. You teach new generations of writer-screenwriters, developers of series, producers of series. You are at the frontline, providing the tools and the knowledge to new generations of BIPOC TV writers, of storytellers in general.

PM: It is putting my money where my mouth is. If you hear it said that there aren't enough Latinx writers—as did the showrunner for *Hawaii Five-0*, may his name never be mentioned ever again—well, this is not true. I'm helping open doors for new generations of Latinx writers, producers, and showrunners. I'm very pleased and honored to do this.

FLA: Knowledge and use of this knowledge. Learning and practice. Pen and sword.

PM: I'm excited tonight. It's the night before school starts for me. I'm preparing my lectures for tomorrow. It's my second year at ASU, and it feels great. It's funny, some students wonder why I'm teaching—in addition to all the work I do in L.A. I'm here because someone like me needs to be here.

FLA: Speaking of vital new spaces, where is the vitality in TV today?

PM: It is in the nooks and crannies. I need to go backward ten years to go forwards: HBO didn't want *Mad Men* (2007–15). It had one of the writers from *The Sopranos*. They still turned it down. Matthew Weiner had to go to AMC, which was doing movie reruns, and get them to take a chance on it. Or, think about Kevin Costner's *Yellowstone* (2018–). TNT and TBS didn't want it. Paramount Network picked it up. It's the biggest show on cable.

The vitality is in the nooks and crannies. It's finding what you love in a nook and a cranny and then celebrating it. There's so much out there now, that you can do that. One of my favorite shows that I'm watching now with my son is *Better Call Saul* (2015–). That's like a victory lap show. That's a victory lap of someone who created something that, again, was in a nook and a cranny when it first came out: *Breaking Bad.* No one expected *Stranger Things* to be big. Netflix didn't. They for sure didn't. Netflix thought for sure that Ryan Murphy's *Hollywood* miniseries was going to be huge. And it wasn't.

I'm always suspicious of the biggest billboard and the biggest promo campaign for a new show because that's usually a sign that it's got a lot of splash but not a lot of treasure inside.

FLA: So do you think that the streaming platforms have allowed for these nooks and crannies to find their way to audiences?

PM: That is tricky. There's a lot of people who have shows on Netflix that no one's ever heard of. It requires engagement, if you're a consumer. You need to really engage with your community, with your friends—and in an old-school, word-of-mouth way. Nobody thought *Stranger Things* was going to be big. The love that those creators had for Spielberg and eighties was palpable. You could feel it. I hope the fans of *Mr. Iglesias* can feel our love for Gabe and our love for the mission of a guy saving students. You've just got to find the good shows by making friends and talking about what you like to watch. Like you and I do.

FLA: Thank you, Peter.

PM: Thank you so much. This has been a pleasure, and not just a trip down memory lane. It's been a great way for me to focus and be verbal about what I believe.

CONTRIBUTORS

FREDERICK LUIS ALDAMA, also known as Professor Latinx, is the Jacob and Frances Sanger Mossiker Chair in the Humanities at the University of Texas, Austin, as well as the award-winning author of over forty-five books, including an Eisner Award for *Latinx Superheroes in Mainstream Comics*. He is editor and coeditor of nine academic press book series, including editor of Latinographix, which publishes Latinx comics. He is creator of the first documentary on the history of Latinx superheroes and founder and director of UT's Latinx Pop Lab. He recently published the Spanish translation of his kids' book *The Adventures of Chupacabra Charlie* and debuted his animation film that follows the continued adventures of Chupacabra Charlie.

STACEY ALEX is assistant professor of Spanish at Morningside College, Sioux City, Iowa. She has published on undocumented Latinx immigrant narratives, Latinx folklore, and Latinx pop culture. She created an online oral history project, *Latinx Stories of Siouxland*, and she is the coauthor of *Mi idioma, mi comunidad: Español para bilingües*, an open-access textbook for heritage language learners of Spanish that centers on students' experiences with language, identity, and belonging in the Midwest.

MELISSA CASTILLO PLANAS is associate professor of English at Lehman College in the Bronx, New York, specializing in Latinx literature and culture. She is the author of the poetry collection *Coatlicue Eats the Apple*, editor of the anthology *¡Manteca! An Anthology of Afro-Latin@ Poets*, coeditor of *La Verdad: An International Dialogue on Hip Hop Latinidades*, and coauthor of the novel *Pure Bronx*. Her most recent book project, with Rutgers University Press's new Global Race and Media series, *A Mexican State of Mind: New York City and the New Borderlands of Culture*, examines the creative worlds and cultural productions of Mexican migrants in New York City.

PEYTON DEL TORO is a Chicana lesbian PhD student in the Department of English at the Ohio State University. Her scholarship focuses on Latinx lesbian literature and representation in pop culture using postcolonial and feminist theory.

MAURICIO ESPINOZA is assistant professor in the Department of Romance and Arabic Languages and Literatures at the University of Cincinnati, where he is also affiliate faculty with the Niehoff Center for Film and Media Studies. His scholarship focuses on Latinx popular culture, migration, and Central American literary and cultural studies. He's also a translator and poet.

LAURA FERNÁNDEZ is currently a visiting assistant professor in the Department of Hispanic Studies at Bates College. She completed her PhD in Latin American cultural and literary studies with a graduate interdisciplinary specialization in Latinx studies at the Ohio State University. She is currently working on a book project based on her dissertation, "Giving the Midwestern White Gaze a Latinx Spin: Mediated Latinx Lives in the American Heartland." She is a specialist in Latinx popular culture, with research interests in Latinx and Latin American twentieth- and twenty-first-century literature, rural Latinx narratives, and the intersections of race, ethnicity, and gender of Latinx representations in U.S. film and television.

CAMILLA FOJAS is Foundation Professor and director of the School of Social Transformation at Arizona State University. She is the author of numerous books, including *Border Optics: Surveillance Cultures on the US-Mexico Frontier*. She is coeditor of numerous volumes, including *Mixed Race Hollywood* with Mary Beltrán and *Transnational Crossroads: Remapping the Americas and the Pacific* with Rudy Guevarra.

YADIRA GAMEZ is a PhD student at Texas A&M. Yadira specializes in post-WWII multiethnic American literature and culture. She has published in the *Houston Chronicle* and is currently working on publishing a book of her Latinx creative fiction.

CARLOS GABRIEL KELLY GONZÁLEZ is a PhD candidate in the Department of English at the Ohio State University. He specializes in Latinx studies and video game studies and has published in the areas of Latinx cultural studies and video game studies.

LAWRENCE LA FOUNTAIN-STOKES is professor of American culture, Romance languages and literatures, and women's and gender studies at the University of Michigan, Ann Arbor. He was born and raised in San Juan, Puerto Rico, and received his BA from Harvard and his MA and PhD from Columbia. He is author of *Queer Ricans: Cultures and Sexualities in the Diaspora*. His book *Translocas: The Politics of Puerto Rican Drag and Trans Performance* is part of the Triangulations: Lesbian/Gay/Queer Theater/Drama/Performance series. Larry has performed in drag as Lola von Miramar since 2010, and has appeared in several episodes of the YouTube series *Cooking with Drag Queens*.

J. V. MIRANDA is assistant professor of English and media studies at Bentley University. His research and teaching focuses on the intersections of Latinx and Indigenous literature, narratives of (im)migration, and border studies. He is currently working on a cross-disciplinary study of border-crossing narratives tentatively titled "Border Transits: Desert, Bridges, and Networks."

JOSÉ A. MUÑOZ is associate professor of sociology at California State University, San Bernardino. He has published articles in *Social Movement Studies*, *Hispanic Journal of Behavioral Sciences*, *Sociology Compass*, *Migration and Development*, *Migration Letters*, *Journal of Public Child Welfare*, *Humanity & Society*, and the *Journal of Hispanic Higher Education*. He teaches courses in qualitative methods, theory, Latino health, Chicano social stratification, migration, and social movements. Muñoz's current research project seeks to understand the experiences of Latinos in academia, examining how first-generation and working-class statuses, mentorship in graduate school, and family support impact Latinos' presence in the professoriate. The project expands on Muñoz's research as part of the American Sociological Association's Task Force on First-Generation and Working-Class Persons in Sociology.

PETER MURRIETA is a TV producer, writer, and comic book creator, and has earned an Imagen Award and multiple Emmys. He is best known for his *Wizards of Waverly Place*, *Wizards of Waverly Place: The Movie*, and work on *Lopez*, *One Day at a Time*, and *Mr. Iglesias*.

WILLIAM "MEMO" NERICCIO is the director of a West Coast-based cultural studies program called MALAS, the Master of Arts in Liberal Arts and Sciences, at San Diego State University. Nericcio is a film studies and cultural critic best known for *Tex[t]-Mex: Seductive Hallucinations of the "Mexican" in America*. His latest book, coauthored with Frederick Luis Aldama, is *#BrownTV: Latinas and Latinos on the Screen*. He is also the director of SDSU Press and publisher of Amatl Comix.

DANIELLE ALEXIS OROZCO received her PhD from the Ohio State University. She researches and publishes on U.S. Latinx media and literature. She uses an intersectional and decolonial feminist framework and queer BIPOC methodologies to study pleasure activism and disability justice. She has published in *Latinx Ciné in the Twenty-First Century*, *American Book Review*, *Studies in 20th & 21st Century Literature*, *Image [&] Narrative*, and *¿Qué Pasa? Ohio State*.

HÉCTOR J. PÉREZ is associate professor of audiovisual narrative at the Universitat Politècnica de València (Escola Politècnica Superior de Gandia). He studies the role of corporeal narration in film, TV series, and opera. He also brings a cognitive aesthetics lens to his analysis of television series. His most recent book is *Cine y mitología: De las religiones a los argumentos universales*. He is editor of *SERIES—International Journal of TV Serial Narratives*.

LYDIA PEREZ-PALENCIA is an independent scholar. She graduated cum laude with a BA in sociology from California State University, San Bernardino. Lydia plans on earning an MA degree in applied behavior analysis and working with autistic children.

NICOLE PIZARRO is a PhD student in the English Department at the Ohio State University, where she also served as associate director of the Digital Media and Composition Institute. She researches and publishes in the areas of film and adaptation studies and digital media studies. She is recipient of the Eric Walborn Award for Excellence in Digital Media and English Instruction. She publishes on film and comics in journals such as *The Middle Spaces, Latinx Spaces,* and *New Approaches to Contemporary Adaptation.*

RYAN RASHOTTE is assistant professor of English at Lakeland University Japan, and the author of numerous articles as well as the book *Narco Cinema: Sex, Drugs, and Banda Music in Mexico's B-Filmography.*

ANAHI REYNOSO-FRANCO is an independent scholar. She graduated with a BA in sociology from California State University, San Bernardino.

CRISTINA RIVERA is a PhD candidate at the Ohio State University. She researches and publishes on Latinx representation in children and young adult literature and media. She teaches classes on race, culture, and identity in the United States through literature and media for young people. She is a High School Hub Coordinator for OSU's LASER: Latinx Space for Enrichment and Research and works on culturally sustaining pedagogies for the Writing Across the Curriculum program at OSU.

MATHEW SANDOVAL is an Honors Faculty Fellow at Arizona State University's Barrett, The Honors College. His current research concerns large-scale celebrations of the transborder holiday Día de los Muertos (Day of the Dead). He examines the ways this holiday has developed from ancient Mesoamerican ritual to American popular culture. He teaches courses on cultural studies, performance studies, popular culture, and critical race theory. He is also a performer, storyteller, and documentary filmmaker.

DAVID SCHMIDT is an author, podcaster, and multilingual translator who splits his time between Mexico City and San Diego, California. His books include *Three Nights in the Clown Motel, Holy Ghosts: True Tales from a Haunted Christian College, The Tiny Staircase* series, *Más frío que la nieve: Cuentos sobrenaturales de Rusia,* and *Tunguska: Luces en el cielo sobre Siberia.*

KATLIN MARISOL SWEENEY is a PhD student in the Department of English at the Ohio State University. She specializes in U.S. Latinx studies and popular culture studies. Her scholarly work focuses on prison media, DIY culture, comics and zines by women of color, and media portrayals of Central Americans in the United States. She is the central coordinator of SÕL-CON: The Brown, Black, and Indigenous Comix Expo and an executive team leader with the Latinx Space for Enrichment and Research (LASER) at the Ohio State University. She has published in *The Routledge Companion to Gender and Sexuality in Comic Book Studies, Cultural Studies in the Digital Age, American Book Review, and Revista de Estudios Hispánicos.*

SARAI TOVAR is a graduate student at Azusa Pacific University. She graduated with a BA in sociology from California State University, San Bernardino.

IRMA J. ZAMORA FUERTE is a PhD student in the Department of English at the Ohio State University. In her research she uses a queer, feminist, and unDACAmented analytic lens to examine the representation of immigrant stories in the national sociopolitical narrative; she also analyzes how different storytelling formats (testimonios, cuentos, autobiographies, autoethnographies) impact power structures for marginalized communities.

INDEX

criminalization, 78, 155–56, 226–27; and the Deferred Action for Childhood Arrivals (DACA), 21, 211–12, 215, 228, 231, 241–42, 243, 249; and deportability, 39; and the Development, Relief, and Education for Alien Minors Act (DREAM), 215, 227, 228, 243; and the Illegal Immigration Reform and Immigration Responsibility Act (IIRIRA), 216; and Immigration and Customs Enforcement (ICE), 211–12, 214–15, 221; and the Immigration Reform and Control Act (IRCA), 227; and presidential administrations, 214, 226–27; and raids, 211, 214–15, 226–27; and rhetoric, 152, 227–28, 241, 242–43, 249, 253, 275–76; and undocumedia, 21, 215, 216–17, 221–22. *See also individual titles*

incarceration: in popular media, 75–79, 92–93, 93n1; and the prison industrial complex, 75, 76–77, 78–79, 85–86. See also *Orange is the New Black*

Indigenous: characters, 346, erasure, 21–22, 253; forms of knowledge, 135–37; holidays, 160–61, 171n1; production, 354

intersectionality, 138, 186–87, 204, 224–25

Jane the Virgin, 9, 113–14, 118–25, 137–39, 229, 243–46, 253; "Chapter 8," 244; "Chapter 10," 229, 245–46; "Chapter 27," 229; "Chapter 30," 229; "Chapter 55,"119–20; "Chapter 56," 120–22; "Chapter 61," 229; "Chapter 62," 244; and immigration, 21–22, 229, 243–46; and mental health, 20, 118–25; reception of, 244

Kant, Immanuel, 58, 59, 61
Karp, David, 106–9
Kohan, Jenji, 81–82

La casa de las flores, 341–42, 354
L.A. Law, 176
language: and code-switching, 31–33; policing, 11, 153; and radical bilingualism, 152–54; Spanish, 31–34, 38, 153, 188, 195–96
Las crónicas del taco, 347
La Serenata, 18
Latinx: actors, xiv, 15, 21–22, 58, 79–80, 173–74, 176–80, 193–94, 343, 346; consulting, 148, 150, 162; criminalization, 76–79, 156; erasure, xiv, 10, 12, 50–51, 117, 146, 148, 150–51, 154–55; production, 337–38, 339–40, 344, 350–51, 353, 355, 366; representation, 5–6, 11, 71–73, 76–78, 83, 105–6, 113–14, 137–38, 173, 179; threat narrative, 8–9, 15–16, 78–79, 98, 115–16, 270,

272–73; writers, 12–13, 378. *See also* Afro-Latinx; *and individual persons and titles*
Law on the Border, 214
Law & Order, 177, 179
Law & Order: Special Victims Unit, 20, 103–4, 179–85; "Amaro's One-Eighty," 181, 189; "Forgiving Rollins," 184; and mental health, 103–4; "October Surprise," 182–84; "Poisoned Motive," 103–4; "Spring Awakening," 181
Legion, 194
Leguizamo, John, 12
lesbians: as hemisexual lovers, 286, 287–88; and the Latina lover, 285–98; and the myth of authenticity, 292
Level Up, 375–76
Living Undocumented, 21, 212–14, 215–22, 228; "A Prayer in the Night," 213, 218–19; "The World is Watching," 219–20
Lopez, 374
Los Briceño, 348
Los Espookys, 14–15, 351–53
Love, Victor, 16
Lower Classy, 52–53
L Word, The, 22, 285–97; "Livin' la Vida Loca," 288–92
L Word: Generation Q, The, 17

Magnum P.I. (2018), 179
Mandalorian, The, 21, 192–93, 195–206; "The Child," 196–97; "The Gunslinger," 202–3; "The Mandalorian," 195, 197–98; "The Prisoner," 195; "Redemption," 195, 199–200, 204; "Sanctuary," 195
Mandingo, 358–59
masculinity: and the Latina lover, 290, 291–93, 296–97; and the Latin lover, 286; and the male gaze, 27–28; reimagining, 197–200, 203–5, 286; and sports, 294; and stereotypes, 180–82; toxic, 16
Mateo, Alexis, 327–28
Mattel, 149, 154–55, 157
Mayans M.C., 180
Mehrez, Samia, 151–53
mental health: and ADHD, 113, 119, 124–25; and anxiety, 109, 113–14, 119–21, 122, 126–31; and community support, 122, 125, 126–27, 129–31, 137, 138–39; and coping strategies, 120–21, 122, 124, 125, 127, 128; and depression, 100, 106–9, 126–31; and diagnosis, 113–14, 124–25; and grief, 119–20; and Indigenous forms of knowledge, 135–36, 137, 139; and psychosis, 274–75; and PTSD, 101–3, 106, 119, 123; and schizophrenia, 131, 132–34, 136; and